Machine Modernism, Masculinity, and the Trauma of War

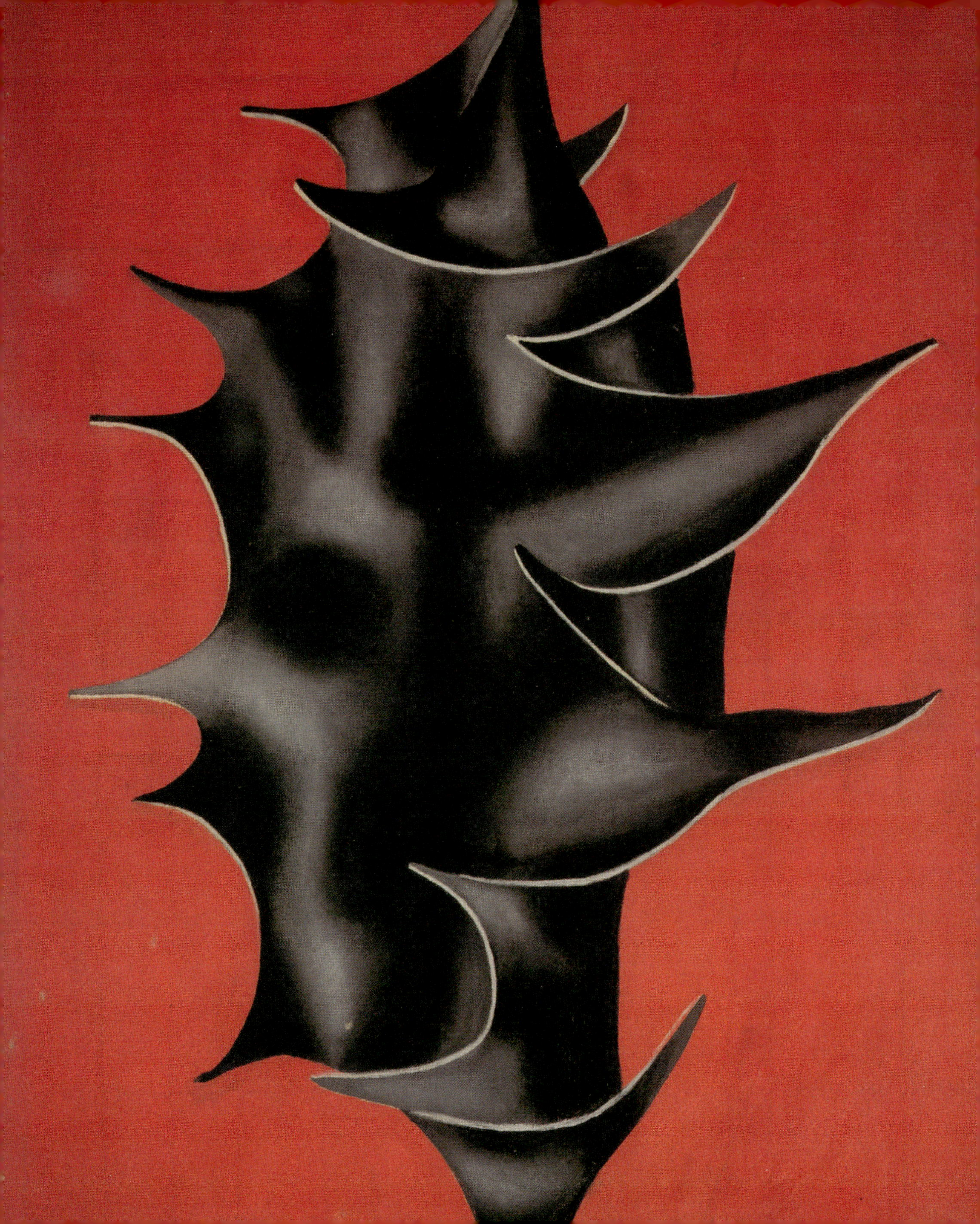

Machine Modernism, Masculinity, and the Trauma of War

The Art of Fernand Léger

Maureen G. Shanahan

The Pennsylvania State University Press | University Park, Pennsylvania

Library of Congress Cataloging-in-Publication Data

Names: Shanahan, Maureen G., author.
Title: Machine modernism, masculinity, and the trauma of war : the art of Fernand Léger / Maureen G Shanahan.
Description: University Park, Pennsylvania : The Pennsylvania State University Press, [2024] | Includes bibliographical references and index.
Summary: "Investigates the artwork of Fernand Léger, one of machine modernism's leading figures, as a case study of the aesthetic's origins in World War I, its unstable production of masculinity, and its collapse in the context of surrealism, economic crises, and the revival of war memories"—Provided by publisher.
Identifiers: LCCN 2024005986 | ISBN 9780271096858 (hardback)
Subjects: LCSH: Léger, Fernand, 1881–1955—Criticism and interpretation. | Painting, French—20th century. | Modernism (Art)—France. | War in art. | Psychic trauma in art. | Masculinity in art.
Classification: LCC ND553.L58 S53 2024
LC record available at https://lccn.loc.gov/2024005986

Printed in the United States of America
Published by The Pennsylvania State University Press, University Park, PA 16802–1003

The Pennsylvania State University Press is a member of the Association of University Presses.
It is the policy of The Pennsylvania State University Press to use acid-free paper. Publications on uncoated stock satisfy the minimum requirements of American National Standard for Information Sciences—Permanence of Paper for Printed Library Material, ANSI Z39.48–1992.

Frontispiece: Fernand Léger, *Holly Leaf*, 1928 (fig. 34).

Dedicated to Diana E. Haddad

Contents

Illustrations

Acknowledgments

As the network of citations in this book will attest, my analysis is in dialogue with many other scholars and writers to whom I am profoundly indebted. This book has been an intellectual journey that owes its arrival to many people beyond those remembered in these acknowledgments. Numerous museums, archives, and libraries provided invaluable access to images and documents. These include the Art Institute of Chicago, the Bibliothèque Kandinsky at the Centre Pompidou, the Bibliothèque nationale de France, the Dansmuseet in Stockholm, the National Gallery of Art Library, the Musée national Fernand Léger, the Museum of Modern Art in New York, and the US Library of Congress. I am particularly grateful to Nelly Mailland, former director of the Musée national Fernand Léger, for her recommendations. Residencies and speaking engagements provided important venues for intellectual exchange. At the Camargo Foundation, I met the late Jane Marcus, who became an early mentor, and Juliette Rogers, who has provided support and advice for many years. During a second Camargo residency, Elizabeth Wingrove, Robin Walz, and Jennifer Jones offered collegiality, critiques on argumentation, and insights on the writing process and French histories; I am grateful, too, to Alia Al-Saji for our conversations on philosopher Henri Bergson and to Toril Moi for her sage advice. At the Five College Women's Studies Research Center, Amrita Basu and Sura Levine helped me refine questions about masculinity and sexuality, and the late Robert Herbert shared his enthusiasm for and recommendations on Fernand Léger. Generous colleagues have provided invitations to present talks at their institutions, permitting dialogues that refined, corrected, and sometimes refocused my questions: Defne Turker at Haliç University, Istanbul; Martin Hurcombe at University of Bristol; Jennifer Kilgore at Université de Caen, Normandy; and Anna Lena Lindberg at Lund University. Didier Francfort at Université de Lorraine has been particularly welcoming over the years with his many invitations. I am grateful for his long-standing friendship and for his community formation in Nancy and Lunéville.

This book would not have been possible without the critical eye of the press and its reviewers. My gratitude goes to Jonathan Eburne, the Refiguring Modernism series editor, Ellie Goodman, Maddie Caso, and the many staff at the Pennsylvania State University Press for their investment and patience in shepherding this book through to completion. To the anonymous reviewers of the book, I hope you will find that your insights and advice have improved the argumentation. I am especially grateful to Lisa Regan for reading through the entire manuscript and for her encouragement and commentary throughout its revision.

My interest in art history and visual culture began during my youth in the shadow of Hollywood with an AP Art History course and regular visits to the Los Angeles County Museum of Art. Early careers as a lawyer and museum fundraiser taught me advocacy and grant-writing skills that continue to inform my work. Dissatisfied with law's positivism and "rational man" paradigm, I pursued a new life in art history at the University of Michigan, Ann Arbor. There many professors modeled the practices of visual analysis, critical inquiry, gender and sexuality studies, and anticolonial criticism. Beth Genné's wonderful class on the Ballet Russes introduced me to Fernand Léger's designs for the Swedish Ballet and launched my inquiry into the artist and era. My dissertation committee—Matthew Biro, Joel Isaacson, Sharon Patton, and Patricia Yaeger—guided my research and supported many grant and job applications, helping me to secure a Samuel H. Kress Foundation travel grant, an American-Scandinavian Foundation fellowship, a Joel Isaacson Dissertation Award, a Henry P. Tappan Dissertation Grant, my first Camargo award, an affiliation with Stockholm University's Gender Studies Center, and my first professional position at SUNY Oswego. Many other Michigan scholars supported my career with reference letters, advice, introductions, and friendship, including Laura Lee Downs, Pat Simons, Z. S. Strother, and Dror Wahrman and his family.

My home institutions, first at Oswego and now James Madison University (JMU), have supported this book financially and intellectually. Oswego provided regular funding, an affiliation with the Einaudi Foundation at Cornell University, and a semester sabbatical. At JMU, the College of Visual and Performing Arts, the JMU Libraries, and the School of Art, Design and Art History have been especially crucial in funding and educational leaves. Friends and colleagues from Michigan, Oswego, JMU, and elsewhere have kindly listened to talks, read chapters of this book, or otherwise advised and supported me on the book's development. These generous auditors and readers include Greg Abrahamson, Mary Kay Adams, Adérónké Adésolá Adésànyà, Temma Balducci, Anne Birien, Lara Blanchard, Sarah Brooks, Matthew and Julia Friday, Doris Gray, Paul Gradvohl, Shah Mahmoud Hanifi, Laura Henigman, Laura Katzman, Patrick Murphy, Margaret Mulroney, Lisa Langlois, John Ott, Sue Peabody, Mary Perramond, Ana María Reyes, Karyn Sproles, Mary Thompson, Siân White, and Helen Zakin. Very special thanks go to Kirstin Pai Buick, Libby Otto, Roberto Tejada, and Carol Zemel, who have been friends and supporters of this book and other projects. I profoundly respect their individual ethics, intellectual rigor, professionalism, and mentoring, which have been influential for me in many aspects of my life and career.

Throughout, family has guided and supported me. My mother, Louise Shanahan, and her sister Maryanne Rebic of Cleveland, both now deceased, were each important in distinct ways. My mother encouraged my intellectual interests with museum trips and beautifully illustrated art books. My aunt fostered a curiosity about people and the world and a love of languages. My sister Moira encouraged the transition from law to the arts and supported me financially and emotionally over the years. The Thompsons and Haddads have provided the shelter and joy of family. Most of all, my beloved partner in life and favorite scientist, Diana E. Haddad, has sustained me in this journey with love and laughter. This book is dedicated to her.

Introduction

In Fernand Léger's biographies, his World War I experience has become what historian Dominick LaCapra calls a "founding trauma," typical of national origin myths.[1] In 1946, after returning to France from exile in the United States, Léger recalled his experience decades earlier as a soldier during World War I: "It permitted me to discover the people and renew myself entirely . . . the engineering corps was a corps of laborers, road workers, and miners."[2] Léger expressed an identification with the working-class male while asserting shared virtues of loyalty, strength, and courage: "I was strong as well and I had no fear. I became comrades with them. Even when I was offered a position in camouflage, far from the front, I didn't want to leave them. 'I'll stay,' I said."[3] Codified in midcentury biographies and by the French Communist Party after he joined in 1945, Léger's story of fraternal solidarity is a trope of masculine heroism that denies or easily overcomes the trauma of war and the fear of death. Such anecdotes of choosing to stay with one's company and of courage in the face of death were a common feature of war stories across the political spectrum, appearing in the letters and diaries of Léger's contemporaries on the left and right—from socialist Henri Barbusse to fascist Benito Mussolini.[4] These war stories, marked by a discourse of male heroism, converged, in Léger's case, with a racialized and gendered mythification that began early on in his career when Guillaume Apollinaire cast him as belonging to "those tall Normans, blond, a bit heavy, shrewd, and prudent."[5] Léger's apparent survival of the war unscathed, combined with his peasant roots and sturdy build, motivated friends, curators, art critics, and dealers to compare him to symbols of virility and strength: an English boxer (Serge Romoff, Ragnar Hoppe, Georges Bauquier), a race car driver (Romoff), a Viking (Guy Dornand), and a Norman oak (Daniel-Henry Kahnweiler, Georges Bauquier).[6]

His war stories only contributed to his public persona as figure of national resilience, psychic equilibrium, and racial fortitude.

World War I, invoked as the originating experience of Léger's identity, generated a crisis of masculinity at the individual, collective, and national levels while also motivating Léger's machine aesthetic. From the time that Léonce Rosenberg's Galerie de l'Effort Moderne first exhibited Léger's monumental war painting of three card-playing soldiers, *The Card Party* (1917) (fig. 1), in February 1919, Léger famously and repeatedly claimed that his new aesthetic was inspired by the "breechblock of a 75," the loading cylinder of the 75 millimeter French artillery cannon (hereafter "75mm cannon" or merely the "75") credited with winning the war.[7] This tale became Léger's machine aesthetic origin story, regularly invoked by art critics and art historians. Yet Léger produced the painting prior to the Armistice in November 1918, during his hospitalization for nerves when he assumed he would be returned to the front. I propose interpreting the painting as a confrontation between the living or revivified, represented by the soldiers at left and center, and the dead or deadened body, signified by the gray, colorless figure at right. My interpretation foregrounds Léger's deployment of his prewar Cubist forms to depict the survivors' inscrutable yet fractured faces and their internal turmoil, features that differentiate them from later figures. I argue for the painting as an example of Cubist simultaneity in which the temporality of the trench, recalled by a small aerial view at top left, overlaps with hospital time, signified by the medals awarded to those who lost limbs and were typically bestowed in a hospital or homefront context. Survival and fraternity are, I propose, contingent not upon metallic hermetic bodies but ruptured faces, internal agitation, and the confrontation with death.

Fig. 1 Fernand Léger, *The Card Party*, December 1917. Oil on canvas, 129 × 193 cm. Kröller-Müller Museum, Otterlo, the Netherlands. © 2024 Artists Rights Society (ARS), New York / ADAGP, Paris.

Léger's well-crafted and late-career war stories suppress the less heroic private version he had told during the immediacy of the war and that only came to light half a century after his death. Not published until 1997, Léger's wartime letters to his childhood friend Louis Poughon contradict the persona Léger sought to create. The letters reveal moments of intense fear, a desire to flee the front, repeated efforts to transfer into the camouflage unit, and hospitalization for nerves. As early as 1915, Léger described the war as a tragedy dividing his new self from the prewar era and his prewar self: "Do you know what it means to feel fear overtake your entire body and to be uprooted from a secure shelter, flung outside at death's door like an imbecile? No, you cannot know that; you did not make war. You will remain a 'prewar man' . . . [while] I despite my thirty-four years, my life and work already begun, [that] this tragedy has broke in two . . . [will be] one of the great *postwar* generation."[8] In interpreting the war as a temporal and experiential rupture constituting his new self, Léger foregrounds a corporeal fear that overtakes the body. Fear, provoked by the threat of imminent death and a powerful loss of agency, arose at the

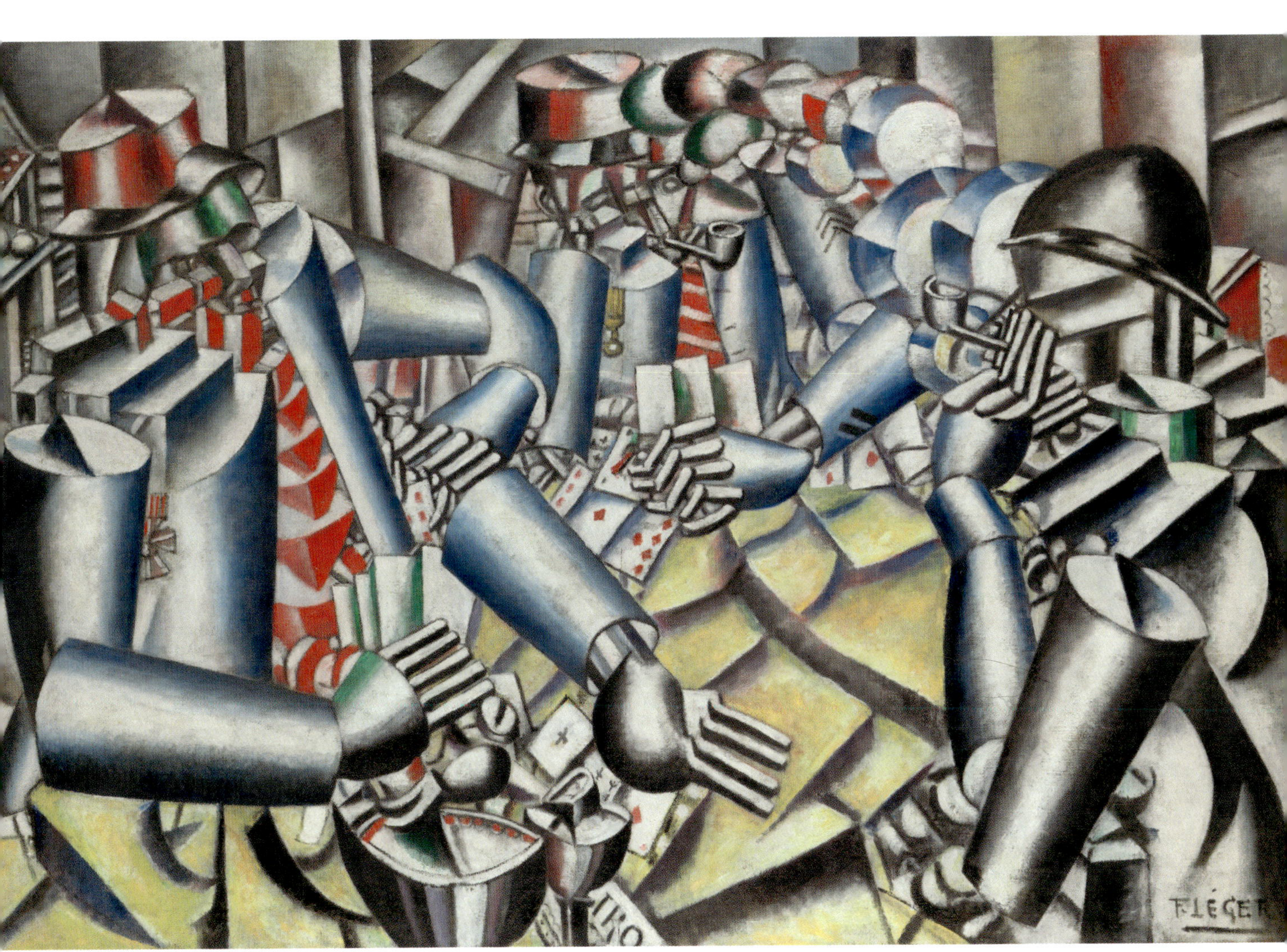
F. LÉGER

moment he was flung by an explosion from a shelter to "death's door"—perhaps into no-man's-land or near the battle zone. Not surprisingly given the repeated shock of near-death experiences, Léger was hospitalized for a "crisis of nerves" after three years of service. He was seen by neurologists at the Hôpital Pitié-Salpêtrière (hereafter Salpêtrière) in Paris and initially diagnosed with "nervous gastritis" but was later released from service and assigned a rest cure.[9] Finally, the letters also reveal what might have been perceived as a failure of solidarity in that, contrary to the story of fidelity, Léger repeatedly but unsuccessfully sought reassignment away from the front lines, including to the camouflage unit.[10]

The social and psychological conditions of World War I—its mass production of death, amputation, and disfiguration and its psychic trauma—created a national trauma that was felt by Léger and his circles. As feminist writers have argued, the war's epidemic of male hysteria and dramatic reversals in gender roles generated a historical crisis of masculinity that undermined the symbolic order.[11] Soldiers suffered mental breakdowns that manifested in symptoms of numbness, rigidity, detachment, depression, nightmares, paralysis, and more, provoking debates within medical communities across the combatant nations about causes and therapies. Trauma to the psyche was, in fact, understood and misunderstood through a wide array of wartime medical diagnoses and treatments that shifted according to beliefs about the origin of the malady, national neurological and psychiatric practices, the exigencies of war, the class status of the soldier, and other factors.[12]

This book takes the recurrence of war trauma and crises of masculine subjectivity as a lens for a reconsideration of Léger's career and its intersections with major artistic and social movements of his era. It argues for Léger's art as both symptom of and therapy for the crises of masculinity that he experienced on an individual level as well as those he shared at the collective and national levels. In situating his experience within larger discursive contexts, the book uses Léger as a case study of the often contested and contradictory ambitions of the machine modernisms he engaged with, notably the Purist art movement of the 1920s. While Léger's engagement with a utopian machine aesthetic is well known, his and Purism's battle with neurasthenia and death are, I argue, also crucial for understanding the anxious masculinity of the era. The failure and breakdown of the machine aesthetic in the late 1920s and early 1930s, evident in little-discussed examples of Léger's art, occur at a pivotal moment when the spectacle of masculine ruination could no longer be symbolically overcome. In 1940, the Nazi invasion of France, the nation's social collapse, a massive internal exodus, and Léger's exile in the United States were crises registered in Léger's artistic production in ways not previously acknowledged. Only in his late work does Léger encode risk and male death while mediating losses that nevertheless cannot be fully known or represented. In foregrounding periods of war and historical trauma in the life of a leading modernist, this book engages with modernism's conflicted traumatic-utopian desires and with the limits of knowing and representing trauma.

The war and psychic breakdown that divided Léger's life in two provoked transformations in the history of medicine and psychiatry. In France, Joseph Babinski, head of neurology at Salpêtrière during the war, established a new diagnosis of pithiatism that became prevalent and that interpreted most breakdowns as a failure of masculine will.[13] Babinski rejected the hysteria diagnosis and its claim of a neurological basis as developed in the late nineteenth century by his teacher, Jean-Martin Charcot, whose photographic documentation of his female patients later became important to Surrealists. Charcot's hysteria diagnosis proposed a universal definition across class and gender, but Babinski's new diagnosis of pithiatism was highly gendered in that it asserted that the soldier's condition was a failure of will that could be corrected through persuasion and a virile medical model. Babinski's assault on the hysteria diagnosis meant that shocked soldiers were more likely regarded as malingerers who sought to evade military duty. By contrast, Sigmund Freud's theory of "war neurosis," published in 1919, interpreted the malady as a conflict within the psyche or ego, advocated a talking cure, and criticized the electroshock therapy used by Babinski and others.[14] But Freud's theory was too late to be deployed even by the Central Powers, and then it was neglected for a generation. Yet even in France, where Babinski's theory dominated, not all neurologists agreed with the presumption of shirking that it assumed.[15] Seen by Charcot students at Salpêtrière, Léger avoided any stigmatizing diagnosis and instead gained release from service in June 1918 on the grounds of chronic congestion. At the same time, his doctors prescribed a rest cure more typical of nervous maladies.

Rather than citing the 75mm cannon as a model while he was working on *The Card Party* in 1917, Léger only invoked the nationalist symbol of combative virility after his release from hospitalization and military duty. In honor of Léger's exhibition of *The Card Party* and new paintings of mechanical elements, factories, mechanics, tugboat captains, and typographers, Léger's good friend, the poet Blaise Cendrars, wrote "Construction" (1919), which, like Léger's statement that year, invoked the 75mm cannon. Cendrars was a Swiss-born poet who volunteered in 1914 and lost his right arm in September 1915; his medical record was marked by "folie" or madness.[16] The poem praises Léger's use of color, his hardening of the liquid earth, and his painting as "an enormous thing that moves . . . the machine, the human soul, the breech of the 75[mm cannon], my portrait."[17] But Léger's portrait of Cendrars, one of five drawings for an earlier poem *J'ai tué* (I Have Killed; 1918), is not a militarized image of a machine man composed of metallic tubing but a naturalistic black-ink drawing of Cendrars's gaunt face, his eyes nearly completely blotted out in a kind of symbolic

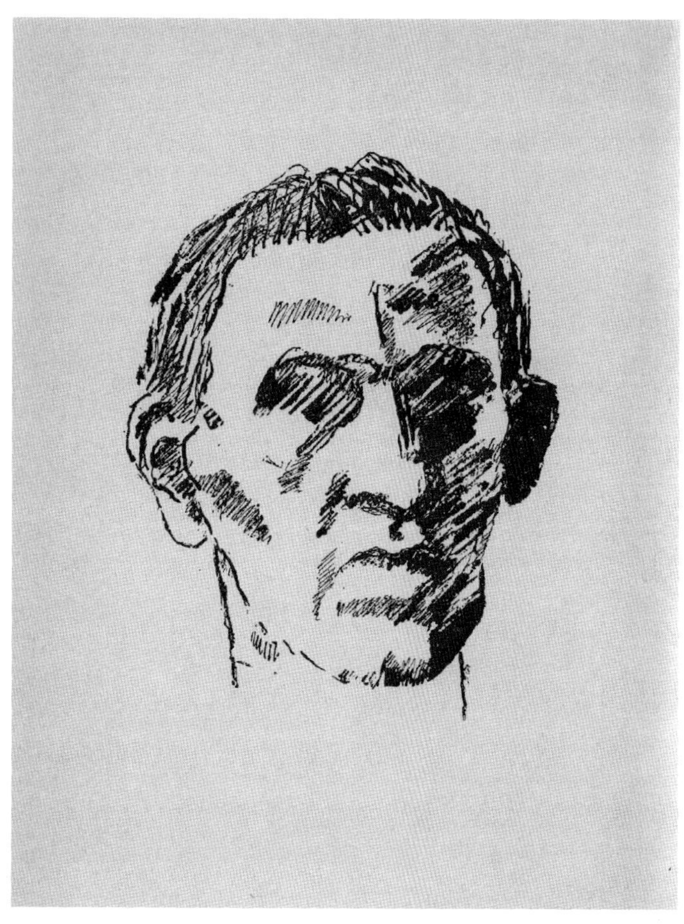

Fig. 2 Fernand Léger, portrait of Blaise Cendrars, frontispiece for Cendrars's *J'ai tué* (Paris: Crès, 1918). Ink on paper. Courtesy of the Bibliothèque nationale de France. © 2024 Artists Rights Society (ARS), New York / ADAGP, Paris.

blinding against amputation (fig. 2). Cendrars's *J'ai tué* telegraphs the war as a collective global effort of men and materials. Assaulted by the sounds of battle, including the "mad wail of the 75[mm cannon]" arching overhead, the narrator, his "nerves tense, muscles strained," crosses no-man's-land and, though struck by a "mad fear" on arriving in the German trench, overcomes it to engage in an anachronistic hand-to-hand knife combat, killing a German. In a 1919 edition of Cendrars's poem, Léger's portrait of Cendrars has been replaced by an image of a soldier, his eyes hidden by his helmet, who opens his mouth wide, baring his teeth, in a bestial howl (fig. 3). Fragments of Cendrars's name and the poem's title, *J'ai tué*, appear in stenciled lettering in this new frontispiece. Ambiguous tubular shapes, circular and crescent forms, and horizontal bars make up the soldier's dissonant and fragmentary world. In adopting the militaristic discourse of the era, Léger and Cendrars express a paradoxical identification with the aggressor's weapon and its imagined potency despite their vulnerability to the enemy's counterpart weapons. The contradictions between Cendrars's and Léger's identification with the 75mm cannon and their personal experiences raise questions about the uses of art and fiction in constituting a resilient self.

How might we account for the contradictions between Léger's militaristic invocation of the 75mm cannon, his wartime fears, and his postwar silence about his hospitalization for nerves? Historian Stéphane Audoin-Rouzeau calls attention to the "determining role of fear [of death] . . . that cannot be mastered" as a crucial finding of Hungarian psychoanalyst Sandor Ferenczi, in his study of soldiers suffering from nerves.[18] The profound fears to which Léger and Cendrars testified are also ones they constantly sought to overcome or negate through art and fiction. According to psychiatrist Boris Cyrulnik, resilience can include making believe, "lying as protection," and the power of fiction in which art and writing are forms of repair.[19] Historian Ruth Leys links "current stalemates" in the nature and treatment of trauma to psychiatry's historical impasse between two possibilities: one in which the traumatic experience can never be consciously remembered or a second in which hysterics "tend to lie," and thus the "truth" of their past cannot be known.[20] Emphasizing the irresolvable dilemma of passively received memory and actively constructed recollections, phenomenologist Paul Ricoeur has raised the problems of the "truthful status of memory" and the "truth claim of history," both productive and destructive in their processes.[21] As historian Dominick LaCapra and literary theorists Cathy Caruth and Shoshana Felman have argued, at the heart of trauma is a "crisis of truth" in which witness testimony or experiential memories contest historical narratives, making the crisis not only an individual problem but also a historical dilemma.[22] Trauma disrupts the ego or psyche from within and without, and trauma's inaccessibility to consciousness (at least initially) calls into question whether it is possibile to identify and narrate the traumatic event and whether any event is ever registered in memory. Leys's genealogy of trauma and her critique of hypnosis therapy has, for example, cast profound doubt on the capacity for the individual or historical narration of trauma. Her criticism of Caruth's writing has resulted in a significant dispute over the nature of trauma and potential therapies.[23] Caruth, Felman, LaCapra, and others nevertheless argue for the possibilities of poetics, literary, and artistic forms to represent the traumatic experience or at least its dynamics, even if only in fragmentary, incomplete, or displaced forms.

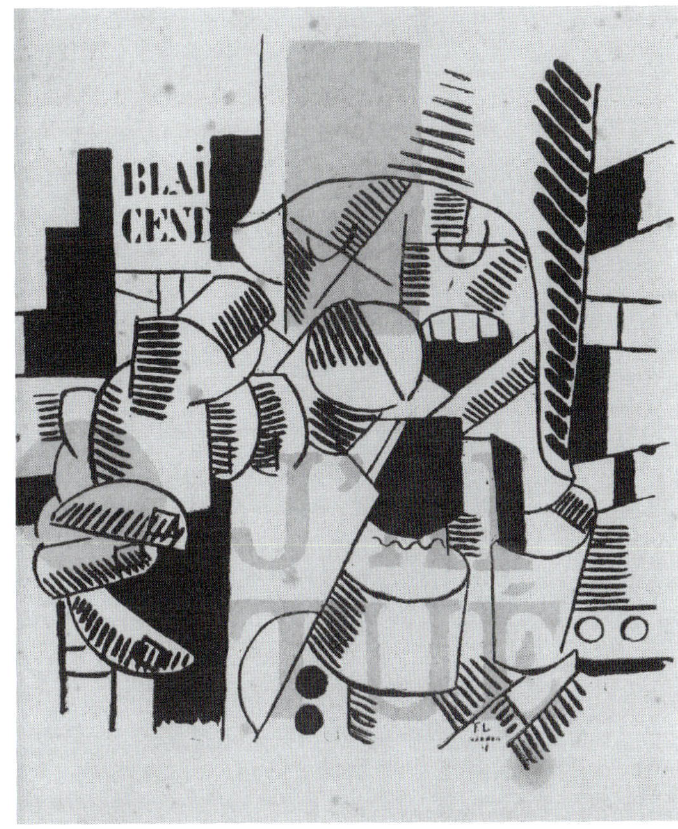

Fig. 3 Fernand Léger, frontispiece for Cendrars's *J'ai tué* (Paris: A la belle edition, 1919). National Gallery of Art Library, David K. E. Bruce Fund. © 2024 Artists Rights Society (ARS), New York / ADAGP, Paris.

Complicating questions about the "truth" and retrievability of trauma are the conditions for resilience. As Cyrulnik and others claim, resilience is contingent upon human relations and social institutions.[24] However, social institutions tied to the state or the artistic collective may only reinscribe normative and even authoritarian social and sexual orders, such as the denial of the fear of death as part of masculine subjectivity. As Griselda Pollock has observed, theories of subjectivity show that the self is a fiction, but historical and political formations of nation, ethnicity, class, gender, and so on "constantly produce such powerful illusions of identity."[25] In analyzing the memory and commemorative practices around World War I, Jay

Winter has called attention to "collective memory" as a social or cultural formation that can contest individual memory and so prove to be unstable.[26] Commemorative practices linked to the production of collective memory can, for example, be contingent upon what gender theorist Judith Butler describes as the "regulation of affect" by "regimes of power" that limit which lives are grievable and in what ways.[27] The contestations among individual and collective memories are further complicated by the contingencies of memory, forgetting, and representation, a dialectic theorized by Ricoeur. Rather than assessing Léger's public statements and private writings in terms of historical or veridical truth, this book borrows from the analysis of testimony and witnessing to understand where and how traumatic memory might be registered—even if only in fragmentary form. The book interprets Léger's art and writings in terms of the libidinal energies and affect discharged as well as the gaps, omissions, or displacements that demarcate the limitations of cognition and representation. My analysis seeks to understand Léger's subjectivity within intersubjective social, psychic, and discursive formations at the national, individual, and collective levels. For example, how did Léger position himself in relation to a nationalist reconstruction iconography and ideology and to Purism's desire to forget the war? How might he, even unconsciously, have resisted or disturbed these forms of memory and forgetting?

Léger's writings and artistic work operate not simply as the self-conscious fashioning of a public persona but also as sites that register "forgetting" and silence as conditions for survival. In the 1920s, Léger participated in Purism, the art movement organized around the journal *L'Esprit Nouveau* (1920–25), founded by three noncombatants: artist Amedée Ozenfant, architect Charles-Edouard Jeanneret (better known as Le Corbusier), and poet Paul Dermée. Purism responded to the war's devastation and the fracture of Cubism by advocating for a "spirit of reconstruction," effecting an "upbeat amnesia" in which civilization was constituted by turning away from the sight of the fallen soldier.[28] The periodical engaged with a virile masculine discourse of economic recovery that Léger adopts in his writing. Yet, I argue, Léger's machine-era works are haunted by psychic battles of wartime and postwar economic uncertainty, and his art is conditioned by the larger cultural silences of the interwar era. Even the emerging fields of psychiatry and psychoanalysis were complicit in these cultural silences. René Laforgue and René Allendy, two little-discussed founders of French psychoanalysis, contributed numerous articles to *L'Esprit Nouveau* and introduced Freudian ideas, yet their work scarcely addressed the war's psychic impact.

As I will show, Léger's ambivalence about a militarized aesthetic emerges even in his most canonical writings, notably in the second of his two "Machine Aesthetic" essays.[29] While the first essay, published in 1923, exalts the mass-produced object as a new form of beauty challenging and surpassing easel painting, the second essay, published in 1924, both develops these themes and raises the specter of death. In this second essay, Léger turns not to the 75mm cannon but to a row of kitchen pans as his model, situating the reader within the peacetime production of domestic commodities for the feminine sphere. Even more, the essay concludes with the stunning assertion that his valorization of the mass-produced object has as its origin the heightened value of objects scavenged at the warfront—a nail, candle stub, or shoelace—that could, in the process of their collection, cost a man his life. Léger makes contradictory claims that states of war are "more normal and more desirable" than states of peace, yet the state of war inflates value and breaks men down: "men and things are seen in all their intensity, their hypertrophic value, examined in all its sides, [and] stretched to breaking." Rather than constituting a hardened masculinity forged in war, Léger's new postwar man might be better understood, I argue, as a hypertrophic man who is both aggrandized and "stretched to breaking." How the specter of war, death, and psychic breakdown haunt Léger's machine aesthetic have, however, scarcely been discussed.

In existing literature, twentieth-century machine modernisms have been divided between those identified with aggressive fantasies fetishizing technologies and armoring the body, such as Futurism, Vorticism, and Constructivism, and, on the other hand, those that place trauma, shock, or castration on display, notably Dadaism and Surrealism.[30] In these examples, the male body alternates between the fascist—hybridized machine-men, the valorization of war as the only hygiene, or Nazism's hypermuscular male heroes—and the antifascist displays of damaged and castrated male bodies. Often understood through the lens of his machine aesthetic in the 1920s, Léger's art metamorphosed over the life of his career. This book offers a study of the trajectory of his art and writing, which shows the complexities and contradictions of his work. Despite celebrating the state of war in his second "Machine Aesthetic" essay, Léger privately expressed a profound sense of economic embattlement and melancholic loss about the "sentimental value" of the organic male body, a view that persisted throughout his writing.[31] Léger's role in machine modernisms aligned with Italian Futurists and Russian Constructivists has contributed to interpretations of him as surviving the war unscathed or of his art as fascist fantasies. However, Léger's case can be understood as not only a story of psychic threat to an embattled ego or art as a form of therapy but also a rich field for inquiry into the psychic, social, and historical conditions for the making and unmaking of masculinity and resilience.

The twentieth century has sometimes been described as a century of trauma, one that has generated new genres—the memoir and witness testimony—and a modernist aesthetics of the fragmentary.[32] Modernism's rejection of an authoritative and positivist vision lends itself to the problem of trauma and its representation, as Lisa Saltzman and Eric Rosenberg have argued. Trauma's language is visual in that it is composed of flashbacks, dreams, the primal scene, and screen memory. Modernist aesthetics can, they propose, assume the "paradoxical status of a form that was made visible but, at the same time, negated, or offered up as unknowable."[33] In addition, modernism's visual fragmentation and rejection of pictorial narratives—the anecdotal, the sentimental, and academic history painting—align with immersive forms of traumatic memory that relive rather than narrate trauma. I argue that, starting with *The Card Party*, Léger's art repeatedly returns to traumatized subjects while desiring to overcome or master trauma. *The Card Party* and many of his iconic machine aesthetic pictures of the 1920s stage a shocked subjectivity by refusing to "know" interiority while simultaneously enacting the disorienting spatial and temporal conditions of traumatic experience. In this sense, the traumatic is registered not so much in a literal or mimetic fashion but in what Griselda Pollock describes as "an affective process . . . allowing some movement, never a cure," and what art critic Jill Bennett has described as an "affective dynamic internal to the work."[34]

Léger's machine aesthetic engages in the collective memory and cultural silences forged by the Purists and by national ideology. On the one hand, the interwar era was a period of "permanent mourning," an era of monument building and commemorations dedicated to the war.[35] On the other hand, France's interwar silences and forgetting produced an aftermath culture in which mourning could never be completed. As philosopher Walter Benjamin claimed, many men returned from the war "grown silent—not richer but poorer in communicable experience," a claim that was true for many soldier-artists and -writers who refused to explicitly reference the war for decades.[36] André Masson, gravely injured and suffering a history of mental breakdowns, resolved never to speak of the war until he broke his silence in 1932 with the *Massacres* series.[37] Georges Braque never represented the war in his work and, after World War II, only commented on his experiences as a soldier enough to say that his memories remained in no-man's-land, where he had been injured and abandoned for hours.[38] Louis Aragon, who survived being buried alive and was decorated for his war service, wrote in 1964 that "our silence seemed to be a means of effacing the war."[39] And, after his hospital release, Léger remained largely silent about his breakdown and the war's horrors. Yet even without explicit reference to the war, the war's aftermath emerges in the work of these artists through configurations of displacement, disavowal, or allegory.

Understanding France's reconstruction era as an aftermath culture opens up questions about how Léger's machine aesthetic engages with artistic and national discourses that discipline the body and suppress affect even as they promise an image of resilience. Léger's compulsively repeated stories, such as the story of the

75mm cannon, and his repeated forms of the *mécanicien* are, I argue, an anxious and ambivalent engagement with the machine. They operate in a dialectic oscillating between the repetition compulsion that Freud identified as a crucial feature of war neurosis and another form of repetition aimed at masculine mastery, two forms of repetition that critical theorist Kaja Silverman sees as interdependent and contingent. In Silverman's terms, masculine mastery depends upon "subordination to the order of discourse" yet is vulnerable to the death drive.[40] She draws from feminist analyses of World War I in her readings of post–World War II film that engage with that era's crisis of masculinity and displays of male lack. Art historical studies of Dada and Surrealist art by Brigid Doherty, Amelia Jones, Amy Lyford, Hal Foster, and others extend and deepen the historical context through analyses of castrated masculine subjectivities.

This study argues that in the 1920s, Léger's work both knows and refuses to see the traumatized male subject. It argues that new historical traumas in the 1930s and 1940s undermined Léger's faith in resilience and reconstruction while also reviving war memories. Rather than aiming for a definitive biography of Léger and his oeuvre, this book offers a discursive analysis of his gendered and traumatized subjectivity understood within larger cultural networks. In doing so, the book aims to show the *longue durée* of trauma, even among those like Léger who suffered no physical injuries from the war. The belatedness or latency of trauma's symptoms after someone gets away "apparently unharmed" is, according to Caruth, crucial to the "peculiar incomprehensibility of human survival."[41]

The book is organized chronologically around key works and stylistic shifts occurring at crucial periods of historical trauma. Chapter 1 argues that the manifesto painting of Léger's war experience, *The Card Party* (1917), holds in tension a traumatized masculine subjectivity that both comes together and falls apart. The chapter situates the painting within the context of its production—that is, Léger's hospitalization for nerves and what he thought was neurasthenia. Léger's war letters, too, repeatedly describe not metallic surfaces but grayness and colorlessness as signs of psychic numbing, exhaustion, and death. Two of the figures incorporate color, which Léger repeatedly wrote about as a therapeutic. While prevailing interpretations rely upon his post-hospitalization statements about the influence of the 75mm cannon as his inspiration for the machine aesthetic that emerged beginning in 1918, my interpretation argues for a closer analysis of his letters and his conception of the new man as a hypertrophic man stretched to breaking. The painting can, I propose, be understood as a conflicted representation of survival. It draws upon philosophical discourses of vitalism and unanimity or a collective spirit while also encoding signs of facial and physical wounding, a confrontation with death, and tensions between a hardened but fractured exterior and an agitated interior. The painting's radical use of Cubism's ruptured spatialities and temporalities registers the affective dynamics of the traumatic condition.

Chapter 2 situates the art and writing of Léger's machine aesthetic era within the context of an embattled economic recovery and the discourse of Purism. Modeled on industrial magazines and capitalist distribution systems of the era, the Purist periodical *L'Esprit Nouveau* produced an interdisciplinary and international coverage of the arts, economics, and politics. Purism repeatedly grapples with the legacy of the war and social disintegration by recruiting machine modernisms, including Léger's art, to gain mastery over neurasthenia, revolution, and other social ills. Léger's mechanics and machine art from the 1920s contributed to the Purist iconography of reconstruction and its campaign of overcoming economic and psychic crises. Yet Léger's art and writing from the era betray an ambivalence toward reconstruction ideologies and reveal fragmented and displaced signs of war experiences. The chapter interprets Léger's machine aesthetic iconography as an incomplete and paradoxical process of working through the war's legacy.

Chapter 3 interprets the end of Léger's machine aesthetic and the emergence of a new still life iconography during the late 1920s and 1930s. His new work evidences a study of his Surrealist contemporaries, an awareness of Freudian symbolism, and collaboration with the Belgian Surrealist periodical *Variétés*. Biomorphic forms, primordial tools, naturalia, and butchered meat work through the value of the body, which appears in displaced forms. The castrated masculinity on display in Surrealist art, the memoirs produced in the context of the tenth anniversary of Armistice in 1928, and the spectacle of homelessness and unemployment resulting from the global economic collapse all generated trauma to masculine value. Léger's writing expresses a new skepticism about rationality. Melancholic expressions in Léger's writing betray a conflicted masculine subjectivity, even as many of Léger's advocates discursively constituted him as a figure of corporeal virility in opposition to Surrealist effeminacy.

Throughout his career, Léger's art returns to the primitive forms, primal formlessness, and screen memories that are trauma's visual language. Chapters 4 and 5 consider Léger's artistic responses to the new historical traumas of the Nazi invasion of France and his exile in the United States. Manifest scenes of leisure—the divers (*plongeurs*) series discussed in chapter 4 and the cyclist series analyzed in chapter 5—encode a sense of national dissolution, exile, and loss. Léger's *plongeurs* series is a collection of paintings and drawings based upon Léger's last memory of France in 1940, as he went into exile in the United States. Scenes of androgynous divers in indeterminate watery spaces, the *plongeurs* series can, I argue, be understood within a prevailing discourse of the German invasion as a flood. Even as the series draws from a wide range of traumatic scenes, it also abstracts and empties referential elements in a dissociative process. In chapter 5, I read Léger's wartime production of the cyclist series, particularly *Big Julie* (1945), as contradictory scenes of survival, nostalgia in the context of exile, and mourning signified by masculine absence and *Big Julie*'s iconic diptych structure.

My aim throughout the book is to offer an interpretation of Léger's painting and writing that accounts for both his experiences of historical trauma and the contingencies of his resilience or survival. This book renders more ambivalent Léger's embrace of the machine aesthetic in the 1920s, accounts for its discontinuation in the 1930s, and interprets his later work as a response to new historical traumas. Just as repetition can function either as a form of immersion into an unknowable trauma or as a form of mastery, Léger's artwork oscillates between these poles, revealing a conflicted and contested subjectivity. Léger's work repeatedly grapples with threats of death and crises in masculinity, making his artistic production a constant struggle aiming for the release of libidinal energies in search of a new equilibrium. His identity as a man of the people, so bound up with a persona of virility and masculinity, is equally shaped by that which it refuses or displaces. Léger's case suggests that history is not only about the repetition of trauma, forgetting, and return but also a series of renewed challenges to the dominant fictions of masculinity. Léger's final motifs—his acrobats, divers, and constructors—rarely find solid ground and instead imbue leisure, spectacle, and (re)construction with uncertainty and the threat of death. In doing so, Léger's final works convey a heightened consciousness about the fragility of bodies and the contingency of a modernist subjectivity operating in worlds that are paradoxically utopian in their desires and anxious and melancholic in their affective dynamics.

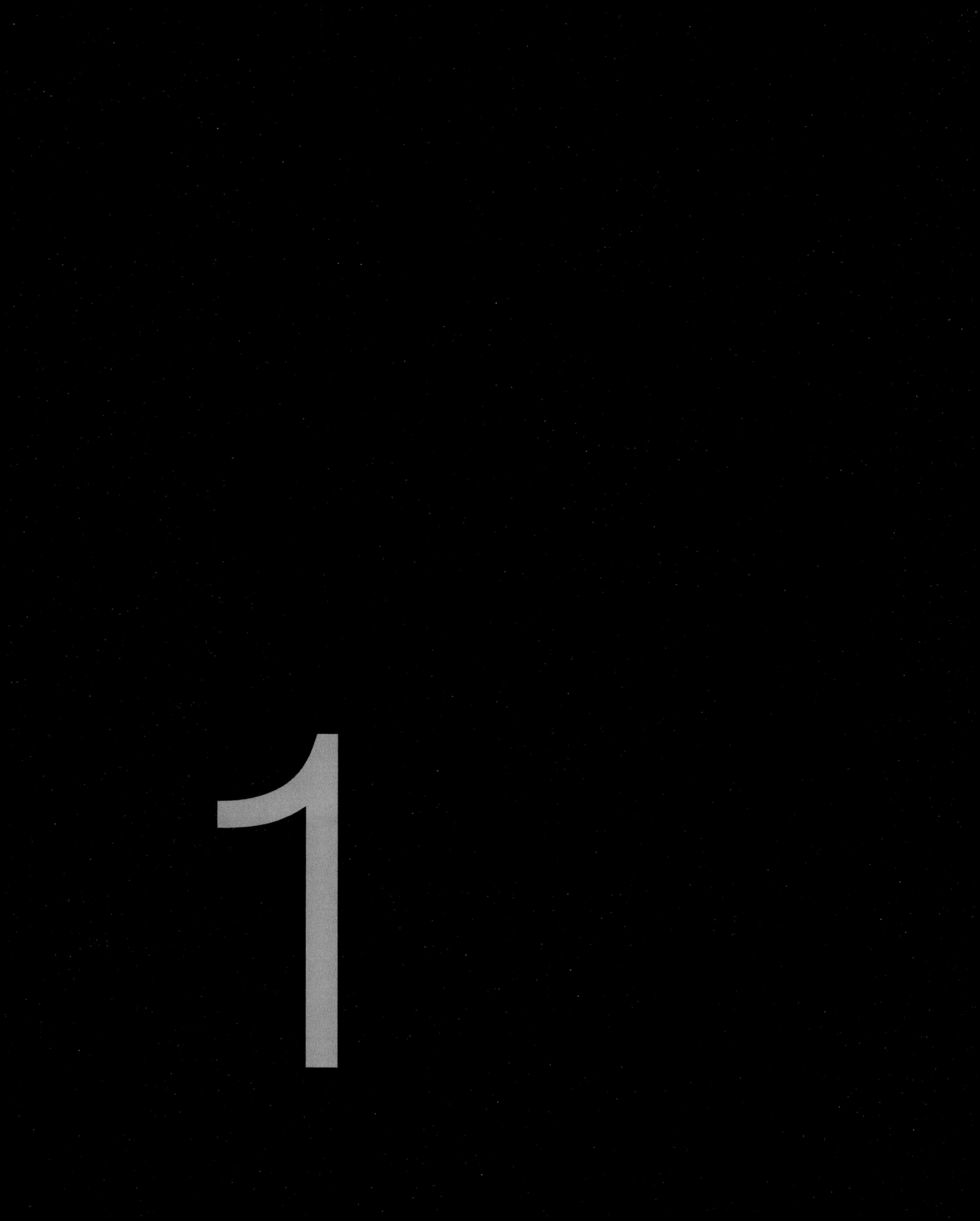

1

The Confrontation with Death

World War I broke Fernand Léger. Then he began reassembling himself. Mobilized at the age of thirty-three in August 1914, Léger served for three years, longer than many of his artist peers, and survived battles in the Argonne Forest and Verdun. During his fifth leave, starting on July 31, 1917, he was almost immediately hospitalized in Paris with what he initially described as *une crise de rhumatisme* and *les reins en compote* (kidney failure) and severe weight loss but later explained as a *crise de nerfs* (nervous crisis) and a *fort cafard* (profound fatigue or depressed state), even neurasthenia, symptoms that today have been understood as post-traumatic stress disorder.[1] In September, Léger wrote to his future dealer Léonce Rosenberg, telling him of the hospitalization and asking to meet on a Sunday, his free day. The meeting eventually took place in late November and launched negotiations for a three-year exclusive dealership contract signed in July 1918.[2] Léger produced mostly black-and-white drawings and only a few small paintings during the war, but his hospitalization provided him with the time to return to painting and to testify to his war experience through a large-scale work: *The Card Party* (1917) (fig. 1). He completed the painting in about three months, noting on the reverse the context of hospitalization: "made in Paris during convalescence, December 1917." He sold it for 3,000 francs on December 5, 1917, to Rosenberg, who resold it three years later to Helene Kröller-Müller. The monumental painting became one of Léger's most iconic works, evidence of his discovery of the French nation in the trenches of the war and his solidarity with his fellow compatriots.

The painting's trio of card-playing soldiers seated around an oddly rutted yellow table is a genre scene inspired by Paul Cézanne's multiple card player paintings but also by the theme in wartime painting, illustration, and photography. Card playing signified fraternal solidarity, and during the war, it depicted a period of waiting or resting at the front lines between battles or in hospital during convalescence. Because Léger's wartime sketches of card-playing soldiers depict them in dugout shelters, the setting has long been assumed to be a similar shelter. I argue for a more complex image of spatial and temporal simultaneity, including the spaces of the warfront shelter and the homefront hospital ward. One of the largest paintings Léger made to that date, *The Card Party* tightly frames the three greater-than-life-size soldiers within the picture's borders. By comparison to the looser, more sketch-like style of Léger's prewar paintings, its finished technique seals off the surfaces, yet the cylindrical forms of the torsos are opened. The gray-brown planks across the upper frame and behind the heads of the three soldiers represent the timbered wall of a frontline shelter. However, unlike Léger's wartime sketches where timbered supports define and divide interior spaces conveying three-dimensional interiors, the spatial setting of the painting compacts the figures together and compresses them toward the picture plane. The framing truncates their bodies and cuts off the human legs and table legs that appear in the sketches. At the base of the painting, on the threshold of the depicted space, are two cup hilt handles of anachronistic swords. Rendered upright like chalices, they lead the gaze to a metallic ball that is the central figure's right hand. Wedged between the smaller of the cup hilts and the bottom frame is the word fragment, "iro," a gesture to the photography journal *Miroir* that was a source for some of Léger's wartime drawings but also a foil in his battle against mimeticism.

Fig. 4 Fernand Léger, *The Staircase*, 1914. Oil on canvas, 144.5 × 93.5 cm. Moderna Museet, Stockholm. © 2024 Artists Rights Society (ARS), New York / ADAGP, Paris.

While the painting's prevailing view is of a compressed interior space, Léger also incorporates a marginalized and fragmentary aerial perspective that lends itself to overlapping temporalities. Framing the left figure's cap, head, and stepped right shoulder is a bird's-eye view of a trench, with its characteristic zigzag line of plank walls juxtaposed with tiny horizontal rungs that might be a boardwalk or a ladder to the soldier's near-certain death in no-man's-land, the terrain between enemy lines. The zigzag signifier of the trench leads to the left soldier's stepped shoulder and agitated red forms, revising Léger's prewar *escalier* (stairs) motif. Perhaps responding to Marcel Duchamp's *Nude Descending a Staircase, No. 2* (1912), Léger adopted the motif in paintings that he made before the war, such as *The Staircase* (1914) (fig. 4), but not to suggest the successive temporal moments of Duchamp's nude or Jules-Etienne Marey's chronophotography. To do so would have engaged more closely in Futurist temporalities suggesting chronological time and an aesthetics of force lines. Instead, for Léger the prewar *escalier* is an architectural fragment mounted by conical figures, effecting pictorial energy through geometric contrasts. But in *The Card Party*, the stepped forms are embedded within the soldier's immobile body, conveying not autonomous dynamic movement through space as in the

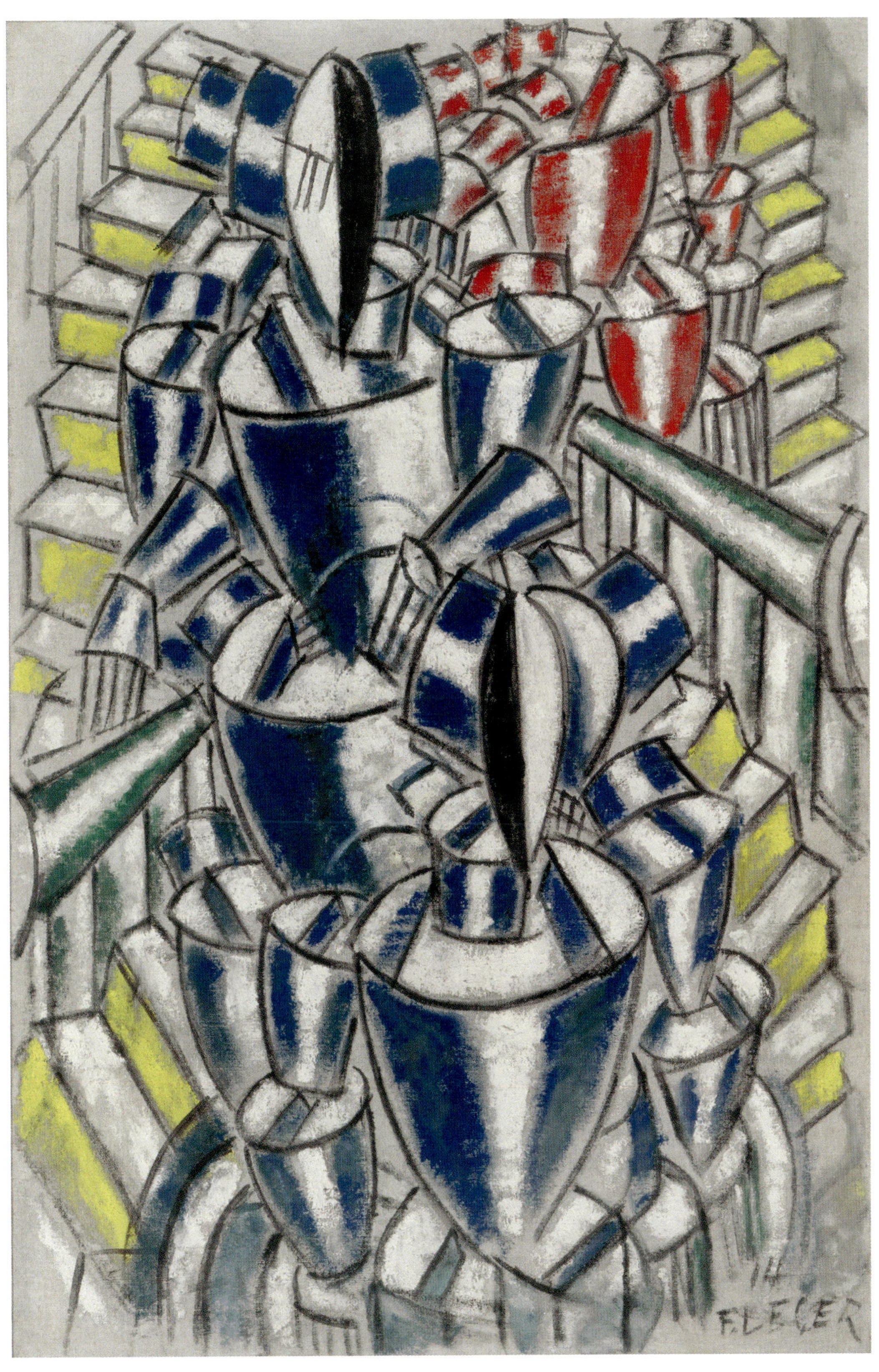
F.LEGER

prewar paintings but a fragmentary "sense-memory" of the past action of going up and over the top.[3] The trench fragment may be spatially and temporally behind the soldier, but the stepped motif reconstitutes that site within the soldier's body. Unlike Duchamp's mobile mechanomorphic nude, Léger's soldiers are visually amputated at the waist, disabling spatial movement. While the timbered wall and noxious yellow table or ground might recall the physical space of a frontline shelter and the color of poison gas, the aerial perspective conveys another view, that of aviation reconnaissance photography published in journals like *Miroir*.

Complicating the compressed space and time of the trench are references to the context of convalescence and hospitalization. The soldiers' war medals signal the contexts of hospitals and the homefront, where decoration ceremonies typically took place. The left figure wears the *Croix de Guerre*, created in 1914 by legislation authored by the novelist and politician Maurice Barrès, while the center figure wears three chevrons near his left shoulder and wrist, indicating his presence in the war for eighteen months. He also wears a *médaille militaire*, often awarded to soldiers due to loss of a limb in combat or on their deathbed.[4] By fall 1917, many of Léger's friends and peers had been awarded such medals: poet and art critic Guillaume Apollinaire, writer Cendrars, and painters Braque and André Denoyer de Segonzac all had received the *Croix de Guerre*. Both Apollinaire and Braque suffered head injuries and underwent trephinations. Cendrars, who lost his right arm in September 1915, was also awarded the *médaille militaire*.[5]

Corporeal ruptures mark the faces and bodies of all the figures, recalling the *gueules cassées* (broken faces) and *mutilés* (amputees) that Léger had rescued in his duties as a *brancardier* (stretcher-bearer) and that he saw in his hospital contexts. As a *brancardier* from spring 1916 until his hospitalization in August 1917, Léger was a frontline witness and first point of rescue for men suffering devastating wounds. Facial destruction due to gassing, shrapnel, and bombing were wounds that almost never appeared in *Miroir*. Nor were such photographs publicly distributed until after the war, when the *mutilés* led the Victory parades in July 1919. Rather than a naturalistic representation of disfiguration, Léger's soldiers present a Cubist version of facial wounding. The leftmost soldier wears a red columnar cap, a soldier's *képi*, whose undulating gray brim is echoed in his forehead and brow, where the two arched forms become a pair of tubular cavities for his recessed eyes. Turned in three-quarter profile to face his comrades, he displays for the viewer his right cheek, composed of red blocks disrupting the face the way gas or explosion disfigured many soldiers. No mouth, ears, neck, or chin are delineated, lost in the facial brickwork that descends past the stepped shoulder into a column of inverted red pyramids enclosed within the "blue horizon" jacket, the color of the French soldier's uniform.

The central figure, also wearing a *képi*, has an even more inscrutable face. Asymmetrical, pupil-less eyes appear on either side of a nose that is not a projecting mass but a black T-shaped splice, like a facial splint that links the "nose" to a clay pipe marking the site where a mouth should be but is not. His right cheek extends in stepped forms from his eye to his shoulder and jacket, eliminating any reference to a neck and creating the effect of a man sunken down into his clothing. His blue cylindrical body is legible as a jacket due to the lines marking buttonholes, suggesting the red diagonal stripes could be braid or shirt stripes. His left hand, with its articulated fingers and tubular wrist, animates the center of the canvas, while his right arm bisects the canvas vertically. Visually interrupted at the elbow and surrounded by cards and the left figure's fingers, the central figure's right forearm resembles a detached prosthetic submitted as a prize in the card game. This soldier holds up three cards, with their blank backs to the viewer, while face-up cards, now put into play on the table, girdle his waist. He leans back toward the comrade at his right (the viewer's left) to turn his attention to the third soldier (at the viewer's right).

Unlike his two comrades, the gray soldier at right displays no war medals or chevrons marking his service, and his identity has been fully obliterated: his facial features have been replaced by a patchwork of planks. The head of Léger's featureless soldier has been reduced to a profile view of a steel Adrian helmet, introduced in 1915 to protect infantrymen from shrapnel and head injuries. It replaced frontline use of the red *képi* that had called enemy attention to the French soldier. The helmet hangs upon a narrow pole, effecting an abstracted version of the familiar makeshift warfront grave marker. One such example appears in Paul Jouve's *Tomb of a Serbian Soldier at Kenali* (November 1916) (fig. 5), commissioned by the French Army and exhibited at the Musée de l'Armée. This abstracted soldier is a precursor to the unknown soldier that the war produced and that was first formally commemorated in France with the Tomb of the Unknown Soldier on November 11, 1920. The "unknown soldier" emerged as a new wartime discourse that commemorated the common man while accommodating the grotesque fate of half of all the dead, whose bodies became fragmented and unidentifiable.[6] Positioned in profile as suggested by the arc of his helmet, the right soldier in Léger's painting seems only to observe; unlike the other two, he holds no cards, or perhaps they have been swept up by another soldier. It is tempting to say that he is a melancholic figure who, contemplating the living, rests his chin on his left hand as he also holds his pipe, except that no eyes, chin, or mouth are visible. Nor do they seem possible in this abstracted face, where a row of narrow digit-sized logs fills in the gap between the hand and "chin." The stepped motif again appears, this time where shoulders should be on either side of the green neck. On one side, they lead to the yellow table and on the

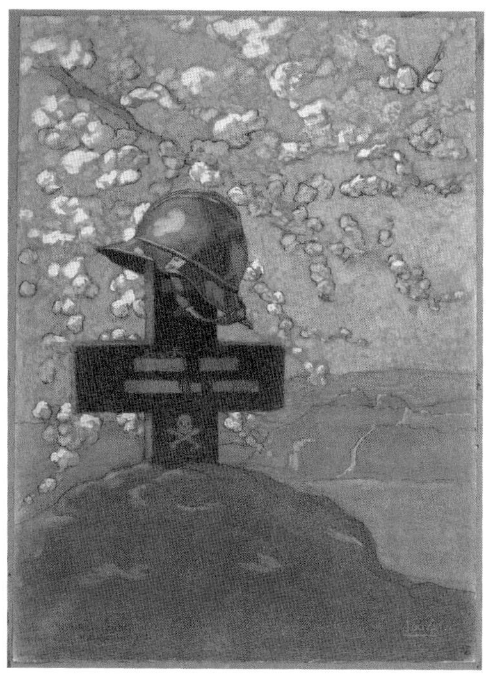

Fig. 5 Paul Jouve, *Tomb of a Serbian Soldier at Kenali*, November 1916. Charcoal, gouache, India ink, vellum paper (imitation), 57 × 409 cm. © Musée de l'Armée, Dist. RMN-Grand Palais / Art Resource, New York. © 2024 Artists Rights Society (ARS), New York / ADAGP, Paris.

other to bits of red planks marked by barbed wire–like loops. In the absence of eyes to represent his gaze, it is his left arm, hand, and pipe, positioned in the foreground and parallel to the picture plane, that establish the orientation of his body toward the two other soldiers and make him something more than a memorial. Yet he lacks his comrades' cylindrical torso-jacket, and his body dissolves in several passages into gray disks and, at the bottom right corner, into black arcs terminating in Léger's signature: "F. Léger."

This memorialized or melancholic soldier is connected to the living through several pictorial devices that constitute the group as a collective body. His pipe emits a chain of smoke in the form of blue rotator disks that lead to the gray spherical puffs produced by the middle figure's pipe. Their connection is reinforced by the axial alignment of their respective pipes. Writing in 1914 about the smoke motif in his prewar *fumée* paintings, Léger argued for the "multiplicative intensity" of "curved and rounded smoke" as "living forms" rising between the "dead surfaces" of the architecture.[7] Other art historians have emphasized how Léger's smoke motif blurs boundaries between animate and inanimate figures or between interior and exterior spaces.[8]

Léger's motif borrows from writer Jules Romains, who used smoke in his prewar poetry and novels to convey his unanimist philosophy of the interconnectedness of human beings and their collective consciousness or memories. Léger probably met Romains through the Cubist artist and theoretician Albert Gleizes and through their prewar participation in the Abbaye de Créteil and Closerie des Lilas café discussions; in the 1920s, Léger praised Romains's theater.[9] Like Romains's novel, *Death of a Nobody* (1911), in which the death of a "nobody" motivates fragmented, unspoken memories, overlapping temporalities and shared spaces, Léger's gray soldier is an anonymous figure who is connected to his comrades through the "living form" of smoke even as his body disintegrates and is memorialized as a "dead surface." Romains, like many of the poets and writers in Léger's prewar networks, including Georges Duhamel, Yvan Goll, and Romains Rolland, had a prewar reputation for pacificism, and, as French literature scholar Nancy Sloan Goldberg's research has shown, their wartime poetry continued in direct criticism of the war.[10] Their calls to fraternity and their epitaphs, elegies, and requiems may inform Léger's painting. Like Léger, many pacifist poets had ties to Vladimir Lenin and Leon Trotsky, who opposed the war.[11] Although Léger never mounted a direct criticism of French leadership or engaged in moral appeals to the public during the war, he later joined interwar pacifist movements and argued that people should not become "pawns . . . of the powerful . . . [and their] economic interests."[12]

The card-playing scene represents a deciding moment in the game when the left and center figures have laid down their aces and high cards and confront the figure at right. In the painting's game of chance, the agitated living show their cards to a melancholic shocked or dead figure, but the question of who wins and who loses remains unanswered. Perhaps representing *manille*, a favorite card game of the trenches, the painting invites in the viewer as a player seated on the end of the yellow table titled forward into our space.[13] The monumental scale of the painting and compressed space brings the viewer into the scene even as Léger's Cubist vocabulary works against identification with the figures. Produced during an anxious period between the promise of health and recovery and the risk that recovery would mean a return to the front, Léger could have believed that the painting was not only his manifesto work on his war experience but also possibly his last. What kind of response to the war's trauma does the painting represent? And to what ends does it deploy Cubism?

The Mythification of the 75mm Cannon

Despite the visibility of his soldiers' fractured faces, severed and prosthetic limbs, pictorially amputated torsos, and the scene of camaraderie between the living and the dead, the painting has never been interpreted in terms of physical injury or psychic confrontations with death. Instead, it has been primarily understood through the lens of Léger's postwar statements about the machine aesthetic and the 75mm cannon. From the time that *The Card Party* was first exhibited at Rosenberg's Galerie de l'Effort Moderne in February 1919, Léger famously and repeatedly claimed that his new aesthetic was inspired by the "breechblock of a 75[mm cannon]." A year and a half after producing the painting, almost a year after his release from service in May 1918, and a few months after the November 1918 Armistice, Léger adopted the discourse of French triumphalism. Rosenberg resumed prewar debates between the Cubists and the Futurists by sending artists' statements, including Léger's, to *Valori Plastici*, an Italian Futurist magazine founded in 1919. Léger wrote: "I like the forms imposed by modern industry, and I use them: steel with a thousand colored reflections is more subtle and more closed than classical subjects. I maintain that a machine gun or the breechblock of a 75[mm cannon] are better subjects to paint than four apples on a table or a Saint Cloud landscape and that without being Futurist."[14] For Colonel de Grandmaison, France's leader of military strategy, the 75mm cannon was "God the Father, God the Son, and God the Holy Ghost," a mythification and sacralization of the weapon that France credited with winning the war.[15]

Yet the "glorious 75" also had a reputation for backfiring and, according to historian Jacques Meyer, was "never so menaced, more indispensable . . . and more decried" than at Verdun.[16] By 1919, the homefront climate of a bellicose nationalism was such that even Spaniard Juan Gris was, according to Braque, producing "patriotic paintings" of "our little 75" and heads of *poilus*, the soldier become hairy due to frontline service.[17] Paradoxically, Léger's stated preference for "the machine gun or the breechblock of a 75" as subjects contradicts his pictorial output, including *The Card Party*, where the only weapons are outmoded sabers. Munitions rarely appear in Léger's oeuvre, and the 75mm cannon never does. In his war letters to his childhood friend Louis Poughon, Léger only briefly mentions the 75mm cannon and not as a reflective surface for color and light but for its power in "cleaning up" the Germans and for the deafening noise of the "75 zone."[18] Indeed, the glint of light on the metallic surfaces of aircraft, cannons, and other military equipment made them deadly targets of enemy attacks, motivating the development of the camouflage unit.[19] Léger's invocation of reflective metallic surfaces more closely correlates with the images of homefront industry, peacetime machinery, and factory tubing depicted in the new machine aesthetic paintings he began in 1918.

For Léger and his friend Blaise Cendrars, the 75mm cannon engaged with a dominant discourse of phallic armoring even as they both had been marked by nerves. A Swiss-born poet and writer, Cendrars was the pseudonym that Frédéric Louis Sauser adopted in 1912, a year after meeting Léger. They became lifelong friends and collaborators. Less than a year after he volunteered in December 1914, Cendrars lost his right arm in battle. From September 1915 to May 1916, he was hospitalized at various locations, including Maison Blanche in Paris, where he was fitted for prosthetics and which was also an important center in charge of *psychonévroses de guerre* (war neurotics).[20] While his dossier includes mention of *folie*, or madness, Cendrars never explicitly acknowledged having nerves or receiving psychiatric assessment.[21] His account of his wartime experiences and his amputation did not appear until decades later, in *La Main coupée* (1946). However, his fictional accounts of mad soldiers and the psychiatric institution make him, according to psychiatrists Julien Bogousslavsky and Laurent Tatu, a "first-rate witness of neuropsychiatry."[22] After the war, Léger, too, remained silent about his wartime "nerves" and neurasthenia for the rest of his life.

Expressions of fear and vulnerability became shameful in the public eye. For both Cendrars and Léger, their postwar writing negates their wartime testimony of fear. In 1916, when hospitalized, Cendrars reported that at the time he was injured, he heard his own "unrecognizable voice" crying in fear: "I was so ashamed at having howled like an ox."[23] Much later, Cendrars wrote only about other soldiers' profound fear of death.[24] In 1946, Léger claimed he had "no fear."[25] Yet his wartime letters describe moments of intense fear, "fear [that] overtake[s] your entire body," such as once in 1916 when he was trapped in an isolated, muddy patch of Verdun.[26]

Cendrars's multiple invocations of the 75mm cannon shift from an identification with the aggressor weapon to the weapon as a sign of the war's sensory fragmentation. In February 1919, when Rosenberg's gallery first exhibited *The Card Party*, Cendrars declaimed his poem *J'ai tué* (1918), in which the narrator crosses no-man's-land as the shells of the 75mm cannon whizz overhead. In "Construction" (1919), Cendrars describes Léger's new painting as equivalent to "the 75mm breech."[27] But in July 1919, Cendrars published an essay about Léger's new postwar art, signaling that the 75mm cannon was not so much part of a literal representational mode but rather a new fractured and contradictory sensory experience. Léger's eye, he writes, moves among the war matériel, from "airplane squads" to "truck convoys," "American motors . . . English preserves, international soldiers, German chemicals, the breech of the 75, everything marked by a formidable unity."[28] Yet many of the motifs Cendrars lists do not appear in Léger's wartime artwork. Rather than representing "airplane squads," Léger's watercolor of a downed French plane undermines his earlier idealization of aviation, famously narrativized in his visit to the prewar Aviation Salon with Constantin Brancusi and Duchamp. By the time of Cendrars's essay in July 1919, Léger had been released from service and shifted to new themes of tugboat captains and fantastic factories. Cendrars interprets these paintings, with their montage of geometric forms, colors, and graphic signs, as an aesthetic informed by the war: "picturesque detail becomes part of a grand ensemble absorbed into outrageous contradictions . . . whether he paints the street or the factory, he [Léger] will never forget this complex unity born of the war." For Cendrars, the 75mm cannon may have become more of a metaphor for the war's sensory montage of "outrageous contradictions."

Despite the contradictions within *The Card Party*, its absence of guns, the compressed space and confinement limiting agency, and the corporeal breaches and ruptures, art historians often read the figures as armored bodies inspired by the 75mm cannon and as hardened survivors. On the centennial of the painting in a major Léger retrospective, Centre Pompidou curator Ariane Coulondre wrote about the painting as an image of "roboticized humanity," whose bodies announce Léger's machine aesthetic informed by the 75mm cannon.[29] In his survey on the war's production of art, Richard Cork describes the scene as a card game among "robot" players who have banished "unnecessary sentiment" and "flesh and blood" for "machine-age geometry," thus demonstrating the soldiers' "iron resolve" and Léger's "ability to recover from the trauma of war-injury."[30] Christopher Green, who has published extensively on Léger, once described *The Card Party* as "a precision machine" whose figures have a "metallic shine."[31] He has also written that

Léger's postwar machine-men are "essentially positive reactions" to the war due to their "constructive rather than destructive" worlds.[32] Yet, more recently, Green has emphasized *The Card Party* as deconstructive figures "burst apart by the forcefully contrasting elements from which they are built . . . no call to order here."[33] Art historian Philippe Dagen, who sees Léger's wartime images as an exception to a French artistic "silence" about the war, nevertheless emphasizes Léger's inability to paint the body in decay, the wounded body, its suffering and death. Cubism, Dagen concludes, was inadequate to represent the damage of mechanized war.[34] I propose examining the ways Léger's soldiers "burst apart" and how Léger, a long-standing opponent of imitative arts, deploys Cubism in his *Card Party* painting.

Fig. 6 Gino Severini, *Cannon in Action*, 1915. Oil on canvas, 50 × 60 cm. © 2024 Artists Rights Society (ARS), New York / ADAGP, Paris. Photo © Rheinisches Bildarchiv Cologne, rba_c013068.

Several art historians align Léger and *The Card Party* with a fascist refusal to imagine the disintegration of the organic body, but these readings neglect crucial aspects of the soldiers' faces and the memorial aspect of the right soldier. "There is no *Guernica* by Léger," art historian Rainer Rochlitz asserts; for Rochlitz, Léger's art and writing are not far from Filippo Marinetti's vaunting of war and dream of a metallic body as expressed in his Italian Futurist manifesto.[35] Yet Léger's painting responds to the Futurist conception of war, represented by the noncombatant Gino Severini in *Cannon in Action* (1915) (fig. 6), exhibited in early 1916, by rejecting the depiction of cannons, active warfare, and the convergence of the soldiers with the big guns they fire. Eric Michaud reads Léger's painting as blocking out what he describes in his letters; Michaud writes that it is "difficult, if not impossible to see the card players as a critique of the war that transforms soldiers into robots."[36] Yet Léger produced the painting at the height of wartime censorship against images of French death and disfiguration. Could *The Card Party* be read as deploying Cubist fractured aesthetics both to preclude naturalism's representation of the organic and still permit recognition of the war's destructive capacities?

Although many scholars have accounted for the psychic shock of the war in Léger's writing, how these conditions, including Léger's hospitalization, informed his conception of Cubism is less discussed. After Léger's war letters to Poughon were published in 1997, many scholars saw a profound contradiction between the horrors of war described in the letters and artwork that seems alienated from physical trauma.[37] A rare exception is Peter de Francia, who wrote that *The Card Party* "would seem to result from and certainly induce a strong traumatic shock," an interpretation in accord with the argument I make here.[38] Similarly, Daniel Marcus reads Léger's war drawings as a "pictorial materialism, a figure of the *poilu*'s phenomenology" and part of Léger's deployment of Cubism, "its weak abstraction—in defiance of the superior abstractions of war and capital."[39] Dorothy Kosinski describes the letters as a Surrealist "écriture corporelle," and concludes that *The Card Party* "avoided dramatizing or glorifying combat . . . in order to confer force and dignity to the figures of

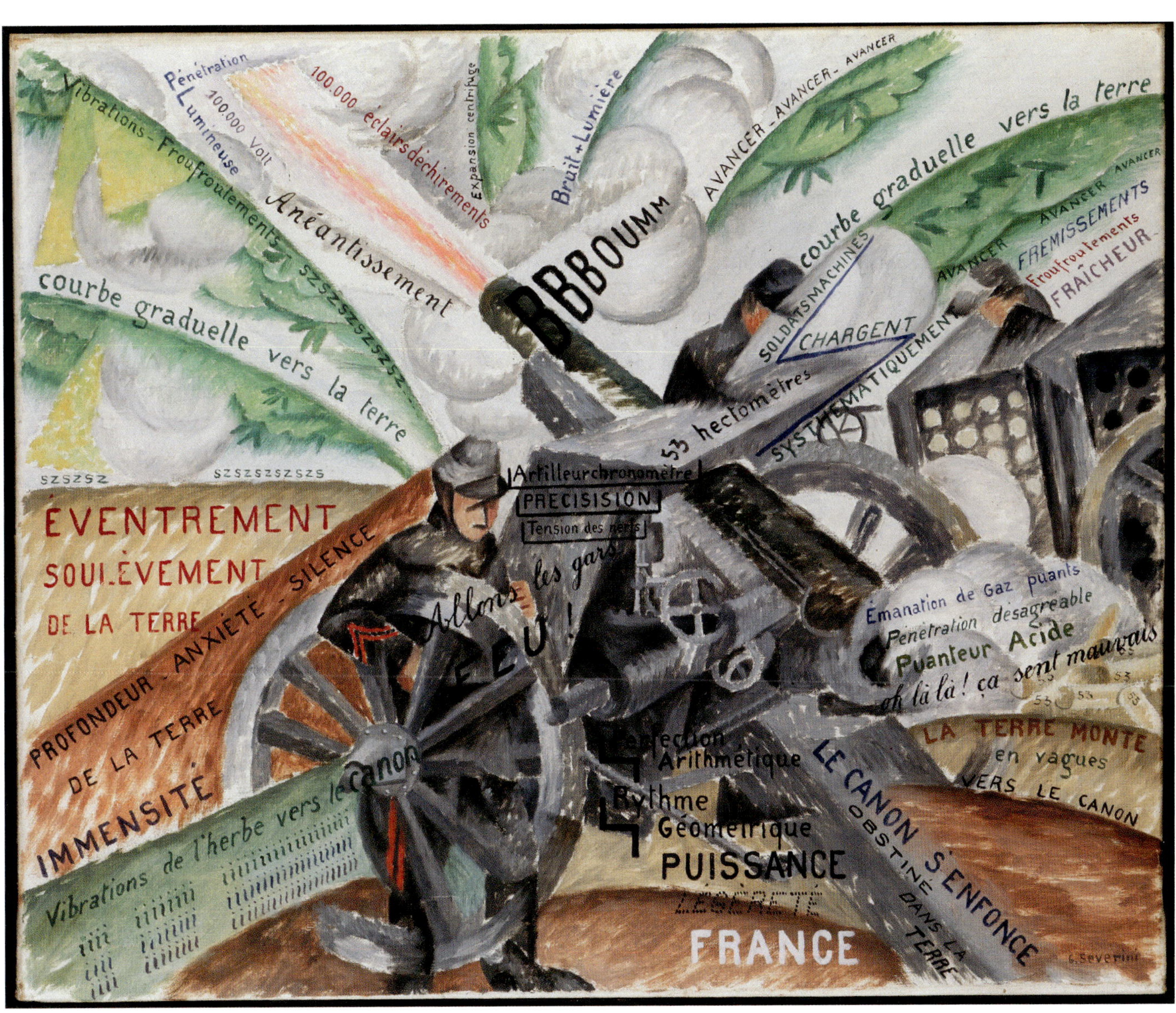
Vibrations - Froufroutements
Pénétration Lumineuse
100.000 Volt
100.000 éclairs déchirements
Expansion centrifuge
Bruit + Lumière
AVANCER - AVANCER - AVANCER - AVANCER
Anéantissement
BBBOUMM
courbe graduelle vers la terre
courbe graduelle vers la terre
AVANCER AVANCER AVANCER AVANCER
FREMISSEMENTS
Froufroutements
FRAÎCHEUR
SOLDATS MACHINES
CHARGENT
SYSTEMATIQUEMENT
53 hectomètres
Artilleurchronomètre
PRECISISION
Tension des nerfs
ÉVENTREMENT
SOULÈVEMENT
DE LA TERRE
PROFONDEUR - ANXIÉTÉ - SILENCE
DE LA TERRE
IMMENSITÉ
Allons les gars
FEU !
Emanation de Gaz puants
Pénétration désagreable
Puanteur Acide
oh là là ! ça sent mauvais
LA TERRE MONTE
en vagues
VERS LE CANON
Vibrations de l'herbe vers le canon
Perfection Arithmétique
Rythme Géométrique
PUISSANCE
LÉGÈRETÉ
FRANCE
LE CANON S'ENFONCE
OBSTINÉ DANS LA TERRE
G. Severini

the soldiers."[40] Historian Stéphane Audoin-Rouzeau interprets the symptoms Léger describes in his letters as characteristic of post-traumatic stress disorder, while art historian Claire Maingon and psychiatrist Laurent Tatu group Léger among "neurologically wounded" artists based upon his medical records.[41] Of these, only Marcus proposes a theory of Léger's wartime Cubism, and none extend their interpretations to consider how *The Card Party* is distinct from Léger's postwar machine aesthetic.

Returning *The Card Party* to the context of its production—Léger's hospitalization for symptoms of shell shock—helps us assess the painting prior to national victory and instead during a period of national and individual anxiety when Léger's diagnosis and future were uncertain. At that moment, a stigmatizing diagnosis of nerves was as possible as a return to the front, motivating Léger's repeated appeals to his friends to find him a position in the camouflage unit led by Guirand de Scévola.[42] In late 1917, at the time of Léger's hospitalization, French troop morale was at a low, and "combatant fatigue," or *le cafard*, was high. The war's longevity and brutality compounded anger at censors and motivated mutinies in May and June, while the Russian Revolution and defection from the war in October and the Italian defeat at Caporetto in November made the historic moment more grim for those left fighting.[43] Léger's gray-metallic soldiers in *The Card Party* should, I argue, be interpreted in terms of the shocked and numbed survivor of war rather than as conflations with the weaponry of war that emerged in Léger's postwar discourse. Instead of glorifying war, Léger's war letters repeatedly return to his observations of soldiers' confrontation with death and their shock registered as grayness or a lack of color.

How might Léger's *The Card Party* soldiers testify to the psychic shock he repeatedly observed at the front and to the survivors—the *gueules cassées* and *mutilés*—he encountered during hospitalization? How do the affective dynamics internal to the work—that is, Léger's Cubist aesthetics—register the experience of trauma as well as a desire for survival and resilience? I propose that the three soldiers present three states of being: the shell-shocked soldier at left whose agitated interior is encased in a hardened exterior but whose face and torso incorporate the "steps" of the trench and the memory of its zigzag space, the disabled and prostheticized body in the center whose damaged face and disjointed arm emphasize his reconstructedness, and the comrade at right whose grayness, lack of facial features, and helmet-pole body make him a signifier of loss and shock. My analysis explores how Léger deployed prewar Cubist techniques to represent interconnectedness and fraternity, temporal simultaneity and multiplicity, and a connection and confrontation between the living and dead. Returning to the cultural and psychic conditions of the painting's production and to the shifting national and aesthetic discourses between 1917 and the early postwar years offers an alternative context for Léger's Cubist vision.

Historical Trauma

The Card Party responds to three crucial contexts: the historical trauma to the nation, the trauma to Léger as an individual, and the trauma to the collectives he identified with, including his military company and intellectual circles. In interpreting Léger's wartime painting in the context of trauma on the national, individual, and collective levels, I have turned to trauma theory and its uses in humanistic interpretations of artistic production. Psychic breakdowns—the "nerves" that Léger and Cendrars suffered from—became epidemic in the trenches and provoked debates among French neurologists. Historians since have characterized the period as a crisis for masculinity. Wartime French neurological debates about trauma help explain Léger's diagnosis, his understanding of his condition, and his long silence about his hospitalization for "nerves." Freud's theories about war neurosis have had the most long-standing impact on our understanding of trauma. His concepts of "war neurosis" and "repetition compulsion," articulated in 1919 and 1920, continue to inform psychoanalytic studies about the psychic mechanisms of trauma. Drawing upon Freudian thought and feminist scholarship about World War I's crisis of masculinity, Silverman's research provides an interpretative frame for analyzing how "dominant cultural fictions" about masculinity can be undermined by a "historical trauma" such as war.

Freud's definition of "war neurosis" in his 1919 essay has remained influential in describing the symptomology of individual trauma as a response to the threat of death and a conflict within the ego. Overwhelmed by the threat or proximity of death, traumatized soldiers or subjects become numb to the world, and their responses emerge as nightmares, hallucinations, mutism, paralysis, and other intrusive phenomena.[44] Freud explained the concept of repetition compulsion suffered by the "war neurotic" in *Beyond the Pleasure Principle* (1920), a crucial analysis that informs my interpretation of Léger's artwork as a return to the site of his traumatic experience. Freud's essay sets forth his argument for an economic theory of the libido and his explanation for why the pleasure principle fails to function in the case of the war neurotic. The pleasure principle, the libido's aim for constancy or stability, is a process of binding free-flowing internal energy into a "quiescent state" to create a "coherent ego." But the pleasure principle fails to function in the case of the war neurotic, whose dreams compulsively return him to "the situation of his disaster." Traumatic shock is both an external breach of the psyche, producing symptoms such as paralysis and reoccurring nightmares and numbing, and an internal stimulus resulting from "memory-traces" in the unconscious that bring an "overplus of pain." This free-moving or unbound energy internal to the psyche strives for discharge or binding, but failing these, it motivates the psyche to regress to "an earlier condition," a process that is the death drive. The psyche's repeated disequilibrium results in an "oscillating rhythm" between the sexual drive (Eros) and the death drive (Thanatos), both of which emerged "at the beginning"—that is, at the origins of biological life.

Silverman's research brings together an analysis of trauma to the individual and the nation through a feminist inquiry into cultural forms of masculine subjectivity. Building upon feminist scholarship on World War I, Silverman proposes that historical trauma such as war can call into question, even if temporarily, dominant cultural fictions or "what a society assumes to be its master narratives."[45] Citing feminist scholarship on the crisis of masculinity produced by World War I, Silverman argues that an epidemic of "male hysteria" or mental breakdowns can undermine assumptions of masculine mastery over the rational mind. In Silverman's analysis, war constitutes a "historical trauma," which she defines as an event that "brings a large group of male subjects into such an intimate relation with lack that they are at least for the moment unable to sustain an imaginary relation with the phallus, and so withdraw their belief from the dominant fiction."[46] War's destructive capacities, as documented in Léger's letters, repeatedly and overwhelmingly brought him in close proximity to the threat of death, the dead, the dismembered and mad, and forms of lost or annihilated masculine potency.

Central to Silverman's analysis is her interpretation and critique of Freud's theory of repetition compulsion and the death drive in *Beyond the Pleasure Principle*. Silverman claims that Freud fails to sufficiently differentiate between two competing forms of repetition. In her reading of Freud's text, one form of repetition leads to mastery (a binding or coherence of the ego), and the other is the traumatic repetition of the death drive (an unbinding or breakdown of the psyche). The death drive is best defined as a compulsion to repeat "experiences of an overwhelming and incapacitating sort," while mastery results when those same experiences are "linguistically rather than affectively reprised."[47] She points to Freud's example of the *fort/da* (gone/there) case, in which a child (Freud's grandson) repeatedly throws away objects to gain pleasure and mastery at their reappearance. The child's repeated throwing away of the object reenacts the unpleasurable experience of the mother's departure to gain its return and so mastery over the loss of the mother. In Silverman's reading, Freud frequently conflates these active forms of repetition (the *fort/da* example) and passive forms of repetition (e.g., recurring nightmares), one leading to the binding of the ego and the other to its unbinding or psychic breakdown. Freud's error, she argues, means that he misunderstands that mastery "exists in a parasitic or anaclitic relation to the death drive."[48] Masculinity is therefore "particularly vulnerable to the unbinding effects of the death drive because of its ideological alignment with mastery."[49]

Following this analysis, I argue that *The Card Party* returned Léger to the situation of his disaster—that is, the warfront context and living with the dead—but that the painting's production was also a process aimed at mastery over the war experience. The painting might be understood as a palimpsest of memories in which hospital time recalls wartime, not as a "linguistic reprisal" or narrative form but as a form of affective visual reprisal. If, as Silverman argues, repetition aiming for mastery has an anaclitic relationship to the death drive, how do these two forms of repetition operate in connection with the painting and Léger's artwork more generally? As I will show, Léger's linguistic reprisals of the war, his writings and public statements from 1919 and after, often adopt a triumphalist and bellicose tone at odds with the more contradictory dynamics of the painting's Cubist techniques. The painting is, I propose, structured around the tension between a scene of compensatory fraternal bonding and the body's fragmentation and dismemberment, suggesting a psychic conflict around the war's capacity to unite and destroy.

Wartime Iconographies

World War I was a historical trauma for France that radically undermined the dominant fiction of masculinity. France experienced what historians claim to be the highest per capita number of casualties among combatant nations. Some eight million French men went to war, and about 1.3 million died. Another 2.8 million, or 40 percent, returned wounded, of which at least 300,000 suffered a catastrophic loss of limb and became *mutilés*.[50] An estimated 11–14 percent of French wounded were *gueules cassées*, whose facial wounds meant they suffered what medical historian Sophie Delaporte has called a "double violence," a physical injury combined with the psychological loss of self identified with the face.[51] The physical damage to the male body was compounded by an indeterminate but significant number of cases of psychological trauma, a "mass outbreak of mental disorder" as George Mosse called it, that raised the specter of male hysteria.[52] At the same time that trench life and disability could imprison men physically and psychically, women gained new wartime freedoms and autonomy by assuming labor roles that men had vacated.[53] During and after the war, French women also had the contradictory new duties of being both breadwinners and caretakers for disabled veterans.[54] Many men feared a permanent reversal of gender roles. In 1917, Apollinaire expressed these sentiments: "Without a doubt, after the war, men will be occupied at home. They will do the housework, cooking, and mending, while women will work at the workshop and in the office."[55] Cartoons and caricatures often ridiculed working women depicted as displacing men in the labor force.[56] Silverman interprets this wartime homefront management without men as a "symbolic impotence" and a second historical trauma of the war.[57]

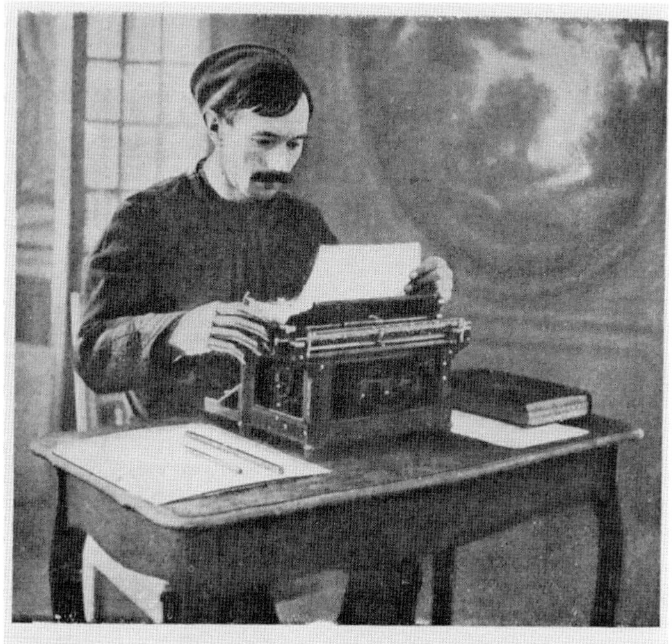

Fig. 7 Jules Amar, "Crippled Typist Using Mechanical Arm." In Jules Amar, *The Physiology of Industrial Organisation and the Re-employment of the Disabled*, translated by Bernard Miall (London: The Library Press Limited, 1918), 302, fig. 108. Courtesy of the Library of Congress.

Reconstructing the damaged male body to return to prewar labor became a design and engineering project subject to state regulation, surveillance, and control. Since masculinity and citizenship were interdependent, men were understood as "the state," and the male body signified the health of the nation. Jules Amar, a French physiologist and expert on fatigue and labor power, represents the French investment in what he called the "human motor." Amar's publications *La Prothèse et le travail des mutilés* (1916) and *Organisation physiologique du travail* (1917) were quickly translated into English and published in England and the United States in 1918 and 1919 respectively. He argued that some 80 percent of disabled men could be reeducated. He designed class-based artificial limbs, adopted in many combatant nations that served Taylorist efficiency and industrialization by replacing the lost labor function with hands in the shapes of tools or with articulated fingers to serve the work of typists, violinists, and accountants.[58] In *The Card Party*, the arms and fingers of Léger's left and central figures resemble the kind of prosthetic that Amar developed with articulated fingers (fig. 7). In practice, prosthetics were not always comfortable or easy to use. In 1916, Cendrars was fitted with an aluminum prosthetic with articulated fingers due to his profession as a writer, but he soon abandoned it in a train station, preferring instead to learn how to write with his left hand.[59]

For those with facial wounds like Léger's left and center soldiers, serious disfiguration could remain even after multiple reconstructive surgeries, resulting in a belief that face masks could help men return to their masculine claim upon public life, fatherhood, and productivity. Léger's representation may respond to debates over reconstruction's aims. Léger's soldiers, with their ruptured, stepped, and blocky red cheeks, splint-like noses, and eyes without pupils, reject the mask and its ideology of a return to a prewar self. By contrast, American artist Anna Coleman Ladd established a Paris Studio for Portrait Masks making handcrafted, painted copper masks with reconstructive aims. Located at 70 rue Notre Dame des Champs from November 1917 to January 1919, Ladd's studio was only a couple blocks from Léger's studio at 86 rue Notre Dame des Champs, making it likely he saw her subjects regularly. Ladd's masks, based upon plaster molds of the soldier's damaged face, covered what surgery could not fully repair (fig. 8). Only about 1.5 percent of facially wounded soldiers received such masks, while many men rejected the masks and others remained hidden from sight; reportedly, women and children would burst into tears at the sight of the disfigured.[60] Eventually, the masks fell into disuse due to deterioration and the disconnect between the idealized face of a mask and the aging face of an organic body. In Julie Powell's analysis, the mask signified an ideology of a classicizing and conservative view of an essential, unchanging France, while the soldiers who refused masks and called themselves *les gueules cassées* adopted a more modern position of a changeable national and masculine body.[61] Léger, who described himself as part of the "great postwar generation," may have sought to present the damaged face as both a type of injury as well as a refusal to return to a prewar self.

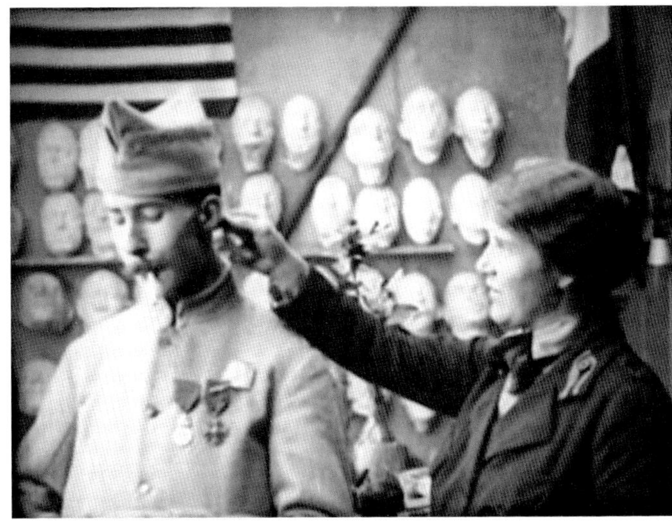

Fig. 8 Film still from *Red Cross Work on Mutilés, At Paris* (1918). 4mm film. OHA 252. Otis Historical Archives, National Museum of Health and Medicine, Armed Forces Institute of Pathology.

The maladies that were perhaps the most destabilizing to masculinity were "nerves" or psychic trauma identified with feminine irrationality, male dependence on women, and masculine infantalization. Prior to the war, the most acute symptoms of psychic trauma—muteness, tremors, paralysis, and nightmares—had been associated with Jean-Martin Charcot's diagnosis of hysteria and were largely attributed to women.[62] Although the wartime epidemic initially caused a revival of Charcot's hysteria diagnosis and hypnosis therapy, the official French position on mental breakdown was established by Joseph Babinski.[63] A Charcot student and the wartime head of neurology at Salpêtrière Hospital in Paris, Babinski rejected a neurological basis to hysteria and was suspicious of the suggestibility of hypnosis therapy. Instead, Babinski developed a diagnosis he called pithiatism, which was supposedly curable by the persuasion of a virile medical authority and which was widely adopted by the French military. By 1916, Babinski had established a policy prohibiting women from entry into the neurological units, fearing "demoralizing influences" and "collective hysteria."[64] In the context of war, the symptomology of trauma, especially its unclear etiology, motivated debates about how widespread the problem was, what its origins were, and whether men used the condition as a way to evade conscription.[65] Shell-shocked soldiers like Léger who had no other physical wounds were often perceived as malingerers who sought to avoid frontline duties; such perceptions of cowardice motivated decades and sometimes lifetimes of silence.[66]

Léger's letters from the front report on soldiers going mad but never adopt the psychiatric language of hysteria. One soldier, Léger writes, was singing at the top of his lungs and had to be carried away in a rain of bullets. Another was in "a state of unconsciousness that made him indifferent to all around him," and a third went out into the trenches "half mad."[67] In his earliest letters from 1914 onward, Léger adopts the discourse commonly used in soldiers' letters and in trench journals, writing of a *cafard* or *un fort cafard*, meaning exhaustion or depression, that he and his fellow soldiers felt.[68] As Jean Nicot's analysis of soldiers' letters shows, complaints about "combatant fatigue" were particularly acute in 1917 due to the length of the war.[69] "Trench journals," or soldiers' presses like *La Baoinnette* and *Le Crapouillot* that were directed by soldiers and officers, initially sought to respond to the *bourrage de crâne* (brainwashing or propagandistic lies) and were full of full of stories of fatigue, depression, and "morbid anecdotes" of bodies split apart "like horrible puppets."[70] *Le cafard* was so widespread and so frequently linked to other symptoms such as hallucinations that it became medicalized in a series of books published in 1917 and 1918 by the frontline doctor Paul Voivenel.[71] Even after being hospitalized, Léger primarily references exhaustion, nerves, and neurasthenia in his letters—not hysteria or pithiatism—engaging with a more popularized discourse rather than the more stigmatized and newer medical diagnoses.

Officially sanctioned exhibitions indicate the range of motifs and the ways dominant culture largely suppressed the war's traumas. The Musée de l'Armée operated continuously during the war and exhibited a diverse range of objects, including commissioned paintings, maps, insignia, and war trophies (e.g., flags, munitions) seized from the enemy.[72] Individual and group exhibitions of amateur and professional soldier-artists took place throughout the war and increased after 1916. One of the largest such exhibitions, the Salon des Armées (December 1916–February 1917), represented common themes: soldiers in their trenches, caricatures of the enemy, and ruined landscapes.[73] In the art displayed, wounded soldiers lean on canes or have bandaged heads, but none display amputation or disfiguration. Léger could have seen the exhibition or read about it in the press, since it occurred at the time of his fourth leave in Paris. Then in December 1917, while hospitalized at the Hôpital Italien on the Quai d'Orsay, Léger was close to Les Invalides and the Musée de l'Armée. An undated letter from late 1917 shows that he was aware of the iconography disseminated by the museum, that he planned to bring a friend some of the museum's reproductions, and that several of his war drawings had entered the museum's collection that August, all of which make a visit likely.[74]

Military history paintings were, in Léger's view, outmoded genres unsuited to modern life. Trained at the École des Arts Décoratifs as a student of Jean-Louis Gérôme and Gabriel Ferrier in 1903 and 1904 but rejected from the École des Beaux-Arts, Léger was familiar with academic art traditions and naturalism. Before the war, he had criticized academic art and the genre of history painting. In 1913, Léger proclaimed that the few workers he once saw standing before Edouard Detaille's Franco-Prussian War battle scenes (in the Musée de l'Armée) and Jean-Paul Laurens's historical narratives were now going to the movies.[75] Nevertheless, Detaille's student Georges Scott, a member of the Société des peintres militaires, was a prolific artist and illustrator widely credited with renovating the genre of history painting. Scott regularly exhibited at the Musée de l'Armée and published in a leading illustrated weekly magazine, *L'Illustration*, making him one of the best-known wartime artists, such that Léger was undoubtedly aware of his work. Scott's pictures participated in an iconography of the confident *poilu*, hand-to-hand combat, ruined villages and churches, and sacralized death that largely served military propaganda. His *The Soldier of 1915* (1915) (fig. 9), published in the December 16, 1915, issue of *L'Illustration*, exemplifies the type he perpetuated. Dressed in full uniform, with his pack on his back, his rifle upright and at the ready, and a pipe in his mouth, the soldier stands in three-quarter profile, dominating a low horizon line. Earlier that year, before official censorship set in, Scott had produced a remarkably disturbing image of an explosion in an enemy unit, severed limbs flying about. Published in *L'Illustration* (May 29, 1915), it was an anomaly in his oeuvre. By 1916, Scott acknowledged to the novelist Henri Barbusse that the truth of the war was just too horrible to paint.[76] Another Beaux-Arts student, Adolphe Willette, the architect of Le Moulin Rouge and an artist who wrote to Léger during the war, similarly chose to imagine the soldier as a virile figure embracing his lover in a poster created for the *Journée du poilu* (1915).[77]

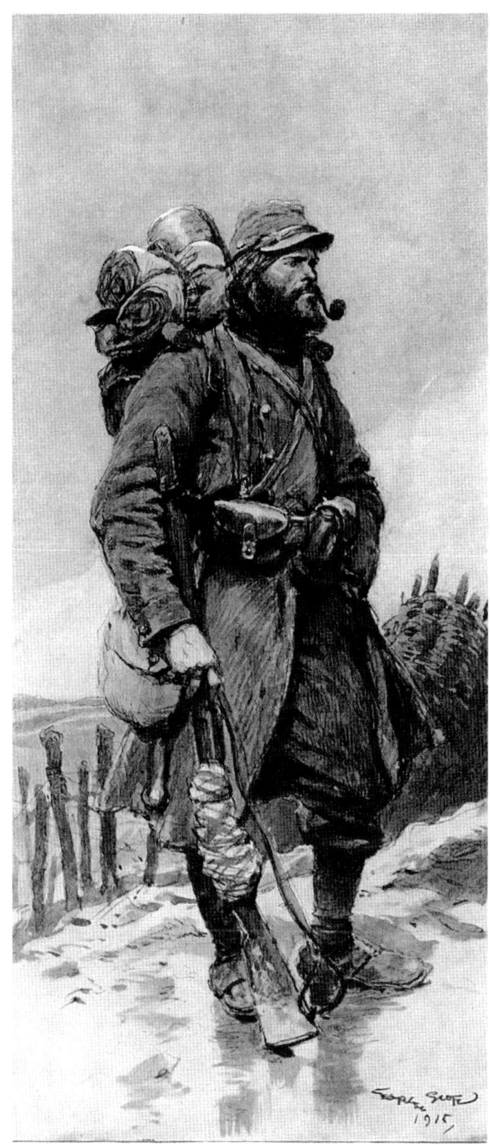

Fig. 9 Georges Scott, *The Soldier of 1915*. In *L'Illustration*, no. 3757 (March 6, 1915), 251 (in black and white) and in *L'Illustration*, no, 3850 (December 16, 1916), n.p. (in color). Image © *L'Illustration*.

Prominent galleries, such as the Bernheim-Jeune Gallery, which Léger knew for its prewar exhibitions of Cézanne (1910) and the Futurists (1912), organized patriotic exhibitions during the war. In January 1915, the gallery hosted a "fraternity of artists" exhibition under the patronage of Raymond Poincaré, the president of the republic, and under the leadership of Léon Bonnat, a professor at the École des Beaux-Arts. Their first album of painting, watercolors, and drawings published contributions by leading Impressionist and Fauvist artists as well as academicians.[78] These artists envisioned the successful prosecution of the war for a larger French public: the heroic French soldier or *poilu* remains an intact body; allegorical French symbols Marianne and a personification of "La Marseillaise" lead the troops charging into battle; women pray and knit for their men at the front; or mothers cradle their infants as signs of faith in the future. In scenes of trumpeting angels flying over the fallen or officers surveying the dead, the message is one of necessary sacrifice and heroic death, leaving an image of largely intact if wounded bodies.

The contemporary avant-garde, too, had to prove its patriotism and adapt to the nationalist iconography, as Kenneth Silver has argued. Cubism came under attack as German dealers Daniel-Henry Kahnweiler and Wilhelm Uhde left the country and had their collections confiscated by the French state. New periodicals Paul Iribe's *Le Mot* (November 1914) and Ozenfant's *L'Elan* (April 1915) sought to adopt a patriotic posture while defending the avant-garde. Probably thinking of illustrated weeklies like *Le Miroir*, Ozenfant reprimanded the French press for its gore and cadavers and proposed averting the gaze: "When you [the French soldier] fall, lamentably, isn't it more decent to turn away?"[79] He praised soldier-artists like André Denoyer de Segonzac, whom Léger corresponded with during the war, for the ability to maintain "perfect possession of all their faculties" even while drawing at the front.[80] Segonzac's drawings, included in an exhibition in November 1918 sponsored by *Le Crapouillot*, depict the dead soldiers as sleeping and the living survivors as intact bodies.[81] As Silver shows, even Cubism's leading theorists modified their stance. In Pierre Reverdy's *Nord-Sud* (1917–19), Paul Dermée announced a new classicism, and Apollinaire praised the great men of France. Jean Metzinger, a leading prewar Cubist theorist, sought to defend artistic liberty while also turning to motifs of a loyal citizenry, such as his female *Nurse* (1914–16) reproduced in *L'Elan* (December 1, 1916).[82] Jacques Villon, the oldest of the Duchamp family of artists, whom Léger knew from prewar artistic gatherings, produced a naturalistic drawing of an officers' card game: *At Ease* (*The Officers' Bridge Game*) (1915). In the December 1916 issue of *L'Elan*, Ozenfant published Pablo Picasso's *Portrait of Max Jacob* (1915) and Severini's *Maternity* (1916), two artworks exemplifying the return to an "Ingres-style" naturalism and a rejection of vanguard aesthetics. In Severini's case, this new painting reversed his Futurist war imagery exhibited in February 1916.

In his book *Le Silence des peintres* (1996), Philippe Dagen has argued that painting turned away from the war's horrors just as it was eclipsed by the new media of photography that even official state artists like Scott learned to rely on. Photography gained much wider audiences through mass distribution. New periodicals such as *Le Miroir*, the magazine referenced in Léger's painting, as well as *L'Illustration*, *J'ai vu*, and *Sur le vif*, provided visual narratives of the war often using Army photography.[83] Even after official state censorship set in, some periodicals like *Miroir* published gruesome images of brutalized women and dead enemy soldiers.[84] Serialized photography albums published by Agence ROL and *L'Illustration* and single-issue color photography albums by Jules Gervais-Courtellemont on the battles of Ourcq, the Marne, and Verdun sought to narrate the war for popular audiences. The war photography album rationalized and organized the war hierarchically, spatially, and chronologically by grouping photographs into portraits of the political and military leaders and their public meetings; new weaponry and big guns, including the 75mm cannon, that would defeat the enemy; staged scenes of troop preparations; colonial subjects and soldiers as ethnic types; destroyed towns and churches as evidence of enemy savagery; and entertainment, leisure, and medical care of the soldiers. As Joëlle Beurier has shown, the capacity to depict the dead, primarily envisioned as the enemy, declined after spring 1915, which she attributes not just to the initiation of state censorship but also to entrenchment and the unheroic passivity of soldiers' bodies. In her analysis, photography shifted to two categories of images that sought to repress death: first, the daily life of soldiers, entertainment at war, and other soldierly activities that exclude danger, and second, mass death envisioned not as bodies but in the Battle of Verdun as an apocalyptic landscape viewed through aerial photography or in the Battle of the Somme as "an enormous rubbish dump."[85]

In early 1915, France organized state censorship and propaganda campaigns to contain the representation of mass casualties and to generate a new visual reality. Established in April 1915, the Section photographique de l'armée française reached a staff of more than ninety photographic reporters and, by the end of the war, produced some 170,000 photographs. The Army controlled access to the front and, in November 1915, issued specific instructions distributed to frontline photographer-soldiers requiring images to valorize French military power and the machinery of war and to document soldiers and their daily life as well as war damage to churches and cultural patrimony. Certain subjects, such as mutinies and executions of soldiers, were never represented.[86] The military's Section cinématographique de l'armée, also created in spring 1915, made the newsreel a mass phenomenon and produced more than one thousand films in collaboration with the major film studios. In Laurent Véray's analysis of the military film archives, he argues that film, like other visual media, displaced French death and dismemberment through an iconography of debris-ridden landscapes and ruined churches.[87] The weekly newsreel *Les Annales de la Guerre* (1917–19) and films such as *La Puissance militaire de la France* (1917)

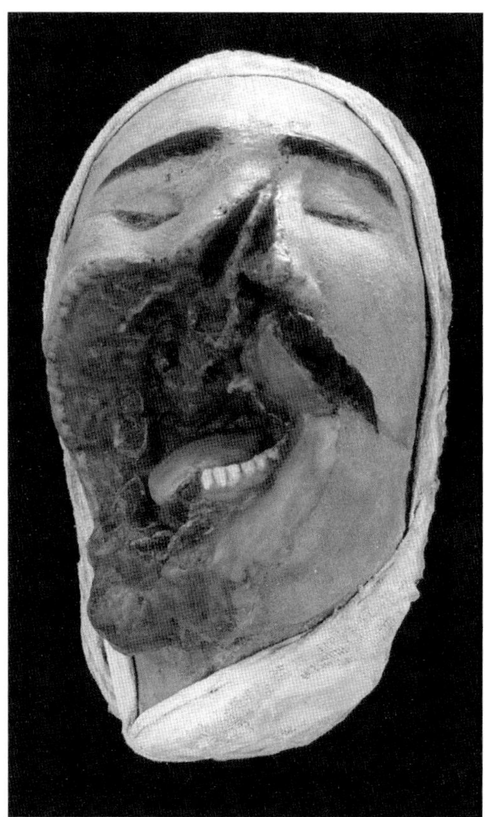

Fig. 10 Face mutilated by shell, substantial loss of right part of face, notably superior and inferior maxillary, wound before treatment, 1914–19. Polychrome plaster and wax facial mold. 35.8 × 21.5 × 15 cm. © Musée du Service de santé des armées, Val-de-Grâce, Paris, Inv. no. 2006.4408.

depict soldiers at work and leisure or display the weaponry of war, organization of troops, and supply and health services. Due to risks as well as technical difficulties, cameramen and photographers rarely captured firing lines or active combat, yet film could offer a privileged view from the trench between battles.

Army film and photography also sought to visualize the reconstruction and rehabilitation of amputee soldiers, but many of these were not publicly distributed. For example, the Army used both media to document the efficacy of the reconstructed body, as in the case of French amputees whose prosthetics permitted them to perform agricultural labor.[88] But during the war, the military maintained a general prohibition against publishing images of the *mutilés* without their prosthetics.[89] As Lyford argues, photographs of the amputee risked emasculation of the subject, resulting in restricted circulation for medical use. In her analysis of a series of censored photographs from June 1916, a double amputee appears with and without his prosthetic arms, oscillating between an image of corporeal reconstruction and one of dependence on a female nurse.[90]

With rare exceptions, severe disfiguration did not appear in publicly disseminated images until 1919, when five *gueules cassées*, or "broken faces," attended the signing ceremony for the Treaty of Versailles and led the Victory Parade on Bastille Day. However, Léger's experience as a *brancardier* starting in spring 1916 meant he saw such wounds immediately after the injury rather than in the aestheticized context of reconstruction. The stepped faces, spliced nose, and missing eyes of Léger's left and center soldier in *The Card Party* suggest his interest in compelling the viewer to see facial wounding as Cubist fracture. In an exception to the suppressed sight of facial disfiguration, a new museum at the Val-de-Grâce military hospital in Paris opened in July 1916 with the aims of overcoming the distressing image of war wounded and narrating national regeneration. Lyford's research on the new hospital shows that its exhibitions displayed lifelike painted wax and plaster casts (*moulages*) of facial damage, before and after surgery photographs, and full-size mannequins wearing prosthetic limbs (fig. 10). Reviews show that the journalists were both disturbed by the realism of the *moulages* but also interpreted them within the museum's narrative of recovery and reconstruction.[91] Léger may have seen these displays, since Val-de-Grâce and its new museum were only a ten-minute walk from his studio, and his third leave in August 1916 occurred a month after the museum's opening.

Fractured Bodies and Temporalities

Léger's use of Cubist visual language in *The Card Party* permitted a representation of injury that circumvented prevailing military censorship of French injury and death while still borrowing from innovative forms of photography. Existing scholarship notes Léger's reference to *Le Miroir* through the fragment "iro." But other parts of the painting might also be informed by *Le Miroir*'s new photographic forms, which published multiple views of the zigzag trench construction, such as its panoramic maps of Verdun and an aerial view of Fleury, both of which were sites described in Léger's letters from the ground level.[92] Léger's use of aerial photography's perspective of the zigzag trench in the framing elements around the left soldier in *The Card Party* demonstrate his interest in photography's new abstracting modes of vision. Aerial photography, as Paula Ahmed has argued, signified not only in terms of power, mastery, and control but also in terms of Cubist imagination and history or the *longue durée*, even geological time.[93] As Green has shown, Léger's ink drawing of two dead French soldiers in a trench quotes and inverts a photograph published two weeks before on the cover of *Le Miroir*.[94] Léger must have known that Cendrars contributed photographs to *Le Miroir*, motivating his study of the periodical. Léger's *The Card Party* may, too, have drawn from *Le Miroir*'s scenes of card-playing soldiers, such as one of French soldiers playing *manille* in the trench between battles or another of two Germans killed in the midst of their card game.[95]

Where war photographers most often aimed for a propagandistic verism, Léger borrowed from photography to convey a temporal and spatial simultaneity. An elusive Cubist concept arising from French philosopher Henri Bergson's concept of *durée* (duration), simultaneity was first theorized by Metzinger and Gleizes in *Du Cubisme* (1912) and adopted by Léger in paintings like *The Wedding* (1912).[96] Bergsonian *durée* is antithetical to measurable time or space and instead is time experienced as a constant flux and felt at the level of intuition.[97] Simultaneity signified multiple temporal moments and overlapping spatialities, ideas that had informed Léger's prewar paintings. For example, David Cottington describes *The Wedding* as a "unanimist event" in which the spiraling motion of smoke and vapors "have no perceptual origin" but "anticipate the dizzy-spin device of Hollywood film 'flash-backs.'"[98]

In *The Card Party*, Léger converges photography's aerial perspective and direct view, borrowing from the aviator's perspective at the time of bombing but also a reader's view of an illustrated magazine like *Miroir*. His soldiers bring together moments that photography represented as distinct: the fraternal time of card playing and the traumatic time when an attack arrests play and produces death. Léger's Cubist reworkings and inversions of photography's documentary mode permitted his assertion of another "reality" of time, space, and national survival. In 1914, Léger argued against "visual realism" and for a modern "realism of conception."[99] Painting, he claimed, responded to modernity's speed, its visual stimuli "one hundred times more" than in the prior century, with the "rupture of forms" and "violent contrasts" that are "multiplicative" and "dissonant." Léger's multiplicative temporalities deploy prewar Cubist simultaneity to imagine the new realities of the war.

Léger's iconography of fraternal solidarity engages not only with *durée* but also with Bergsonian concepts of *esprit de corps* and *élan vital* (or vitalism) that led to an upsurge of nationalism even before the war. Bergson's theories of time and memory, creativity and perception had informed Léger and his artistic circles in the prewar era.[100] That Léger continued to read Bergson during the war appears in his letters.[101] Bergson's collectivist and vitalist concepts became important to a wide range of actors invoking nationalist sentiments, as art historian Mark Antliff has discussed.[102] French scholars have shown that during the war, the discourse of *esprit de corps* was a way of unifying diverse classes and populations and a vehicle for keeping up morale and combating depression.[103] By 1917, Bergsonian discourse permeated military discourse and disciplinary systems in the service of nationalism. Ozenfant, for example, invoked Bergson's *élan vital* in the name of his journal, *L'Elan*, as a means of promoting patriotism. Bergsonian vitalism offered a philosophical and artistically informed notion of survival. Bergson's concept of *élan vital* became what historian Jay Winter cast as a "cult of the offensive."[104] Art historians Mark Antliff and Patricia Leighten interpret the vitalist discourse in the formation of the French soldier as a compensatory "psychological weapon."[105]

Producing *The Card Party* during his convalescence may have had a therapeutic function for Léger, since the painting images a confrontation with death as well as survival in the form of the collective body. Léger's soldiers engage traumatic time and space: they are both fractured and reassembled, in trench and in recovery, bound together in fraternity and separated by death. The painting brings together three kinds of trauma that informed his artistic choices. First, mobilization separated him from his artistic community. Second, at the front, he witnessed death, the body turned to meat, and psychic suffering. Third, he manifested the symptomology of psychic trauma, for which he was hospitalized. Léger described each of these experiences using the language of trauma, shock, and nerves.

For Léger, mobilization in August 1914 was the first form of trauma he experienced, separating him from his avant-garde community and rupturing his persona or identity. He wrote: "Imagine the shock: I left my studio, the frontiers of art, and I fell into a crowd of road workers."[106] He had networked with an international community, a bourgeoning arts press, and an avant-garde exhibition culture: the communal life of the Abbaye de Créteil collective led by Gleizes, the meetings at the Montparnasse café Closerie des Lilas, soirées at the Puteaux and Courbevoie studios of Villon and Gleizes, and lectures sponsored by the Russian expatriate Marie Vassillief and her Académie. The war put a halt to many of the exhibition venues Léger had participated in. The Salon d'Automne did not resume until 1919, the Salon des Indépendants suspended operations until 1920, and the Section d'Or group was only briefly revived in 1919. After his first solo exhibition in fall 1912 at Kahnweiler's gallery, Léger did not have another solo show until February 1919, at Rosenberg's gallery. The war interrupted the growing international networks and reputation Léger had gained as part of group exhibitions with Der Sturm in Berlin in 1910, the Jack of Diamonds exhibition in Moscow in 1912, and the Armory Show in New York in 1913.

The war's dislocation and dispersal of the avant-garde groups could not be repaired during his short periodic leaves. Prewar partnerships between Picasso, a noncombatant Spaniard, and Braque, who suffered a serious head injury, and between Robert Delaunay, who went to Spain, and Léger, who went to war, were permanently ruptured or estranged. Cendrars saw Delaunay as abandoning France and flaunting his wartime artistic successes such that Cendrars refused to see Delaunay again.[107] The war aborted the Puteaux group meetings and dispersed its founders and members, the three Duchamp brothers. Marcel was disqualified from service due to a heart murmur and spent the war years in the United States, while Jacques went to the front, and Raymond served as a medic but tragically contracted typhoid fever and blood poisoning and died in 1918.[108] Like many other combatant-artists—André Mare, Segonzac, and Gleizes, as well as contributors to trench journals like *Le Crapouillot*—Léger's wartime artistic production was limited. Aside from a few small humorous paintings on board as gifts for his commanding officers, he produced drawings in ink or charcoal while at the front and only two extant paintings on canvas: *Soldier with a Pipe* (1916) and *The Card Party* (1917).

The second phase of trauma for Léger was his experience at the front and the confrontation with death registered individually and collectively. His accounts are documented in letters to his childhood friend Louis Poughon and to his lover and later wife, Jeanne Lohy. Within months of the start of the war, in October 1914, he wrote to Poughon that he "saw trenches where the 75[mm cannon] had cleaned up the Germans," but "the phase of horror has long since passed for me. You get used to it all." In a kind of gallows humor, he wrote, they would hand out "prizes for the most morbid grimaces."[109] War was no longer "heroic" and no longer had "the thrill of action," since soldiers had been made into "machines" and war had become an "abstraction."[110]

The threat of death was a constant anxiety and reality. Léger often wondered: "Will I be alive this evening?" His letters describe the men in his company who died, sometimes in a slow, painful death as in the case of one soldier who could not be safely rescued but lay in agony in no-man's-land, calling out the names of his friends, his wife, and daughter for twenty minutes: "Never in my life have I been so disturbed. This trench warfare is made of little assassinations like that."[111] In a letter from November 1914, he reports being "affected" by the death of a childhood friend, Duchène, and the "sinister" execution of a deserter, whom Léger describes sympathetically as a kind of "Montéhus de Caf conc," an anarchist singer who sang of class solidarity between soldiers and demonstrators.[112] In January 1916, Léger reported on the death of a friendly corporal.[113] After that, he no longer mentions the names of the dead, as though individual death and mourning has become so overwhelming it can no longer be registered. During the Battle of Verdun in October and November 1916, death is collectivized, totalizing, anonymous, desacralized: "everywhere human debris"; bodies become a "mix of rotten meat and mud."[114] At best, the dead are types; at worst, their corpses still have utility. Léger had to dig a trench among the dead and discovered a wooden cross marked "colonel" at one end of a body whose feet served as coat hooks.

The third wartime type of trauma for Léger was the period of his hospitalization when he painted *The Card Party*. Hospitalization provided an anxious reprieve that nevertheless held the threat of return to the front. Admitted on the last day of his leave in July 1917 due to an attack of rheumatism, Léger expected to be treated for only a month and then returned to duty. Writing to Poughon, he reports hopefully about a prospective new art dealer, but at the same time, he assumes he will have to return to the front before he can produce new art: "Will I manage to get off! I doubt it."[115] His use of the verb *m'embusquer* (to make myself a shirker) betrays a sense of guilt about evading service or anxiety about being seen as a shirker due to hospitalization without any obvious injury. Even as his hospital stay lasted much longer and he began to lose weight in September, Léger still expected to return to the front, writing that he was "making of neurasthenia a brief delay. You'll see me sent back to the front in this state."[116]

In October and December 1917, Léger was examined by two neurologists. Their diagnoses avoided the most effeminizing categories of psychic shock while still indicating that they interpreted his symptoms as a case of nerves. Emile Parmentier, who had interned with Charcot, examined Léger at the Hôpital St. Joseph and initially diagnosed Léger's condition as nervous gastritis. He imposed a "strict regimen" of "calm, countryside" and an additional "two typed pages" of instruction.[117] By December, Léger still had not improved and suffered from a "generally depressed state," claiming that "never in my life have I lacked so much energy."[118] Sent to Salpêtrière, he saw Charles Chatelin, a specialist who had published extensively on paralysis, brain injury, and head trauma. Chatelin had coauthored a book that included discussion of *commotion cérébrale*, a neurological injury to the brain caused by explosions. Chatelin sought to differentiate *commotion cérébrale* from other kinds of "functional, emotional, pithiatic, or simulated" nervous disorders.[119] In doing so, Chatelin both acknowledges Babinski's pithiatism yet disagrees with his dismissal of *commotion*. Many French doctors accepted *commotion* and used it more widely, since it focused on a neurological cause that left open the possibility of healing over time.[120]

Léger was lucky in his care and diagnosis, since he managed to avoid the most authoritarian doctors and stigmatizing interpretations of his case. Léger's letters show that he thought he suffered from neurasthenia, which accords with Parmentier's remedy of calm and countryside. Neurasthenia was originally developed in the United States as a diagnosis of nervous exhaustion for overworked men, while during the war, the diagnosis extended to cultivated or sensitive men who grew depressed. But neurasthenia diagnoses also raised questions about a predisposition to psychic instability.[121] Breakdowns among the women in Léger's family could have lent to medical interpretations of familial degeneracy and effeminacy, especially since, as Léger reports, Parmentier had also cared for a female cousin.[122] The year before, in November 1916, Léger's future wife, Lohy, had confided to the Swedish painter Nils Dardel that she had been sick for two months and that there had been talk of placing her in a *maison de santé*, or asylum.[123]

In France, neurasthenia became a neurological malady that particularly afflicted middle and upper classes, including artists. Around the same time that Léger was hospitalized, Francis Picabia, too, was hospitalized in Switzerland for neurasthenia provoked not by frontline service, which he evaded, but by his New York life or what Amelia Jones describes as a "self-imposed state of nervous exhaustion caused by excess socializing and drug and alcohol abuse."[124] But whereas the fragmented soldiers in Léger's *The Card Party* are alternatively survivors or memorialized, Picabia's ironic portraits and feminized light bulbs ridicule sublimation to the machine. After the war, when Dada's mechanomorphic bodies made their mark on the Paris scene, Picabia mocked the military's production of war dead as heroes.[125] Perhaps Picabia's distance from combat permitted his Dadaist stance, while Léger registered the shock of the war and sought to overcome it. In May 1916, Léger wrote to Poughon that since he could not paint at the front, he used letter writing to "kill neurasthenia."[126] For Léger, the war damaged his nerves, and his artistic practice during hospitalization permitted a return to painting that had a therapeutic role.

At the end of Léger's hospital stay, the supervising physician who signed Léger's medical release in early 1918, a Dr. Bigard, expressed a strong interest in Léger's art, and Léger dedicated a 1917 still life to him.[127] By releasing Léger with a diagnosis of "chronic congestion" rather than one of the many diagnoses associated with mental breakdown, including neurasthenia, Bigard may have been motivated by a mix of other factors as well: Léger's three years of service, deference to Léger's status as an artist, and a belief that he needed rest but would recover. The result was that he saved Léger from diagnoses that could have permanently damaged Léger's public persona and self-image.

Cubism and Trauma

In the context of the war and hospitalization, what did Cubism mean for Léger? In November 1916, he described the war as an "academy of Cubism" that produced jarring recombinations—a chair perched on top of a tree—which "please[d] his Cubist soul."[128] Late in life, Léger told artist André Verdet that Verdun's "destruction, [its] walls in ruin . . . [and] signs in the streets" entered his compositions "where he tried to better render a sensation of shock in lines and planes."[129] Stephen Kern has described World War I as a "Cubist war," aligned with new modes of seeing, and Cubism as an "excellent means for portraying a war that broke all the rules of traditional combat."[130] As Kenneth Silver has shown, Cubism succeeded at the front even as it came under attack in Paris. Léger's wartime pencil sketches insist upon the war's physical, temporal, and linguistic disruptions. They often show soldiers in the ruins of houses or towns or destroyed buildings interspersed with bits of signage.

For Léger, Cubism was the visual language that broke the rules of academic convention and a language that he shared with his fellow artists but also one that represented the conditions of the war. On his first leave in August 1915, Léger made a point of visiting with fellow soldier-painters who had been part of the prewar Cubist circles he had exhibited with. He saw Roger de La Fresnaye and Albert Gleizes, who fought until the end of 1915, and Juliette Roche, who married Gleizes in late summer that year.[131] Before the war, La Fresnaye had deployed Cubism in nationalist and militarist paintings like *Artillery* (1911) and *Conquest of the Air* (1913). In *The Soldier Drinks* (1910), Marc Chagall, who had known Léger since 1909 when they both lived in La Ruche, combines Cubist planes in the face and hands of the soldier with a folkloric iconography to suggest multiple times and places in the man's life. During the war, Gleizes produced Cubist woodcuts such as *The Return* (1915), published in *Le Mot* (July 1915), and portraits, including of his brother-in-law Jacques Nayral. Léger also kept in touch with his childhood friend and onetime studio mate, André Mare, who collaborated on the Maison Cubiste at the Salon d'Automne in 1912 and became more Cubist in his wartime drawings. Léger used his leaves to stay abreast of the avant-garde art scene in Paris. At the time of his August 1916 leave, he wrote to Poughon telling him that he had several paintings on exhibition "at rue St. Honoré in the gallery contiguous to Poiret . . . the anonymous organizer of the exhibition."[132] The month before, in July 1916, André Salmon organized the Salon d'Antin exhibition that included Léger's *14th of July* (1914) and the first public showing of Picasso's *Les Demoiselles d'Avignon* (1907).[133] That summer, Severini's naturalistic *Portrait of Jeanne* (1916) and *Maternity* (1916), too, appeared in the rue St. Honoré gallery, marking a reversal of his Futurist *Cannon in Action* (1915) exhibited earlier that year. As Silver has shown, the summer of 1916 was a pivotal period when critics attacked Cubism and announced its demise as vanguard artists like Severini abruptly shifted from antimimetic art (in his case, Italian Futurism) to a new naturalism more palatable to a wartime public.[134]

By late 1916, when Léger returned to Paris for his fourth leave, many avant-garde artists began abandoning the fracture of avant-garde aesthetics even as he hewed to Cubism. Two wartime advocates for classicism were Ozenfant and the Belgian writer Paul Dermée, later founders of *L'Esprit Nouveau* (1920–25) and the Purist art movement Léger joined postwar. Ozenfant's wartime magazine, *L'Elan* (1915–16), promoted the return to Ingres-style naturalism represented by Picasso and Severini in late 1916. In December 1916, Ozenfant redefined Cubism as "a movement of Purism" and argued against prewar analytical Cubism.[135] Léger's perpetuation of Cubism even came under attack by Ozenfant, who exasperatedly but privately accused Léger and other artists of "perpetuating and advocating . . . BOCHE PAINTING."[136] Ozenfant's reaction exemplifies what Silver has described as a split between Cubism's "vitality in the trenches" and its rejection in Paris.[137]

During this contested period for Cubism, Léger produced his first painting of the war, *Soldier with a Pipe* (1916) (fig. 11), which represents a Cubist *fantassin* (infantryman) antithetical to Scott's virile, gun-toting *poilu* and Willette's lascivious soldier. A year earlier, Léger wrote that he wanted to represent the shadowy *fantassin* in a state of shock and war as "a mechanization from which all emotion is excluded."[138] Doing so posed the problem of picturing a negation—that is, the absence of emotion or feeling. Rather than transform his sketches of *foreurs* (drillers) with their phallic machines into painting, he chose instead to depict a pipe-smoking, battle-weary soldier who leans on a crutch and whose right shoulder maintains a tenuous ligament-like connection to the arm. This soldier has no weapon at his side but is a wounded man whose facial injury is abstracted into a dramatic red trapezoidal form. In representing the soldier in this way, Léger invites injury into the frame in a way that circumvented censorship of disfiguration. While rejecting any explicit displays of affect and blocking the sight of destroyed flesh, the soldier's facial injury nevertheless recalls a shrapnel-sheared face. Its formal and corporeal contrast is the soldier's mouth, sutured shut in an X, as he clenches down on the pipe as if to avoid crying out in pain or perhaps unable to do so. Facial disfiguration, equally important in *Soldier with a Pipe* and *The Card Party*, could produce mutism due to the

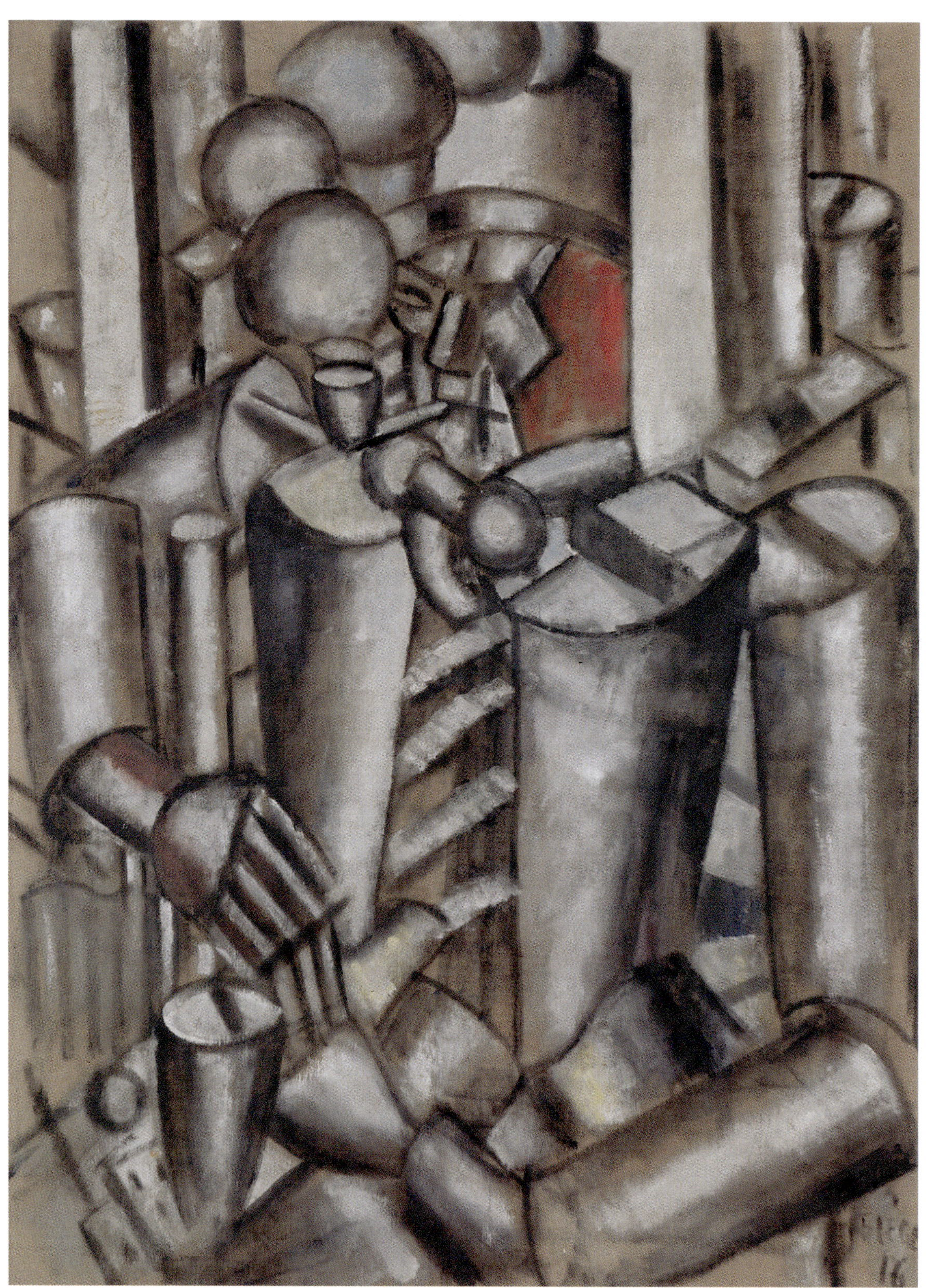

damage to muscle and bone structure.[139] As aesthetician Elaine Scarry has observed: "Pain does not simply resist language . . . [it] actively destroys it."[140] In her examples, the gaping mouth as tortured scream reoccurs in art: from the alienated subject in Edvard Munch's *Scream* (1893) to the mother watching her child's carriage descend into a fatal fall in Sergei Eisenstein's film *The Battleship Potemkin* (1925). Léger's mute soldier with his sutured X of a mouth denies both language and the atavistic cry of suffering. Such a suppression of emotion accords with wartime censorship blocking emotional expressions of grief.[141]

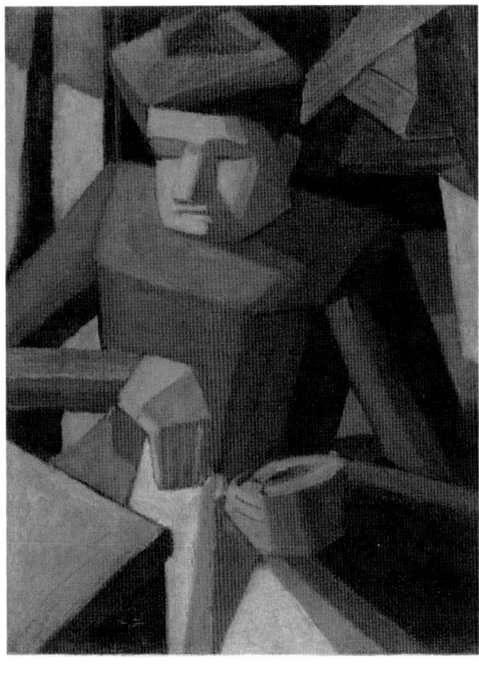

Fig. 11 | opposite Fernand Léger, *Soldier with a Pipe*, 1916. Oil on canvas, 130 × 97 cm. Photo: bpk Bildagentur / Kunstsammlung Nordrhein-Westfalen, Düsseldorf, Germany / Art Resource, New York. Photo: Walter Klein. © 2024 Artists Rights Society (ARS), New York / ADAGP, Paris.

Fig. 12 Fernand Léger, *The Seamstress*, 1909–10. Oil on canvas, 72 × 54 cm. Photo: Philippe Migeat. Musée national d'art moderne / Centre Georges Pompidou, Paris, Inv. no. AM1984-578. Digital Image © CNAC/MNAM, Dist. RMN-Grand Palais / Art Resource, New York. © 2024 Artists Rights Society (ARS), New York / ADAGP, Paris.

Léger's passive soldier is, paradoxically, an emasculated figure who adopts the silent, emotional, and spatial constraint that Léger's prewar paintings had attributed to conditions of femininity. Unlike Scott's swaggering *fantassin* or Picasso's confident Apollinaire, Léger's soldier is not a propagandistic imagery of masculinity as bravura and action. Several art historians interpret *Soldier with a Pipe* as an exception to Léger's vision of a hardened masculinity.[142] But its use of Cubist abstraction to represent physical injury and its spatial constraint reoccur in *The Card Party*. The painting reworks compositions from prewar paintings *The Seamstress* (1909–10) (fig. 12) and *Woman in Red and Green* (1914), in which women gaze downward at their sewing or clasped hands. Such poses were adopted in depictions of knitting and sewing women as icons of loyal femininity that academic artists put on display in the Bernheim-Jeune exhibition in 1915. The blocky hands and bowed posture of Léger's seamstress might signify her position as a type of laborer in a system in which she has little agency. Similarly, Léger's soldier folds inward, adopting the posture of lost agency. Like the seamstress's hands unsuitable for tiny needles, the soldier's tubular digits are ill designed for holding cigarettes or pulling triggers. But like the stylized hands of Picasso's *Girl with a Mandolin* (1910) that seem to dissolve into the instrument, the hands of Léger's soldier are a synecdoche for the machinery of war he has become part of.

Writing from Verdun after watching exhausted soldiers returning from days at the front, Léger claimed that only "an incredible sculptor could ever immortalize the *fantassin*."[143] In the same letter, Léger expressed the desire to depict the soldier at the moment of deadened indifference before "life returns to them" yet also the inability to find the forms to do so. The medium of painting or his skills as an artist

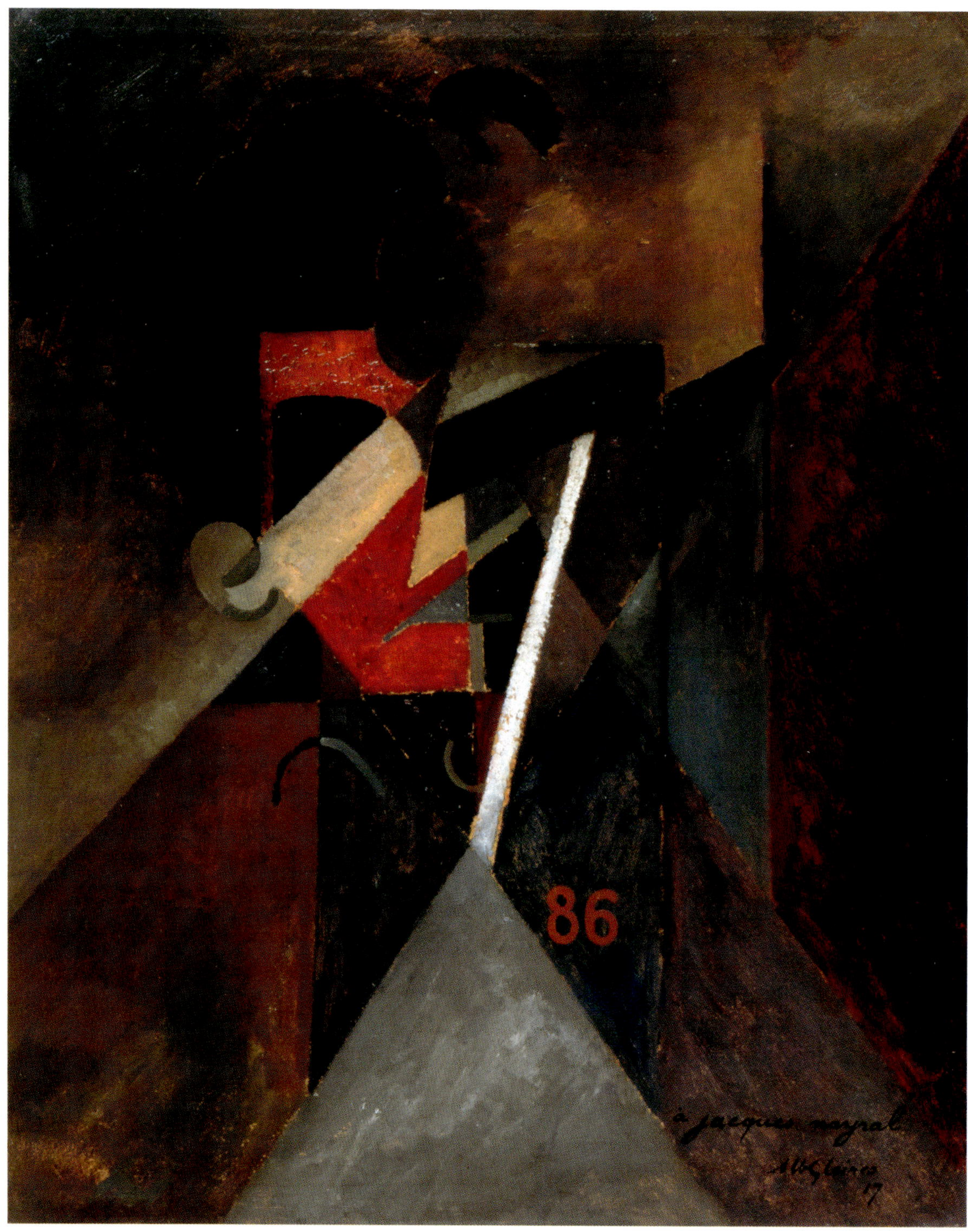
86
à jacques nayral

were not up to the task. Léger felt that the soldier's affect on returning from the front was necessary to see but impossible to represent, writing: "you have to see them here and not elsewhere." He wrote about them as having unforgettable "bony faces with dead eyes" such that everyone moved out of their way to let them pass "like shadows." Paradoxically, their muteness and emotional detachment provoked in Léger "one of the strongest emotions of the war." Before the war in 1914, Léger had written: "Painting, because it is visual, is necessarily a reflection of exterior and not psychological conditions."[144] But even if Léger did not want to represent emotional states, his desire to represent the soldier in his most shell-shocked state suggests a contradictory attraction to profound psychological stress that numbs and evacuates feeling. In fall 1917, while making watercolors and drawings, Léger described the other hospitalized soldiers in similar terms to his Verdun comrades, as immobile and inscrutable like "very curious hospital pillars, hard to follow, real foxes difficult to unmask."[145]

Fig. 13 Albert Gleizes, *To Jacques Nayral*, 1917. Oil on board, 76 × 60 cm. Gift of Howard D. and Babette L. Sirak, the Donors to the Campaign for Enduring Excellence, and the Derby Fund. Columbus Museum of Art, Ohio. © 2024 Artists Rights Society (ARS), New York / ADAGP, Paris.

Rather than engaging in a heroic or truth-telling naturalism, Léger is instead more closely aligned with the practices of Cubist portraiture, which depended both on masking and an often intimate relationship between the viewer and subject. Art historian Marcia Pointon claims that Cubist portraiture relies on the tension between the desire for recognition and the mask's capacity for "the oblique and the hidden," making the Cubist face a mask that leaves the viewer unsatisfied.[146] In the same year that Léger made *The Card Party*, Gleizes produced a wartime portrait of his brother-in-law, whose death deeply depressed him: *To Jacques Nayral* (1917) (fig. 13).[147] Léger, too, undoubtedly knew Nayral, who had been important to Cubism as a publisher. In a Cubist prewar portrait of Nayral (1911), Gleizes depicted Nayral in a moment of contemplation, his bony hands fingering a manuscript (probably *Du cubisme*, which he helped publish). In the wartime portrait, Nayral's face has become a carnival mask engulfed in darkness. Less a commemoration of the individual "Nayral," the portrait's death mask is a montage of the nighttime battle that destroyed him: a searchlight beam sweeps across his brow, and the number eighty-six identifies Nayral's military assignment. The non-naturalistic, fractured faces of Léger's card-playing soldiers similarly refuse to reveal individualized identity but suggest a hidden, unknowable interior. As Léger wrote about stunned soldiers returning from days of combat, they have an "interior life, very silent but real."[148]

Léger's *Soldier with Pipe* is, like *The Card Party*'s rightmost soldier, a gray rather than metallic body that accords with Léger's wartime perspective on shock and death. His letters chronicle the war as gray and grayness as a sign of death, deadened feeling, and a kind of numbness resulting from the confrontation with death. On October 15, 1915, Léger wrote that the war is a "mechanization from which all emotion is excluded."[149] In January 1916, he described war as a "gray and colorless thing like an immense cemetery where innumerable gravediggers all dressed the same kill and bury mechanically."[150] A year earlier, he wrote about two battalions of infantrymen returning from having spent twenty-nine days on the front lines: "Everything was written on their ravaged sweaty mugs. Twenty-nine days! They were gray and colorless, their expressionless eyes all the same. They didn't even react. There were two who came in last . . . I told them there was some wine but they didn't even respond. I will always remember that procession."[151] The mechanized and industrialized production of death marked the body with grayness and transformed soldiers into gravediggers alienated from their task and drained of feeling. In contested border regions, such as la Meuse, the villagers whose lands had been overtaken were hungry, gray, and melancholy. Léger wrote: "La Meuse is Corsica without the grandeur but with the thin and shabby face of the poor. The people are sad and gray."[152]

So, too, "hardness" signifies not as metallic surfaces or the 75mm cannon but an outer numbing and silence that hides inner suffering. In the same letter about la Meuse, Léger describes the response of the corps to a comrade's death: "their faces hardened and they listened in silence . . . these men were marked by death." The war causes exhaustion and a kind of numbing of the mind. In 1916, Léger writes of himself as "asleep rather than worn out," a kind of shutting down of his mind.[153] He recognizes that the numbing, deadening of nerves, and detached or impersonal air are the results of repeated exposure to the threat of death and that they mask an interior life difficult to access. He wrote that the Verdun soldiers had a "dead and impersonal air . . . nothing about the war shocks them, they have seen it ten or twenty times . . . [and] their nerves are dead."[154] As Léger repeatedly observed, only wine or alcohol revive the "hardened" soldier. Anesthetized from the horrors by drink, speech returns and color enters into gray faces.[155]

Léger's *The Card Party* shares the silent fraternity of injured men depicted in Georges Duhamel's writing. Duhamel, an army surgeon during the war, had been part of the Abbaye de Créteil group and knew Léger from that prewar context. Coincidentally, Duhamel operated on Léger's childhood friend André Mare in March 1918 when Mare was wounded by shelling.[156] Although he never mentions it in his letters, Léger likely knew of Duhamel's successful novel *La Vie des Martyrs, 1914–1917* (1917). Published by the monthly literary review *Mercure de France* and advertised regularly by the paper, the novel was released in April and was positively reviewed or mentioned in many leading presses. Like Léger, who believed the generation who fought the war were new men, Duhamel's narrator claims that "these men are no longer those you so lately knew."[157] Like Léger's Verdun soldier who has a "dead and impersonal air" yet also an "interior life, very silent but real," Duhamel's soldier has "a soul which does not readily reveal itself," whose interior is unknowable.[158] The novel closes with a scene that could have inspired Léger. Two soldiers, Houdebine and Panchat, play a game of "dummy *manille*" referring to a third absent player as a "dummy" or "dead" hand. The novel justifies dummy *manille* "because no one in this ward can get up, and communication is only easy for those in adjacent beds." *Manille* was often played *muette* or as a "silent game" to avoid giving away players' positions, a strategy that served Duhamel's Panchat, who had suffered a bullet wound in his neck. Léger's soldiers, like Duhamel's, are immobilized men with affectless exteriors that mask unknowable interiors, suggesting that Duhamel and Léger shared similar perceptions about men who were traumatized psychologically as much if not more than physically.

With its tension between masked psychic states and exposed vitalist interiors, *The Card Party* enacts Léger's response to the war as "four years without color."[159] His repeated argument for color as a cure sees the absence of primary or vibrant colors as a sign of debilitating and life-threatening conditions. The material conditions of wartime artistic production were such that for many soldier-artists at the front, including André Mare, Segonzac, Gleizes, and Léger, the only available media were pencil, charcoal sketch, and ink drawing. Monochromatic drawings and print forms have historically lent themselves to depictions of war's miseries and brutalizations, including artists whose work Léger knew: Jacques Callot's etchings *The Major Miseries of War* (1633), Goya's etchings and engravings *The Disasters of War* (1810–20), and Frans Masereel's woodcuts in *Stand up, Dead* (1917). During World War I, French and British painters—Marcel Gromaire, Stanley Spencer, Paul Nash, even William Orpen—often depicted the war, especially the soldier's body, in a palette of grays, blues, browns, or muted tones. In postwar Germany, several leading artists recalled the war in monochromatic media: Käthe Kollwitz's *War* woodcuts (1922–23), Otto Dix's *War* (1924) etchings series, or Ernst Friedrich's photography book *War against War* (1924). Some turned away from color as hedonistic or joyful, as critic Carl Einstein argued about Max Beckmann, whose work Léger knew as early as 1913 due to their shared ties to the dealer Alfred Flechtheim.[160] Beckmann's *The Night* (1919) (fig. 14) uses a limited palette of browns and greens punctuated by reds to depict a grim scene of torture and degradation within a compressed, even collapsing spatial context.

Where *Soldier with a Pipe* used a red, geometric form to suggest a wound, in *The Card Party*, color has a vitalist role. Primary colors in the revivified survivor at left are juxtaposed against color's absence in the gray figure at right. Contemporary viewers saw *The Card Party* as a colorful painting antithetical to the image of war, neglecting the figure at right. When Rosenberg first exhibited Léger's *The Card Party* in January 1919, the art critic André Salmon saw Léger's use of color in the painting as a response to the grays and greens of wartime. Salmon begins the review by

Fig. 14 Max Beckmann, *The Night*, 1919. Oil on canvas, 133 × 153 cm. Photo: bpk Bildagentur / Kunstsammlung Nordrhein-Westfalen, Dusseldorf, Germany / Walter Klein / Art Resource, New York.

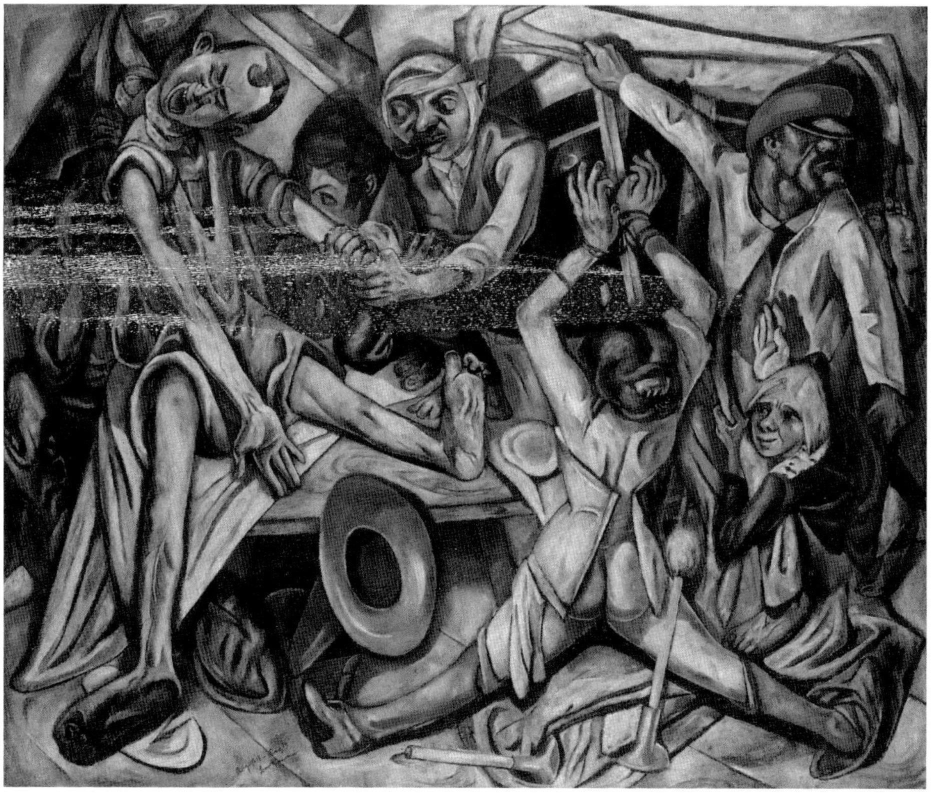

repeating a misguided question he overheard from one visitor: "Had Léger become a Fauve?" That viewer seems to have seen Léger as out of step with Cubism's usual muted palette. Léger's paintings, Salmon writes, are the antithesis of Picasso's Cubist palette, with its greens, grays, and ochers, which are "the colors of war! The exact colors of the front at the line of fire."[161] In Salmon's interpretation, it is the use of bright color more than the machine that is salubrious, regenerative, revivifying, even humanizing. Salmon interpreted Léger's Cubism in the context of the emerging classicism adopted by Picasso. Léger, he wrote, "humanizes . . . figures that are further from nature than those Picasso tranquilly dared to construct." For Salmon, humanizing is not equated with naturalism but an animation of the figures. The bright color, particularly the reds in the left and center figures of *The Card Party*, compete with the "colors of war" represented by the rightmost soldier.

Léger understood color not only as a vitalist antidote to the war and to grim lives but also in therapeutic and utopian revolutionary terms. Léger, who responded to Georges Seurat's use of color to develop his own conception of "multiplicative contrasts" of form and color, was undoubtedly aware of the impact of chemist Michel Eugène Chevreul's theory of simultaneous contrasts and art critic Charles Blanc's ideas about complementary colors and optic mixing.[162] As early as 1922, as part of the organizing committee for the failed Congress of Paris led by André Breton, Léger proposed a list of questions, including one about the "psychological value" of color and "a multicolor hospital (cure through colors)."[163] Two years later, in 1924, he expanded his ideas, writing that "color and light have a necessary social function," arguing for the "polychrome hospital . . . [the] colorist doctor."[164] In an interview in 1929, Léger criticized hospitals with their "gray walls," arguing that patients love flowers because "their intense colors are a sort of bridge between their mortified flesh and the great fresh rhythm . . . of nature. . . . It should be possible to establish [color's] psychological value as well as its physiological importance."[165] Léger recalled that at the time of his release from military duty, posters provided a "colorful disorder" counteracting the war. He saw color as "a vital necessity . . . a primary material indispensable to life, like water and fire."[166] In 1946, in the wake of World War II and before working on a ceramic facade mural for the Hôpital Saint-Lo (1954), Léger again returned to the theme of color as therapeutic, arguing for "the polychrome hospital [and] cure through colors" with "restful rooms in green or blue for [cases of] nerves [and] other rooms in yellow and red for the depressed or anemic."[167] In the late 1940s, he claimed he invented the idea of a "polychrome city" during World War I when he met Trotsky on one of his leaves, an encounter that could have taken place in 1915 or early 1916, before Trotsky was expelled from Paris, a meeting mostly likely facilitated by the Russian artist Marie Vassilieff, later imprisoned for being a Bolshevik sympathizer.[168] In linking the "polychrome city" to his encounter with Trotsky and the war, Léger aligns color with utopian and revolutionary possibilities that would transform grim lives.

Léger's statements on color as therapeutic repeatedly recall World War I, the hospital context, and the nervous or depressed person. As Maurice Fréchuret's analysis of Léger's writing shows, Léger's therapeutic ideas position him within a long history of color theory dating from antiquity to writing by theorist Johann Wolfgang von Goethe, spiritualist Rudolf Steiner, and Bauhaus artists.[169] But there are also specifically medical and psychological ideas that might have informed *The Card Party* painting. Before the war, Léger must have known of Wassily Kandinsky's *On the Spiritual in Art* (1912), which, as art historian John Gage shows, references experimental psychology and the treatment of mental illnesses with chromotherapy.[170] Léger and Kandinsky had exhibited together at the 1912 Salon des Indépendants, and during that period, both were close collaborators with Robert Delaunay, who had Kandinsky's book translated into French. At the time of the war and in its wake, England and Germany investigated the uses of chromotherapy in the hospital context. By

1918, such ideas gained enough currency that a British paint manufacturer invoked chromotherapy in its advertisements, proposing that London hospitals use yellow and blue on walls as a "colour-cure" for "shell-shock and nerve cases."[171] By the 1920s, Léger may have known about the psychological theories of color that Kandinsky introduced into the Bauhaus curriculum, reinforcing his belief in color as therapy or cure.[172]

State of the Nation

In addition to its national impact, the war was traumatic in different ways for two collectives that shaped Léger's public persona and identity: his artistic community and the "French people" he claimed to discover in the trenches. Léger's *The Card Party* negotiates between the wartime iconography of the soldier and his frontline observations of physical and psychic trauma. The shift from the portrait of a type, *Soldier with a Pipe*, to a trio of card players foregrounds this negotiation as manifested in two competing desires: the desire to claim his status among the *corps* of combatants with whom he had spent three years and the wish to reengage with the artistic community that had been fragmented by mobilization.

In 1900, when he first moved to Paris, Léger had left behind a largely provincial peasantry that he rediscovered at the front. He repeatedly claimed to have discovered the French nation during the war. Some 70 percent of the infantry were peasant class, who had rarely traveled far from home and were deeply invested in the defense of the land.[173] Léger's letters describe some of these men as particularly memorable comrades. One Tavernier, a "Gaudissart perfectionné," who, like Honoré de Balzac's comic salesman, had an answer for every question, knew how to do everything, and so "kills neurasthenia."[174] Another, nicknamed Chouya-l'arbi, was a survivalist who always seemed to have a rabbit or candle stub in his pack and so saved the day when supplies were low. Yet these men were favorites of the group rather than close to Léger individually. Léger admired rather than identified with the common soldier. Léger wrote that the ordinary soldier "never shows effort, but they're always adequate at their job, their life isn't complicated; ours is more complicated."[175]

In his prewar milieu, Léger had been viewed as an intellectual and artist with valuable ideas, but in the wartime context, he was clumsy and inadequate. His account of his relationship with his comrades shows his failure to conform to their expectations despite his admiration for them. He sensed that they were the real soldiers and he was just a "disoriented civilian": "They don't muddle up what they know. I don't dare mix up anything [and] any initiative I might take is off and they can tell right away, so they have no confidence that what I do is right. They see things much more simply than me, and it disappoints me; I am in a rude school. They have little esteem for me. I'm useless and not 'on track.' I'm just a disoriented civilian and who has for them . . . inexplicable admiration."[176] Rather than finding himself a brother among comrades, Léger was the outcast, disoriented and unassimilated.

Léger found friendship and solidarity not as much with the working classes he admired but with a trio formed by his commanding officer, a major whom he tried to "initiate slowly into Cubism," and Corporal Bienvenu-Martin, the son of a radical Minister of Labor.[177] After Léger nearly lost his life digging sap trenches, the major reassigned him to *brancardier* (stretcher-bearer) service, which meant he also served as the major's secretary, handling his calendar and reports.[178] Tragically, the major died in February 1915, and the corporal, who lent Léger a Bergson book, was also killed on July 13 that year.[179]

The war forged a new collective identity founded in trauma and survival. In a letter dated April 1915, Léger wrote to his friend Poughon, describing the war as a "tragedy" that broke his life in two, leaving behind the "prewar man," such as his noncombatant friend, while making combatants part of a "great *postwar* generation" of new men.[180] Dominick LaCapra has proposed that traumatic historical events have become "founding traumas," serving as a basis for collective or personal identity.[181] This is the case for Léger, who shaped his persona through public statements about identification with "the people" or "the French nation." In asserting his allegiance to the French Communist Party after joining in December 1945, Léger addressed an audience of party members and cited his immersion in the French engineering corps as his introduction to the French nation: "It [the war] permitted me to discover the People and renew myself entirely . . . the engineering corps was a corps of laborers, road workers, and miners."[182] Yet, in claiming camaraderie, Léger simultaneously disavowed individual trauma: "I was strong as well and I had no fear. I became comrades with them."[183] In fact, Léger's anxieties about a return to the front drove him to make repeated appeals to his friends Mare and Poughon to transfer him into the camouflage unit.[184]

Léger's production of *The Card Party*, an image of soldierly fraternity, served as a process of envisioning survival and reconstituting collective identity. As many scholars have argued, trauma should be understood not only in terms of the threat of death but also what Caruth calls the "enigma of survival."[185] Holocaust and genocide studies have shown that trauma's latency, gaps, and omissions in memory have produced a "crisis of truth." Trauma calls into question whether the traumatic experience was merely forgotten and can be retrieved therapeutically or never known and so irretrievable by the conscious mind and unavailable to representation. Paradoxically, Léger's *The Card Party* painting claims witness status while at the same time deploying Cubism's antimimetic devices that block any access to the soldiers' interior life. Referential elements—the aerial view of a trench, the war medals, the caps and helmets, the broken face of the central figure, the prosthetic arm—mix with metaphorical passages—the stepped shoulders, the agitated red vertebrae, the gray figure at right. Witness testimony or experiential memories, like Léger's painting and statements about the war, contest historical fact and national narratives, making the crisis not only an individual problem but also a historical dilemma. Drawing upon Klaus Theweleit's classic study of the German Freikorps and the "constant dissolution" that threatened the psyche of the soldier at the front, Silverman argues that the psychic binding that fails at the level of individual ego occurs at the level of the group. However, removed from the front, the soldier risks psychic breakdown.[186] Binding on the cultural level, she argues, involves "the gradual reaffirmation and reconstitution of the dominant fiction." At the pictorial level, Léger's *Soldier with Pipe*, with its open torso, abstracted facial wound, and grim mouth, conveys an individual vulnerability that *The Card Party* remedies through collective solidarity.

In choosing the card players theme, Léger foregrounds collective solidarity while solidifying his position within a French tradition and challenging Italian Futurism. Cézanne's card player series has been credited as a model for Léger, who repeatedly cited Cézanne as the artist who liberated painting from tradition.[187] Shortly before Léger's hospitalization, in June 1917, Cézanne's *Card Players* (1890–92), now in New York's Metropolitan Museum of Art, had been exhibited at the Bernheim-Jeune Gallery. *The Card Party* provided Léger an opportunity to return to Cubism's prewar debate with Futurism and respond to Severini's representation of war. The year before, from January 15 to February 1, 1916, Severini, a noncombatant whom Léger had known before the war through the Abbaye de Créteil artists' commune, had exhibited his war paintings at the Boutet de Monvel Gallery in Paris. Picasso, Gris, and Ozenfant attended. Severini, who describes Léger as the "most amicable" of the Cubists, does not identify him as a visitor.[188] Yet Léger had leave in late January or early February and certainly must have known of the exhibition. As Green has argued, Léger's *The Wedding* (1912) was a reaction to the first Futurist exhibition in Paris in February 1912 at the Bernheim-Jeune Gallery.[189] Despite his collegial rapport with the Italians, Léger rejected any claims of a debt to Futurism and never adopted Futurism's conception of temporality as successive moments. In 1913, he directly responded to Boccioni's claim that the French "plagiarized" from the Italians and asserted that his inspiration for the contemporary subject came from French artists, especially Cézanne. He quoted Cézanne's letters, stating that one must make objects "turn, move away, and live," thus accounting for the animation of his figures. Instead, Léger argued, the Italians owed a debt to France. Léger wrote that "contemporary painting was born in France" and had produced "universal concepts" serving all sensibilities: "the Italian Futurist movement is one such proof."[190] In 1919, Léger's dealer, Rosenberg, sought to revive these prewar debates when he submitted Léger's statement about being inspired by "the breechblock of the 75 [mm cannon]" to the new Italian Futurist periodical *Valori Plastici*.

Severini's solo exhibition in 1916, entitled *The First Futurist Exhibition of the Plastic Art of War*, sought to fulfill Filippo Marinetti's glorification of war, first announced in the Futurist's manifesto of 1909. Severini's "plastic synthesis" of war, such as *War* (1915), depict war as a multisensorial, multiperspectival experience where human bodies are eliminated. The work juxtaposes the words "antihumanisme" and "effort maximum" in a T-formation over an aerial map of trenches, mathematical calculations, and graphs; a factory smokestack and its tiled roof appear above text referencing poison gasses such as "gaz asphyxiants" and "hydrocarbures." Several paintings and drawings—*Sea = Battle* (1914–15), *Flying over Rheims* (1915), *Crash* (1915)—present aerial perspectives indicating Severini's awareness of new photographic techniques. Others, such as *Armored Train in Action* (1915), draw directly from war photography albums and Severini's view of Paris's Denfert-Rochereau train station from his studio. Severini's *In the North-South* [1916], a revision of a prewar motif, was published on the heels of the exhibition in Pierre-Albert Birot's *S.I.C.* (April 1916) using Futurist *parole en libertá* ("ttoum ttoum," "tta tta tta," "szszsz") to invoke the firing of large munitions and whizzing bullets, as does *Cannon in Action* (1914–15) (fig. 6).

The distinctions between Léger's *The Card Party* and Severini's Futurist ideas of war emerge from their different wartime experiences as well as their competing notions of Bergsonian time and space. Severini was a noncombatant, while Léger had survived three years at the front. Severini's art focuses on the machinery of war—the cannons, trains, factories—and an image of war as speed, noise, and action, while Léger foregrounds the body of the soldier at a point of stasis, silence, and inaction. Despite his many letters describing the noise of battle in slang terms as a *bastringue* (noisy band), *tintamarre* (cacophony), *boucan* (racket), *marmitage* (pots banging), and a *fête de bruit* (noise party) that prevented sleep for days, Léger chose not to represent the sounds or terrain of battle but rather soldiers in a moment of constrained waiting.[191] In Severini's painting, sound is indexical for a sped-up time, while Léger's card game, his soldier's damaged faces, and the word fragment "iro" signal limited, telegraphic speech, if any. Where Severini's art invites an imagined movement via train or plane speeding across French territory, Léger's soldiers have nowhere to go and no means to get there but instead are compressed within a shallow depth of field that can be alternatively understood as dugout, hospital, or homefront. For Severini's viewer, aerial perspective offers visual mastery over the terrain it depicts, but for Léger's viewer, the aerial view of a trench juxtaposed with the soldier's stepped shoulder, face, and interior links what can be known through photography to what cannot be known of the survivor's interiority. Where

Fig. 15 Fernand Léger, *The Three Comrades*, 1920. Oil on canvas, 92 × 73 cm. Collection Stedelijk Museum, Amsterdam. © 2024 Artists Rights Society (ARS), New York / ADAGP, Paris.

Severini diminishes the male body to incorporate it within the machinery of war, Léger monumentalizes the soldiers' bodies in a painting about three times the size of Severini's *Cannon in Action*. The two paintings engage with different temporal and spatial moments regarding soldiers' nerves. Severini's use of "tension de nerfs" at the center of his canvas implies that the reverberations caused by the cannon could rattle nerves, sharing the logic of *commotion cérébrale* that claimed neurological damage as the origin of "nerves." Léger's painting imagines the traumatized soldiers' numbed affect as a mode of survival registered by his masked subjectivity and interior agitation. Finally, Léger's *The Card Party*, unlike Severini's *Cannon in Action*, foregrounds the interaction among the figures, the play and chance of the game, and solidarity symbolized through the *fumée* motif.

Conclusion

The most significant way that Léger's *The Card Party* departs from Severini's Futurist aesthetic of war is that Léger's collective is contingent upon loss. The fraternal trio in *The Card Party* is bound together by an exchange of gazes between the living soldiers and a figure of death, shock, and loss. The centrality of absence or a kind of ghosting among three veteran comrades reoccurs in at least two other Léger paintings. In *The Three Comrades* (1920) (fig. 15), a white sphere appears between a fez-wearing African holding a cane and a blue-capped, pipe-smoking worker. Unlike his comrades, the central third figure has neither facial features nor limbs; instead, his "body" is a collage of forms that overlap the other two figures. Together, the three confront the viewer and stand in front of a small gray table in the lower right corner, yet their torsos are flattened geometric planes of color and none has legs. Similarly, in *Man in the City* (1919), the central figure is a ghostly silhouette positioned behind tubing that could be a detached prosthetic arm, a cane, or scaffolding. In these paintings, the body is apprehended as obscured and abstracted, subject not to a sustained gaze but one that is occluded and fragmentary, transformed into a colorful graphic language in an otherwise gray world. The gaps and blank passages in *The Three Comrades* and *Man in the City* gesture to that which is blocked from sight as a form of knowledge or unavailable to consciousness in order to mourn.

As the largest painting addressing his war experience, Léger's *The Card Party* enacts both a repetition of the traumatic encounter with death and a desire for mastery. With his fate uncertain and still anxious about being returned to war, Léger adopted the genre scene of card playing, a subject with a long history in French art that adapted to the new media of photography and film and served to represent the arbitrariness of survival in war's game of chance. The monumental size and the scale of the painting immerse the viewer within the scene, yet its Cubist vocabulary

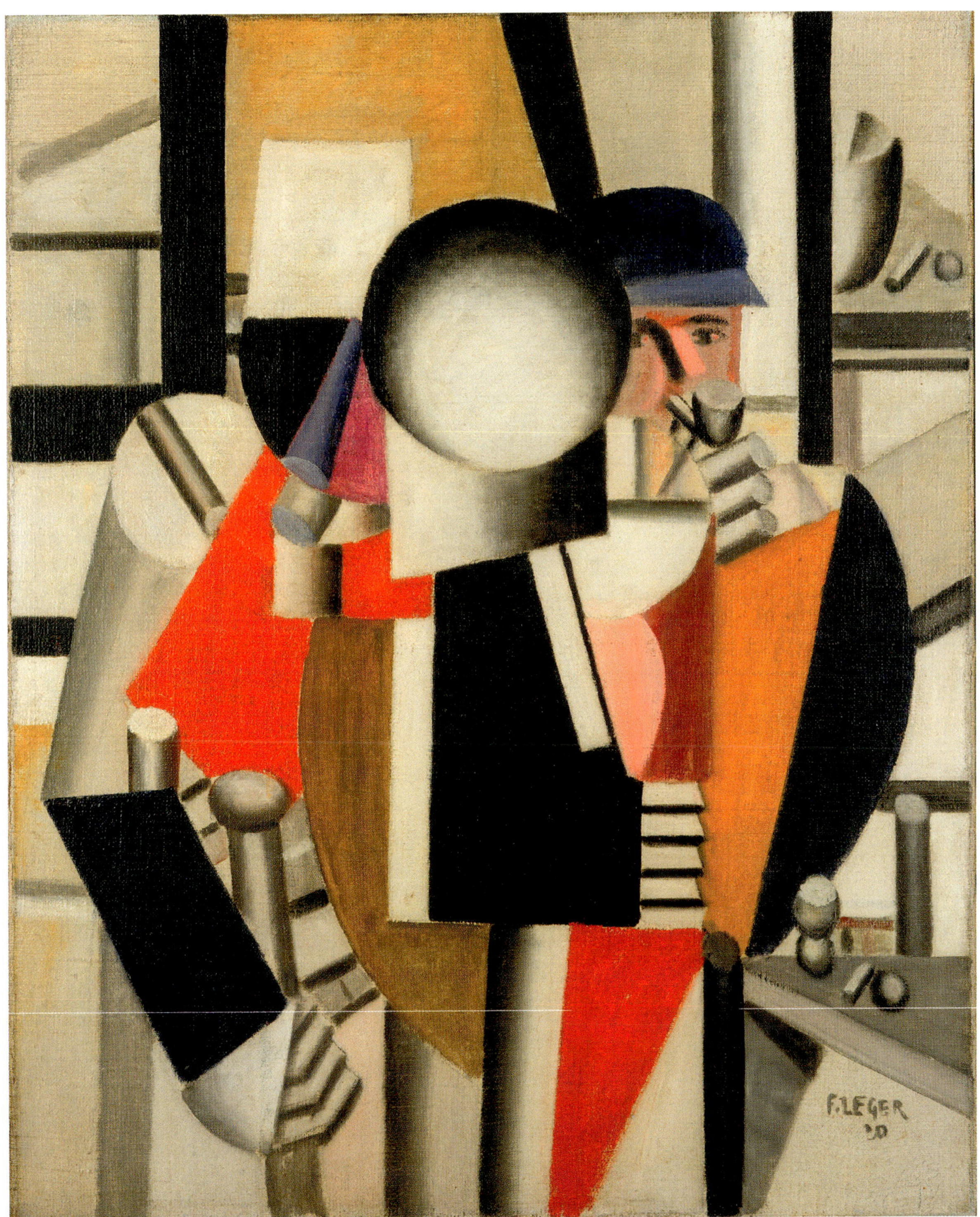
F.LEGER
20

masks the capacity to identify with or recognize the depicted figures. The painting testifies to the spaces and times that preoccupied Léger during his treatment: the trench space that frames the painting in the form of the fragmentary aerial view at left and the memorialized figure at right; the hospital space and time of decoration, reconstruction, and rehabilitation signified by the medals, the stepped and splinted faces, and the prosthetic limb. By using multiple perspectives and signaling multiple spaces, Léger deployed Bergsonian simultaneity to represent a moment of confrontation with death that is also a scene of solidarity with the numbed or dead comrade. In doing so, Léger created an artwork that registers the affective dynamics of traumatic memory as always partial, incomplete, and unspoken, yet connecting the group like the unanimist puffs of smoke. Addressed to his dealer and to his artistic and intellectual circles—Cubists, neoclassicists, Futurists, and others—Léger stakes his claim as part of the "great postwar generation," unlike the noncombatants (Poughon and Severini) who "cannot know."

Léger advances himself as a colorist doctor, signifying regeneration and even resilience by using the painting to respond to war's production of grayness, death, and shocked subjectivities. His soldiers may have, like those he observed at Verdun, a "dead and impersonal air," but they also have an "interior life, very silent but real."[192] But resilience is paradoxical, as the shocked, commotioned body at left retains the trench experience within, and the rehabilitated body at center may reject the state's prosthetic limbs and classicizing reconstructions. While imitative art signified by *Le Miroir*'s photography is inadequate to represent a psychic interiority that cannot be known, the antimimetic art of Léger's Cubism, with its truncated bodies, fractured corporeal forms, and fragmented language, acknowledges the limits to totalizing forms of knowledge. Fear and grief, with their howls and cries, are censored and silenced. Masculinity may be protected by a hardened shell, but that uniformed, bemedaled shell is also breached corporeally, revealing its fragility. Fraternal bonding may be envisioned in the genre of the game, but the game is also a contest that only one can win and where death's hand remains unknown.

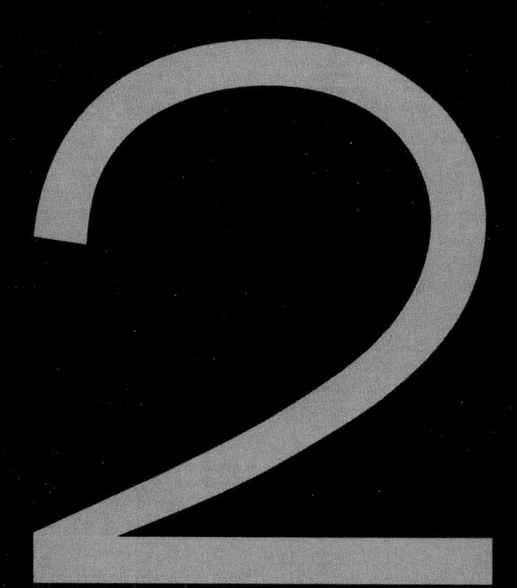

The Machine Aesthetic and Aftermath Cultures

Temporarily discharged from military duties in June 1918 after eleven months of hospitalization and time in a "military sanatorium," Léger retreated to the "little silent town" of Vernon for rest and recovery until the end of the summer.[1] Located on the Seine River about seventy kilometers north of Paris, Vernon was the birthplace of Lohy, the woman Léger married in December 1919. Vernon also provided an escape from the ongoing bombardment of Paris that had struck close to Léger's hospital in March 1918.[2] In relocating, Léger followed the advice of his neurologist, Dr. Parmentier, who in October 1917 had prescribed a "strict regimen" of "calm [and] countryside," a rest cure in accordance with a neurasthenia diagnosis.[3] The official diagnosis, signed in March 1918 by Dr. Bigard, was "chronic congestion," unsurprising for soldiers made to withstand waterlogged trenches and for Léger who had, at the time of his required military service in 1906, received a diagnosis of a congested right lung.[4] Bigard, who Léger described as "enlightened about art" and interested in his work, supported his discharge proposal. Although not a final release from military duty, the diagnosis helped relieve Léger's anxieties about being returned to the front. He had complained about doctors who try to "dope us up" to send soldiers back to the front or as a means of avoiding pension payouts.[5] After December 1917, when Léger made the last of many appeals to Poughon for help transferring to the camouflage unit, his writing to Poughon slows down, and his communication with his new dealer Rosenberg increases, marking a shift in focus to his artistic career.[6] With his temporary discharge and move to Vernon, Léger gained the time, space, and calm for focused attention on artistic production.

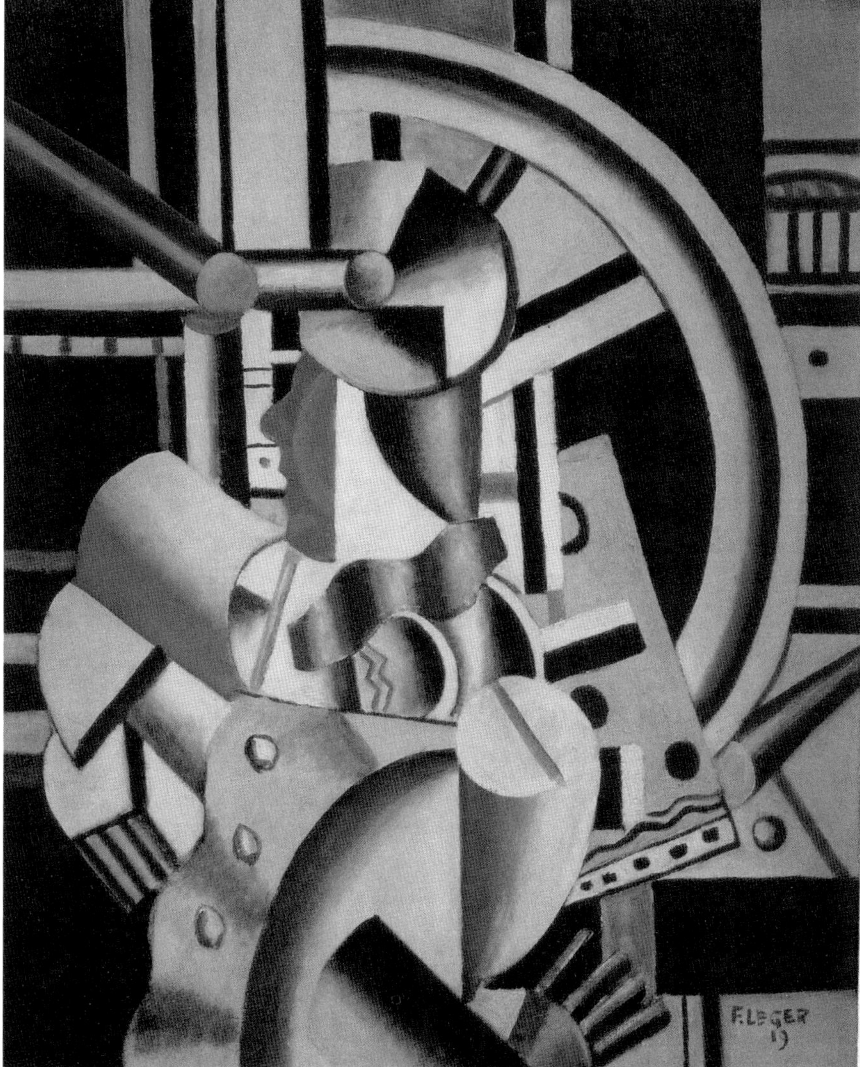

Fig. 16 Fernand Léger, *Man at the Wheel*, 1919. Oil on canvas, 97.42 × 92 cm. Collection of Mr. and Mrs. William Jaffe. Bauquier, *Catalogue raisonné*, vol. 1, fig. 177. © 2024 Artists Rights Society (ARS), New York / ADAGP, Paris.

With the threat of being returned to the front largely removed by his temporary discharge, Léger shifted from the traumatic time of *The Card Party*, which condenses the spaces and experiences of trench and hospital, to historical time and a national iconography. In July 1918, Léger and Cendrars made the short trip from Vernon to Monet's gardens at Giverny, a visit that reaffirmed Léger's long-standing rejection of Impressionism. In contrasting Monet's gardens, where there was "not one line," Léger wrote that his own garden was composed of rows of vegetables that *s'architecture* (are structured and geometric).[7] During this period, Léger produced five ink drawings illustrating Cendrars's poem *J'ai tué* and paintings such as *The 14th of July at Vernon* (1918) and *Armistice* (1918). The paintings join the nationalist fervor by prominently displaying the French *tricouleur* flag and a stenciled "R.F." (République Française). Léger's work largely turns away from war, death, and any suggestion of mourning, negating any representation of the losses he continued to experience, such as the deaths, on October 9 and November 9, 1918, respectively, of two fellow artist-combatants: Raymond Duchamp-Villon, brother of Marcel Duchamp, and the poet Apollinaire. Instead, Léger's new paintings self-consciously rework or reverse the corporeal damage evident in *L'Homme à la canne* (1920), the last explicit reference to a wounded veteran. As Green has observed, Léger's wartime sketches of wounded soldiers became compositional paradigms to be reimagined as productive man-machine bodies in *The Typographer* (1919) and in *Man at the Wheel* (1919) (fig. 16); so, too, warfront aviator drawings of planes blown apart are refashioned into postwar aviator images that "[replace] the memory of wrecked flying machines with an image of power kept under control."[8]

Léger's postwar art and writing reveal a tension between an awareness of damaged masculinity and a desire to negate or reverse death in an imagined resilience. Where Léger's soldiers and veterans are passive, constrained bodies in an abstracted war that was no longer "heroic" and where being a "machine" meant lost agency and the lost "thrill of action,"[9] Léger's postwar men reinterpret the machine in the service of national reconstruction yet often anxiously so. Léger's wartime men had rarely been depicted with, or as masters of, weaponry, but his *mécanicien* (factory workers, mechanics, or engineers), typographers, tugboat captains, and stokers claim their potency from machinery. Some are hybridized as in the profiled figure whose French tricolor head merges with a metal disk and lever in *Man at the Wheel*, suggesting a desire to overcome the organic body's frailty by merging the body with the machine. But more often, they are anonymous puppets, robots, or silhouettes in proximity to fantastical machinery such as *The Mechanic* (1918) (fig. 17). Léger's hybridized machine-men might be read as Freudian "prosthetic gods" caught between "psychic castration" and faith in a "technological phallus," as Foster has argued about the contradictions of machine modernisms.[10] But Léger's robotic new men, dominated in scale and energy by the city, factories, and engines of economic recovery, also risk becoming what Léger described as a "victim of the machine" that causes the new man to be in a constant "physical and moral tension."[11]

In turning away from the body of the wounded soldier, the sight of death, and the memory of war, Léger participated in a larger cultural shift that has been cast as a cultural amnesia about the war in a *retour à l'ordre* or return-to-order era. As the body is reconstructed, threatened annihilation and death are reversed, a fantasy that French psychoanalyst Boris Cyrulnik identifies as a method of resilience.[12]

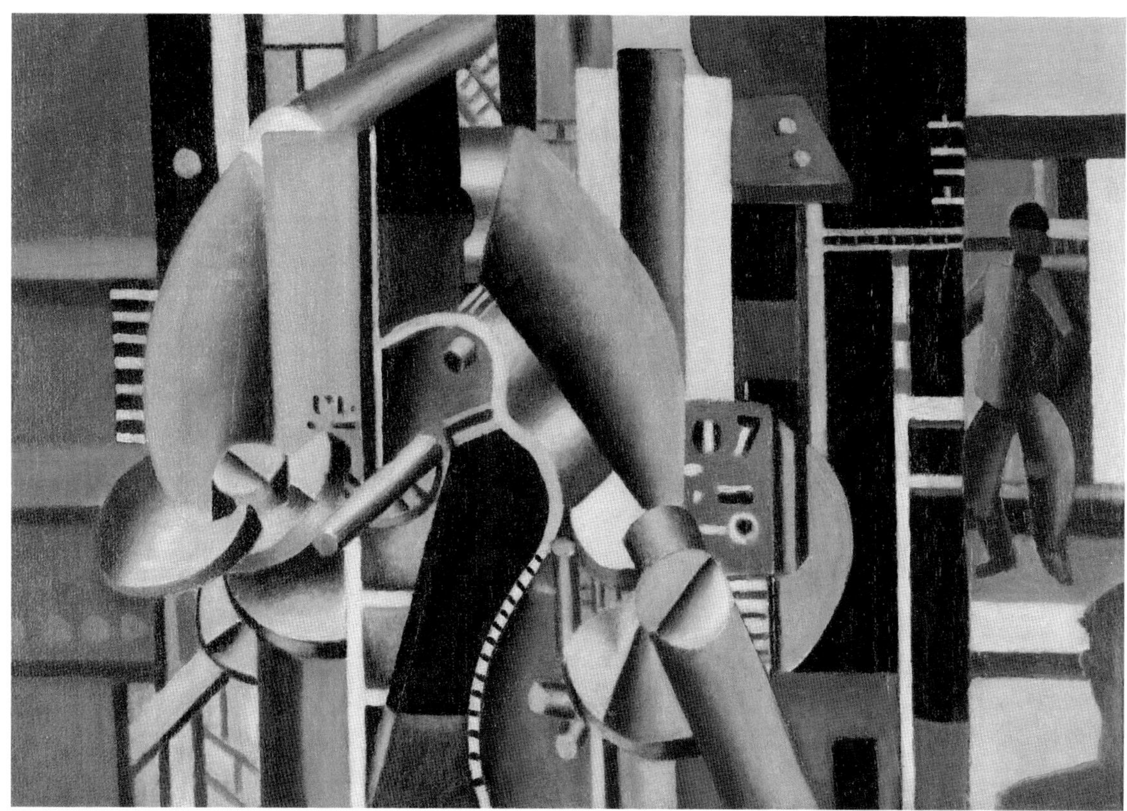

Fig. 17 Fernand Léger, *The Mechanic*, 1918. Oil on canvas, 45 × 64.135 cm. Munson-Williams-Proctor Arts Institute / Art Resource, New York. © 2024 Artists Rights Society (ARS), New York / ADAGP, Paris.

In 1919, Léger created untitled illustrations for Cendrars's poem *La Fin du monde filmée par l'ange de Notre Dame* (The End of the World Filmed by the Angel of Notre Dame; 1918), published as a book and written as a film scenario; it portrays God as an American who blows up Paris as a circus stunt and ends with the angel of Notre Dame blowing his horn. In a postscript, the film is rewound, reversing the destructive impact of war. In another fantasy of reversing death, Léger's set design for the protagonist's laboratory in Marcel L'Herbier's film *L'Inhumaine* (1924) is the stage for the Swedish engineer to demonstrate his capacity to bring back to life his lover, a singer, to demonstrate to her the power of radio and film as transcendent media overcoming death and distance.

Amnesia and Reconstruction

With the Armistice on November 11, 1918, and the Treaty of Versailles on June 28, 1919, France became a victorious yet visibly castrated nation and entered an aggressive but embattled era of reconstruction officially lasting until 1927. The unprecedented and massive scale of injury, death, and psychological trauma constituted a historical trauma that destabilized dominant cultural fictions about gender and sexuality. About 1.3 million French men had died and twice as many returned wounded, including the disfigured and amputees.[13] As Laura Frader has observed, the contrast between the male *mutilé* and female wholeness exposed the fragility of hegemonic meanings of masculinity and femininity.[14] The reconstruction era was a social, economic, and psychic process of stabilizing hegemonic meanings radically disturbed by the war. The male body's reconstitution was bound up with an ideology of the male provider and father as the center of the family, the economy, and the nation, roles that many injured men could not return to.[15] The women that Apollinaire feared would displace men in the workplace were largely demobilized to prioritize men's access to paid labor. As feminist historians have shown, women lost the prewar momentum toward female suffrage, not gained in France until 1944.[16] After the French president Paul Deschanel suffered an embarrassing mental breakdown, he was compelled to resign in September 1920, and the country elected a conservative new government. Responding to long-standing anxieties about depopulation and a desire to prepare for the next war, they enacted natalist policies criminalizing abortion and limiting access to contraception with an aim to increase the national birth rate.[17] Postwar biopolitics imposed heteronormativity and reproduction as the path to national renewal, policies that competed with the sense of liberation and mobility many women had gained during the war.

At the same time, a cultural practice of silence about the war's damage to national and psychic coherence followed France's wartime censorship of the sight of death and cries of grief. In Paul Ricoeur's analysis, the collective can be conditioned by silence; official statements ending civil wars and later codified as part of France's national identity required "institutional forgetting" or amnesia, as in the example of Henry IV's Edict of Nantes in 1585, which forbade subjects to "retain any memory" of the prior conflict and required all "to live peacefully together as brothers, friends, and fellow citizens."[18] Drawing from Ricoeur and others, historian Jay Winter argues that silence is never total but a social construction that can be alternatively liturgical, complicit with forgetting in order to end open conflict, or contingent upon circumscribed forms of privileged speech.[19] On Armistice Day 1919, France initiated the "moment of silence," a secularized quasi-liturgical ritual marking the end of conflict and contingent upon the privileged speech of political and military leaders.[20] France developed a cult of the dead through war memorials, monuments, and commemorations that proliferated in towns and cities across the country, many dedicated to the new concept of the "unknown soldier."[21] As Stéphane Audoin-Rouzeau and Annette Becker show, psychological suffering lacked language. This period of memorialization paradoxically produced a "mourning taboo," since to "grieve too long or too intensely was to betray the dead, betray the cause for which the heroes had died" and so to undermine the idealized cause and sacrifice justifying the war.[22]

The taboos of France's aftermath culture included a stigmatizing silence about its psychological impact. Medical interest in psychological trauma declined after World War I and was not significantly revived until the post-traumatic stress diagnosis developed in the United States in 1980.[23] Gregory Thomas's research has offered a rare study into the treatment of traumatized French veterans and the shame and attendant silence around psychiatric damage from the war.[24] Unlike in England, veterans suffering from shell shock or nervous disorders were not covered by France's pension law of 1919 unless they were institutionalized, in which case pensions paid for their care in state hospitals but did not support their families.[25] Alcoholism increased during the interwar years as did admissions for grief disorders, such as melancholy and depression, especially among women. Veterans in overcrowded mental asylums were known as *morts vivants* (living dead), hidden away and forgotten.[26]

In Léger's circles, Ozenfant had launched a wartime call to "turn our backs [away from] agony" and so initiated what Kenneth Silver has called a "self-conscious forgetting" that characterized the return-to-order classicism.[27] Léger's new dealer, Rosenberg, became an important driver of the new classicism and synthesis of form aligned with the national project of reconstruction and economic regeneration. Through his Galerie de l'Effort Moderne (1918–41) and periodical *Bulletin de l'Effort Moderne* (1924–27), Rosenberg promoted his artists, including Léger, in a series of solo exhibitions and in a permanent group show, *Masters of Cubism*, that foregrounded the postwar crystal or synthetic Cubism. This new form of Cubism, led by Juan Gris, Metzinger, and Jacques Lipchitz but also practiced by Picasso, aimed for equilibrium and stasis. It retained prewar Cubism's genres of still life and portraiture but retreated from the faceting and figure-ground oscillation of analytical Cubism and banished collage for painted simulations of collages and transparent layers. By May 1919, Cendrars announced that the cube had crumbled—*le cube s'effrite*—and that Rosenberg's gallery represented the "return-from-the-front" generation wanting to "construct."[28]

Rosenberg secured his postwar leadership because he was able to sign exclusive contracts with Kahnweiler's former clients—Léger, Picasso, Braque, and Gris—as well as other Cubists who had exhibited in the salons before the war. By 1920, Rosenberg took on Severini and added Dutch De Stijl leader Piet Mondrian to his fold. Rosenberg benefited, too, from the state reparations auctions of Kahnweiler's stock. Kahnweiler, Léger's prewar dealer and promoter of analytical Cubism, had been compelled to leave France in 1914 due to his German citizenship, after which the French state appropriated his stock of paintings. Rosenberg bought up some seven hundred paintings at these auctions, solidifying his position as a leading avant-garde collector and dealer but also intervening significantly in the economic and cultural value of Cubism.[29]

Two other artists who became important to Léger and to the discourse of construction and reconstruction were Ozenfant and C. E. Jeanneret, who refashioned himself as Le Corbusier during the 1920s. They founded Purism, the art movement Léger affiliated with in the early 1920s. Léger probably met Ozenfant during the war and Le Corbusier in 1920 or early 1921.[30] Léger's collaborations with Ozenfant and Le Corbusier were formative and long-standing. Léger and Ozenfant together later directed the Académie Moderne (1924–29), after which Léger ran it alone until 1938; the academy attracted students and instructors from Europe, Asia, and the Americas, extending Léger's renown and networks. Léger collaborated, too, with Le Corbusier on architectural projects, starting with the Pavillon de l'Esprit Nouveau at the Exposition des arts décoratifs in 1925.

On Armistice Day 1918, Ozenfant and Jeanneret launched the Purist movement with the publication of *After Cubism* (1918).[31] The war was a "great competition" that swept away "aging methods," but now with the war over, "factories rise." They called for an end to an "era of strikes, demands, and protests where art was but an art of protest" and the start of a new "spirit of construction" and synthesis of form. Their manifesto invests in a French history of art represented by Nicolas Poussin and Jean-August-Dominique Ingres and in the rationalized industrial production known as Taylorism or Fordism. Capitalist economics became aestheticized through "manufactured products that are so perfect that they give labor teams cause for collective pride" and engineering feats—"bridges, factories, dams." Purism sought to discipline social orders and libidinal energies, aiming to "conquer chance and channel emotion" to achieve an aesthetic and psychic "equilibrium." With the founding of their periodical, *L'Esprit Nouveau*, in 1920, Ozenfant and Jeanneret advocated for "Purism" as an aesthetics of logic, rationality, and the "perception of order."[32] Histories of Purism and the few exhibitions dedicated to the movement emphasize its discourse of aesthetic hygiene, cleanliness, and purification. Art historian Tag Gronberg has read its culminating project, the 1925 Pavillon de l'Esprit Nouveau, as a set of practices assuaging anxieties over lost male control.[33] More recently, art appraiser and critic Pierre Guénégan has focused on the rise and fall of Ozenfant and Le Corbusier's relationship as "enemy brothers of Purism" initiated by their homoerotic wartime intimacy.[34]

L'Esprit Nouveau promoted Léger as an exemplar of the new spirit, regularly reproduced images of his artwork, and published reviews of his solo and group exhibitions at Rosenberg's gallery and elsewhere. The first article on Léger was in issue four, an essay by art critic Maurice Raynal, who had known Léger since 1909 when they lived together in the artist's colony La Ruche (the beehive). Raynal cast Léger as a resilient survivor of war engaged in the productive energies of the postwar era and a utopian machine iconography.[35] He saw Léger as having "survived" the "frenetic hours of war" and "profited from the war" in that his postwar work had a new "intensity and purity." He interpreted Léger's agitated urban scenes as *nature vives* (living nature), "dynamic spectacles" full of "colliding contrasts," animated wheels, "flying stairs," and *cocardes* (the French tricolor rosette) that nevertheless always "guarantee equilibrium" and have a "center of gravity." Yet Léger's letters exchanged with Rosenberg also reveal the ongoing anxieties of the era, extensions of prewar debates between French Cubists and Italian Futurists as well as wartime battles between the avant-garde and their xenophobic detractors. In a letter to Rosenberg, Léger wrote that the war's "hard convulsion" and the "Russian social evolution" disturbed societal "equilibrium" and led to a "hypertrophy [or swelling] of temperaments" such that only now (in September 1919) had "the frightened public" cautiously returned to the art scene.[36]

Léger scholarship regularly posits him as exemplary of Purism's postwar classicism and reconstruction ideology, yet rarely do these accounts consider how Léger's art manifests the traumatic legacy of the war and ambivalence about the exigencies of corporeal and national reconstruction with its reconstitution of normative gender roles.[37] Why, for example, were Léger's *nature vives*, as Raynal described Léger's agitated worlds, not seen as at odds with the *natures morts* (still lifes) and equilibrium promoted by Rosenberg's gallery and produced by Ozenfant and Jeanneret? How might Purist "equilibrium," invested with Platonic statics in Le Corbusier's work, have signified differently for Léger, who sought to register the shock of modernity in his art? How might Léger's aesthetic, which did not conform to the return-to-order's use of chiaroscuro, linear perspective, and naturalism, encode the affective dynamics of trauma? Nor have the gendered implications of Léger's forms of classicism been considered within the context of postwar discourses. John Golding, Green, Robert Herbert, Kenneth Silver, and other art historians typically hold out Léger's depictions of women, especially *Three Women*, as examples of his classicizing turn. In Green's analysis, Léger's hybridization of classical forms with machine elements aligns with Purist paradigms: just as Le Corbusier paired images of the Parthenon with Ozenfant's Hispano-Suiza automobile, Léger's *Nudes on a Red Ground* (1923) converges the female nude and the factory machine.[38] Yet Léger's female figures, sometimes bald and rarely maternal, are in many ways an uneasy fit with the postwar ideology of femininity and maternity represented by Severini or Picasso's suckling mothers. Further, the *femme-machine* (machine-woman), a widespread phenomenon in postwar spectacle, could also operate as a displacement of the mechanized and dehumanized soldier and as a sign of masculine fears about technology and sexuality.[39] Alternatively, art historian Amelia Jones has proposed reading Picabia's feminized spark plugs and light bulbs, such as in the *American Girl* (1917), as "the feminizing effects of rationalization on his own body and mind."[40]

In this chapter, I examine how Léger's art could be at odds with the Purist project, and I argue that his participation in the symbolic reconstruction of France was always partial, desirous of turning away from the trauma of war and contingent upon an incomplete process of forgetting. Focusing on five arenas of reconstruction—the economy, the male body, the city, the female body, and the landscape—I show that Léger's position in postwar classicism and his investment in machine modernism engaged in contradictory claims to resilience while also manifesting an incomplete process of mourning. Other scholars, too, have remarked upon the contradictions between Léger's and Le Corbusier's aesthetics. Simon Richards sharply differentiates Léger from Le Corbusier and Ozenfant, arguing that Léger's new reality was "disruptive and traumatic," while Le Corbusier's and Ozenfant's still lifes aimed for "static order" disinterested in "the potential chaos and flux of contemporary existence."[41] In analyzing Le Corbusier's and Léger's still life paintings, art historian Nina Rosenblatt interprets Léger as producing a subjectivity antithetical to Le Corbusier's "anaesthetic subjectivity." She reads Léger as representing modernity's "incessant shock and dissipation of perception" through techniques like montage and fragmentation, but, Rosenblatt argues, this was "not synonymous with the numbing, normative models" adopted by Le Corbusier.[42] My analysis affirms these insights and documents how Léger's art could be "disruptive and traumatic" in contravention to the "numbing, normative models" that Purism sought.

Economic Wars

For veterans like Léger and for the avant-garde more broadly, the war's military battles and wartime aesthetic conflicts were perpetuated in the postwar art market. A volatile postwar economy intensified the arbitrary value of the commodification of art. Before the war, the hostile criticism of Cubism appearing in mass-circulation newspapers traded in racist and xenophobic attacks and depictions of Léger, Metzinger, and Gleizes as criminal types.[43] While Apollinaire, Raynal, Salmon, and others had responded with positive reviews, the wartime xenophobia intensified and motivated a retreat by the avant-garde. By 1918, the art critic Louis Vauxcelles, publishing under the pseudonym Pinturrichio, perpetuated his prewar battle against Cubism, cheering the departures of Diego Rivera and André Lhote from Rosenberg's gallery as signs of the failure of Cubism.[44] Léger was so upset that he wrote to Rosenberg describing the aesthetic fight as "our war" and bitterly cursing Vauxcelles as "the kind of man the war should have killed."[45]

By fall 1919, Léger interpreted his era as a period of "sped-up human development" where the "prewar extremes" had become far more fraught in "battle[s]" over "equilibrium," battles represented by the Russian Revolution on the international scale and by the artistic debates evident in Rosenberg's gallery. Responding to Rosenberg's characterization of the era as "an era of construction . . . discipline, order, [and] measure," Léger insisted that he was "the most conscientious mason . . . a constructor," as Cendrars had described him in a poem of the same year. But Léger also went on to assert that he had "a terror of too much control" and that "an excess of equilibrium [is] the point of death, 'the motor stopped.'"[46] In Léger's terms, the aesthetic debates over the life and death of Cubism were bound up with the social upheavals of war and the Russian Revolution. Paradoxically, both states of war and an "excess of equilibrium" could result in death.

Léger's writing betrays a profound ambivalence about the new economic and aesthetic wars and their impact on modern man. On the one hand, in "The Machine Aesthetic" (1924), Léger expresses a preference for the state of war over a state of peace, writing: "I find the state of war more normal and more desirable than the state of peace. . . . The state of peace is life in a slowed-down rhythm; it is a situation of getting into gear, behind drawn blinds, when everything is really happening in the street where the creator must be. There life reveals itself—accelerated and profound and tragic."[47] In this opposition, "war" is the street that is the source of creativity and life's acceleration, profundity, and tragedy, while "peace" is cast as interior spaces, the home or studio, the state of preparation, and "a slowed-down rhythm." On the other hand, in "Le Spectacle" (1924), Léger writes about World War I as "four years of paroxysm." The postwar period of economic anxiety is, he writes, "a social order that is not peace, but another plateau where the economic war leaves him [the ordinary man] no respite, another state of war as implacable as the first."[48] The modern city's sensory stimuli functioned like a war that could be alternatively threatening and invigorating. Léger goes on to argue that modern man should not be made to be a "victim of the machine" but its beneficiary, effectively recognizing the risks of the industrial order and its capacity to destroy. In reflecting back upon the postwar years, Léger wrote in 1937: "The man of 1921, returned to normal life, keeps in him this physical and moral tension from the hard years of war. It had changed; the economic battles replaced the battles at the front."[49] Here, the veteran returning to civilian life retains the tensions of war within his body and psyche, revived by economic stresses and uncertainty in a form of psychic disequilibrium.

Postwar reparations produced a specific economic war that directly impacted Léger and destabilized the monetary value of his art. The French state had confiscated the art collections of German dealers Kahnweiler and Uhde and, in 1921, sold their collections as part of German war reparations. The sales included over fifty paintings by Léger, which sold for 300 to 1,000 francs each, and two hundred of his drawings, which sold from 70 francs on up.[50] The sales prices at auction brought the battles about the "value" of Cubist art to a crisis, as Green has observed.[51] *L'Esprit Nouveau* and *Bulletin de l'Effort Moderne* provided extensive coverage of the sales, including price listings and articles discussing their significance for artists.[52] Although Rosenberg bought Léger's and others' art for his Galerie de l'Effort Moderne stock, Léger felt disenfranchised from the auction process. Artists were not compensated directly, and Léger could not afford to buy back his own work. He complained to Rosenberg that the law acted contrary to "the vital interests of men who had fought in the war."[53] In the inaugural issue of his *Bulletin de l'Effort Moderne*, Rosenberg defended the acquisitions by arguing that auction prices were much higher than expected and so increased the value of future work by artists like Picasso and Léger.[54] However, it took years for Léger to reap the benefits, and initially, he was not a gallery favorite.[55] By 1922, the Purists accused the art critic Vauxcelles of manipulating the market in favor of Impressionist art dealers and double-dealing by writing for Cubism under one pseudonym and against it under another. The battle escalated into charges of anti-Semitism, countercharges by Ozenfant and Le Corbusier for defamation, and ongoing debates about the devaluation of Cubist art.[56] Kahnweiler even complained that the sales at the auction house Hôtel Drouot were a "disaster" and that he bought back one painting for some 300 francs after he had originally paid 3,000.[57] The debates around these sales brought attention to the power of institutions that made and unmade an artist's value: the dealer system, the critical review, and the state as buyer, seller, and market manipulator.

As economic historian Stephen Schuker has argued, economic warfare in the form of France's demand for reparations from Germany supplanted military warfare, complicated national recovery issues, and resulted in the decline of France as an economic power. The early 1920s saw, he claims, "an economic and psychological crisis as great for the victors as for the vanquished" in which France was "often misinterpreted as bellicose" but was actually "nervous and defensive."[58] Léger's anxieties about the value of his art and his statements about multiple forms of "war" align with this larger national mood. Purism's engagement in the economics of artistic recovery also reveals this bellicose yet defensive posture.

For Léger, the artist's vulnerable status as a pawn of market manipulation during a national economic crisis perpetuated the crisis of human value that the war had provoked. In a letter to Poughon in 1915, Léger wrote that: "It [the Great War] is as rotten [*vache*] as the economic battles in times of peace and not much different; the only difference is that you can push the result a little farther, just a bit farther:

instead of ruining good men, you kill them. That [difference] is a sentimental value. I can assure you that it is nonexistent. It does not serve anything because it is not worth anything."[59] In Léger's writing, the difference between the financially ruined man and the dead man is his living body, a bit of "sentimental value" that is "not worth anything." Léger's cynicism is a shocking and melancholic expression of lost faith in the organic male body. Before the war, Léger had rejected "sentimentality" in painting, meaning the cloying narratives and emotional drama of an outmoded academic aesthetics that he saw as unsuited to a modern era of fragmentation and "dynamic divisionism."[60] In the postwar period, Léger's machine aesthetic writings use the beautiful mass-produced object to displace the "sentimental," a fetishization of the commodity that simultaneously negates lost bodies and refuses to mourn.[61] Man's body, stripped of military or economic value, leaves only a sentimental value, a failed masculinity useless to the prosecution of the war or the project of reconstruction. Léger's engagement with Purist economic discourse operated as a form of compensation for this lost value.

Purism asserted a dominant position in the volatile economic context by envisioning a virile world of male elites as the leaders of national reconstruction. A discourse of masculine potency emerges in *L'Esprit Nouveau*'s iconography, economic plans, and intellectual debates. The first issue announced in its opening pages: "The elite individuals who compose the world of industry and business and who live as a consequence in this virile atmosphere where they create works of undeniable beauty, think of themselves as far from aesthetic activity; they are wrong, because they are among the most active creatures in contemporary aesthetics."[62] Economic leaders are both virile industrialists and aesthetic makers. A year after its founding, the review proclaimed its aim to be an "indispensable connection among elites" who should "advance, cultivate, civilize, and stabilize societies" in a tumultuous era.[63] Again in *Toward an Architecture* (1923), Le Corbusier's influential architectural and urban planning text, engineers are "healthy and virile, active and useful, moral and joyful."[64] As art historian Mark Antliff has argued, *L'Esprit Nouveau* promoted a technocratic modernism and "hoped that the extension of capitalist rationalization worldwide would result in the creation of a world federation able to guarantee global stability."[65]

Le Corbusier's vision rejected prewar Cubism's simultaneity and Bergsonian flux and instead, as Antliff claims, combined modernist technology with a regenerative ideal that led in the 1930s to a "fascist productivism."[66] *L'Esprit Nouveau* imagined virility and potency enacted by the dissemination of its publications and articulated in a capitalist economic system and patriarchal social structure. Imitating the monthly industrial trade magazine *La Revue industrielle*, from which Le Corbusier amassed numerous clippings, images, and ideas, the Purist editors imagined *L'Esprit*

Nouveau as a corporation with a worldwide distribution network. Like *La Revue industrielle*, *L'Esprit Nouveau* announced on the inside cover of the first issue that it was a *société anonyme* (private corporation) capitalized to 100,000 francs. Its masthead lists the countries and sites of its distribution, and the journal published charts and maps showing the scope of its sales. Corporate advertisers in *L'Esprit Nouveau*, too, generated income for the periodical and fostered an image of the arts and architecture as collaborators with industry and the manufactured object.[67] Le Corbusier's famous dictum, "architecture or revolution, revolution can be avoided," envisioned social control by appropriating the voice of women in an imaginary housing manifesto that would demand a Corbusian model of mass housing and so ward off a class- and gender-based revolution.[68]

Léger's writing shares Purism's discourse of virility, its investment in a capitalist economics, and the dissemination of ideas as artistic capital. In multiple essays published in France, Germany, Belgium, and elsewhere, Léger developed his postwar machine aesthetic, notably in two essays titled as such and published in 1923 and 1924. Léger imagined economic regeneration and social renewal by arguing for the mass-produced object as a thing of beauty in competition with fine arts. Beauty, Léger claimed, was subject to a "law of supply and demand," and the spectacles of the city were "raw material" that the artist needs to put into production or *mise en valeur*.[69]

Well-known passages of the second of Léger's "Machine Aesthetic" essays declare his investment in the fetishized object of mass production: "the manufactured object is absolute, polychrome, clean, and precise, beautiful in itself . . . beauty is everywhere, in the arrangement of a set of saucepans on a white kitchen wall as well as in a museum."[70] Léger's *Ballet mécanique* (1924) (fig. 18), a short film made in collaboration with photographer Man Ray, filmmaker Dudley Murphy, and musician George Antheil, exemplifies Léger's economic and aestheticized valorization of mass-produced objects.[71] Rows of kitchen pots, their lids, pie pans, soup ladles, and wine bottles all appear in their most purified and commodified state: new, isolated or in assembly-line rows or shop displays untainted by food or liquids that might putrefy. While the emphasis on culinary objects might seem antithetical to an art inspired by the 75mm cannon, the militarized rows of kitchenware seem to refashion the deafening cacophony of Verdun cannons that Léger described as a *marmitage* (pot banging).[72] The "pots" of war, clanging and banging in their deadly firing, are now silenced, made harmonious in their regularized dance and orchestrated into a symphony of light and color. The effect of discordant and coordinated machine sound was a key aspect of Antheil's composition whose orchestra and performance plans variously included two to sixteen pianos, one player piano, electric bells, and airplane motors or fans.[73] Even after Léger abandoned his machine aesthetic, his fame and modernist persona were tied to the innovations represented by the film.

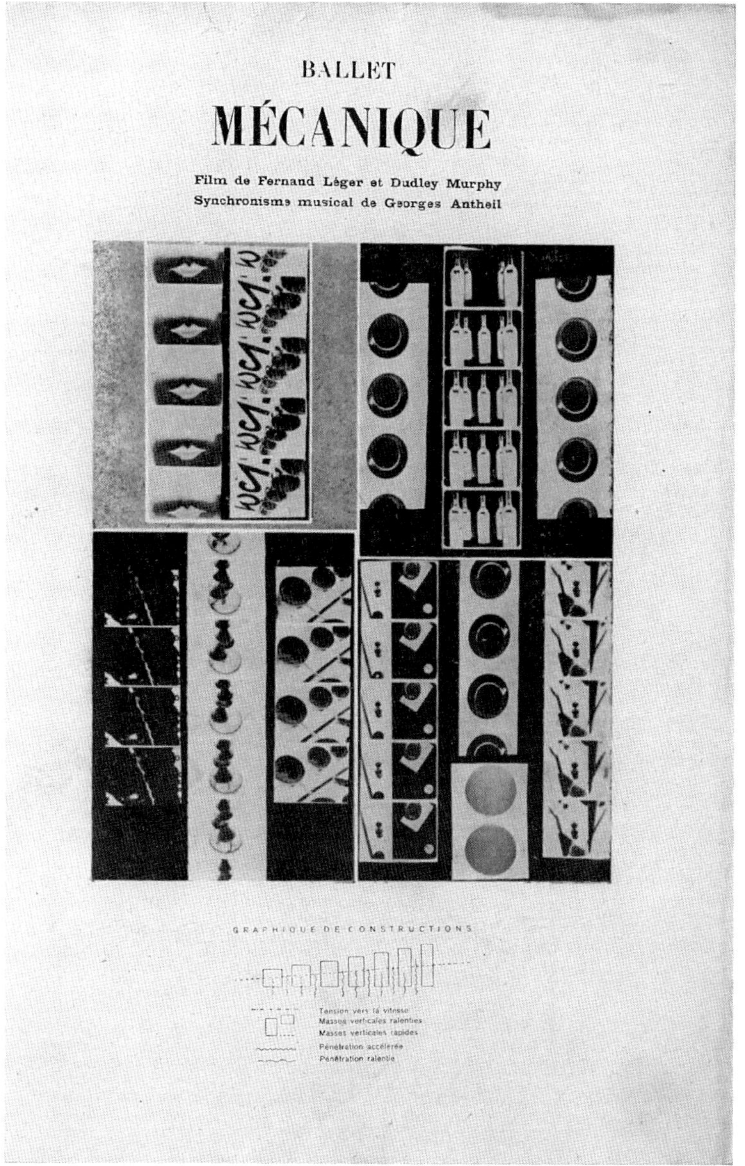

Fig. 18 Fernand Léger, stills from *Le Ballet mécanique*, 1924. In *L'Esprit nouveau*, no. 28 (January 1925): n.p. Inv. no. MNFL Revue–0352/21. Musée National Fernand Léger / Biot, France. © IMEC, Fonds MCC, Dist. RMN-Grand Palais / Léger / Art Resource, New York. © 2024 Artists Rights Society (ARS), New York / ADAGP, Paris.

Léger's investment in the aestheticized commodity became the subject of critique by his contemporaries, including Aragon and Benjamin.[74] Yet Léger's valorization of the commodity and objectification of the body can, I propose, also understood by another, rarely mentioned, part of his "Machine Aesthetic" essay in which he identifies scavenged war debris as the model for the idealized commodity and the abject body as that which it works to disavow. For Léger, the beautiful commodity supplants fine art just as the object scavenged from warfront debris gained unexpected value due to its "cost," which could be a man's life: "A nail, a candle stub, a shoelace can cost a man's life or a regiment's. . . . There is no longer any negligible value . . . the order of usual and conventional values is reversed . . . human-value, object-value, machine-value take their pitiless, natural hierarchy." The factory product's precursor is thus capitalism's wartime waste, a negligible object abandoned due to the death of the original owner and acquired at risk of death by the scavenger. In this neglected passage of his "Machine Aesthetic" essay, Léger self-consciously envisions the commodity as a displacement of death. The inverse relationship between the "object-value" and "human-value" can be understood as the devaluation of human life and specifically the male body that, at best, has only useless "sentimental value." This passage in Léger's "Machine Aesthetic" essay is surprisingly explicit in its processes of blocking male ruination from representation and of displacing investments from a once-idealized masculinity to the new idealized object. Masculinity's de-idealization, as Silverman writes, is a process linked to the mutilation of the male body and to "the void at the center of subjectivity."[75]

Death and Neurasthenia

In *L'Esprit Nouveau*, Léger is posited as a rational man whose machine aesthetic signifies in terms of economic and psychic regeneration in an ongoing battle against madness and neurasthenia, melancholy, and death. By 1920, in the context of French and Purist censorship of psychic breakdown, *L'Esprit Nouveau* vaunted Léger's art as a new classicism of the machine age and interpreted Léger as a survivor of the war with no trace of mental weakness. Raynal wrote that Léger would not, like Gauguin, "flee to Tahiti," or, like Van Gogh, "cut off his ears," casting Léger as a resilient figure who would not fall into the depression, alcoholism, or suicide that plagued Van Gogh and many veterans.[76] Another anonymous article fictionalizes Léger's story of discovering the beauty of the machine at the Aviation Salon to claim his machine art as a weapon against the "disarray [and] neurasthenia" of outmoded forms of painting.[77]

The pages of *L'Esprit Nouveau* demonstrate its constant efforts to manage that void at the center of subjectivity: the threat of financial disaster and the spectacle of death. The difficult economic status of France, the national debt, and fears about depopulation are the focus of several articles.[78] The national economy impacted the periodical, which depended upon funding from the state. The editors had to suspend publication for over a year between June 1922 and November 1923, after which it cut down its monthly publications to ten issues per year.[79] The penultimate issue, in 1925, called for support, noting the difficult situation in Europe and the financial challenges the journal confronted.[80] In a double issue at the end of

1921, the "Direction," meaning Ozenfant, Le Corbusier, and Dermée, defended the economic focus of the journal, arguing that "a law of capital . . . reigns over contemporary activity."[81] The tumultuous forces of the era—"the syndicalist spirit, Bolshevik efforts . . . monstrous anomalies such as war and arms . . . the admirable conquest of machinism . . . social disorganization"—evidence the need for an "immense project" requiring elites to study, debate, and develop a "program of action." The Purist leadership believed that conquest of the machine was a response to "war and arms" but had not yet securely established itself in the "social apparatus" or in "the State," as represented by the ongoing civil war in Russia, which "dies of hunger." The promise of Russian Constructivism, in other words, had not been realized.

In *L'Esprit Nouveau*'s coverage, Russia's machine modernisms compete with death, hunger, economic stability, "wars and arms." The periodical published articles about Russian poetry, music, theater, art, and architecture, including by Ilya Ehrenbourg, who was a contributor, Communist Party loyalist, and friend to Léger; and about Vladimir Mayakovsky, whom Léger met in 1922 and to whom Léger dedicated his first "Machine Aesthetic" essay.[82] Largely emphasizing the revolutionary Bolshevik politics of the new art, *L'Esprit Nouveau* presents the image of a new society in the making. Issue 14 reproduces an image of Vladimir Tatlin's Monument to the Third International (1920), and issue 22 includes an essay by Ivan Puni on Constructivism.[83] Yet, as Puni acknowledges at the end of his essay, "sabotage, lack of manpower, credit, hunger, the drop in the exchange rate, and the hostile attitude toward modern art" have impeded execution of most projects. In a startling photograph of the reality of Russian conditions, *L'Esprit Nouveau* contradicted its mission and Ozenfant's dictate to turn its back on war and death. The photograph, published twice during the Russian Civil War in 1921 and 1922, was part of a Red Cross appeal to aid the Russia that "dies of hunger." It shows bodies piled up in the snow before Russian Orthodox crosses. The text below claims thirty million had already died and another fifteen million people were "condemned to death" due to Russia's civil war and widespread starvation.[84]

In covering the German avant-garde, *L'Esprit Nouveau* articles establish machine modernism as a response to Germany's pervasive "melancholy" and the threat of economic collapse, neurasthenia, and death. The periodical published illustrated articles by the Alsatian poet Yvan Goll on German poetry and theater, the critic Paul Westheim on the visual arts, the founder of the Bauhaus Walter Gropius on architecture, as well as other articles on German philosophy, arts, and architecture. Le Corbusier drew upon contacts he had established when he studied in Berlin in 1909; there, he worked for architect Peter Behrens, met architect and furniture designer Mies van der Rohe, and learned from the Deutscher Werkbund, the German association of artists, architects, and industrialists.[85]

Westheim, the German art critic and editor of *Das Kunstblatt*, contributed an essay on German art to *L'Esprit Nouveau* in which he aligned Léger with Russian Constructivism's "romanticism of the engineer," a path shared with Bauhaus artists Oskar Schlemmer and Willi Baumeister.[86] By contrast, Westheim writes, Dix and George Grosz's "integral verism," the aesthetic strategies of New Objectivity, aim to give the viewer a "violent shock" like "whip lashes." Grosz wants to make painting a "weapon" and drawing "a sort of intellectual machine gun." The conservative critic Waldemar George, too, aligned Baumeister with Purist ideals; Baumeister's art was "anti-Expressionist" and negated emotion and "sentimentality."[87] Léger and Baumeister had their work exhibited together in 1922 at Der Sturm Gallery in Berlin, and Baumeister had been in contact with the Purist leaders. By the time they met in 1924 in Paris, launching years of exchange, both were veterans, although Baumeister was a decorated pilot with little evidence of psychic trauma. In Léger and Baumeister's joint interview that year, Léger expresses his admiration for German "precision" and "cleanliness," citing the German steel helmet that the French adopted during the war and claiming "j'étais artilleur à Verdun" ("I was in the artillery at Verdun").[88] Léger's posturing elides both his actual role as a *brancardier* and the imprecise and unclean mess of fragmented bodies he had to clean up.

In art historian Gottfried Boehm's analysis, both Léger and Baumeister invoke the machine in their writing, incorporate marionette-like figures in their art, and adopt an anti-Expressionist or antisentimental position vis-à-vis the human figure.[89] Yet the era was perhaps less "optimistic" than Boehm sees it and more anxious and haunted. New scholarship offers another way to read Léger's German counterparts. Art historian Paul Monty Paret interprets the encased and constrained dancers in Schlemmer's *Triadic Ballet* (1922) as not simply "half-human, half-mechanical beings" but also as "grotesque combination[s] of [disfiguration] and prosthetic attachments" paralleling war wounded.[90]

Economic instability and fragile reconstruction plans undergird *L'Esprit Nouveau's* reading of historical and racial markers of psychic breakdown. Recalling the debts, bankruptcy, misery, and homelessness of Dutch artists Johannes Vermeer, Rembrandt van Rijn, Salomon van Ruysdael, and Frans Hals, Westheim cautions the modern artist about bourgeois tastes and the threat of "hate and scorn" in the midst of "today's hard times," speculation, and art market bubbles. In an article on German art, critic Paul Boulard casts Albrecht Dürer, Matthias Grünewald, and Hans Holbein (probably the younger) as symptomatic of German "melancholy, sadness, [and] despair" that persisted in the modern era, even in the midst of an architectural and industrial reconstruction and a "new machinism."[91] Modern architecture—Behrens's factories, Josef Maria Olbrich's Dusseldorf department store (1909), Heinrich Tessenow's Garden City in Hellerau (1908), Erich Mendelsohn's Einstein Tower (1922), and Gropius's Municipal Theater at Iena (Jena) (1922)—responds to the threat of "expressionisme, neurasthénie aiguë, détraquement" ("expressionism, acute neurasthenia, madness"). In Boulard's article, these threats are represented by German art such as Otto Dix's *War* (1924), a drawing of a rotting corpse, and Grosz's *Ecce Homo* (1922), an illustration of an old man leering at a naked young girl.

Fig. 19 Otto Dix, *Skat Players*, 1920. Oil on canvas with photomontage and collage, 110 × 87 cm. Inv. no. FNG 74/95. Photo: bpk Bildagentur / Nationalgalerie Staatliche Museen zu Berlin, Germany / Joerg P. Anders / Art Resource, New York. © 2024 Artists Rights Society (ARS), New York / VG Bild-Kunst, Bonn.

Léger, however, blocks the more literal representation of disabled war veterans and prostitutes that Dix and Grosz depict and the physical and moral decay they signify. For Léger to make explicit representations of the disfigured and crippled like Dix or diseased and aged prostitutes like Grosz would have negated the Purist investment in reconstruction and in a utopian Constructivist discourse. Such a mode of representation would have contradicted Léger's long-standing anti-Expressionist, antimimetic position that predated the war. The three amputee and disfigured veterans in Dix's New Objectivity painting *Skat Players* (1920) (fig. 19) catalog visible wounds—facial burns, lost ears, empty eye sockets, the macabre grin of a botched surgical reconstruction—and signify the absurdity of corporeal repair—earpiece tubing, glass eyes that cannot see, exposed metal headplates and jaws, wooden legs conflated with furniture legs—signaling a false investment in the possibility of wholeness on a corporeal or social level. Léger's *The Three Comrades* (1920) (fig. 15), painted the same year as Dix's *Skat Players*, is less explicit about veteran status and injury. As I will show with Léger's *The Mechanic* (1920) (fig. 20), the artist rarely looks closely at the reconstructed male body, and doing so becomes problematic.

Unlike Grosz, who had published a poem declaring "we are all neurasthenics," Léger remained silent about his neurasthenia.[92] Whether Léger met Grosz, who traveled with Baumeister to Paris in 1924, is unclear. Léger certainly knew of Grosz and Dix due to *L'Esprit Nouveau*'s coverage of their work and their shared networks. Both Léger and Grosz knew or collaborated with Einstein, poet Yvan Goll, and Alfred Flechtheim, and Grosz and Léger's mutual friend Pierre MacOrlan wrote a preface to the catalog for Grosz's Paris exhibition in 1924.[93]

The neurasthenia that Léger thought he suffered from when hospitalized in 1917 became, in Purist terms, disparaged as a sign of German melancholy and social and psychic "disarray" antithetical to the virile masculinity needed for the postwar order. Like Le Corbusier, who argued for harmony and equilibrium in aesthetics, design, and architecture, two Purist psychoanalysts—Allendy and Laforgue—advocated for psychic equilibrium and diminished the legacy of war neurosis. Allendy, a close friend to Le Corbusier and onetime analyst to writers Anaïs Nin and Antonin Artaud, organized the Sorbonne lectures that included Léger's machine aesthetic lectures. Little-discussed figures in the history of Purism and the history of psychoanalysis, Allendy and Laforgue were founders of the French Psychoanalytic Society of Paris in 1926 but later were suspected of wartime collaborationism with the Nazis.[94]

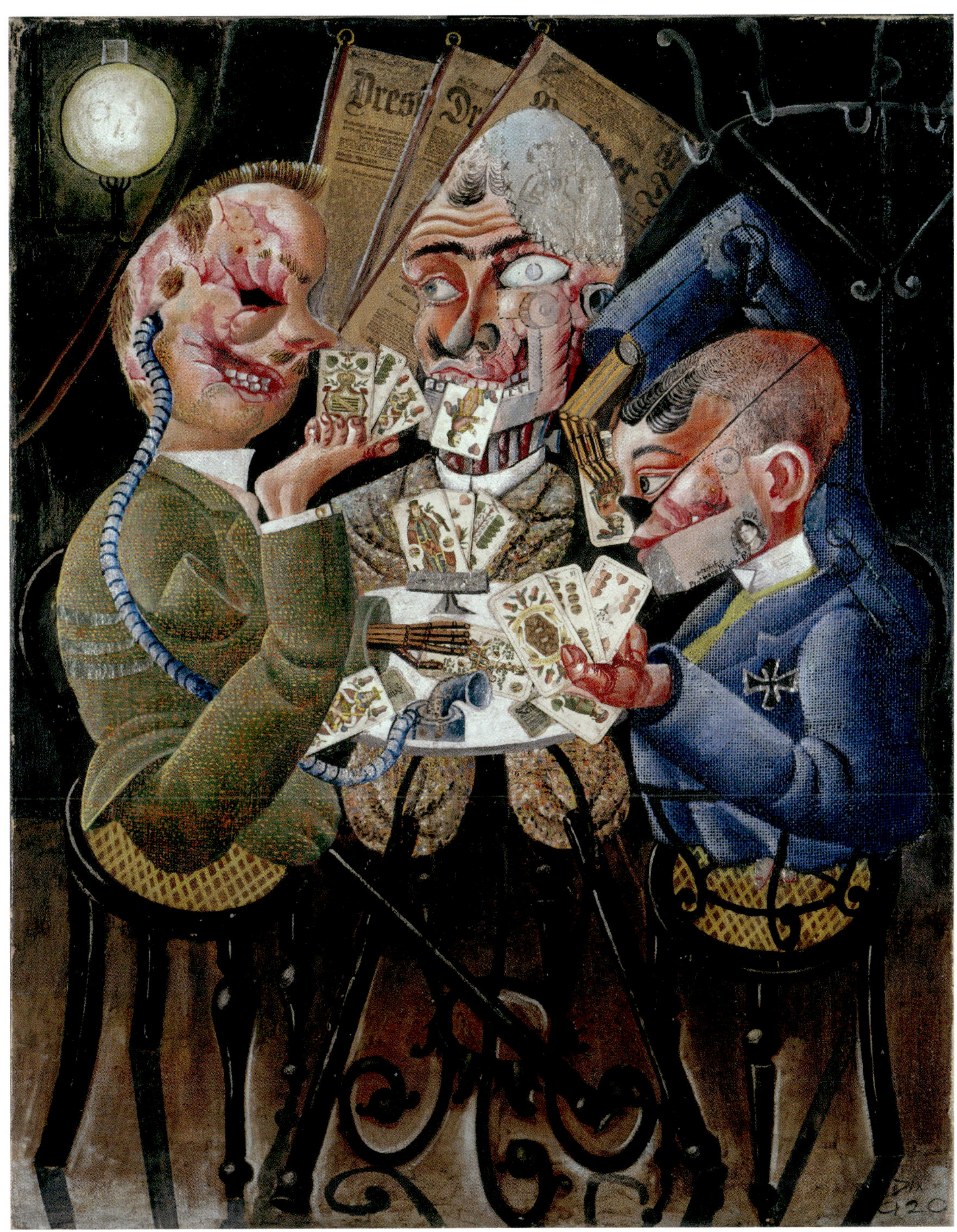
Dix
920

Regular contributors to *L'Esprit Nouveau*, they introduced Freudian terms and ideas but also exemplified the interwar silence about the mental health of veterans and stigmatization of mental illness.

In Allendy and Laforgue's writing, psychic "disequilibrium" was a failure to channel the libido whereas sublimation of the libido is "the principal motor of human progress."[95] The Oedipus complex emerges from a failure of family "harmony" or "equilibrium" exemplified by the case of a man who became a "neurasthenic" after the death of his severe father.[96] In an essay on neurotics, Allendy described a range of symptoms resulting from "psychic shock," including the digestive trouble and insomnia that Léger had suffered in 1917, as well as the paralysis, stammering, ticks, and frigidity that were typical of wartime shell shock.[97] Ironically, this essay was published in the same issue as a reproduction of Léger's *The Card Party*. Yet Allendy never identifies the war as a causal factor for psychic shock. Nor did Allendy or Laforgue discuss Freud's writings on war neurosis or repetition compulsion. Their study on neurotics focuses on frigid women and homosexual men.[98] The few military men who appear in their coauthored book *Le Rêve et la psychanalyse* (1926), are non-neurotics whose dreams are interpreted as signifying minor conflicts with authority that are easily resolved.[99]

Léger's Hypertrophic New Man

In reconstruction-era France and in the Purist world, the competing discourses of "equilibrium" and "neurasthenia" had economic, political, and psychic significations on the national, collective, and individual levels. For *L'Esprit Nouveau*, machine modernisms were repeatedly made to be aesthetic and economic responses to wars, revolutions, starvation, defeat, melancholy, and neurasthenia. In this context, Léger described modern life as precarious: as "accelerated and profound and tragic," causing the modern man's "hypertrophic value" to be "stretched to breaking."[100] Hypertrophy, a physiological term referring to an abnormal swelling or enlargement of a muscle, organ, or body part (often the prostate), signifies in Léger's usage as an aggrandized or inflated value that risks psychic breakdown. Writing to Rosenberg in 1919, Léger described their era as one where "we've lost our equilibrium" and where conflicts manifest as a "hypertrophy of temperaments."[101] Léger rejects the old "hideous hypertrophism of the individual among the false artists of the Renaissance" to valorize a new "hypertrophic" man of the people who lives up to the "maximum effort," suggesting a kind of constant psychic strain.[102] In 1923, he argued that creatives should immerse themselves in the popular milieu "with their rude and hard sides, tragic and comic, always hypertrophic" and avoid the "soft milieu" of the bourgeoisie and aristocracy, whose existence is based on a "minimum of life."[103] Unlike these elite classes, the working classes become hypertrophic by being subjected to modernity's excessive psychic pressures.

In two works from the early 1920s—*The Mechanic* (1920) and the Chaplin puppet (1921)—Léger alternatively aggrandizes the male body and materializes his conception of the hypertrophic body. Léger's portrait-style *The Mechanic* (1920) (fig. 20), located in the National Gallery of Canada in Ottawa, invites the viewer to scrutinize the face and body, a departure from the majority of Léger's *mécanicien* paintings and their small, usually featureless figures in or near a factory. The titles of these *mécanicien* paintings tell us the figure's otherwise inscrutable gender and labor: machine operator, engineer, or mechanic. These bodies are miniaturized according to several typologies: puppetlike figures with dowel-shaped, tapered limbs in *The Circus* (1918), *The Mechanic* (1918) (fig. 17), and *The Black Stoker* (1919); robotic gray bodies with cylindrical torsos and limbs in *The Bargeman* (1918); or even mere silhouettes as in *The City* (1919) or *Discs in The City* (1920). The Ottawa *Mechanic* is an iconic everyman whose profiled, mustached face and three-quarter torso draw greater attention to the male body than any of Léger's other *mécaniciens*. His gaze follows a curious right-angled smokestack that emerges from a tiny factory just above his right shoulder, while his torso is made parallel to and bolstered by a Doric column. His anchor tattoo gestures to a possible wartime maritime career. Read through the lens of Léger's hypertrophic modern man, this factory worker adopts the posture of a confident movie hero even as his body bears the awkwardness of postwar reassembly. As curator Nadine Engel has written, he "seems to be assembled from prefabricated parts, analogously to the serial production" of the factory behind him.[104] In 1920, such assembly invests in the possibility of corporeal reconstruction of the damaged veteran. His hair, forehead, and cheek, divided by a horizontal line at the temple, have the unnatural smoothness and surface sheen of a mannequin or rotator disks. He holds his cigarette with a hinged finger on a four-digit right hand, modeling the functionality of the kind of articulated prosthetic hand Léger's friend Cendrars had been fitted with but abandoned in a train station. And the asymmetry of his rounded shoulders calls attention to what could be read as the inadequacies and irregularities of reconstruction.

In *The Mechanic*, Léger constructs a new face and body for his machine man, reversing the anticlassical position of *The Card Party*, where he represented the ruptured faces of the *gueules cassées*. *The Mechanic*'s self-conscious attempt to reconstruct the male body betrays an ambivalence about new classicism's capacity to recuperate the male body. Green has claimed Léger's *The Mechanic* for interwar classicism and compared the painting to images published in *L'Esprit Nouveau* of Egyptian and Assyrian sculpture in their newly reopened rooms at the Louvre Museum.[105] More recently, Green has called attention to the neoclassical plaster

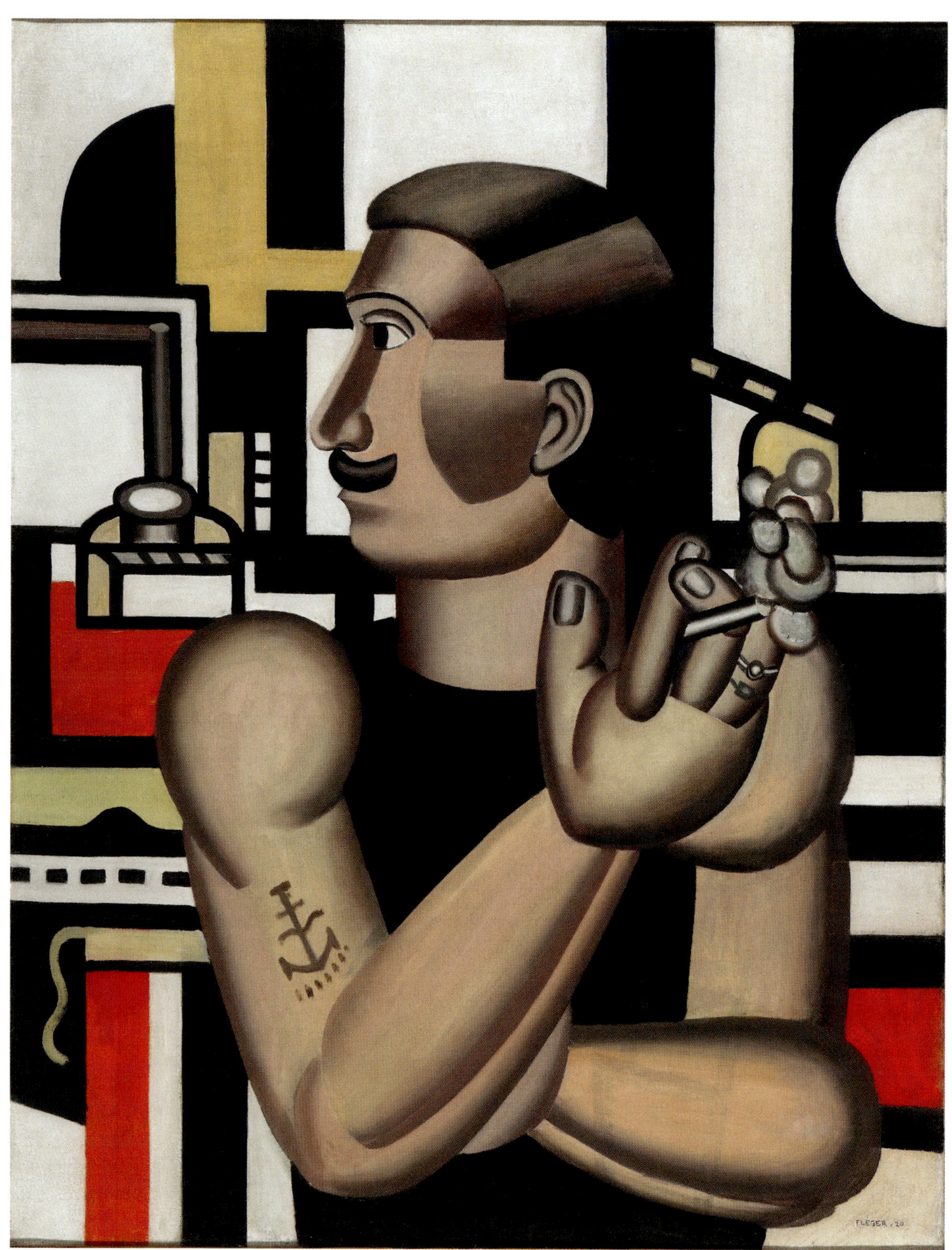
F.LEGER. 20

bust that appears as an idealized form in Picasso and Giorgio de Chirico's paintings.[106] Yet the classical bust and torso were not only inscriptions of an ideal male form; they could also block the fragmented body or signal its reconstruction.

The Mechanic's face, with its apparent seams at the temple, cheek, jaw, and brow, could be read as the reassembled face of a veteran and a sign of a society that could reconstitute itself. Léger must have seen veterans with surgically reconstructed faces in his neighborhood, on his street, or at nearby cafés such as the Closerie des Lilas, located between Léger's studio and the Val-de-Grâce military hospital. In his memoirs, Ernest Hemingway, who lived in the neighborhood in the 1920s, provides a literary counterpart to Léger's painting, describing the men he saw at that café: "I watched how well they were overcoming the handicap of the loss of limbs, and saw the quality of their artificial eyes and the degree of skill with which their faces had been reconstructed. There was always an almost iridescent shiny cast about the considerably reconstructed face, rather like that of a well packed ski run."[107] Léger's *Mechanic*, too, has an "iridescent shiny cast" to his face and forehead. The painting's three-quarter framing presents the body for close examination, sharing Hemingway's attentive eye to the artificiality of reconstruction and a watchful desire for "overcoming" and resilience.

Fig. 20 Fernand Léger, *The Mechanic*, 1920. Oil on canvas, 115.5 × 88.5 cm. National Gallery of Canada, Ottawa. © 2024 Artists Rights Society (ARS), New York / ADAGP, Paris.

Léger's *Mechanic* engages with classicism as an ideology of wholeness while also foregrounding its artifice, inadvertently casting doubt on the ability to return the body to its former self. In her analysis of wartime and postwar prosthetics and surgical reconstruction, historian Ana Carden-Coyne has argued that the ideology and discourse of "classicism" served "cultures of resilience" and provided an "aesthetics of healing" with an appeal to a "mind-body harmony" informed by ideals of wholeness.[108] Léger's mechanic offers up his profiled face for the viewer's scrutiny and proudly displays his hinged finger, but making him "classical" has rendered him rigid and oddly immobilized, outside the factory space rather than laboring within it as Léger's other mechanics and male workers do. For Léger, who wanted to create dynamic, animated worlds, the classical and the masculine seem at odds with each other in that the classical requires a stasis and "peace" that Léger disparagingly attributed to interior spaces and domesticity. The painting wants to depict a masculinity that is not the ruined body of war and economic battles, or what Léger called mere "sentimental value." But Léger's foregrounding of the male body is anomalous in his machine aesthetic period, suggesting an inability to sustain the gaze upon the reconstituted body, perhaps because of the psychic disturbance that close scrutiny brought. That Léger could not sustain such visual scrutiny is suggested by paintings such as *Still Life with Plaster Mask* (1927) or *Four Hats* (1927), which incorporate classical busts with pupilless eyes. Writing about similar sightless plaster busts in De Chirico's *Enigma* paintings, Foster reads them as signs of castration and a melancholic repression of trauma, an interpretation also applicable to Léger.[109] The postwar classicism and Purist project compelled a repression of the damaged male body, which may be registered as a symbolic blindness and psychic conflict in Léger's iconography.

Even more ambivalent and melancholic is Léger's *Cubist Chaplin* (fig. 21), a marionette version of film actor Charlie Chaplin (known as Charlot in French) who doffs his hat to salute the viewer in the opening and closing passages of the *Ballet mécanique* film. In the final sequence, his body collapses and his limbs detach, leaving his head behind. Chaplin's often anonymous characters depicted types—the vagabond, fireman, soldier, boxer—and his repeated gestures accord with the Purist idea of the serialized commodity, as film historian Amy Sargeant has claimed.[110] Like many of his generation, Léger's first encounter with film was with Chaplin films while on leave during World War I.[111] As Cendrars wrote, soldiers returning from leave reported on Chaplin's films and recounted his exploits as if he were a brother-in-arms, providing laughter back in the trenches.[112] Léger produced multiple versions of Chaplin throughout his career, some of which have only recently come to light, but the best known may be the puppet framing the *Ballet mécanique*.[113] Léger praised Chaplin as an artist who, unlike Douglas Fairbanks, did not embody the "star" persona but instead became part of the "moving décor" in which "the human measure . . . disappears [and] man becomes a mechanism like the rest."[114] For Léger, man was but a "human-object" among other objects. Léger wanted to "destroy the subject . . . and the scenario" through cinematic techniques like the close-up that isolates and fragments the object.[115] Although he had originally planned for a "little dancer" in the opening scene of the film, Léger replaced the dancer with the Chaplin puppet, perhaps in part because Chaplin could represent multiple artistic modalities from dance to film and so better interrogate corporeal-mechanical relations, as art historian Juliet Bellow proposes.[116] Yet in the *Ballet mécanique*, Léger's marionette enacts Chaplin's jerky movements signaling the neurasthenic male body that Purism wanted to displace with machine modernism. Léger's film opposes the Chaplin puppet's nervous gestures with the rhythmic and aestheticized movement of rows of manufactured objects. In using Chaplin as a foil for the manufactured object, Léger structures his film as a contrast between two types of movement, one neurotic and nonproductive and the other rational and productive.

Léger's *Ballet mécanique* marionette arose from illustrations he made for Goll's melancholic short story *La Chaplinade*, in which Chaplin signifies as a soldier who lives only as an image. First published in Dresden in 1920, then in Paris in 1921 in *La Vie des lettres*, Goll's story was reviewed in *L'Esprit Nouveau*. Goll envisions Chaplin as an image in a film poster glued to a kiosk who then comes to life and descends into the streets of Paris.[117] He is an everyman whose tale allegorizes the

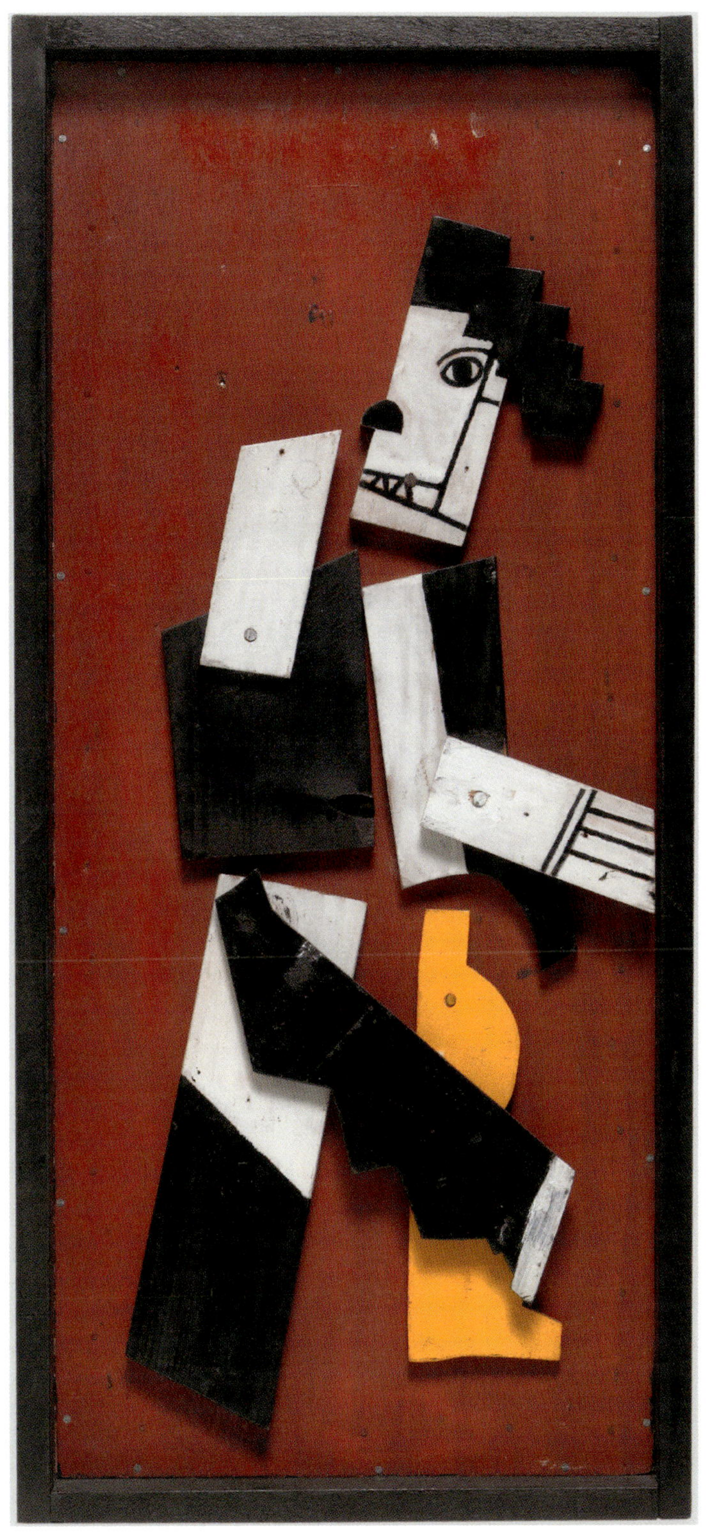

Fig. 21 Fernand Léger, *Cubist Chaplin*, 1924. Painted wood nailed to plywood, 73.6 × 33.4 × 6 cm. AM1985–402. Digital Image © CNAC/MNAM, Dist. RMN-Grand Palais / Art Resource, New York. © 2024 Artists Rights Society (ARS), New York / ADAGP, Paris.

soldier's experience: he enters dark forests, executes an innocent doe, encounters a suicidal widow, and leaves behind a mourning mother. At the end of Goll's story, Chaplin's hat-doffing gesture signals the soldier's earthly death and transcendence as he returns to the representational realm of poster and film.

Despite his tragic-comic persona, Chaplin the artist received positive reviews in *L'Esprit Nouveau*, perhaps because he could be imagined as a French *poilu* and because he always seemed to reconstitute himself in the end. Chaplin's characters engage with two forms of humor that account for his contradictory persona, as both victim of the machine and resilient survivor. He enacted both the corporeal humor that Bergson identified with "mechanical inelasticity" and the gallows humor that, according to Freud, permitted the condemned man heading to his execution to maintain a "tenacious hold upon [the] customary self" and disregard what would otherwise drive him to despair.[118] It is through this duality that many *L'Esprit Nouveau* articles interpreted Chaplin. In the first issue of *L'Esprit Nouveau*, one film reviewer described Chaplin's film about the soldier's life, *Shoulder Arms* (1918), as an example of his genius, writing that Chaplin is an artist who reveals the soul through "poetry, emotion [and] psychology."[119] The art historian Elie Faure similarly interpreted Chaplin as a "clown and a poet . . . a man of sorrows" exemplified by a scene in *Shoulder Arms* when Chaplin rolls out of his bunk bed, yawns, stretches, and then disappears in the waters of his flooded bunker.[120] By the time of Léger's Charlot drawings and puppet, the film director and critic Louis Delluc, who contributed regular articles to *L'Esprit Nouveau*, published *Charlot* (1921), the first book-length study not just of Chaplin but of any film actor. Delluc's book provided an influential interpretation of Chaplin and his character's "immense sadness."[121]

Surprisingly, Léger's marionette enacts not the balletic sequences that sometimes appear in Chaplin's films and would have better aligned with the movement of the manufactured objects but the jerkiness that Léger's contemporaries and historians see as the symptomology of nervous breakdown. In 1921, the film critic and director Jean Epstein, whom Léger knew and whose work Léger praised, remarked on Chaplin's "photogenic neurasthenia." Epstein saw Chaplin's performance as the "reflex actions of a nervous, tired person."[122] The British Vorticist artist Wyndham Lewis deplored Chaplin's "epileptic shuffle" and "puny" tininess.[123] Film historian Susan McCabe, too, has interpreted Chaplin's "spasmodic body" as belonging to an "iconography of hysteria, reverberating as a crisis in sexual embodiment, particularly of masculinity, related to war trauma."[124] Historian Jay Winter compared Chaplin's walk to the tremors of the shocked soldier documented in medical films of the era; at the same time, Chaplin's films served as therapeutic for hospitalized veterans.[125] For Léger to represent such a neurotic Chaplin at all would seem to contradict Purist ideologies. How was this possible?

Chaplin's contradictory body—humorous and neurasthenic—exemplifies Léger's paradoxical "hypertrophic" body representing an everyman inflated in value yet "breaking apart" at the seams. Here, Léger comes closest to the masculine fragility and castrated bodies in Amelia Jones's conception of "neurasthenic modernism." In her analysis, the eight malic molds in the lower register of Duchamp's *Large Glass* (1915–23), which he described as "a cemetery of eight uniforms," are impotent empty shells, "explicitly castrated," and failing in their erotic endeavors toward the "bride" in the upper register.[126] In another version of "hypertrophy," Max Ernst's *Hypertrophic Trophy* (1920) (fig. 22), a collage of five vertically positioned engineering diagrams on three linear axes, the "trophy" might be read as the central form on the highest of the three axes, which tilts slightly upward to the right. Atop the "trophy" and attached by a kind of timing belt is an eight-pointed star (resembling the Iron Cross). It functions like a flag flying upward and to the right, marking the highest point in the composition, while a star and crescent (signs of the Turkish flag, German's wartime ally), hang downward to the left as a visual counterweight. In Foster's reading, the trophy's fragility mocks the militarized discourse of armored bodies and is a sign of war's "hypertrophic" excesses or the way war was swelled or nourished by the death of its "soldier-trophies."[127] Although Léger never parodies corporeal functions as Duchamp did or militarism as Ernst did, Léger's Chaplin is an unusual display of masculine fragility.

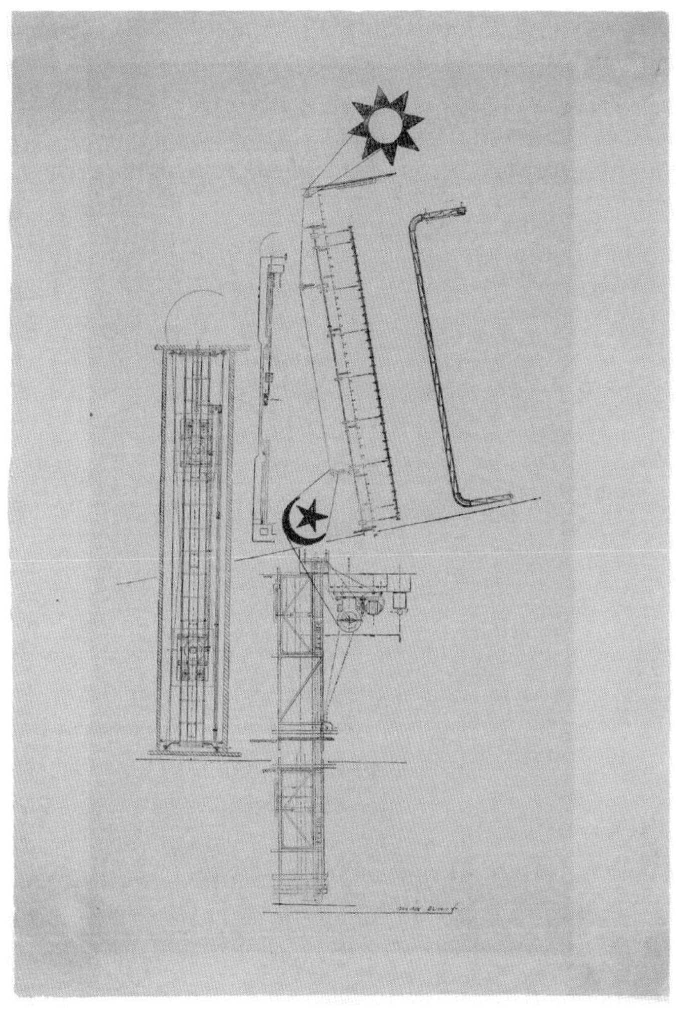

Fig. 22 Max Ernst, *Hypertrophic Trophy*, 1920. Line block print with ink on paper, 41.9 × 28 cm. Gift of Tristan Tzara (72.1936). Digital Image © The Museum of Modern Art / Licensed by SCALA / Art Resource, New York. © 2024 Artists Rights Society (ARS), New York / ADAGP, Paris.

Léger's Chaplin is a melancholic reading of the male body: hysterical in the opening sequences and dismembered into ruination in the closing of the film. Whatever "repair" the film offers through displays of rationalized and aestheticized mass production seems shockingly undermined by its return to Chaplin's sacrificial ruin in its closing, a paradox commentators rarely address. For Léger, who had been both a *brancardier* collecting the body in pieces and a patient hospitalized in a ward of shell-shocked soldiers, the Chaplin marionette condenses the two forms of physical and psychic breakdown that he witnessed: amputation and hysteria. Years later, Léger recalled Chaplin as "a sort of living puppet, dry as a stick, with clickety joints," a rheumatic body.[128] A former student, Pierre Faniest, recalled Léger's string of associations linking Chaplin to the war and its human debris. Léger, he writes, went from talking about Chaplin's "short films to prewar memories then to the war . . . [and] the dislocated bodies that he collected. Curious mix."[129] In the end, Léger's Chaplin marionette is not a survivor and does not reconstitute himself but becomes a ruined body that has only "sentimental value" and must be destroyed. As an object of sentimental investment and aggressive destruction, the marionette brings into view an otherwise unacknowledged sign of castrated masculinity imbued with melancholic loss.

Fig. 23 Fernand Léger, *The City*, 1919. Oil on canvas, 236.5 × 305.5 cm. A. E. Gallatin Collection, 1952. The Philadelphia Museum of Art / Art Resource, New York. © 2024 Artists Rights Society (ARS), New York / ADAGP, Paris.

Disequilibrium and the City

Where Léger's Ottawa *The Mechanic* and Chaplin puppet oscillate between a desired reconstruction and display of ruination, in Léger's cities, a diminished male body is immersed in a state of psychic shock and hypervigilance. In 1923, Epstein aptly compared Léger's paintings to "a hurricane, growing, living, cracking at the joints," suggesting that it is not just the body but also the entire scene that projects an agitated psyche.[130] This is particularly true for Léger's *The City* (1919) (fig. 23), where the city is a modernist version of the romantic sublime, an aggressive and awe-inspiring aural and visual assault that threatens to overwhelm the miniaturized *mécanicien* subsumed by its capitalist energy. In Léger's writing, the artist, who could be "crushed by the enormous mise-en-scène" of the city's colorful spectacles, must be both open and permeable to the city's "raw material" to use it as a resource for his art.[131] Often described as a simultaneist painting, *The City* fragments signs and structures—bits of telegraph poles, metallic columns, bridges, scaffolding, steel girding, staircases, wrought-iron railings, stenciled lettering—a dynamic and potent use of Léger's contrast of form, line, and volume to signify the overwhelming visual stimuli of modern life. The painting condenses the paradigmatic modernist experience as fragmentation and sensory assault in which the city, like the battlefield, can never fully be known, understood, or mastered.

Unlike Léger's noisy, colorful, and incomprehensible city, Grosz's *Grey Day* (1921) (fig. 24) depicts a city where the grayness of war persists, motivating Purist interpretations of Grosz as melancholy and neurasthenic. Grosz's city is, however, much more legible than Léger's. Its grid-patterned industrial architecture and geometric brick wall cannot negate the scars and wounds of war. Léger's city distracts us from its inhabitants. His is a visual cacophony metonymic of an aural one: its disk-shaped

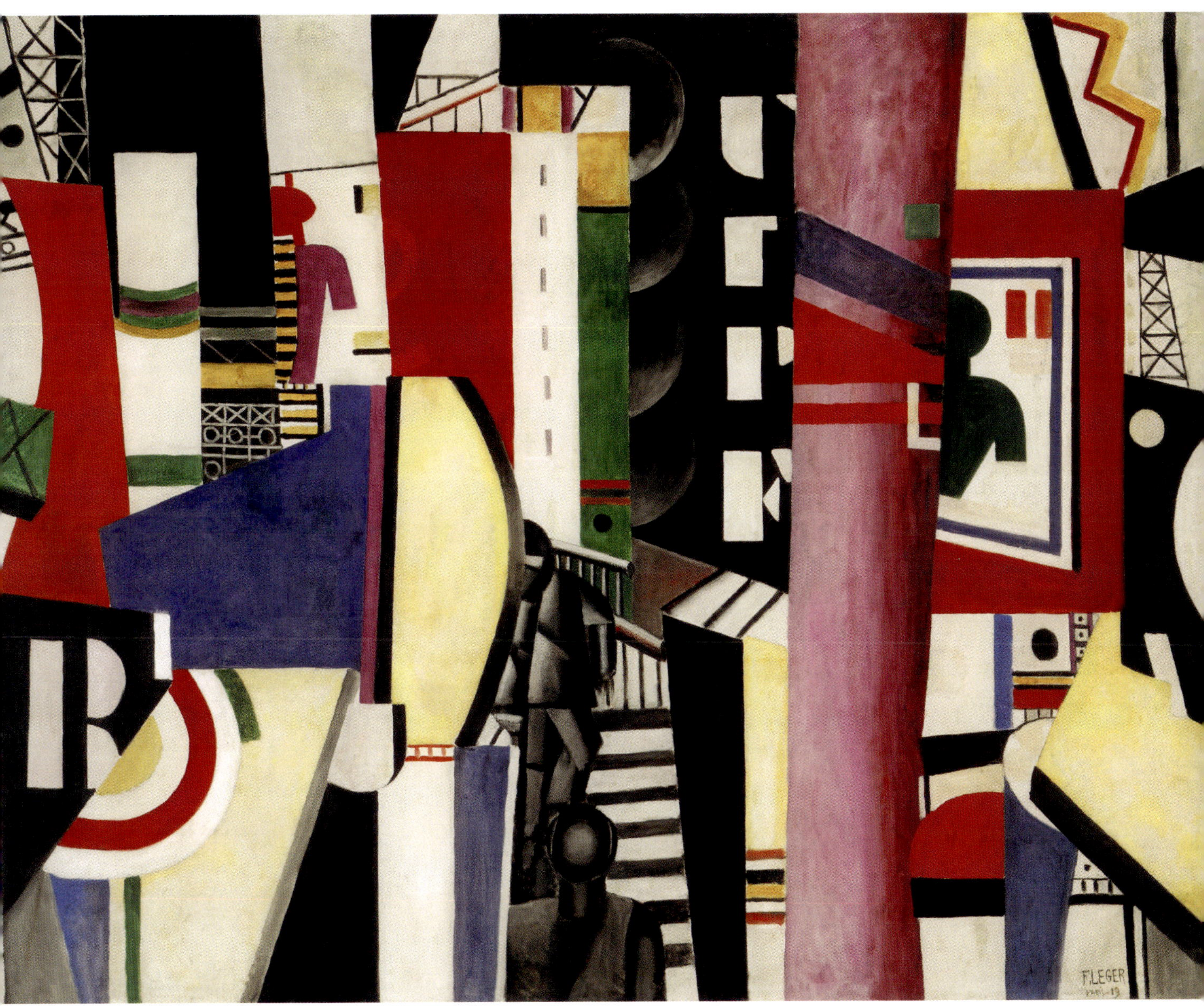
F.LEGER

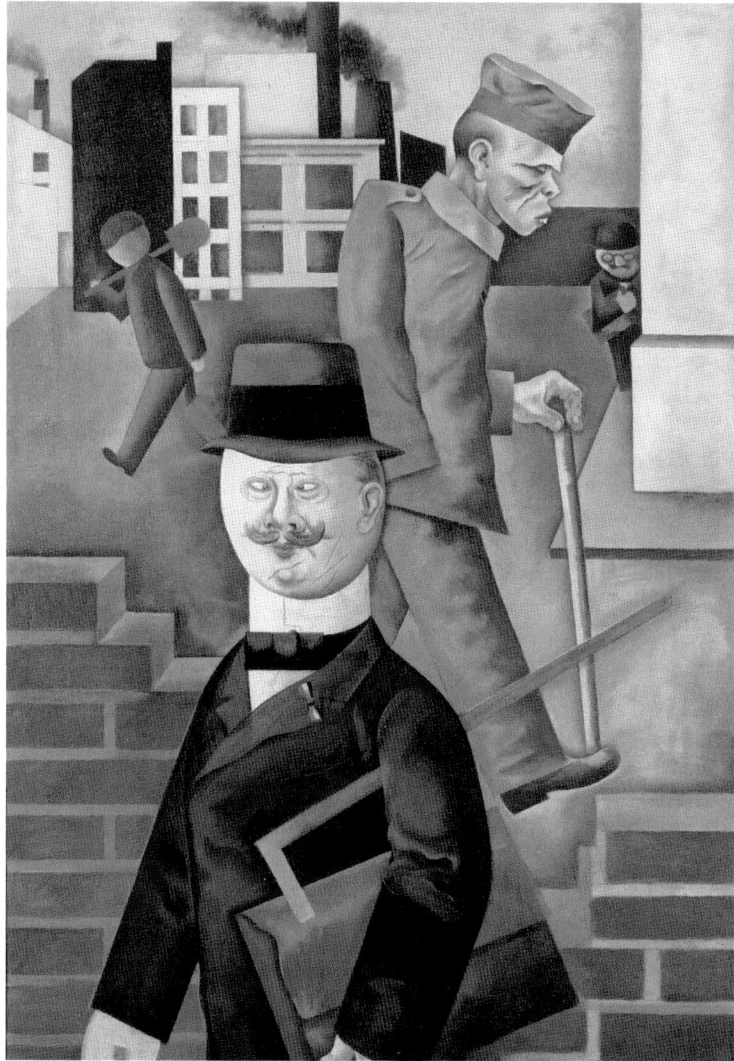

Fig. 24 George Grosz, *Grey Day*, 1921. Oil on canvas, 115 × 80 cm. Bpk Bildagentur / Staatliche Museen zu Berlin / Jörg P. Anders / Art Resource, New York. © 2024 Estate of George Grosz / Licensed by VAGA at Artists Rights Society (ARS), New York.

railroad signals conjure the clanging bells warning of a train's approach; the electrical globe lighting, transmission poles, and telegraph towers could recall for the viewer their incessant buzzing. In Léger's world, the city's sensory bombardment, like the war's, exceeds the capacity of the psyche to absorb and know the terrain in its entirety.

The modernity of the city provided Léger a traumatizing immersive experience that could be mastered through artistic production, an example of the dual forms of repetition described by Silverman: one that aims for mastery while also being contingent upon the repetition compulsion of the death drive. For Léger, the city was a contradictory space, replicating certain aspects of the war while also offering creative material for the artist without the same threat of death. Before the war, Léger had described the city as the site of sensory overload where modern man registers "one hundred times the impressions of an eighteenth-century artist."[132] In Grosz's city, the war's legacy is evident in scarred faces and wounded bodies and in the alienation and class hierarchy of its laborers with their tools, veterans still in uniform, industrialists with their plans, and speculators lurking in the background. But for Léger, cast as a resilient survivor of the war, the city is an immersive state of unbounded psychic energy, alternatively regenerative and destructive. It could be a "state of war" and where "everything is really happening . . . where the creator must be."[133] Or the city could be the space of psychic breakdown where "the intensity of the street shatters one's nerves and drives one mad."[134] With its constant visual and auditory stimuli, Léger's Paris was like the artillery noise that "makes you panic" or the "huge detonations" and "heavy shelling that drive you crazy" and that were strong enough to cover Léger with earth and knock a man off his horse.[135] In the temporality of Grosz's painting, the war is over, the Germans defeated, and the survivors scarred, but in the temporality of Léger's world, the war persists in the city's capacity for psychic overload.

Green has argued that for Léger "the city became the prolongation of the war" and that *The City* suggests "the fractured space of Verdun."[136] Verdun, as Léger wrote in 1916, was a "fête du bruit" in which humans were reduced to shell-shocked "silent shadows."[137] Similarly, Léger's city dwellers are gray and flattened in the urban noise. Two featureless figures descending the stairs in the central foreground are anonymous bodies akin to Grosz's gray worker with a shovel and pail. Two other figures in Léger's city—one at upper left in red and purple and another at upper right in green—are partial bodies, silhouetted figural forms that could represent garments on a clothesline or amputees. Léger's city has effaced emotion and social relations. By contrast, Grosz's amputee veteran displays exhaustion in his gaunt face, hunched body, and cane, while the indifferent industrialist adopts a confident posture, grips his briefcase and carpenter's ruler, and narrows his crossed eyes to focus on his ambitions. Yet Léger's shadowy figures undermine his imagined utopias. To his former dealer Kahnweiler, Léger's figures appeared to be "puppets" and "golem," and to his friend, the film critic Epstein, they were automatons and robots.[138] Such interpretations characterize Léger's figures as artificial bodies who lack individual agency and whose pain and desire are repressed in the service of their maker. Where resilience and reconstruction might be manifested as spectacular economic machinery, Léger's urban body is a site of cultural silence and denied emotional expression.

The City's spatial, temporal, and perspectival simultaneity—its multiple sites, its daytime and nighttime lighting, its aerial and direct perspectives—replicates

Fig. 25 Fernand Léger, *Three Women*, 1922. Oil on canvas, 183.5 × 248 cm. Mrs. Simon Guggenheim Fund. Museum of Modern Art, New York. Digital Image © The Museum of Modern Art / Licensed by SCALA / Art Resource, New York. © 2024 Artists Rights Society (ARS), New York / ADAGP, Paris.

the kind of disorienting "Cubist" juxtapositions—the chair in a tree—that Léger had seen at Verdun. The destabilized ground of Léger's city is reminiscent of his wartime reports of explosions, such as one in which he was twice thrown in the air by the force of 155 millimeter field cannons only 50 meters away.[139] Curator Anna Vallye writes that the painting offers the eye "no reasonable focus and the body no comfortable place to stand" but instead is a "throbbing surface with no point of convergence" in which the self is "pulverized and blown out across the streets."[140] In eliminating any Archimedean point from which to see and know the world in its entirety, Léger imagines the spaces of modernity—the battlefield and the city—as refusing the theocratically ordered, mathematically rationalized space of the Renaissance city. Yet it is the city, not the battlefield, that makes it to the status of painting, since it permits pictorial mastery without the constant risk of death.

Léger's experience of the city as a "state of war" characterized by agitation, hyperstimulation, visual fragmentation, and aural bombardment resonates with sociologist Georg Simmel's interpretation of urban modernity. In his landmark essay "The Metropolis and Mental Life" (1903), Simmel characterized the city as the "intensification of nervous stimulation which results from the swift and uninterrupted change of outer and inner stimuli."[141] Léger's experience of the city as a "state of war" that "shatters one's nerves and drives one mad" accords with Simmel's reading of the city as a site of sensory overload. Impossible to apprehend in its entirety, the city can only be understood as a montage of incomplete and unknowable forms. Writing before Freud's *Beyond the Pleasure Principle* (1920), Simmel does not account for psychic disintegration but anticipates psychic armoring. The "metropolitan type of man," he wrote, "develops an organ protecting him against the threatening currents and discrepancies of his external environment which would uproot him." Simmel's city dweller develops a "hardness" or "matter-of-fact attitude" in response to the city's stimuli. The "gray shadows" of Léger's *The City* convey this urban hardness or psychic armoring in their apparent alienation from each other and acculturation to the city's sights and sounds. They recall the shocked state of soldiers who Léger said "get used to" the horrifying spectacle of war, except that as city dwellers, the veterans' affectless state could be masked by what Simmel described as the "blasé" attitude of the urban man.[142]

As an antidote to *The City*'s dynamism or "state of war," Léger created *Three Women* (1922) (fig. 25), a form of "classicism" that simultaneously aggrandizes, feminizes, and domesticates the body yet also revives the spatial constraints of *The Card Party*. In 1943, when the Museum of Modern Art (MoMA) in New York acquired *Three Women*, Léger described the painting as a "contrary force" to *The City*, explaining the two paintings as exemplifying a long-standing and "uneasy conflict" in his work. He cast the conflict in formal terms as one between mural painting (*The City*)

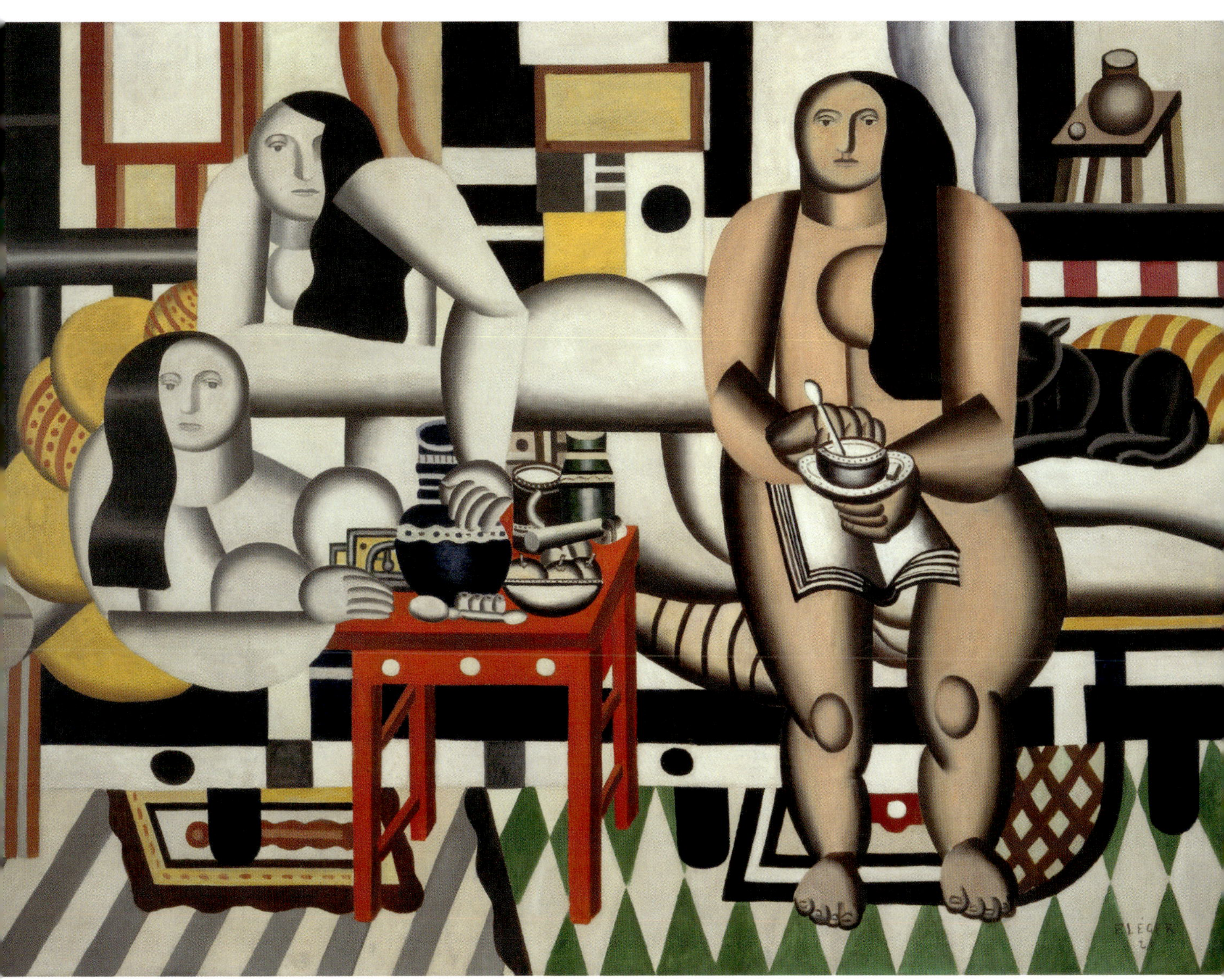
F.LÉGER

and easel painting (*Three Women*) and between the "romantic" that foregrounds the subject and the "classical" that suppresses the subject in favor of the object.[143] In Léger's lexicon, the "subject" aligns with narrative and the "romantic" with a release of affect, while the "object" signifies in terms of emotional suppression and corporeal objectification. In explaining what he meant by subject and object, Léger described the focus on the "subject" as an Italian Renaissance practice while the interest in the "object" is a modern conception.[144] Modern art, he wrote, foregrounds the object that becomes a "principal character."

The Classical and Claustrophobic

Where *The City* foregrounds the psyche's explosive libidinal energy, Léger's *Three Women* brings to prominence what Butler describes as the "regulation of affect." Butler argues that "open grieving is bound up with outrage," which can "disrupt the order and hierarchy of political authority," such that "affective responses . . . are highly regulated by regimes of power and sometimes subject to explicit censorship."[145] In the context of postwar France, the nation regulated affect through the containment of public grief and, in the Purist context, through a stigmatization of nerves and melancholy. Where the miniature puppets and robots of *The City* obscure lost agency and affect within the visual furor of the city, Léger's monumentalized bodies in *Three Women* reveal the psychic strain of Purism's desire for order, equilibrium, and forgetting. As Bennett has argued, trauma is not necessarily located in the manifest content of art but in the "affective dynamic internal to the work."[146] Léger's corporeal and spatial disjunctures register a visual language of trauma and an inability to conform entirely to neoclassicism's mechanisms of constraint.

Léger's best-known *femme-machine* painting, *Three Women* condenses the spaces of sexuality and artistic production in a contradictory representation of the female nude. Three monumental nudes and a pet confront the viewer with glacial stares, as they take tea and toast from a tiny table cluttered with the kinds of domestic commodities that would dance in *Le Ballet mécanique*. They are seated in an interior that can be alternatively read as a brothel due to the nudes' collective display for visual consumption, a studio space where frames stack up behind their sofa, or an industrial exhibition of erotically charged machine bodies. They are neither fully becalmed matrons like the women in Severini's *Maternity* (1916) nor freewheeling, liberated women like Sonia Delaunay's fashionable urbane drivers whose garments coordinate with their automobile design (fig. 26).

Three Women is a successor painting not only to *The City* but also to *The Card Party* in its size, its scene of a spatially confined trio, and in the multiplicity of its perspectival positions. As Green has observed, *Three Women* uses the intuitive perspective of the Mérode altarpiece or a Fouquet miniature to create a dizzying sense of unstable ground, spatial compression, and restricted mobility.[147] In the upper right, a vase sits on a table and a tiny ball balances precariously close to the edge of the tilted tabletop as though the laws of gravity have been arrested to prevent its fall to the floor. The two rugs suspend one-point linear perspective and create contradictory sets of spatial relations: the pulsating diamond-patterned carpet at right is almost parallel to the picture plane, yet the diagonally striped one at left is, like a lowering drawbridge, on a slightly different plane that could easily prompt a misstep. Only the black horizontal bar of the sofa's base and the little red coffee table straddling the two carpets stabilize the "ground."

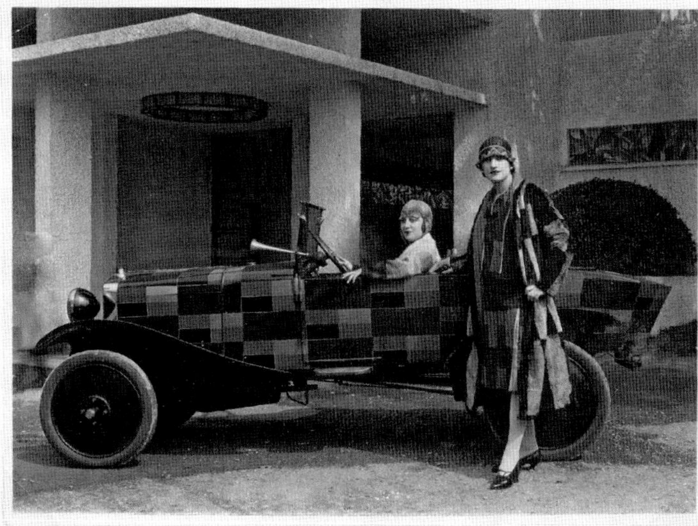

Fig. 26 Sonia Delaunay, dress designs and automobile design, Maison de la Mode, 1925. Photograph. Courtesy of the Bibliothèque national de France.

The horizontality of the left and center figures in *Three Women* reinforces their immobility, while their segmented body parts have the artificial sheen of metallic tubing or prosthetics, recapitulating the surface aesthetics of the limbs in *The Card Party*. The left figure's compass-made crescent arms and bulbous breasts echo the orange and striped cushions she reclines upon, while the rest of her body, interrupted by the red table, continues at the far right, where her legs metamorphose into the furniture that the dog or cat curls up on. The table before her and its mass-produced culinary commodities—manufactured vases, bowls, a spoon—are made central to the painting. Like the impossibly long spines and elongated limbs of Ingres's odalisques or Pontormo's Mannerist aristocrats, Léger's nudes are a hyperbolic commentary on the body. Corporeal ambiguities or doublings—metamorphosing legs, autonomous buttocks, severed torsos—are central to the composition both structurally and thematically. Castrated bodies and anthropomorphized machines, the central and left nudes signify nature subjugated and fragmented by a technological world.

The most coherent and potent body of the three nudes, the single-breasted Amazon at right, seems ready to rise up toward the viewer. The disproportionate scale of her enormous torso in comparison to her shrunken lower legs and inadequate feet foreground a monumental corporeality that has been simultaneously disabled. Presumably seated to read the book in her lap, she is nevertheless poised at the edge of the sofa on or before her sisters' curious legs. With her ambiguous posture between standing and sitting and her diminutive housewares, she recalls Cézanne's

Woman with a Coffeepot (1895). Her open book with its blank pages replaces genitalia unnecessary to a *femme-machine*. What she reads is unidentified, although it is tempting to imagine that her book is Gustave Flaubert's *Madame Bovary* (1856), which Léger read during his hospitalization at Hôpital Villepinte in late 1917 and early 1918.[148] In contrast to her funereal sisters, she is a kind of Emma Bovary constrained by her environment and social conditions yet endowed with energy and desire. Her monumentality conveys the threat that, should she rise to her full height and move through the shifting ground of her domain, she would unleash a fearful Samson-like strength and explode the domestic space that contains her, perhaps even penetrating the viewer's arena.

Although Léger's nudes, odalisques, and domesticated women are typically configured as static, reclining, columnar, and architectural, *Three Women* visualizes a process of animation alternatively seen by contemporaries as ideal movement or as a broken machine. When reading the painting from left to right, the colder gray nudes at left are passive and horizontal, while the terra cotta nude at right rises toward the viewer. Many of Léger's contemporaries and supporters saw his "machine aesthetic" paintings, including *Three Women*, as depictions of ideal functioning machines. These interpretations affirm a fantasized control over the means of production by both the artist and critics. In 1922, in the German periodical *Das Kunstblatt*, Westheim saw *Three Women* as possessing "the energy and intensity of an electric motor in steel production."[149] Two decades later, curator Alfred Barr reiterated Westheim's earlier claims, writing that *Three Women* is "like a great motor running smoothly on sixteen cylinders."[150] But when the painting was first exhibited at the Salon d'Automne of 1921, one reviewer complained that Léger "displays women in pieces . . . with their limbs sectioned into pipe and musketeer gloves," an interpretation focusing on the tubular bodies of the left and central figures and flared forearms of the right figure.[151] The reviewer simultaneously sees their limbs as dismembered ("sectioned into pipe") and militarized (the musketeer was a seventeenth-century infantryman).

The implications for machine movement—productive or disassembled and so arrested—encode Léger's contradictory desire to animate the *femme-machine* while also disabling its threatening potency. In a letter dated March 1922 and published in Rosenberg's *Bulletin de l'effort moderne*, Léger described his artistic process as a mechanical and masculine process of making, identified with a position of agency over the means of production: "A true artist of the twentieth century is the engineer, who extracts from the machine the material for the power of production. With a simple press of his finger, he sets in motion the levers, wheels, propellers, valves; he gives life to inert matter which moves and dilates like a human body with its systole and diastole, its shuddering, its will to create or destroy, and even its desires and its voluptuousness."[152]

In Léger's imagination, the artist-engineer is a secular god, and the feminized machine is an inanimate, nonliving being brought to life through an eroticized touching, "a simple press of his finger," that sets in motion the machine, which "moves and dilates like a human body." The artist, like the engineer, "extracts" or appropriates the machine's power, its fascinating movements and forms (levers, wheels, propellers, valves), its capacity for quantity (mass production), and its economic profitability. The anthropomorphized machine is at first a passive and inanimate object, then like the excited body of a lover, it dilates and shudders, and finally it becomes endowed with the power to create or destroy. The product (the painting as machine), once made, generates an autonomous "will to create and destroy and even its [own] desires and voluptuousness." Léger's nudes as *femme-machines* are then examples of what Foster describes as machine modernism's "fantasy of technological procreation."[153] Yet these nudes also register a conflation of anxieties about machine movement and female agency.

In their machine-classical hybridity, Léger's unnatural women unsettle the viewer and disturb normative femininities. An exchange between Léger and Rosenberg over *Reading* (1924) (fig. 27) reveals the tensions between Léger's *femme-machine* and return-to-order gender roles: "I remember when I brought *Reading* to Léonce, I was short of cash. He looked at the painting and exclaimed: 'But the woman doesn't have any hair! Be reasonable at least, put a little hair on her! She looks flayed, it's disagreeable to see,' he insisted. But I, truly, despite my best intentions, could not. At the spot where her head was, I needed to put a clean round form. I didn't do it purposely, but I could not add hair."[154] Rosenberg's demand for hair was an insistence upon one of the primary characteristics marking feminine sensuality and seductiveness, which Léger refused to offer. Léger's unyielding "instinct" to transform the head into a "clean round form" resembling a steel ball appeared to Rosenberg to be a disfiguration or flaying. Years later, New York art critic Kenneth Rexroth interpreted the female figures in the painting as less Poussin and more "Roman funerary bas-relief."[155] Understood retrospectively, Rexroth's is an apt characterization for a generation of widows and an era of mourning and monuments. Despite Rosenberg's initial reaction to Léger's bald women, he apparently accommodated Léger's vision of "disagreeable" women, because he published *Reading* two months in a row (June and July 1924), the second time with *Woman with a Fruit Bowl* (1924) (fig. 28). In *Woman with a Fruit Bowl*, another one of Léger's bald women appears. A figure whose pleated or fluted skirt renders her columnar, she stands next to (and visually competes with) a table holding an enormous red bowl with gray fruit

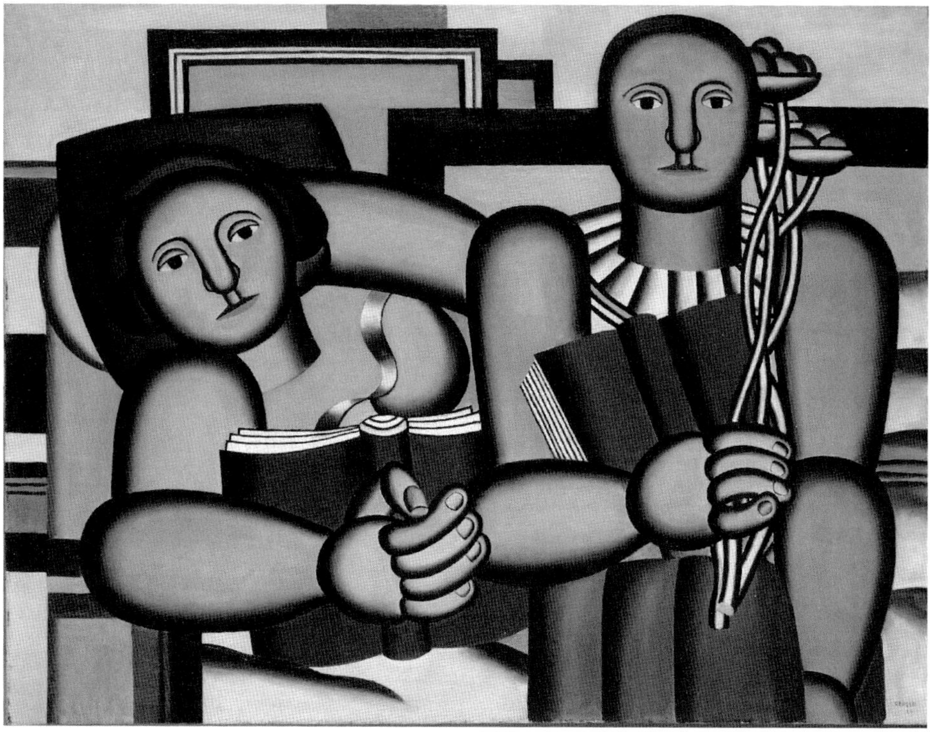

Fig. 27 Fernand Léger, *Reading*, 1924. Oil on canvas, 114 × 146 cm. Photo: Jacques Faujour. Musée national d'art moderne, Centre Georges Pompidou, Paris. Digital Image © CNAC/MNAM, Dist. RMN-Grand Palais / Art Resource, New York. © 2024 Artists Rights Society (ARS), New York / ADAGP, Paris.

that occupies the center of the canvas. She is a static human-object like the objects around her.

That Léger persisted in his disturbing image of the postwar woman registers social anxieties around transformations in femininity. The modern woman was, as historian Mary Louise Roberts has shown, a contested figure in the postwar cultural landscape, whose short hair conveyed virility and sterility and who was seen by detractors as rejecting domesticity and maternity.[156] For example, Sonia Delaunay's urbane and fashionable driver represented the *femme moderne* (the modern woman) or *garçonne* (the boyish girl), a wartime and postwar type characterized by her cropped hair; her corsetless, streamlined, and short dresses; and her autonomy and mobility through the city. By contrast, Léger's domesticated women are typically objects of spatial, corporeal, and affective constraint. Their occasional baldness raised the specter of a diseased or militarized femininity that was a product of the war. For Léger, writing in 1918, bald women signified prostitutes made to shave their hair as a punishment and a warning of their venereal disease.[157] Léger may also have seen *L'Illustration*'s photographs of the White Russian Army's batallion of female soldiers who shaved their heads to fight as men, Madame Botchkareva's Batallion of Death. One photograph shows two such shorn soldiers in a hospital recovering from wounds; their pose, with one reclining on the bed and the other sitting upright, is remarkably similar to Léger's painting (fig. 29). Whether *Reading*'s compositional similarity to the hospitalized women soldiers was coincidental or not, Léger shared a desire to disturb visual pleasure and generate a sexual-social dissonance at odds with return-to-order norms of femininity and domesticity.

Rather than conforming to a repertoire of "happy families," as claimed by Kenneth Silver,[158] motherhood in Léger's painting is an alienated form of labor inconsistent with the return-to-order's iconography. In the 1920s, national policy had not only demobilized women from the paid labor that brought them autonomy but also effectively compelled reproduction. French legislation aimed to repopulate the country after the war and responded to a perceived postwar *grève de ventres* (strike of wombs). Maternity appears only in a handful of Léger's paintings: *Mother and Child* (1919), *Mother and Child* (1920), *Woman and Child* (1922) (fig. 30), and *Persons in a Garden* (1922). Léger's mothers never appear with infants, as in Severini's *Maternity* (1916) (fig. 31) or Pablo Picasso's *Maternity* (1921), nor do Léger's mothers engage in the rapt absorption and embrace of Picasso's. In *Woman and Child*, the mother's gaze and body are turned away from her son rather than attentive to him. Léger's dissonance with normativizing postwar forms of femininity was particularly in evidence when Rosenberg published Severini's *Maternity* in the same issue of *Bulletin de l'Effort moderne* (July 1924) as Léger's *Reading* (1924). Purism prohibited sentiment and emotion in the service of an Ingres-style classicism, as critic Roger Bissière wrote, thus avoiding the hysteria and neurosis Allendy cautioned against.[159] But this meant that maternity could not be represented as affectionate, and instead Purist art silenced and pacified mothers through the violence of a new legal, psychic, and social order.

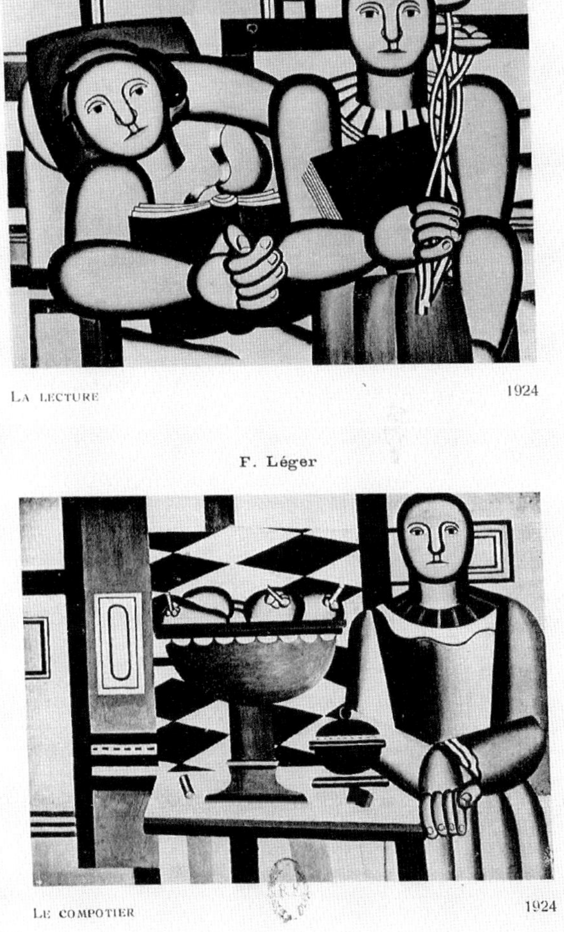

Fig. 28 Fernand Léger, *Reading*, 1924, and *Woman with a Fruit Bowl*, 1924. Oil on canvas, 89 × 114 cm. Reproduced in *Bulletin de l'Effort moderne*, no. 7 (July 1924): n.p. © 2024 Artists Rights Society (ARS), New York / ADAGP, Paris.

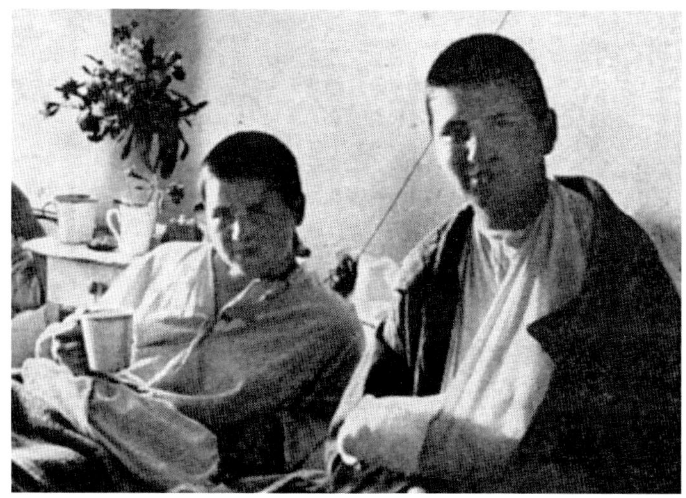

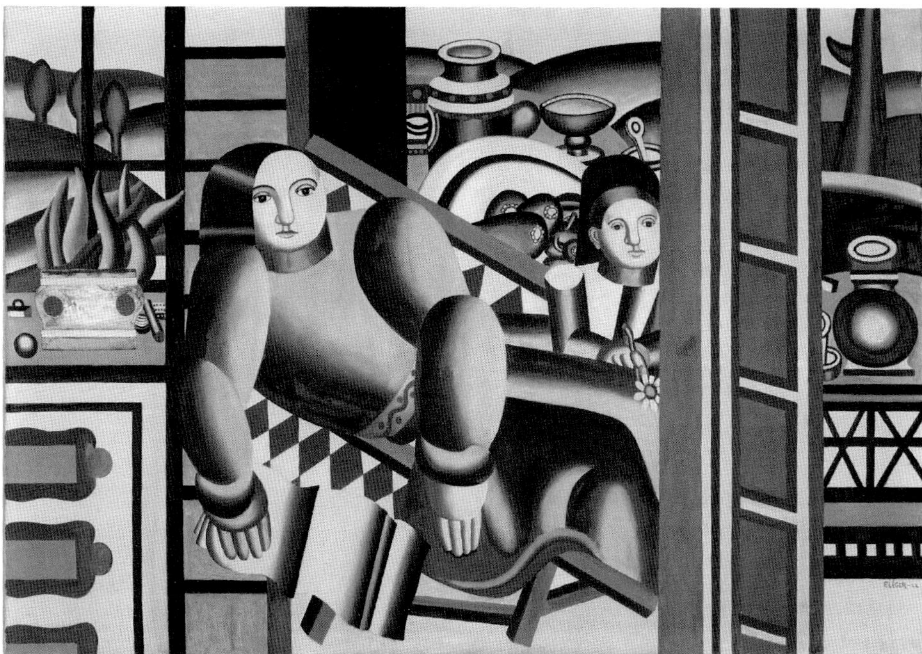

Fig. 29 "Women Soldiers, Wounded in the July Russian Offensive and Cared for in Military Hospital." Detail of photograph. In S. de C., "Le Miracle de Kerensky," *L'Illustration*, no. 3887 (September 1, 1917): 242.

Fig. 30 Fernand Léger, *Woman and Child*, 1922. Oil and canvas, 171.2 × 240.9 cm. Kunstmuseum Basel, Sammlung Online, Inv. no. G 1956.13. © 2024 Artists Rights Society (ARS), New York / ADAGP, Paris.

In Léger's worlds, domesticated femininity embodies what he had described a few years earlier as a "terror of too much control" where "an excess of equilibrium [is] the point of death, 'the motor stopped.'"[160] Paradoxically, to contain the potency of the *femme-machine*, Léger arrests her reproductivity and immobilizes her movements. When Léger's *Woman and Child* (1922) was shown at the 1922 Salon d'Automne, art critic Marcel Hiver was so disturbed that he wrote a review that, as Green observes, could equally have applied to *Three Women*: "Léger, would you like to live in the world your paintings evoke, that crystalline, metallic world, which has the frozen emptiness of planets without atmosphere, where living beings like things, exist petrified in the precise, mechanical stillness of a film suddenly stopped. Why do you treat a human face exactly like that porcelain pot . . . why those arms in pressed steel?"[161] The world Hiver sees is one in which time has stopped and organic matter has been eviscerated. Léger's "worlds," his domestic interiors, are "frozen" and "petrified," lacking the warmth of a maternal embrace or an inviting hearth. The trace of breath or physical movement has been suppressed to "petrify" the body in a deadly stasis.

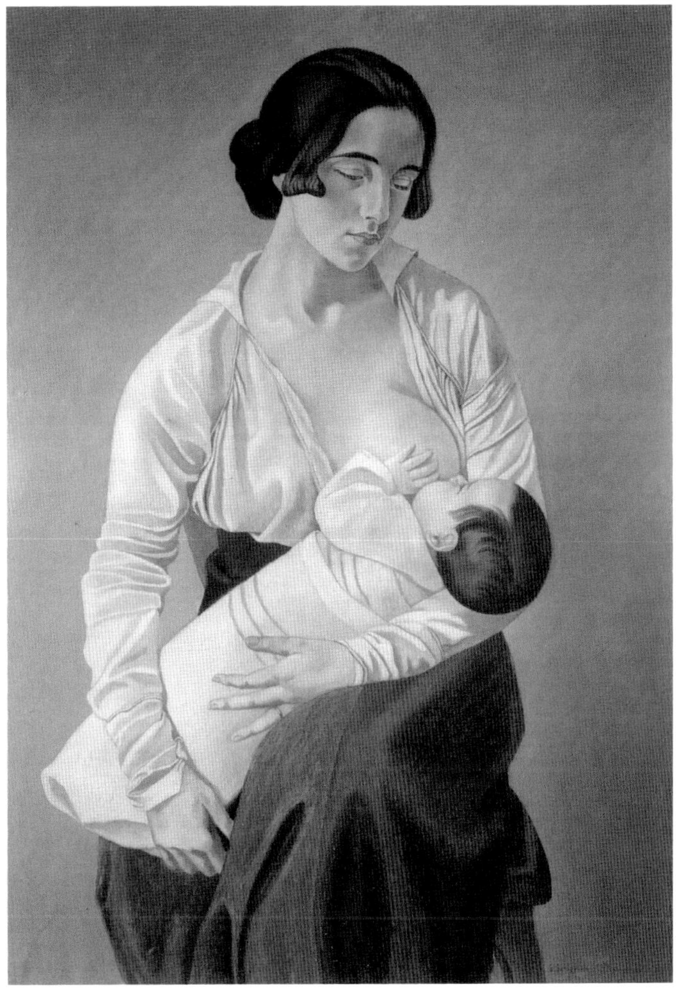

Fig. 31 Gino Severini. *Maternity*, 1916. Oil on canvas, 65 × 92 cm. Museo dell'Accademia Etrusca e della Città di Cortona, Italy. © 2024 Artists Rights Society (ARS), New York / ADAGP, Paris.

In explaining why he treated the "human face exactly like that porcelain pot" and arms as "pressed steel," we can turn to Léger's theory of the spectacle. He wrote that the human face should appear "frozen, fixed, rigid, metallic" so that "human material" can contrast with the rhythm of the *décor-mobile*, Léger's term for the artistic recomposition of the urban spectacle.[162] Like Léger's portrait-style *The Mechanic*, his objectified female bodies are static bodies with puppetlike limbs. The "frozen, fixed, rigid, metallic" faces of Léger's reclining mothers float before their sleek black hair and bright clothing, detached from their bodies and dislocated from their collars. In addition to their masklike faces, the women's hands—wooden and puppetlike—invite comparison to postwar prosthetics made of wood or aluminum. Léger's immobilized, domesticated femininity thus risks slipping into the representation of the confined body of the disfigured or amputee veteran.

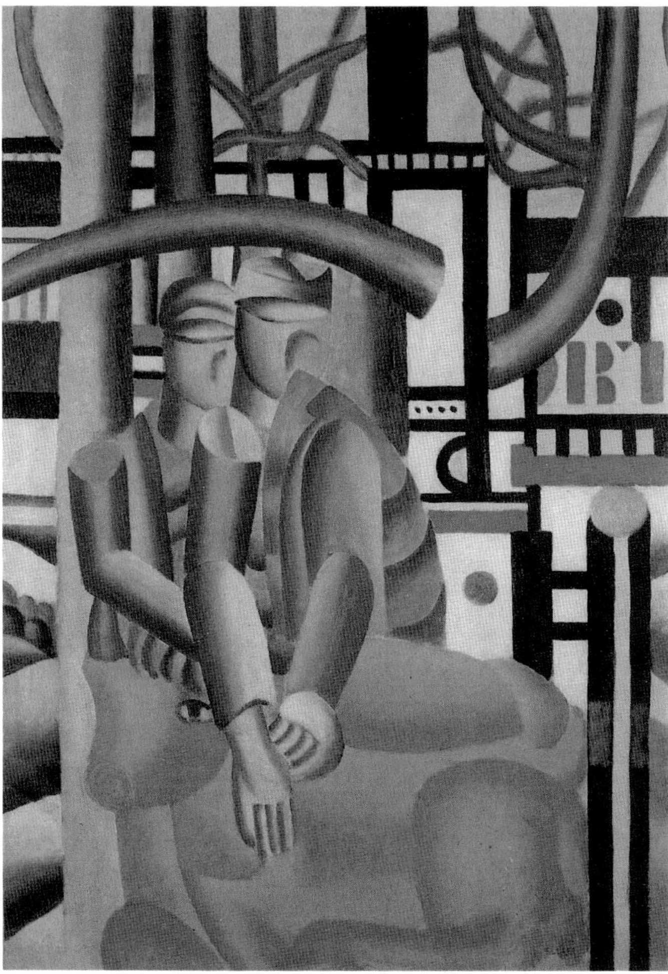

Fig. 32 Fernand Léger, *The Cattle Merchant*, 1921. Oil on canvas, 90 × 63.5 cm. Collection of Leray W. Berdeau. Bauquier, *Catalogue raisonné*, vol. 2, fig. 283.

Sentient Oxen

With *The Cattle Merchant* (1921) (fig. 32), Léger converges the economic anxieties of a volatile postwar economy with signs of a castrated subjectivity in a rare display of protection and affection. Set within Léger's urban iconography of geometric fragments, tubular forms, and stenciled lettering ("ORT" for port), the painting depicts an ox, foregrounded and centered as the main character. His owners, framed by an arched tree limb above and two columnar trunks on either side, shelter him with a protective gesture. The bodies of the figures converge, creating a moment of fraternal solidarity and intimacy. One wears a blue jacket reviving the "blue horizon" color of the soldier's uniforms. While the soldiers are featureless and sightless, blinded to the imminent slaughter of the ox, the animal engages directly with the viewer. *The Cattle Merchant* is the culmination of a series of about twenty paintings that share compositional elements and suggest Léger's preoccupations not simply with graphic signs and their mutability but also with commerce and commodified beings. Part of that series, the Musée de Grenoble's *Tugboat* (1920) suggests the moment of the merchant's arrival at an urban port: set amid the disks, metallic columns, and graphic signifiers of Léger's city, a male figure at lower right gestures toward a reclining animal the size of an ox, as if presenting the sacrificial being to the viewer.

Léger's series of landscapes and cityscapes seem to trace the travels of man and animal through the countryside until, with *The Cattle Merchant*, they become merchants whose ox goes to slaughter, although neither the slaughter nor the market is ever depicted. The series includes the *paysages animés* (animated landscapes) from 1920 and 1921, which despite the titular reference to landscapes, are not obviously set in the countryside. Juxtaposed among arced and curving lines representing hills, trees, bushes, and aloe vera–like plants are always geometric forms recalling modernist architecture. But, unlike the built structures that dominate over the figures in *The City*, these buildings are human scaled, perhaps meant to represent the markets, cafés, bars, and homes of small towns. In many, their facades are marked by reference to the word "commerce." Stenciled letters of incomplete text blocked by graphic elements appear repeatedly: "comm" in *Man with a Cane* (1920), "comme" in *Man and Dog* (1921), or simply "-O" in *Animated Landscape* (1921) (fig. 33).

The Cattle Merchant's precursor landscapes suggest the temporal moment before violence occurs and before the ox is taken to the urban slaughterhouse. Three types of figures occupy the *paysages animés*: one or two standing figures; a reclining figure, sometimes with a book, typically signifying female figures in Léger's work; and one or more animals in ocher or grays. Sometimes imagined as a dog in *The Dog* (1921) or *Man and Dog* (1921), a larger version of the same form also appears in other paintings to be the scale of an ox. For example, *Animated Landscape* depicts a curious neo-Oedipal triad, composed of an erect figure at left, a reclining body in the foreground, and an ocher-colored ox at right. Behind the reclining figure, who might be read as a female nude, are tiny crypt-sized houses, whose black entrances almost entirely consume their facades.

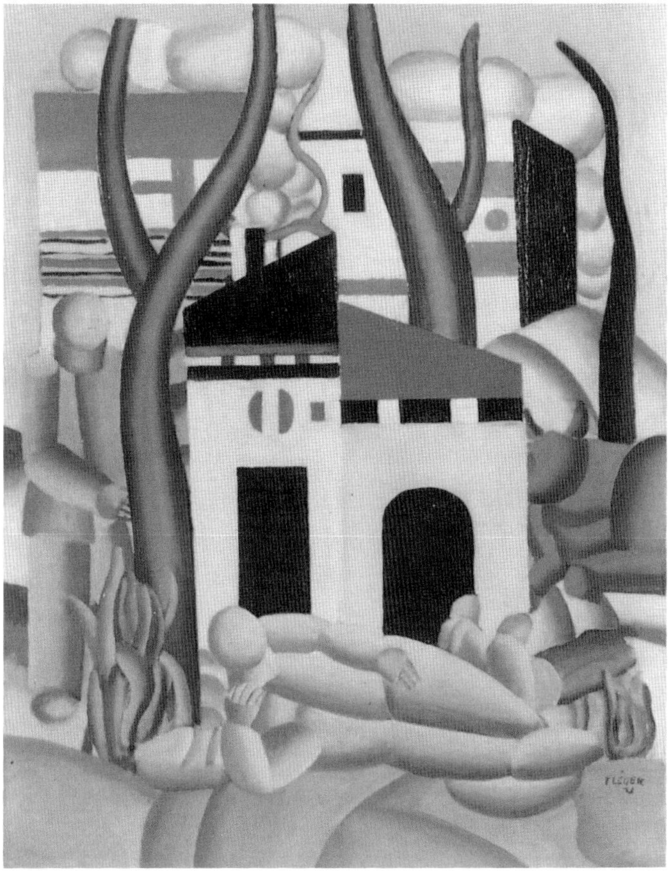

Fig. 33 Fernand Léger, *Animated Landscape*, 1921. Oil on canvas, 65 × 50 cm. Private collection. Bauquier, *Catalogue raisonné*, vol. 2, fig. 271. © 2024 Artists Rights Society (ARS), New York / ADAGP, Paris.

Invested with a patriarchal referent to Léger's father, who was a cattle merchant, the series seems preoccupied with the passage through countryside and small towns that became the site of wartime slaughter only to arrive at an urban scene, the new postwar battlefield. Léger's father, who died at age thirty-eight in 1884 when Léger was only three years old, transported cattle from Argentan to the market and slaughterhouse of La Villette in the nineteenth arrondissement of Paris. In his second "Machine Aesthetic" essay, Léger recalled his father's role in the marketplace to explain fluctuating postwar prices and the value of insignificant objects: "Before the war, my father would take his oxen to La Villette under the guard of dogs who bit at their ankles."[163] During the war and three decades after his father's death, objects of "negligible value" such as "a nail, a stub of candle, a shoelace"—and implicitly the ox shin—gained value. But the cost of such objects could, as Léger remarks, come at the risk of the scavenger's life.

The cattle merchant and *paysage animé* series revive the wartime metaphors of cattle as innocents being sent to a brutal, bestial death. In 1916, soldiers heading into battle at Chemin des Dames mooed and baaed like cattle and sheep, and the French used the word *boucherie* (butchery) to describe the Battle of Verdun.[164] By the early twentieth century, La Villette, which had been transformed into a cattle market in the 1860s under Napoleon III, gained the nickname Cité de Sang (City of Blood).[165] With the war in 1914, it became a site of mobilization, as the Fauvist artist Maurice de Vlaminck recalled in 1919: "The trucks, which only two weeks earlier had been taking cattle to the slaughterhouse of La Villette, were now taking men to slaughter."[166]

Blocking direct representation of the scene of slaughter in favor of affection and fraternity before the final moment of loss, *The Cattle Merchant* instead calls attention to the ox's gaze suggesting that the consciousness of suffering can only manifest in displaced form. In her interpretation of the shaft paintings in the Cave of Lascaux, art historian Kristine Stiles reads the bison's gaze, directed toward the viewer and at its own dismemberment, as the projection of the artist's consciousness. The psychological effect of the animal's appeal to the viewer is "to witness and remember" the pain and suffering of dying, Stiles argues.[167] Léger's ox is a still-intact body, yet its gaze combined with a last fraternal embrace conveys a collective resignation and submission to the production of mass death. Léger's iconography of the cattle merchant secularizes the national discourse justifying slaughter as sacrifice for redemption of the fatherland, a discourse that had become part of memorialization practices.[168] Dominick LaCapra has argued that sacrifice is a mode of "performatively re-enacting the traumatic scene" and that trauma can become valorized as a "secularized displacement of the sacred," giving rise to Christian and Oedipal stories in which "sacrifice creates a victim in order to have regeneration."[169] Caught between Christian iconography signifying transcendence and capitalist economic machinery signifying reconstruction, Léger's *The Cattle Merchant* creates a victim (the ox) in service of economic regeneration, condensing Léger's ambivalence about the exigencies of the war and postwar era.

Conclusion

Léger's alignment with Purism offered him a discourse of masculinity and symbolic reconstruction, but it did so at the cost of affect and in submission to a disciplinary order that suppressed emotion. In an era of interwar silence about grief and prolonged melancholy, Purism's economic imaginary deploys machine modernisms to overcome the constant threat of death and psychic breakdown. Yet in the context of these conditions for resilience and reconstruction, Léger's art and writing are often contradictory and ambivalent. Léger's sense of economic embattlement in the postwar era meant that new states of war—the sensory assault of the city—were a threat only overcome when interpreted as raw material to be harnessed for artistic production. At the same time, the economic arena was a battlefield destroying good men and leaving the male body an empty shell with only a debased "sentimental value." The male body is alternatively a puppet or robot denied affect in the service of a larger economic recovery or, in the case of the Chaplin marionette, a hypertrophic body breaking at the seams and a sign of the male ruination displaced by the mass-produced object. When pictorial attention foregrounds the body, it risks revealing the artifice of reconstruction and compels a deathly stasis to achieve a classical equilibrium. Despite their utility for Purist discourse, Léger's machine-era paintings are haunted by the legacy of war: amputated silhouettes, plaster masks, wooden and metallic limbs, immobilized and feminized bodies, sacrificial oxen, and blinded faces. In oscillating between an immersive recapitulation of war's traumatic assault and a specular mastery of objectified bodies, Léger is trapped between a traumatic repetition compulsion and a repetition aimed at mastery. By the late 1920s and early 1930s, when Léger abandoned his machine aesthetic, the affective dynamics of his work took a new turn.

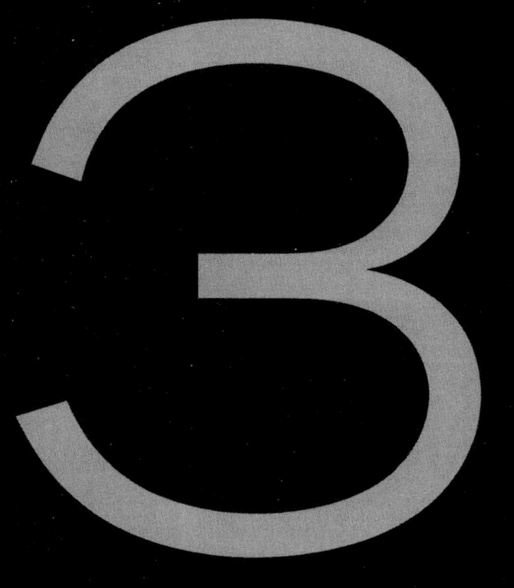

Lost Bodies and Revived Memories

By the late 1920s, Purism's regulation of affect and faith in a technological order came under challenge. New spectral forms of photography, Surrealist interest in the unconscious, revived memories of the war, and the worldwide economic crisis challenged Purism's campaign to overcome wars, arms, and neurasthenia. *L'Esprit Nouveau* ceased publication in 1925 after its government subvention was withdrawn and due to a falling out between Ozenfant and Le Corbusier.[1] Rosenberg discontinued his *Bulletin de l'Effort moderne* in 1927, marking an end to the primary venues promoting Purism and new classicism. Starting around 1928, Léger turned away from his machine aesthetic, the factory, and the *mécanicien* to produce still lifes populated by isolated aestheticized objects and biomorphic, dissolving forms. Léger's new advocate became Christian Zervos, a Greek critic trained in philosophy at the Sorbonne who published a monthly arts magazine, *Cahiers d'Art* (1926–41), that continued the dialogues Purists had had with the avant-garde in Russia, Germany, and elsewhere, while expanding coverage to Surrealism and photography. Its regular articles on Léger were illustrated with large color reproductions that helped make him an internationally renowned artist, although Léger sold little between 1927 and 1934.[2] After 1924, he taught at the Académie Moderne with Ozenfant and the Russian artist Alexandra Exter, attracting students from around the world. He expanded his artistic connections, especially with the German Bauhaus and Russian avant-garde, and traveled widely in Europe and to the United States. During the same period, the Belgian arts magazine *Variétés* (1928–30) reviewed Léger's exhibitions; published his writings, paintings, and drawings; and became another crucial venue where Léger's work appeared alongside Surrealist art and ideas.

In this post-*mécanicien* period, Léger largely suppresses representation of the male body in favor of still life images in pencil, ink, and oil painting. These work through corporeal dissolution, disfiguration, and distortion, manifesting new anxieties about the male body in crisis. Amorphous forms appear as clouds, indeterminate backgrounds, or dissolving statues. Holly leaves resemble fractured metal; spectral comets swerve through undifferentiated space; flint rocks appear uncannily similar to skull fragments; worn garments leave human traces; and quarters of beef hang in sacrificial display. As Rochlitz has observed, Léger's "dream" of mass reproduction "suffers disturbing alterations," while his new art incorporates "shadows, intestinal clouds . . . menacing fissures . . . [and] barriers where ropes, acrobats' clothing or nudes drape."[3]

Even Léger's contemporaries recognized such "disturbing alterations" in his work. Zervos's many reviews of Léger's artwork, including the new still life pictures, show that even as he and other critics wanted to claim Léger as a rationalist opposed to Surrealism, they nevertheless also saw Léger's new work as marked by expressions of emotion and anxiety. In 1929, Zervos wrote that Léger's still life pictures represent his "dreams and anxieties," yet they also "preserve" the viewer from psychic inquiry due to his "classic tendency."[4] A few years later, Zervos characterized Léger's artwork as a "constant call to emotion," possessing "tenderness" despite Léger's "rough appearance."[5] In 1934, Zervos reviewed Léger's Galerie Vignon exhibition of drawings and gouaches of roots, flint rock, quarters of lamb and beef, corkscrews, pants, cheese, and nuts, describing these as representing "the poetry of the object."[6]

What accounts for the new "anxieties," "lyricism," and "poetry"; the shift away from the architectural, the mechanical, the commodity, and the male body? How might we explain the apparent release of affect and emotion in Léger's work? How and why did Purism's regulatory control and Léger's investment in the suppression of feeling in the immediate postwar era give way to a new visual environment? Many scholars trace the emergence of Léger's biomorphic forms to cinematic practices and Surrealist techniques foregrounding the isolated found object and photographic doubling.[7] A Centre Pompidou exhibition in 1984 emphasized Léger's turn to organic objects during a period of numerous exhibitions by Surrealist artists, including Hans Arp and Joan Miró.[8] Recent scholarship on biomorphism shows that it emerged from prewar scientific and philosophical debates about form, life, evolution, and the nature of history and then developed in the interwar years as a middle ground between geometric abstraction and Bretonian Surrealism.[9] Some art historians tie Léger's organic and pastoral motifs to vacations at the family farm in Lisores that he inherited from his mother in 1922.[10] Art historian Romy Golan positions Léger within an "organic retrenchment" in France that affected even the Purists and that was only accentuated by the Depression.[11] Curator Isabelle Monod-Fontaine attributes the new "tenderness" and "strange poetic effects" in Léger's drawings to Léger's relationship with a young Belgian woman, Simone Herman, which lasted from 1931 to 1940.[12] Yet existing scholarship has not addressed how Léger's shift away from the machine aesthetic might figure within revived memories of the war and new crises in masculinity and corporeality.

This chapter argues that Léger's more poetic, affect-laden works show not only his engagement with Surrealist motifs and new techniques in photography but also his working through a crisis of value, especially the value of the male body and masculinity. Phallic Freudian symbolism—keys, umbrellas, hats, female nudes—serve as compensation for male ruination. Figuration appears as castrated classical forms, hollowed-out plaster busts, and sightless silhouetted profiles. The organic body is feminized, primitivized, and miniaturized, for example, as dancing female nudes with rubbery limbs. Naturalia—holly leaves, flint rock, and comets—render time static, prehistoric, or apocalyptic. The slaughtered body emerges as racks of beef and lamb, sometimes with hollowed-out clothing foregrounding the absence of a human body. The male body only briefly reappears during the Popular Front era (1936–38), a left-wing coalition government that Léger supported. In monumental paintings, such as *Adam and Eve* (1935–39) and *Composition with Two Parrots* (1935–39), Léger condenses many of the motifs from his object studies while introducing a nonmechanical male type. In this chapter, I propose considering Léger's new motifs through the lens of trauma's latency, and I argue that the era marks a new consciousness of corporeal fragility and artistic risk in the social order.

As Caruth has emphasized in her writing, it is the latency of trauma (*Nachtraglichkeit* or "afterwardness") that is one of its crucial characteristics. The victim, who is "never fully conscious" during the traumatic event, gets away "apparently unharmed" and "forgets" that which was not known in the first place. The failure of consciousness precludes direct access to the event, and memories do not appear in recognizable forms but as a troubling image, dream, or other symptoms.[13] In Leys's analysis, the "irretrievabilty of the traumatic origin" means that forgetting or failures of memory are formative of how one narrates the self and so, too, the process of self-recognition.[14] Caruth and Leys have profound disagreements on whether and how traumatic memory might be retrieved and enter the realm of cognition and so representation.[15] Where Caruth argues for the possibilities of art and poetics to represent traumatic experience or at least its structural dynamics even if only in fragmentary, incomplete, or displaced forms, Leys casts doubt on individual or historical narration of trauma, since narration imagines a psychic differentiation between an autonomous subject and an external object.[16] Such debates extend, in Leys's analysis, to early twentieth-century psychoanalysis, for example, in Pierre Janet's view of memory as overvalued and his argument for knowing "how to forget," and in Freud's belief in narrative's value for self-understanding "even in the absence of empirical verification."[17] When and how Léger's artwork might manifest revived memories of war trauma thus raises dilemmas of whether and how a traumatic event or symptomology can be located in an image or when compositional structures might register traumatic dynamics. I argue that Léger's modernist aesthetics lend themselves not to narration but to displaced forms that paradoxically both register and block traumatic experience.

Fig. 34 Fernand Léger, *Holly Leaf*, 1928. Oil on canvas, 92 × 65 cm. Private collection. Bauquier, *Catalogue raisonné*, vol. 3, fig. 543. © 2024 Artists Rights Society (ARS), New York / ADAGP, Paris.

Holly Leaf

An anomalous holly leaf painting that Léger produced in 1928 marks a pivotal moment in the shifting signification of the object, the demise of the commodity, and the disappearance of the *mécanicien*. Appearing occasionally as a motif in drawing and painting, the holly leaf represents, I propose, a displaced form of the body that registers the stasis and colorlessness Léger associated with the war and death. *Holly Leaf* (1928) (fig. 34) displays an isolated leaf on a flat, unmodulated red ground and in an environment purged of any referential location. Léger aggrandizes the holly leaf to about tenfold its size in nature, evidencing his interest in film's capacity for close-up and magnification. He first learned about the close-up when working on Abel Gance's film *La Roue* (1923), a tragic story of a railroad engineer with incestuous desires. Léger assisted with close-ups of the train wheels in motion, then deployed the close-up in his film *Ballet mécanique* (1924) and wrote about it as a form of personification and magnification of the fragment.[18] Personified and magnified, the holly leaf is positioned vertically like a scientific specimen in a display case, its pointed tips extending almost to the edges of the frame. The leaf's left edge forms a scalloped design that contrasts with its right edge, which curls inward and outward, adding a sense of three-dimensionality. The interior of Léger's holly leaf is strikingly antinaturalist, composed of a milky web of lines radiating from a spoke that has no referential connection to the leaf's veining.

The holly leaf reimagines many aspects of Léger's *femme-machine* nudes produced as recently as the prior year. In paintings such as *Nudes on a Red Ground* (1923), *Composition with Three Women* (1927), and *Nude on Red Background* (1927) (fig. 35), the figure is an eroticization and aestheticization of the productive machine Léger described in his 1922 letter to Rosenberg's *Bulletin*. Both the nude and holly leaf are made to be isolated modernist objects centrally positioned on similar red grounds, both drained of fluids, whether corporeal, industrial, or organic. Their red grounds recall the "red velour" backdrops that Léger noticed in trade fair displays of saws, nuts, bolts, and wrenches.[19] Both the *femme-machine* and the holly leaf are static objects: the machine stopped, the leaf petrified. But the holly leaf paintings make a

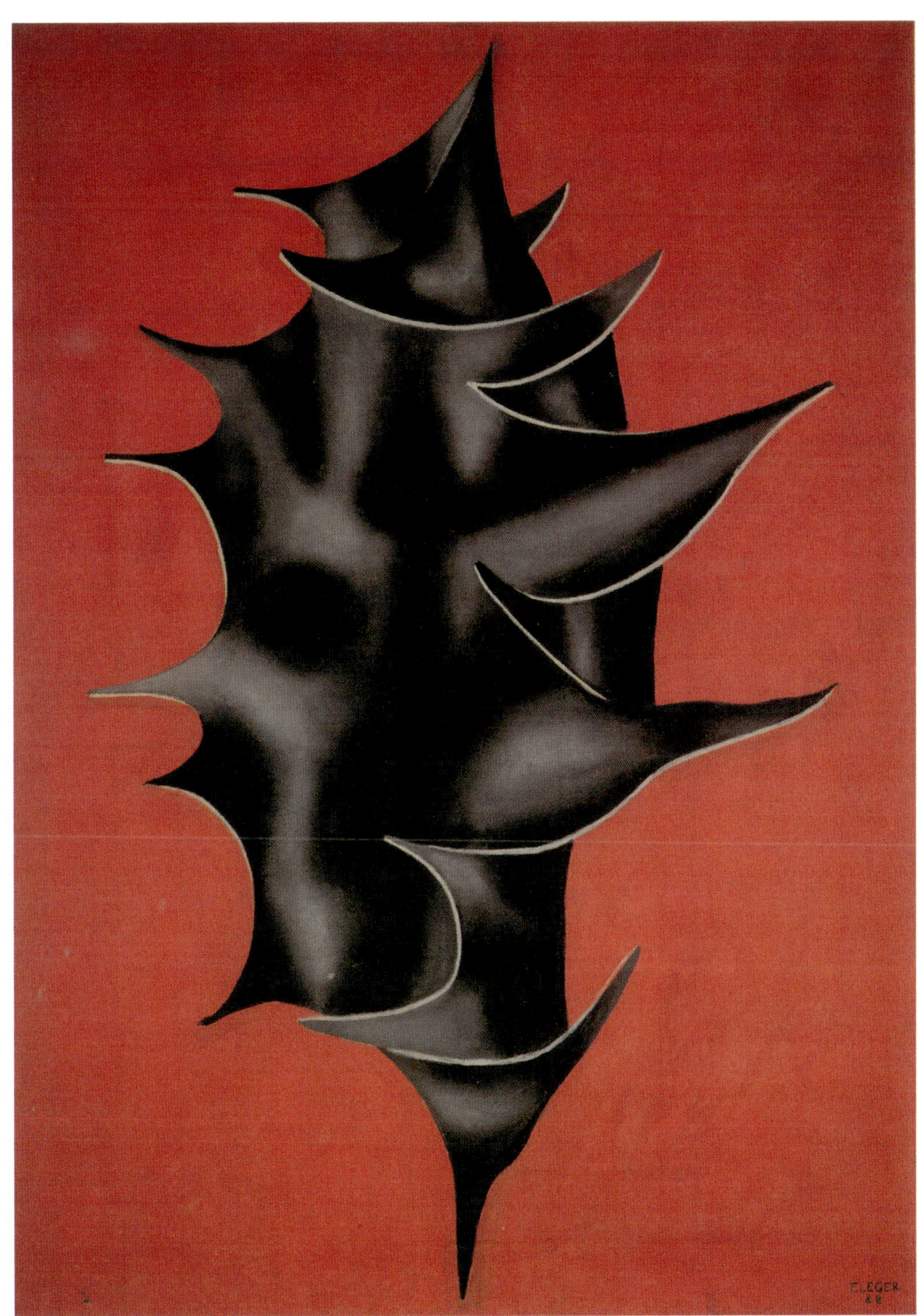
F.LEGER

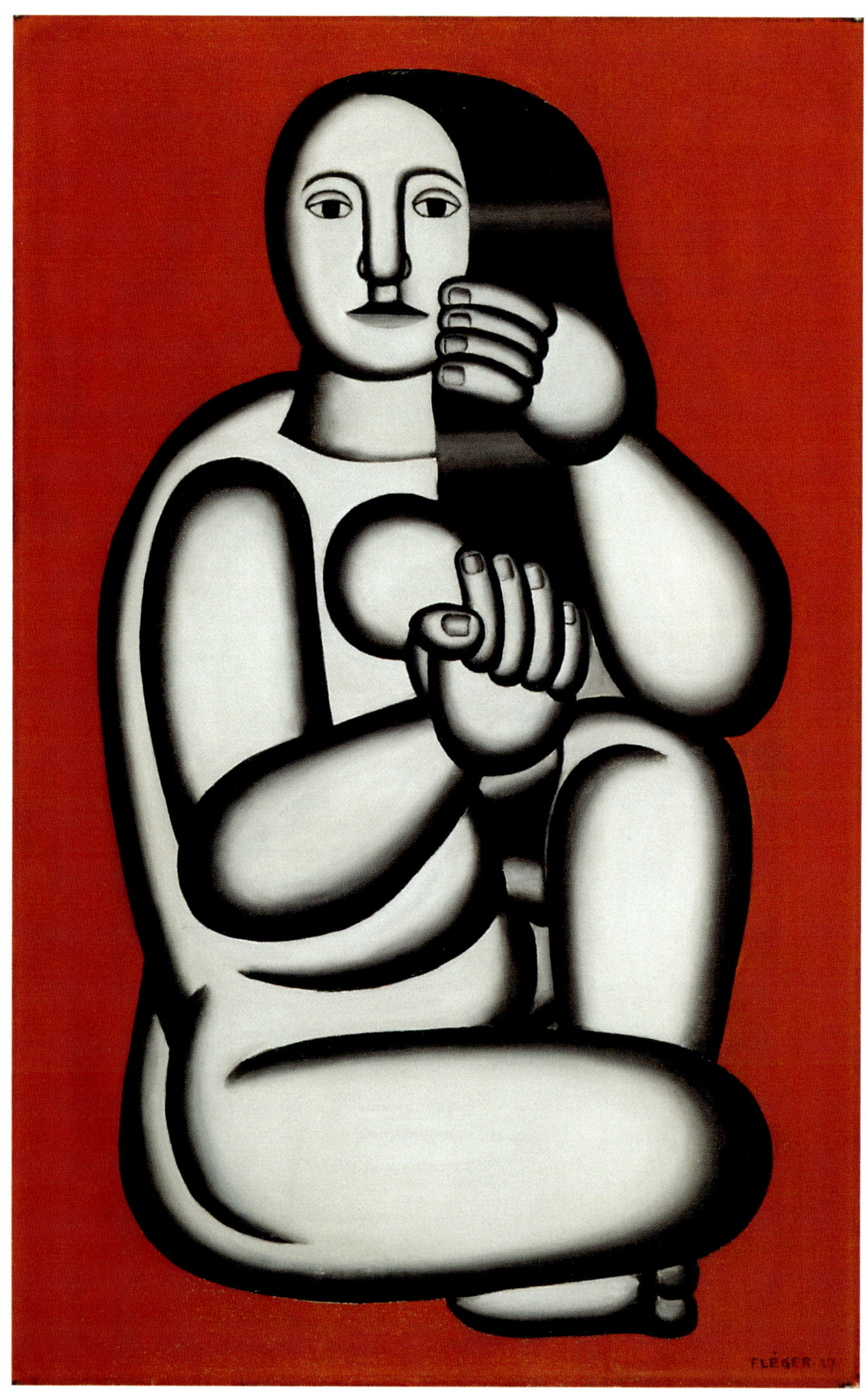

Fig. 35 Fernand Léger, *Nude on a Red Background*, 1927. Oil on canvas, 128 × 80 cm. Gift of the Joseph H. Hirshhorn Foundation, 1972. © 2024 Artists Rights Society (ARS), New York / ADAGP, Paris. Photo credit: Lee Stalsworth, Hirshhorn Museum and Sculpture Garden.

number of formal moves that destroy the machine aesthetic and human figure. The holly leaf's threatening razor-sharp metallic edges replace the nude's smooth rounded limbs and undulating hair. In its combination of a spectral interior and metallic edges, the holly leaf might be read as an exploded machine form or even its ghostly residue. Further, the *Holly Leaf* abandons the kind of lighting that is visible in *Nude on a Red Background* and that prevailed in Léger's machine aesthetic era: high-contrast transitions from darks to lights suggestive of electrical factory lighting.

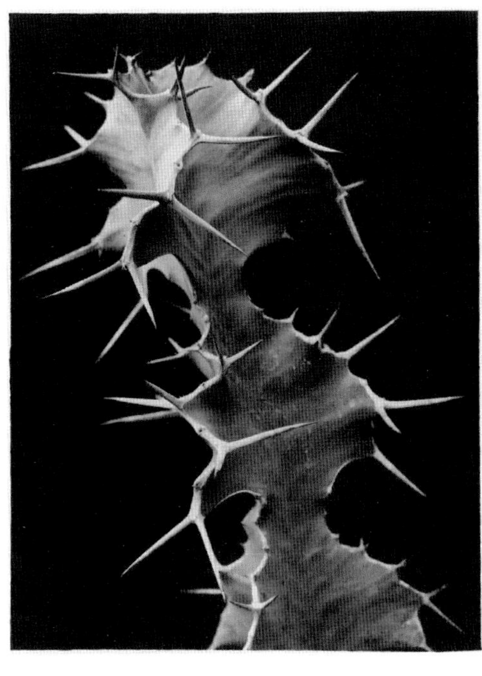

Fig. 36 Albert Renger-Patzsch, *Cactus*, 1923. Published in László Moholy-Nagy, *Painting, Photography, Film* (Cambridge, MA: MIT Press, 1967), 91. Gelatin silver print, 23.1 × 17.1 cm. Photo: Philippe Migeat. Musée National d'Art Moderne / Centre Georges Pompidou, Paris, Inv. no. AM1993-168. Digital Image © CNAC/MNAM, Dist. RMN-Grand Palais / Art Resource, New York. © Albert Renger-Patzsch / Archiv Ann u. Jürgen Wilde, Zülpich / Artists Rights Society (ARS), New York, 2024.

Léger's *Holly Leaf* borrows from new forms of photography but not always in rationalist or scientific ways. Zervos compared Léger's holly leaf paintings to the German naturalist Ernst Haeckel's pen-and-ink prints published in *Kunstformen der Natur* (Art Forms in Nature; 1904).[20] Haeckel's art and writing impacted the development of Art Nouveau's organic iconography and informed a generation of artistic debates about life forms in art.[21] But Léger's monochromatic leaf lacks the crisp line of Haeckel's ink drawings and more closely resembles the close-up plant photography of New Objectivity photographers Karl Blossfeldt or Albert Renger-Patzsch. Formally, Léger's holly leaf paintings participate in an era when photographic vision from the microscopic to the telescopic opened up new worlds and new phenomena. Artist László Moholy-Nagy articulated this "new vision" in *Painting, Photography, Film* (1925), which included Albert Renger-Patzsch's *Cactus* (1923) (fig. 36), a photograph that magnifies the plant and shares the tight framing and spiked edges of Léger's holly leaf.

Yet, instead of the detailed leaf veining in Haeckel's ink drawings or the ridges and volumes conveyed by the lighting in Renger-Patzsch's plant photography, the painterly striations of Léger's *Holly Leaf* replace the veins with the spectral quality of the photogram or cameraless photography produced by Man Ray and Moholy-Nagy. Moholy-Nagy had published several of Léger's paintings in his *Book of New Artists* (1922). That same year, they exhibited together at Der Sturm in Berlin, and *L'Esprit Nouveau* published Moholy-Nagy's sculptures (in issue number 21).[22] They probably met when Moholy-Nagy came to Paris in 1925, and they exhibited together at the Exposition international de l'Art d'aujourd'hui, after which many of Moholy-Nagy's Bauhaus students traveled to Paris to study or collaborate with Léger.[23] Léger, who knew Man Ray well due to their collaboration on the *Ballet mécanique* film, was, by 1928, familiar with Man Ray's photography book *Les Champs délicieux* (1922) (fig. 37). Hailed as a form of Surrealist automatism, Man Ray's rayographs,

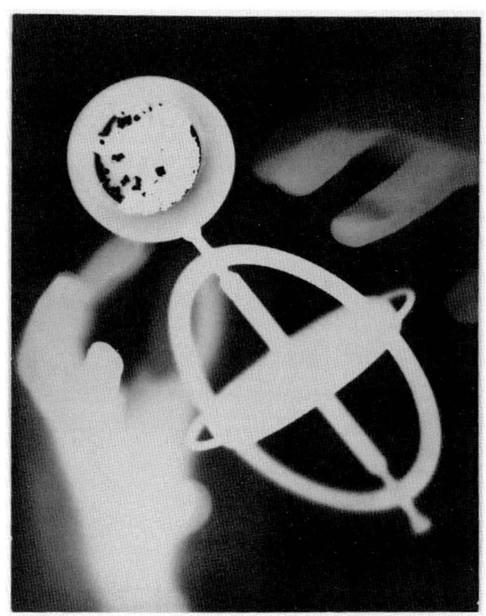

as he called his version of the photogram, produced a new form of still life composed of an array of organic and metallic objects: hands, plants, pipes, keys, and other, often indecipherable items. They rendered all objects—here, hands that reach out to grasp a gyroscope at center—into what Moholy-Nagy called a transformation of the "everyday object into something mysterious."[24] In 1926, Surrealist poet Robert Desnos cast Man Ray as a "master of modern phantoms."[25] French literarature scholar Ramona Fotiade has shown that the critical reception of Man Ray's work in the 1920s emphasized the "poetic disintegration of material reality" and his engagement in an "aesthetics of spectrality."[26] Despite his technological investments, Moholy-Nagy, too, was caught up in transcendentalist spirituality and the "light compositions" of spirit photography, as Elizabeth Otto has argued in her study of Bauhaus spirituality and gender.[27] Léger's *Holly Leaf*, too, seems to engage with the intrusion of the irrational in the technological.

Léger's *Holly Leaf* may also respond to Ernst's art book *Natural History* (1926), advertised and published in the same issue of *Cahiers d'Art* as an article on Léger by Raynal. *Cahiers d'Art* regularly published articles, artwork, and exhibition announcements about both artists, whose work appeared together in a group show at Galerie Myrbor that year. Ernst's *Natural History*, published with an introductory poem by Arp, is a book of thirty-four prints of leaves, plant forms, birds, and eyes, including plate 18, *The Habits of Leaves* (fig. 38). It displays his technique of *frottage* (rubbing), a form of automatic drawing engaging with the kind of free association Breton advocated to achieve poetic liberation. Standing erect between two vertical wood-grain planks, Ernst's leaf overlaps the right plank just enough to cast a shadow while also ever so slightly touching the left plank. Ernst's witty title parodies anthropological and zoological studies, inviting the viewer to read the leaf as a kind of flirtatious and promiscuous being. Where Ernst's erotic leaf uses frottage to express libidinal desires and parody scientific discourse, Léger's leaf is a more sober figure that enacts a painterly appropriation of the photogram, perhaps as an attempted mastery over automatic technique.

Fig. 37 Man Ray, *Untitled* (plate 3), 1922. Rayograph, silver gelatin. *Les Champs délicieux* (1922), page 4. 22.2 × 17.3 cm. Abby Aldrich Rockefeller Fund. The Museum of Modern Art, New York / Art, Resource, New York. © Man Ray 2015 Trust / Artists Rights Society (ARS), New York / ADAGP, Paris 2024.

Fig. 38 | opposite Max Ernst, *The Habits of Leaves*. Plate 18 in Max Ernst, *Natural History* (S/M 807) (Paris: Galerie Jeanne Bucher, 1925–26). Photoengraving from frottage, 42.7 × 26.1 cm. Gift of James Thrall Soby. The Museum of Modern Art, New York / Art Resource, New York. © 2024 Artists Rights Society (ARS), New York / ADAGP, Paris.

The new technologies of photography that inform the holly leaf's spectral interior were, in Léger's thinking and writing in 1928, historically and discursively linked to loss, the war, and corporeal fragility. In March 1928, Léger had presented a talk in Berlin on the occasion of his solo show at Alfred Flechtheim's gallery. Later published in *Variétés*, the talk provided Léger an opportunity to attribute his still life paintings to the influence of new photographic and film techniques—the close-up, aerial photography, the searchlight, the X-ray, and the magnification of the microscopic—known as a "new vision" where "we can actually see through bodies."[28] Aerial photography and the searchlight, both used during the war to identify targets, as well as the photogram and the X-ray, made the new vision imbued with reminders of death and ghostliness. Not surprisingly, even as Léger closed his talk by advocating for a "rationalist plasticism" and "equilibrium," he acknowledges the rationalist's "doubt," "fear," and "uneasiness." Léger's use of the term "new vision" acknowledges Moholy-Nagy's 1925 book and its wide range of new modes of technological seeing: photograms, the magnification of the microscopic, astrophotography, X-ray imagery. Binding together modernity, the war, and the new vision, Moholy-Nagy's book is punctuated by images of war: a German zeppelin, an English airplane squad, and *Militarism*, his photomontage combining advancing tanks, dead bodies, and sports figures.

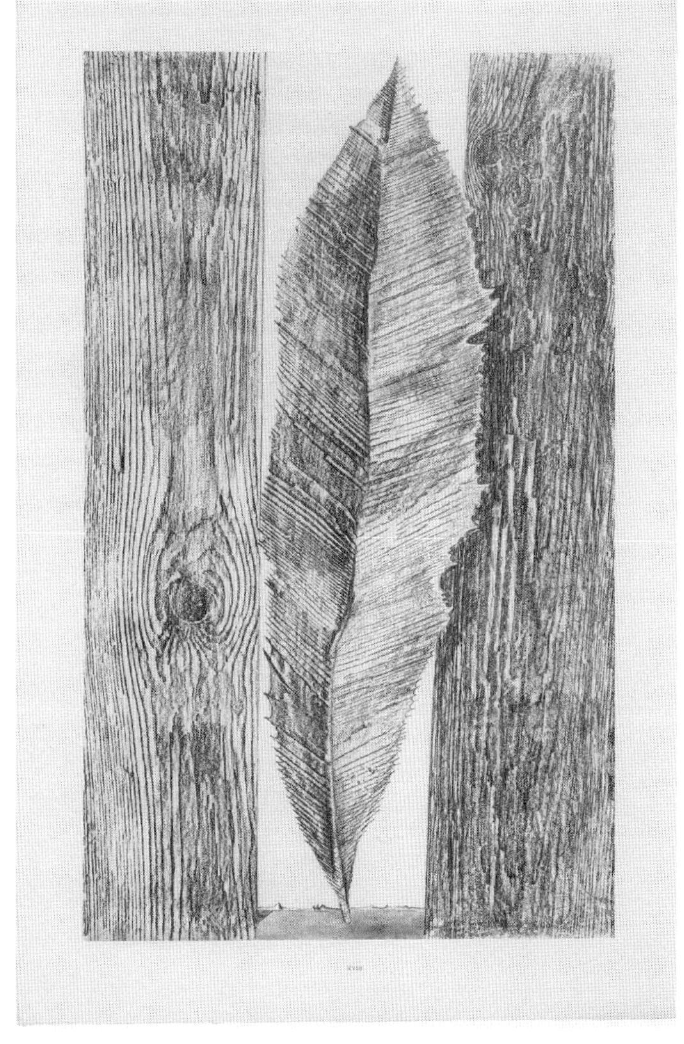

In addition to Léger's Berlin talk, a *Variétés* article published after his trip but not previously attributed to Léger affirms his interest in photograms. Published on November 15, 1928, the article by "F. L." (the initials Léger used to sign his paintings) reviews a major Belgian photography exhibition. It praises Moholy-Nagy and Man Ray for their photograms and techniques of double exposure and superimposition. The review goes on to comment upon photographer Eugene Atget's "tragic facades and desolate banlieue landscapes . . . [that] unconsciously [illustrate] the modern police novel" and the capacity of photographers Germaine Krull, Eli Lotar, and André Kertész to show "power, peace or mystery" in their photography.[29] Published during the week of the Armistice's decennial commemoration, Léger's review invokes photography's capacity to reveal the unconscious, death, crime, mutilated bodies, and a search for elusive causes or criminals. The new vision, in Léger's analysis, can disturb consciousness.

Bretonian Surrealism and Its Defectors

By 1928, the Purist message of combating "wars and arms" with machine modernisms and a virile economics had also come under challenge by Surrealism's revolutionary and hallucinatory poetics. In January 1925, the final issue of *L'Esprit Nouveau* announced Breton's first Surrealist manifesto in which Breton launched an attack upon Purism's "absolute rationalism" and "logical conclusions" and defined Surrealism in terms of Freud's revelations. Surrealism made the physical, psychic, and social effects of the war visible in ways that Purism and other neoclassicisms had wanted to disavow.

Surrealism's iconography of madness, amputation, and the uncanny mark an end to a period of forgetting about the trauma of war. The first issue of *La Révolution surréaliste*, published on December 1, 1924, incorporates stories of soldiers' suicides, such as one who drowned himself and another of a brigadier general who shot himself in the head. These accounts end with the quotation "Les amis de nos amis sont des cimetières" ("The friends of our friends are cemeteries"), foregrounding an intimacy with mortality and funerals. A central Surrealist motif, the mannequin borrows from the Freudian concept of the uncanny in which the object is a nonliving double of the human being, confusing the living and the dead. The cover of the issue dated July 15, 1925, uses Man Ray's photograph of a female mannequin wearing an evening gown and ascending a staircase framed with the words "et guerre . . . au travail" ("and [from] war . . . to work"). Surrealist themes of madness and hysteria revive the corporeal contortions that became visible during the war's epidemic of psychic breakdowns. In March 1928, Breton and Aragon dedicated a special issue of *La Révolution surréaliste* to the fiftieth anniversary of Jean-Martin Charcot's invention of the hysteria diagnosis, first published in 1878 and later revived in debates about male breakdowns during World War I. Breton and Aragon, who had been medical interns with Babinski at Salpêtrière during the war, learned firsthand of the war's impact upon soldiers' minds.[30] Due to his familiarity with Aragon, Breton, and Man Ray, Léger probably knew of these examples. He almost certainly knew of Breton and Aragon's *Variétés* special issue on Surrealism in 1929, which included their coauthored play *Le Trésor des Jésuites*. A dialogue between two allegorical figures of Time and Eternity, the play recalls the sounds of cannons in 1917, the Chemin des Dames battle that year, and the phantoms and madmen who return in 1928.[31]

Léger had known Breton and Aragon, a generation younger than him, since 1920, when the latter two were listed as "collaborators" in the first issue of *L'Esprit Nouveau* and when they started publishing *Littérature* and organizing the Friday events that marked the arrival of Paris Dada. During their Dada period, they contributed articles to the Purist journal and saw their work reviewed there.[32] At the first such matinee, on January 23, 1920, Breton read a text on Léger and introduced his and others' paintings (although Léger was not present), most notably Picabia's *The Double World* (1919).[33] French literature scholar Henri Béhar claims Breton purchased some of Léger's work at the Kahnweiler auctions in November 1921 and July 1922, suggesting an early if temporary rapport.[34] Léger attended multiple Dada events organized by Breton, Picabia, and others.[35] In January 1922, Breton recruited Léger and Ozenfant for a seven-member organizing committee for the never-realized International Congress for the Determination and Defense of the Modern Spirit, better known as the "Congress of Paris," a contest with artist Tristan Tzara over the meaning and origins of Dada that played out in the pages of the arts and entertainment periodical *Comoedia*.[36]

Léger developed closer ties to other Surrealist circles, including many artists who were "excommunicated" by Breton or, in the case of Arp and Miró, aligned with biomorphism or nongeometric abstraction that did not make direct reference to the war's legacy. Arp, who moved to Paris in 1926, may have met Léger through shared friendships with Picabia and Goll; they exhibited together several times starting with art patron Katherine Dreier's Brooklyn Museum exhibition in 1926. Léger may have known of Miró as early as 1921, when Miró's first solo exhibition in Paris was positively reviewed by *L'Esprit Nouveau*.[37] By the 1930s, they became friends and exhibited in group shows together. After Aragon broke with Breton in 1928, Léger and Aragon developed close political ties. They joined the Association des Ecrivains et Artistes Révolutionnaires (AEAR) formed in 1932 and engaged in interwar debates about Socialist Realism in 1936. In those debates, Léger defended Surrealists Ernst and Yves Tanguy and argued for a "new realism" against Aragon's Socialist Realism, which had become Soviet orthodoxy in 1934.[38] Both Aragon and Léger became members of the French Communist Party (in 1927 and 1945 respectively). After 1945, Aragon had a key role in making Léger an icon of the party, gave the eulogy at Léger's funeral, and was instrumental in the founding of the Léger Museum in Biot, inaugurated in 1960. During the 1920s and 1930s, Léger also had ties to art critics engaged with Surrealist circles. Einstein, a German critic and dealer who knew Léger from before World War I, became a coeditor of *Documents* (1929–30) with philosopher Georges Bataille and wrote about Léger in that periodical. Léger, too, knew E. E. Tériade, the Greek critic and publisher who wrote a monograph on Léger in 1928 and later became the artistic editor of *Minotaure* (1933–39), which promoted Surrealism.

A significant body of art historical research has shown how Surrealist aesthetics and motifs emerge from the physical and psychic trauma of the war. As art historian David Lomas argues, Breton and Aragon's wartime medical work with Babinski introduced them to the "poetic capacities . . . unleashed by mental illness."[39]

French literature scholar Mary Ann Caws characterizes Surrealist fascination with disgust and deformation as "stemming from the war experience."[40] She interprets Masson's repeated depictions of the disrupted body as "traces of shell-shock, amnesia and war imagery" motivated by his experience at Chemin des Dames.[41] Foster has argued that the Surrealist preoccupation with mannequins, dolls, waxwork, automatons, and man-machine hybridity embodies the "ghostly doubling" of the Freudian uncanny, while Surrealist depictions of human hybridity with machines are reactions to the capitalist order and the "mutilated or shocked soldier."[42] Art historian Yve-Alain Bois characterizes Bataille's central concept of formlessness, defined in *Documents* (1930), as part of a larger attack upon the ideal, the sacred, and unitary self.[43] Although not explicitly about the war, Bataille's "ethnographic Surrealism" focused on cruelty, sacrifice, and violence. For art historian Sidra Stich, the impact of the war is evident in Surrealism's lost faith in civilization and rationality, its turn to the Freudian primal and primitive, and its investments in antiheroic and impotent states of being. In her interpretation, Surrealism's "bodily forms are tumescent, dissolving, misshapen, molten, dematerialized, and devoid of a structural frame."[44] Lyford, for example, has argued that Kertész's photographic *Distortions* (1926–28), including amputee veterans, and Man Ray's pictures of the cross-dressing acrobat Van der Clyde (known as Barbette) (1934) display the war's legacy of a castrated masculinity.[45] Surrealism's anticlassicism and antiheroism countered the state-sanctioned norms of masculinity and memory, rationality and order.

At the same time as the Pavillon de l'Esprit Nouveau's display at the Exposition des arts décoratifs, Surrealism's display of castrated masculinity confronted Léger directly. In April 1925, the Galerie Simon exhibited Masson's *Man* (1924) (fig. 39) along with works by other artists represented by the gallery, including Léger, whose machine-era artwork Kahnweiler had acquired.[46] Masson, the Surrealist artist most impacted by the war, had been severely injured with a chest wound at the Chemin des Dames offensive in April 1917, left for hours on the battlefield before being rescued, and then hospitalized at the Maison Blanche psychiatric hospital near Paris. Masson's *Man* foregrounds a headless and limbless male torso whose amputated left leg ends in a split-open pomegranate or *grenade*. The *grenade*, a French word that signifies both the fruit and the weapon, became a reoccurring symbol in Masson's art, as did moonlit forests, tombs, ruins, ghostly bodies, and massacres. At the time of the exhibition, *La Révolution surréaliste* published Masson's painting with poet Jacques Baron's short story "Décadence de la vie," a pairing that invites the reader to interpret Masson's painting through the story's dreamlike imagery of burning lava, falling meteors, and human beings "profaned by suffering."[47] Masson's art was, as Einstein wrote a few years later, "hallucinatory," marked by its "destruction of the object," "dissociation of consciousness," and "psychological archaism."[48]

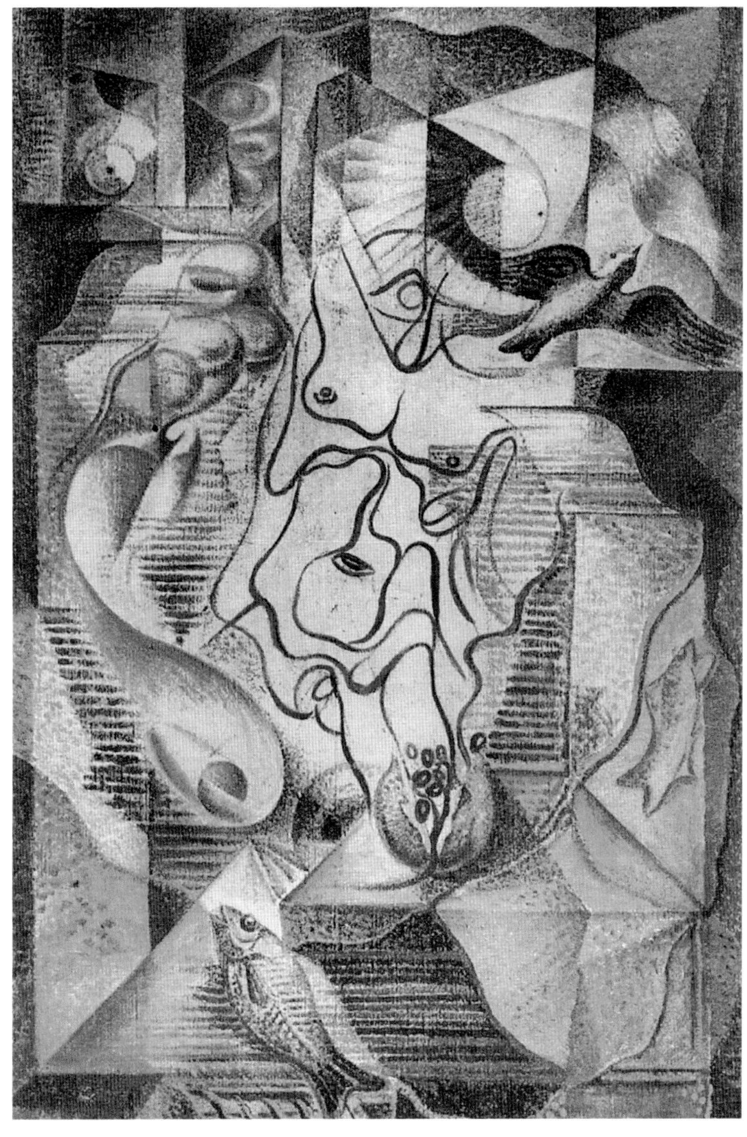

Fig. 39 André Masson, *Man*, 1924. Oil on canvas, 100 × 65.4 cm. Private collection. Dawn Ades, *André Masson: Catalogue Raisonné de l'oeuvre peint, 1919–1941*, 3 vols. (Vaumarcus: ArtAcatos, 2010), 1:200, fig. 1924 * 18. © 2024 Artists Rights Society (ARS), New York / ADAGP, Paris.

By 1928, when Léger produced his holly leaf paintings, however, it was not only Surrealist writing and Masson's imagery that revived the memory of war.

Armistice Commemorations

In November 1928, France commemorated the tenth anniversary of the Armistice, modeling and motivating the production of a collective memory (and forgetting) about the war. The commemorations took place on Sunday, November 11, resulting in several days of articles in all the major daily papers. *L'Intransigeant*, the daily that regularly reviewed Léger's exhibitions and published his articles, described the parades and commemorations that went from the Esplanade des Invalides down the Champs-Elysées to the Arc de Triomphe and the Tomb of the Unknown Soldier. The commemorations included the minute of silence, religious celebrations, and other activities. The paper invited veterans to remember their fallen comrades and where they were when they heard the news, pointing to a cultural practice that shaped what and how to remember.[49] For Léger, who went with Cendrars to Apollinaire's funeral on November 13, 1918, the invitation to remember the Armistice converged national victory celebrations and individual loss.

On November 8, 1928, a few days before the Armistice commemorations, director Léon Poirier's film *Verdun: Visions d'histoire* (1928) opened to national fanfare, with the French president and German ambassador in attendance, its posters papering the city, and reviews in many daily publications. An interweaving of documentary footage with dramatizations of ghostly figures entering the portal of the Verdun memorial, the film sought to narrate the most infamous battle of the war with veterans as actors. Reviewers saw it as a call to "memory." Marshall Pétain, whom Léger cites in his writings as his commander, performed himself, and Antonin Artaud, whom Léger probably knew through their common networks of friends and acquaintances, played an intellectual and the brother of a soldier.[50] That Léger saw the film is evident in his comments, years later, praising it as "really show[ing] the battle."[51] For Léger and those of his generation, the film and the decennial commemorative events shaped what sociologist Maurice Halbwachs in 1925 termed "collective memory," a social concept of memory formed through the nation, religion, and family rather than an individualized Bergsonian or Freudian concept of memory.[52]

How might the encounter with Surrealist art like Masson's and with national commemorative events have competed with or contested what Léger remembered? "Collective memory" became important to successive generations of historians writing on World War I, but recent historians have foregrounded the ways individual memories can complicate, contradict, and intervene in such collective processes.[53] The war memoir, as Paul Fussell showed in his classic literary history of the Great War, is one such intervention.[54] Léger probably knew the work of Jean Norton Cru, a veteran and French historian teaching at Williams College in the United States. Cru published a widely reviewed seven-hundred-page book, *Témoins* (1929), that collected some three hundred veterans' "eyewitness" accounts of the war. War memoirs, however, often blurred the lines between fiction and historical accounts. The claim to authenticity led to accusations of invented narratives and raised questions about truth and historical fact, as in the case of a dispute between Cru and novelist Roland Dorgèles over the latter's war writings.[55] As historian Joan Scott's influential critique of the "evidence of experience" first argued, such war memoirs are highly mediated through the discourses of the era, meaning that the self is not autonomous from events but "constituted through experience."[56]

A decade after the war, the men in Léger's artistic circle recalled the war's brutality and madness in memoirs and novels that were not always directly "historical" accounts, a modernist practice that aligns with Léger's rejection of nineteenth-century history painting. Cendrars published *Moravagine* (1926), a picaresque novel that begins in a French asylum and follows the brutal rapes and crimes of a mad, murderous nobleman who ends up back in Europe just as the war starts. In its closing, the novel states that "the whole world was doing a Moravagine," casting the war as the perpetuation of Moravagine's madness and brutality.[57] Cendrars's description of madness and hysteria at Salpêtrière Hospital motivated psychiatrists Bogousslavsky and Tatu to describe him as a "first-rate witness of neuropsychiatry."[58] Cendrars's writings describe a center for war neurotics based upon Maison Blanche, where he was hospitalized; there, soldiers go "mad," suffer from *le cafard* (intense fatigue), and "acute neurasthenia," and they become "hysterics." In 1929, the Fauvist artist Vlaminck, who had been, like Léger, part of Kahnweiler's prewar stable of artists, published his memoir *Dangerous Corner*. It describes the antiheroic people he encountered in the bicycle corps: ex-cons who became soldiers, starving soldiers who told him how easy it was to become a murderer, wartime prostitutes and madwomen, new recruits coming to the front on the same cattle trucks previously used to take animals to slaughter, insubordinate soldiers subject to summary executions, and a soldier who blinded himself to avoid further service. Novels and memoirs like Cendrars's and Vlaminck's brought into consciousness and representation aspects of the war that official commemorations and Purism had blocked: the degraded morality, the antiheroic, and the irrational.

By 1938, Léger described the era as a battle for survival in a hostile bourgeois social order. He wrote that he wanted to "pay homage to all those unhappy people . . . found in prisons, in asylums, under bridges . . . [an] admirable and fallen humanity" who are "from the same family" as today's "creators and achievers." [59] Soon after the tenth anniversary of the Armistice, this "fallen humanity" became highly visible when France was hit by the worldwide economic crisis, dealing another blow to Purism's postwar economic triumphalism. Starting in 1928, the popular Parisian photographic weekly magazine *VU* and the Belgian arts journal *Variétés* published articles on public drunks, the asylum, the unemployed, and the homeless as photographed by Krull, Lucien Vogel, Eli Lotar, and others. By May 1932, industrial production had declined 20 percent from 1928 levels, a decline from which France did not recover until 1939.[60] Modernist rationalism could no longer contain or suppress the visibility of the homeless and poor, many of whom could have been veterans. These downfallen became the subject of urban public welfare projects by Léger's friends and colleagues. Le Corbusier's most important commission for the period was La Cité de Refuge (1933), a new Salvation Army building in Paris with about five hundred beds. A year before collaborating with Léger on photomontages for the 1937 World's Fair in Paris, architect and designer Charlotte Perriand produced *The Great Misery of Paris* (1936), a monumental photomontage meant to document the urban overcrowding and poor living conditions that city planning would alleviate.[61]

Freudian Symbols

By 1930, Léger turned to Freudian dream symbolism, particularly phallic symbols, demonstrating an awareness of psychoanalytic ideas. But the meaning of these symbols in Léger's work is highly unstable, shifting from signs of compensatory masculinity and phallic dominance to useless found objects. While Léger's interest in Freudian symbols may have been provoked by the emergence of Surrealism, his knowledge of Freud was mediated by *L'Esprit Nouveau*. Film critic Epstein, whom Léger met in 1921, first wrote about Freudian dream symbolism, displacement, and the manifest and latent content of dreams in *L'Esprit Nouveau* in 1922.[62] Even more important were the Purist Freudians Laforgue and Allendy, who contributed regularly in 1924 and after. Léger and Allendy had many shared friends, including Le Corbusier, Miró, Einstein, and Roger Vitrac. Throughout the 1920s and 1930s, Allendy was active in avant-garde art circles and served as a bridge between Purism and Surrealism, making it unsurprising that Léger would turn to Allendy's articles to interpret Freud.[63] In their *L'Esprit Nouveau* essays, Allendy and Laforgue equated Bergsonian vitalism with the Freudian libido and claimed that Bergson advocated the study of the unconscious.[64] In late 1924, Allendy published an article on Freudian dream analysis and symbolism.[65] In two coauthored books on psychoanalysis, Allendy and Laforgue summarize Freud's gendered dream symbolism, including that the phallus is symbolized by umbrellas, scissors, guns, serpents, hats, and keys.[66] In 1926, Allendy used Freudian discourse to write about film. He argued for the "affective value of images" and their "unconscious processes," evident in several films, including Gance's *La Roue* (1923), which Léger had contributed to. Allendy cited films by Epstein and others as "veritable Surrealist productions" that can explain "the most profound mechanisms of our soul."[67] Although there is no evidence that Léger engaged in dream analysis, his exposure to Allendy's writings and his valorization of ordinary objects aligns with Freud's interest in seemingly unimportant things, raising questions about how Freudian analysis provoked Léger's reassessment of the object.

Freudian symbols first appear in Léger's drawings for the Belgian journal *Variétés* (1928–30). These drawings in turn functioned as preparatory studies for paintings such as *Composition with Keys* (1929) and *Still Life, First State* (1929).[68] Informed by the work of Moholy-Nagy and Man Ray's photograms of scattered objects, Léger's new still life compositions move away from the disciplined rows of mass production represented in the *Ballet mécanique*. In these new drawings and paintings, mostly masculine symbols—hats, umbrellas, ribbons, and keys—mix with bits of metallic beams, half a compass or scissors, incomplete design plans such as a grid or cube or Constructivist linear elements, and sculptural forms such as a monochromatic leaf or a chipped plaster hand missing its fingertips. While the hats, keys, and umbrellas reinforce masculinity, other objects—the half compass, partial scissors, and chipped plaster hand—enact the ruination of Russian Constructivism and neoclassicism. As drawings and paintings, Léger's methodically staged compositions run counter to Surrealism's automatic drawings, which attempted to release the unconscious. His compositions may aim instead for the "equilibrium" vaunted by Purism and reclaimed in his 1928 Berlin talk. Léger's objects, no longer serving as signs of mass production or aestheticized displays of commodity culture, render the relationship among the objects often ambiguous. Perhaps legible as the scattered items on an artist's drafting table, the keys might be read as having a home and an owner. But more often their use value disappears, since they are disconnected from any imagined spatial location or portals from which their value derives.

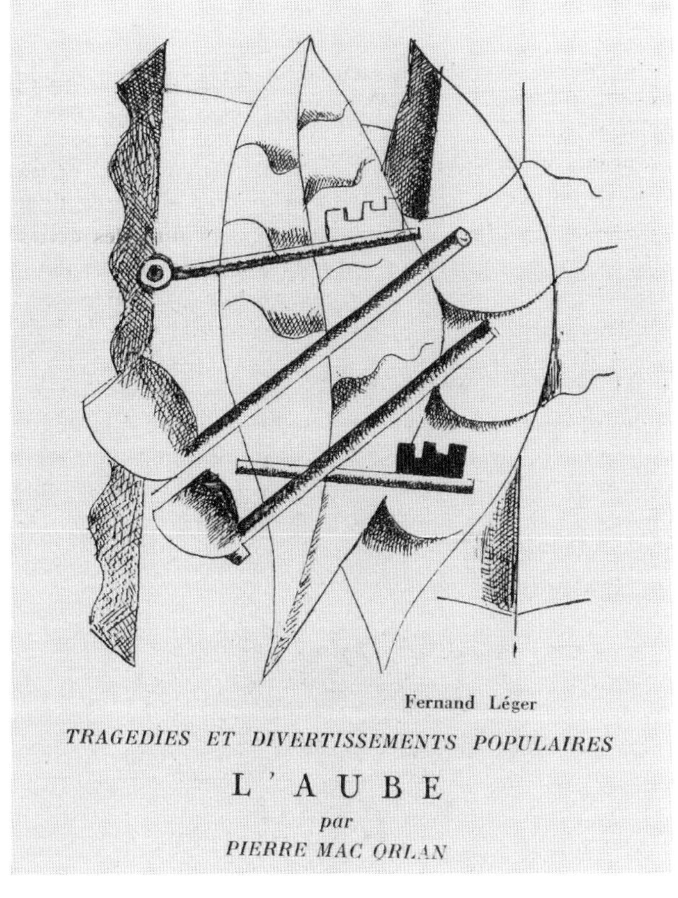

Fig. 40 Fernand Léger, ink drawing of leaves, keys, and pipes, ca. 1928. © 2024 Artists Rights Society (ARS), New York / ADAGP, Paris. Published in Pierre MacOrlan, "Tragédies et divertissements populaires: L'Aube," *Variétés* 1, no. 8 (December 15, 1928): 430. Courtesy of the Library of Congress, Washington, DC.

The ambiguous value of Léger's Freudian symbols and new still life objects emerges in Léger's cover and six still life drawings for *Variétés*. The images are paired with six articles, stories, and book reviews characterized by Surrealist motifs and downtrodden men, raising questions about the contradictory significations the text-image combinations produce. The first of Léger's *Variétés*' drawings, published in December 1928, depicts pairs of leaves, keys, and pipes (fig. 40) and serves as a visual epigraph heading an essay by the critic and novelist Pierre MacOrlan. Léger had known MacOrlan since at least 1924, when L'Herbier adapted MacOrlan's script into the film *L'Inhumaine* (1924), for which Léger designed a laboratory set. MacOrlan's essay describes the "miserable people" of Paris, those Léger later recognized in 1938 as "fallen humanity": the men who are in the soup lines by day and "gray phantoms" by night, who sleep under bridges or on the banks of the Seine or live in abandoned buildings that look like medieval gallows.[69] In MacOrlan's essay, these men prowl around Place Pigalle in the wee hours under electric lighting and monumental advertising looking for "incomprehensible loot" and scrutinizing the gutters for something they see as a "nugget."[70] MacOrlan's characterization radically reenvisions the urban milieu that only a few years earlier had been for Léger the sites of urban spectacle and aesthetic raw material. Read in connection with MacOrlan's essay, the objects in Léger's drawing could be interpreted as the kinds of lost or abandoned items collected by the desperate characters, symbols of their broken masculinity, or perhaps as compensatory signs for male lack. Similarly, Léger's other *Variétés* drawings are paired with stories adopting MacOrlan's nocturnal motifs, such as art historian Paul Fierens's essay on mannequins and shop windows, or essays by Surrealist writers such as Pierre Audard on a "house of sleep" and Vitrac on the ephemeral and phantasmagorical, or about stateless men, such as writer Nico Bost's book review of journalist Joseph Roth's new novel.[71]

Within the visual-textual world of *Variétés*, Léger's keys and still lifes risked being interpreted less as found objects for transvaluation into art than as trash collected by marginalized scavengers and homeless drunks. Immediately preceding MacOrlan's essay are a series of photographs by Krull of alcoholic men on the streets. The same issue included a review of, and stills from, *La Zone: Au Pays du chiffonier* (1928), Georges Lacombe's documentary film of ragpickers living in the shantytowns of Paris's periphery. Both Krull and Lacombe visualized the kinds of desperate people MacOrlan describes. MacOrlan's *Variétés* story exemplifies his concept of the "social fantastic," a term he used, probably for the first time, in his preface to the catalog for Grosz's Paris exhibition in 1924. MacOrlan developed the idea in *L'Art cinématographique* in 1926 and applied it to Atget's photography.[72] For MacOrlan, the "social fantastic" described urban narratives and nighttime scenes in film, photography, and fiction that conveyed a mood of disillusionment, anxiety, and misery. In November 1928, a month before *Variétés* published Léger's first still life drawing, Léger's photography review praising Atget's imagery and other nighttime scenes was almost certainly informed by the work of MacOrlan.

Léger's phallic symbolism is contradictory and ambivalent. In some still life paintings, Léger's keys dominate in position and scale over feminized figures, usually nudes, dancers, or female busts, and so stage a compensatory move that magnifies the phallic sign and miniaturizes the feminine. The dancing nudes in *Composition with Keys*

(1929), published by Einstein and Waldemar George, quote the image Albert Jeanneret, Le Corbusier's brother, used to promote Dalcrozian dance: a photograph of two dancers in midleap published repeatedly in *L'Esprit Nouveau*.[73] Léger's use of the dancing nudes combines signs of physical culture and advertising practice. During this period, Léger, who had written about the aesthetics of the shop window and urban commercial design, taught and wrote about advertising.[74] But the *Variétés*' images of dance as a sign of the healthy body are far outweighed by documentary photography of homeless alcoholics, lynched and starving Africans, war detritus, and other images of debased humanity. While Léger may have wanted the keys and nudes to serve as a phallic iconography of masculinity, at other times, keys fail to dominate the feminine symbol and instead compete with or are dominated by biomorphic forms threating dissolution. In *Statue and Keys* (1930), for example, keys are diminished in size next to an amorphous dark "statue" whose knobby white highlights again revive a painted version of the photogram's spectral forms.

In analyzing these new drawings and still life paintings, Léger's promoters anxiously insisted upon Léger's rationality and consciousness even as they acknowledged that Léger's Freudian symbolism can be read as signs of anxiety. Zervos realized that Léger's new pictures might be read in terms of "dreams and anxieties" but also claimed that they had a "classic tendency" serving equilibrium.[75] In 1930, the German critic and dealer Einstein published an article in *Documents* on Léger and illustrated it with several paintings incorporating keys, including *Composition with Keys*. Like Zervos, Einstein saw Léger as protecting himself and the viewer from confronting the psyche. Einstein wrote that Léger was an extrovert, not an introvert interested in individual subjectivity: "the unconscious for him is equal to nothingness."[76] Perhaps Einstein, who had fought on the western front on the German side and suffered a nervous breakdown in 1917, had greater insight into Léger's psychic defenses.[77]

Certainly, reviewers understood the social-psychic threat of the unconscious and irrational for Léger's art, since they sought to craft Léger's public persona as a virile, rational man. In 1929, Waldemar George wrote that "nothing is more foreign to Léger than . . . the appeal to the forces of the subconscious."[78] Writing about Léger's new still life work, including *Composition with Keys*, George insisted that Léger's art "represents consciousness" and that his objects "remain foreign to affective life." Léger "ignores the obscure sentiment of revolt" in favor of a "standardized and rationalized style"; "the work of art," for Léger, is "a compensation" for modern life.[79] Yet George fails to account for how Léger's scattered compositions turn away from the manufactured object. In 1933, Ozenfant contributed to a special issue of *Cahiers d'Art* dedicated to Léger on the occasion of a major solo exhibition in Zurich. Ozenfant wrote that Léger's "working-class tastes" and "vital power" are a counterpart to the "artistic mentality" of Aragon and Breton and their "Freudism" and occultism.[80] Art

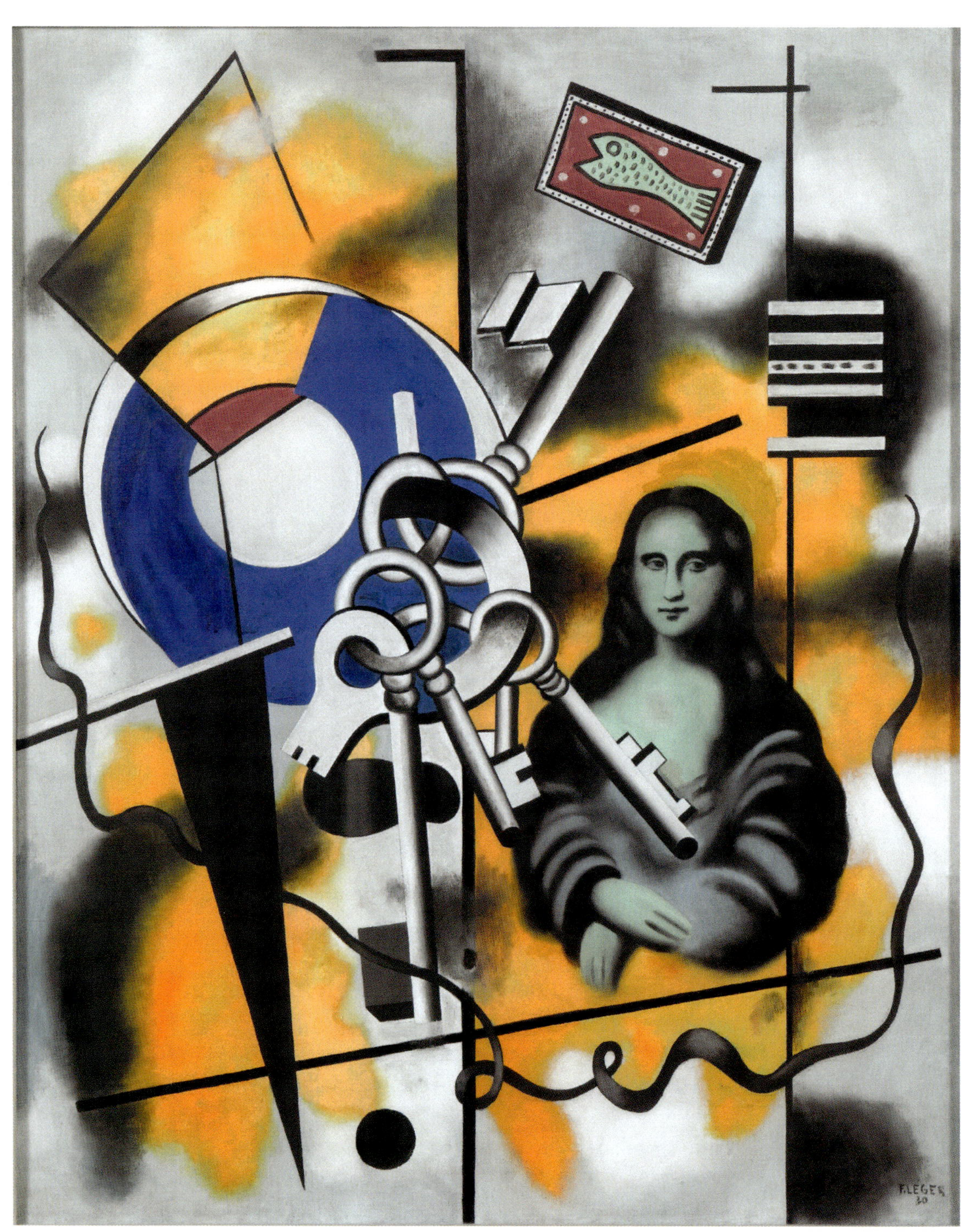
F.LEGER

critic James Johnson Sweeney, too, wrote that Léger's new still life paintings "might remind us of the Super-realists' 'associations of disparate objects,'" but Sweeney then claimed Léger's interest was only in the objects' "plastic aims," reorienting meaning to formal properties rather potential unconscious significations.[81] Such reviews demonstrate the critics' difficulty in reconciling Léger's machine-era work with his engagement with Freudian symbols, motivating their insistence on his purely "plastic" or compositional use of the forms.

By contrast, to detractors, Léger's engagement with Freudian motifs and the photogram's seemingly arbitrary collection of found objects exposed his work to Surrealist interpretations. In response to Léger's depiction of *Mona Lisa with Keys* (1930) (fig. 41), the Italian fascist paper *Quadrante* accused him of being a "rotten Surrealist painter" who has "putrid" taste and fills his pictures with "psychoanalytic symbols."[82] Léger's depiction of the *Mona Lisa* fits within his long-standing criticism of the Italian Renaissance and of academic investment in naturalism.[83] Yet its symbols revive wartime associations. Like his friend Duchamp, whose *L.H.O.O.Q.* (1919) defaced a postcard version of the *Mona Lisa*, Léger mocks the masterpiece as a sign of artistic decay. The Italian reaction understands that mockery but interprets the degradation not as Duchampian wit but as Surrealism's rot, putrefaction, and Freudian symbolism. Léger's *Mona Lisa* pits an icon of fine arts against keys as a found object. Mona Lisa is a cut-out figure removed from her verdant Arno Valley landscape and transformed into a sickly green torso placed before an acidic orange-yellow cloud. A ring of about six keys, some of which merge together, occupies the center of the composition; one of those keys drapes diagonally over the *Mona Lisa*, dominating her in scale. The keys radiate out from the incomplete ring like clock hands; one key with an oddly stepped cut points to a red sardine tin at one o'clock and another to the Mona Lisa at four o'clock. The Constructivist elements—the blue disk and straight-edge lines that run parallel to the picture plane and frame the *Mona Lisa*—contrast with an iconography reviving wartime references: a yellow cloud recalling poison mustard gas, a green body read as a decaying corpse, canned sardines that were a regular feature of the soldier's diet, a stepped key recalling the *escalier* motif in the shoulders of Léger's *The Card Party* soldier, and perhaps even the wristwatch that became standardized in the war to time attacks. In the context of a wartime iconography of found objects, the keys shift from being signs of phallic potency to objects of uncertain value.

Fig. 41 Fernand Léger, *Mona Lisa with Keys*, 1930. Oil on canvas, 91 × 72 cm. Photo: Gérard Blot. Musée National Fernand Léger / Biot, France, MNFL98024. © RMN-Grand Palais / Art Resource, New York. © 2024 Artists Rights Society (ARS), New York / ADAGP, Paris.

Scavenged Things

Whatever compensatory value Léger's phallic symbols might have served in the *Variétés* drawings, when interpreted as found objects, they risk being seen as the useless treasures of the degraded men populating MacOrlan's story, Krull's photography, or Lacombe's film. As scavenged objects, Léger's still life forms approach the debased war trash mentioned at the end of his second "Machine Aesthetic" essay. In 1924, Léger explained his valuation of the manufactured object that surpasses fine art by turning to its imagined other: a system of exchange and labor contingent upon death. In language indicating that he is speaking not about peacetime economies, the beautiful machine, or rows of pots but wartime scavenging practices, battlefield contexts, and a larger crisis in the centrality of man or even humanism, Léger writes: "A nail, a candle stub, a shoelace can cost a man's life or a regiment's. . . . Everything counts, everything competes, and the scale of the ordinary and conventional values is overturned. A nervous officer is finished and a cool-headed noncom[missioned soldier] replaces him."[84] In this passage, Léger makes an abrupt shift from the domestic space of the kitchen with its feminine commodities to the dirty, unpolished, noncommodifiable, and decidedly abject trash of the battlefield, the hysterical officer, and the arbitrariness of "conventional values" or class hierarchies. Léger valorizes the "cool" of the soldier in opposition to the "nervous" officer who apparently cannot carry out his leadership duties and who thus thwarts the war's progress. In arresting the machinery of war, the neurotic officer precedes and prepares for the postwar feminized domesticated bodies—the traumatized veteran and demobilized woman—who cannot perpetuate the machinery of capitalism.

The lack of phallic power disavowed by the fetishized commodity is a deferred confrontation with the experience of war. In his wartime writings, Léger makes the connections between found objects or scavenged debris and the cost of a man's life. In letter dated October 5, 1915, Léger describes one master scavenger, a soldier nicknamed Chouya, meaning a smidgen or tiny bit, perhaps in reference to the man's size or to his small finds. Chouya always "saves the day when supplies are late"; he was sure to have "a rabbit or chicken in his pouch, always a candle stub, when no one else had anything and [everyone] thought that we had rolled through a department or villages that had been burned, pillaged, and bombarded."[85] Scavenging involved discovery amid ruination and an intimacy with, and violation of, the dead. Léger wrote that his comrades "stripped the still warm [corpses] of their shoes; water bottles and socks disappeared as often as wallets." In the same letter, Léger argues for the value of "basic things" in a nonmonetary economy: "no money exists here, all raw materials take an enormous value." Bread, meat, potatoes, wine, trouser buttons, matches, and candles are all objects that suddenly become more valuable than in a peacetime economy due to basic needs and pragmatism. Scavenging becomes indexical of the war's risks, its arbitrariness, its cruelties, and its production of death. A month later, Léger reported in another letter that Chouya was shot in the head reaching for a German helmet, an ironic loss given the utility of the helmet. Chouya's only memorial was the distribution of his belongings, which his comrades discovered included a cache of watches and wedding rings.[86] Signs of interrupted lives and robbed corpses, the war booty was useful in a barter economy for food or wine, by contrast to the homefront's monetary economy where civilians were exhorted to donate their gold rings, watches, and other precious possessions to be transformed into currency.[87]

In Léger's writing, the context of the battlefield scrambled several hierarchies: the monetary economic system was inoperative, supplanted by a barter economy; use value eclipsed exchange value; and class hierarchies were inverted and gendered. The candle stubs, shoelaces, and nails referenced in the 1924 essay, and Chouya's rabbit, chicken, and the other examples in Léger's letter—water bottles, socks, bread, buttons, and matches—take on enormous value. In Léger's letters, Chouya offers gifts to the collective: a rabbit or chicken shared with the group; even his cache of watches and wedding rings end up becoming a bequest to be shared equally among his brothers-in-arms. The utility of the objects is what makes them most valuable: food for the hungry belly; socks, buttons, and shoelaces to repair boots and clothing; a candle stub and matches to read letters or play cards at night; watches to coordinate military attacks. However, wedding rings, like keys, have little use value except for their owner. Military hierarchy, which reinforced class hierarchy, was upended in the scavenger's terrain, where the cool "noncom" or ordinary soldier supplants the "nervous officer." What war showed Léger was not so much a "natural hierarchy," but that the warfront and wasteland broke down those hierarchies imposed through social, legal, and economic systems. Read through the lens of the Chouya story, Léger's paintings with keys might be better understood in terms of the war's destabilization of gender and class categories. Like the scavenged wedding rings, the key rings that populate Léger's still life paintings, particularly when paired with *Variétés*' Surrealist stories, could be interpreted as signs of lost bodies and destroyed homes and relationships brought about by the war's legacy and the economic crisis.

Even the Purist Freudians, who avoided any discussion of hysterical soldiers, linked the close-up and found objects with revived memories of war and death. In 1926, in an analysis of film for its psychological effects and symbolism, Allendy discussed what he called the "affective value of the image-symbol."[88] Allendy cites a séance scene from a now-lost film in which close-ups of ordinary objects such as candles and matchsticks created "a sense of threatening mortal danger." Allendy's examples accord with Léger's drawings and the scavenged war debris (the candle stub) in his second "Machine Aesthetic" essay. Photography, too, could portend doom, as Allendy explains. He recalled that when he served as a wartime infantry doctor, a group of soldiers found a ruined wall with an abandoned mailbox graffitied with the words "La dernière levée est faite" ("The last collection has been taken").

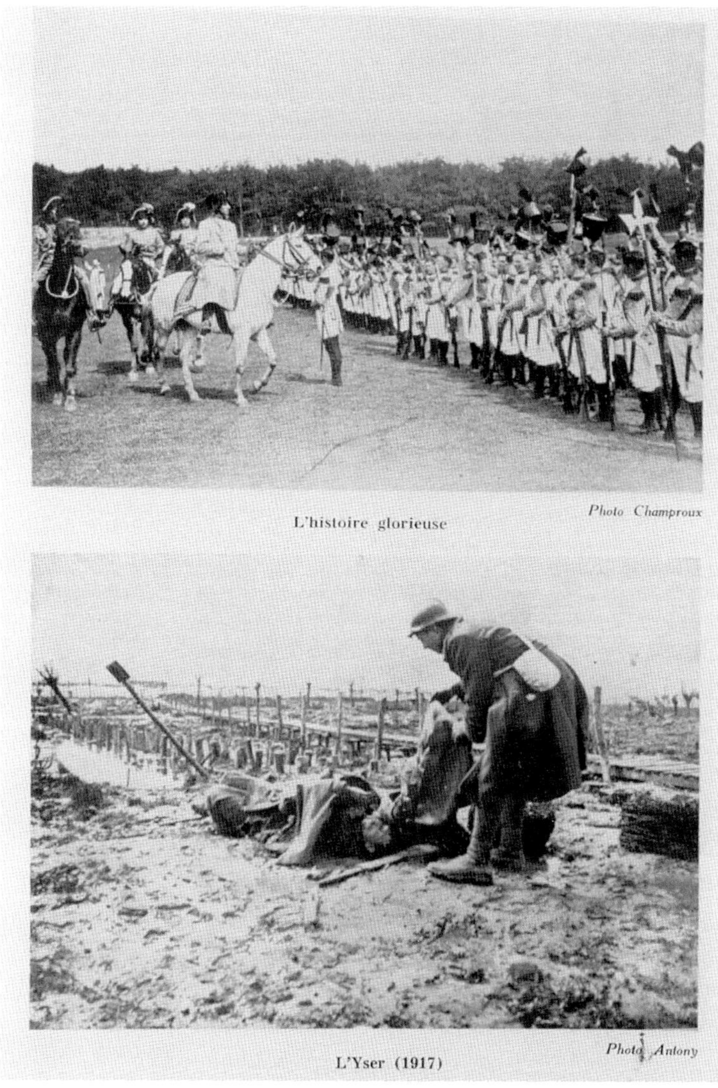

Fig. 42 Photo Champroux, “L'histoire glorieuse,” 1929, and Photo Antony, “L'Yser (1917),” 1917. Photographs, dimensions unknown. In “La paix et la guerre,” *Variétés* 2, no. 8 (December 15, 1929): n.p., after p. 598.

Fig. 43 | opposite Fernand Léger, *Drapery Study*, 1930. Pencil, 27 × 21 cm. Photo: Jacques Faujour. Musée National d'Art Moderne / Centre Georges Pompidou, Paris, Inv. no. AM1981-665. Digital Image © CNAC/MNAM, Dist. RMN-Grand Palais / Art Resource, New York. © 2024 Artists Rights Society (ARS), New York / ADAGP, Paris.

One soldier took his photograph with the ruined mailbox only to be killed a few days later. Ordinary objects—candles and matchsticks, a disused mailbox—increasingly seemed to threaten death and disaster and not just to Bretonian Surrealists.

With the worldwide economic crisis, the dispossessed and déclassé seemed to transform the city into a space of damaged masculinity and revive the war's spectacle of ruin, disturbing even Léger's thinking. The Surrealists recognized the waste of war in the immediate postwar era, but their textual image of scavengers did not enter into visuality until a decade later. In *Les Champs magnetiques* (1919), Breton and writer Philippe Soupault used the term "scavengers of paradise" to refer to "the dreamers and visionaries who pick through the discards of culture,"[89] almost a decade before documentary photography depicted urban scavenging. As Foster argues, Léger's machine modernism became the object of a visual critique of capitalist-militarism in *Variétés* in 1930, where his set design of a fantastic factory in L'Herbier's 1924 film *L'Inhumaine* was juxtaposed with the dysfunctional devices of artist Suzanne Duchamp's imagined factory.[90] A year earlier, a more explicit critique of war and its waste appears in a pair of war photographs published in *Variétés* (fig. 42). At top, an image previously published in *The Paris Times* (June 2, 1929) depicts the "glorious history" of war: a reenactment staged in England of Napoleon on horseback inspecting the Imperial Guard. At bottom, an image entitled "L'Yser (1917)" depicts a soldier bending over a bag or article of clothing in the midst of the vast wasteland of the Belgian front. While the Yser soldier's activity is ambiguous in the *Variétés* publication and might be read as warfront scavenging, it is credited archivally with being a Belgian soldier covering the body of a German.[91] Such photography critiquing staged heroism as spectacle and foregrounding the waste of war may have informed Léger's new themes and writing. By 1934, in a reversal of his machine aesthetic–era thinking of the city's spectacles and mass-produced objects as visual sources for his artwork, Léger wrote publicly that "in the debris, I collected the object that serves as the armature for my current artwork," a statement invoking the specter of scavenging as artistic process.[92]

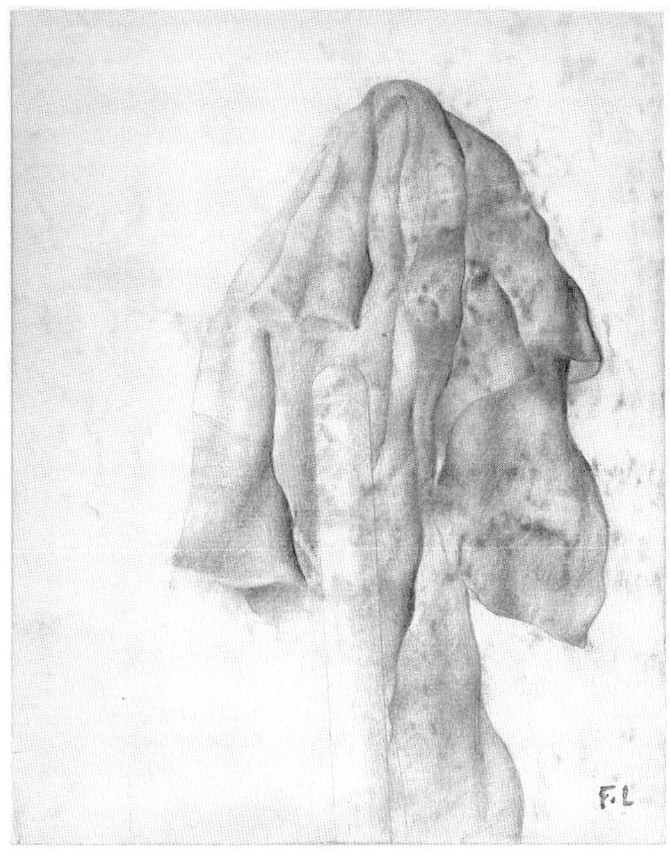

In two still life drawings, *Old Gloves* (1930) and *Drapery Study* (1930) (fig. 43), Léger turned his attention to Surrealist photography's found and outmoded objects signifying lost bodies. First represented in Breton's novel *Nadja* (1928) and essay "Surrealism and Painting" (1928), the Surrealist found object depends upon an unintentional or chance encounter that manifests unconscious processes.[93] In *Nadja*, photographs of Nadja's bronze glove and a flea market piled high with used coats represent the found object and the kinds of sites where they could be discovered.

The narrator pursues Nadja through the streets of Paris, gains sight of her and then loses her in the city. In Foster's analysis, the finding and loss of Nadja is an analog to Freud's *fort/da* repetition compulsion; Nadja's dropped glove is a substitute for the lost love object, and the flea market is the space of the outmoded and ruins of capitalism.[94] Léger's ink-and-pencil drawings borrow from Breton's *Nadja* to capture a sense of loss and ruin. In *Old Gloves*, Léger recapitulates the photograph of Nadja's forgotten glove. The rumpled old coat in Léger's pencil drawing *Drapery Study* could have been pulled from the pile of used clothing in *Nadja*'s flea market photograph. The softness of the pencil drawing and the fullness of the hanging garment endow the form with a sensitivity and sense of corporeal absence. Pictorially, it revives the sense of loss Léger had expressed in his war letters. In 1914, Léger remarked upon the *capote* (great coat) of an anarchist sympathizer shot for desertion: "When they collected his body you had the impression that the *capote* was as empty as the body was broken."[95] Other art historians have interpreted Léger's drapery studies as signs of mourning. Monod-Fontaine has compared the mysterious cloaked and hooded but hollow form in Léger's *La Statuette rose* (1930) to the hooded mourners that support the Tomb of Philippe Pot (1494) and the portentous, faceless draped figure at the periphery of Poussin's *Marriage of the Virgin* (1647).[96] Such hooded figures of mourning were common in contemporary funerary monuments. Unlike the Freudian symbolism of keys, hollowed-out garments become a central motif in Léger's new iconography, persisting well into the 1940s.

Comets and Severed Limbs

Léger's drapery studies are part of the new object images that must have disturbed Léger's advocates who wanted to insist upon his rationality and antithetical position to Surrealism. Zervos, who sought to periodize Léger's study of the object from the machine era to his more recent work, acknowledged that Léger now sought to communicate the "evocative power of the object" and produce a "wide range of associations" or meanings.[97] In two articles published in 1932 and 1934 in *Cahiers d'Art*, Zervos discusses one set of forms—comet paintings, nonmimetic biomorphic "cows," flint rock gouaches—that seem to dissolve the things they manifestly represent and another set of objects—drawings of flint rock, corkscrews, quarters of beef, a window fragment, nuts, clothing—that use pen and ink to secure precision and clarity to form. Between these two articles and on the occasion of Léger's solo exhibition in Zurich in 1933, Zervos dedicated a special issue of over two hundred pages to Léger, republishing numerous reviews and analyses of his work as well as about 150 reproductions from early-career paintings through the machine aesthetic era to the recent still lifes. The special issue served to remind *Cahiers d'Art* readers that

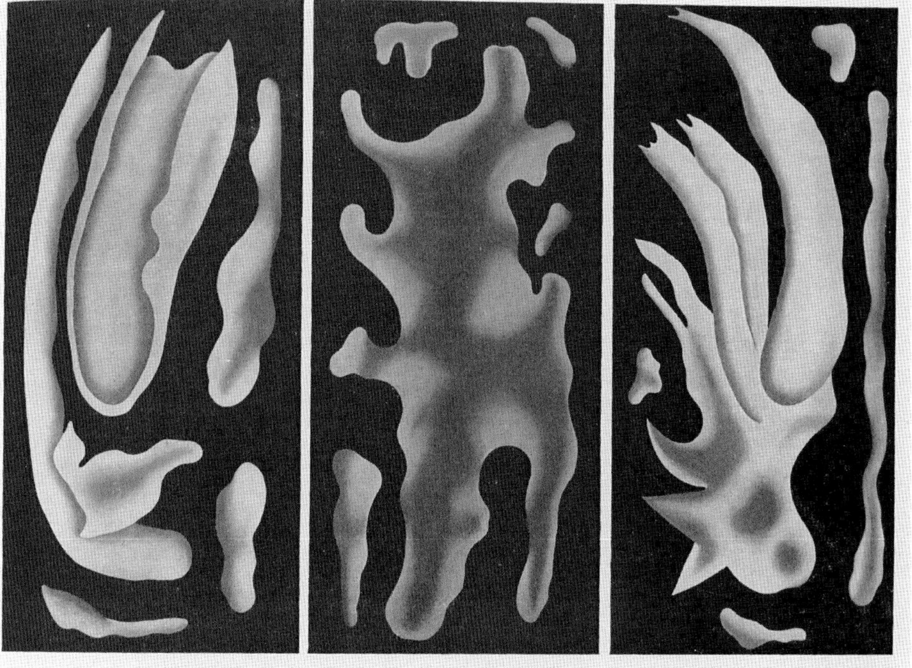

Fig. 44 Fernand Léger, *Comet Tails on Black Ground*, 1930. Oil on canvas, each panel 200 × 270 cm. Galerie Maeght, Paris. © 2024 Artists Rights Society (ARS), New York / ADAGP, Paris. Published in Christian Zervos, "Une Nouvelle étape dans l'oeuvre de Fernand Léger," *Cahiers d'Art* 7, nos. 6–7 (1932): 265. Image courtesy of the Bibliothèque nationale de France.

Léger was a machine modernist and that he sought formal (and psychic) equilibrium, effectively casting Léger's Surrealist-informed compositions and anomalous dissolving forms as an artistic detour.

Perhaps the most startling examples of these dissolving forms are Léger's little-discussed comet paintings, produced from 1930 to 1932 in the context of personal and artistic tragedies. Like Léger's holly leaves, his comet images present a manifest scientific content disturbed by associations with death, dismemberment, and apocalyptic time, yet the monumental scale invites the viewer into an immersive experience of dark canvases. The comet series includes two mural-sized, three-part folding screens believed to have been originally conjoined into one double-sided screen: *Comet Tails on Black Ground* (1930) (fig. 44), published two years later in *Cahiers d'Art*, and *Comet Tails on a Brown Ground* (1931). They were commissioned by the wealthy Americans Gerald and Sara Murphy for the family villa at Antibes, but they were never installed due to family illness and relocation. The Murphys met Léger in 1921 and became important patrons; Gerald Murphy, like Léger, had designed set and costumes for the Ballet Suédois in the 1920s. In October 1929, as Léger was working on the comet painting, his patrons' youngest son, Patrick, was diagnosed with tuberculosis. In the same month, the stock market crashed, impacting the Murphys' fortunes. The family decamped to Switzerland but Patrick died in 1937, by which time their elder son, Boath, too, had died of spinal meningitis.[98]

The years 1931 and 1932 were particularly troubling for Léger and his networks. In summer 1931, after returning from vacationing with the Murphys in the Austrian Tyrol with Patrick, Léger learned of another disaster: the son of his childhood friend André Mare had died in July, and a year later, in November 1932, Mare died of tuberculosis and the long-term effects of mustard gas poisoning.[99] In fall 1932, the Bauhaus in Dessau was slated for closure by the city's Nazi leadership. While Léger never explicitly links the comet paintings to the threat of death and rising German militarism, the paintings' investment in corporeal dissolution makes them perhaps the most antirational, even melancholic, in Léger's oeuvre.

The monochromatic panels combine dark grounds with ambiguous white forms that borrow from the photogram without imitating any referential scientific subject. Léger's fragmented amorphous shapes bear little resemblance to the form of a comet, with its distinctive head, nucleus, and tail. The front screen, *Comet Tails on Black Ground*, is composed of three panels: a left panel of elongated and sometimes rounded white shapes mixed with smaller irregular forms often shaded only at the edges, a central panel depicting a large amoebic mass with multiple protrusions and a dark shadowy interior, and a right panel showing a kind of upside-down body whose rounded "head" and pointed beak dive to the bottom of the canvas, while its "torso" and its multiple elongated "limbs" are merged together, extending to the upper edge of the canvas and terminating in what might be read as several forked comets tails merged into one. One preparatory pencil drawing incorporates elements from the right panel, a birdlike figure, a vertical snakelike form, and an arm with a four-fingered hand (fig. 45). Juxtaposed, the forms in that study invite associations not only with the origins and dissolutions of life but also with the body's dismemberment. A rare theme in Léger's work, the comet in *Comet Tails* completely abandons both the use of color and the formal precision and clean lines more characteristic of Léger's style. In failing to counterbalance the comets with color or another type of object, Léger violated some of his basic design principles aimed at achieving "equilibrium" in his compositions. In Léger's aesthetic theory, color was vitalist, and compositional equilibrium avoided significations of melancholy and death. Why then did he violate his aesthetic practice?

The few critical analyses of the comet paintings understand them as manifesting exceptional expressions of emotion in Léger's work and existential concerns about the nature of life. In 1932, Zervos published the then-untitled comet painting with a caption stating that the panels were inspired by "illustrations from an

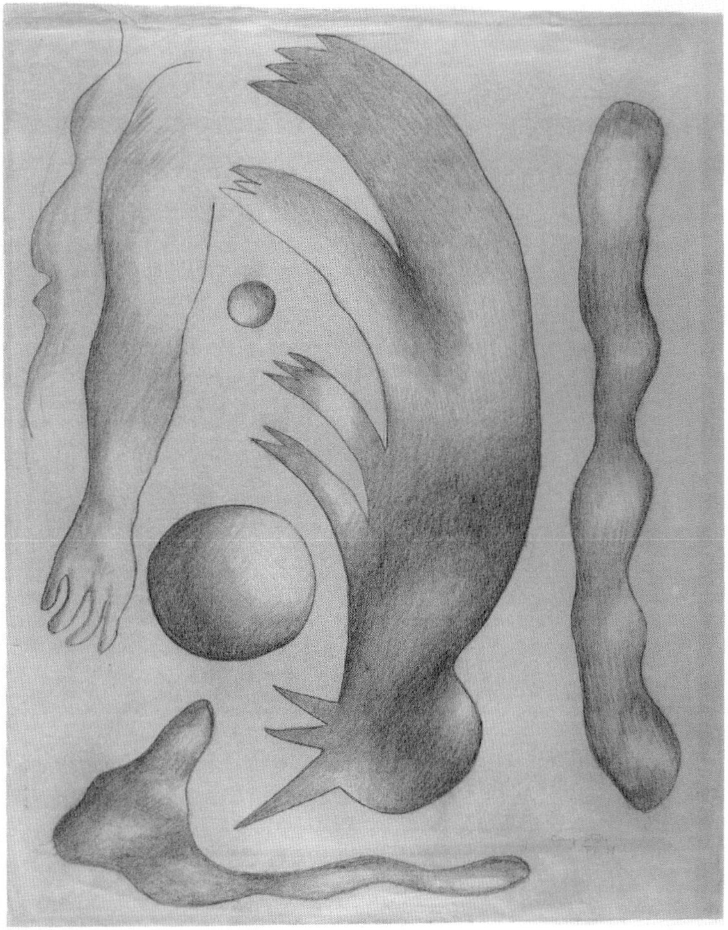

Fig. 45 Fernand Léger, *Composition*, 1931. White chalk and graphite on gray-green paper, 63.2 × 49.5 cm. Musée National d'Art Moderne / Centre Georges Pompidou, Paris, Inv. no. AM1988-613 / Art Resource, New York. © 2024 Artists Rights Society (ARS), New York / ADAGP, Paris.

astronomy book," but the article insists that Léger does not aim to imitate the "morphology" of the object.[100] Léger no longer prioritizes "technical perfection" or craft over "emotion," marking a surprising shift in his aesthetics. Zervos repeatedly describes the new work in terms of emotion and sentiment, interpreting Léger as full of "tenderness and pathos" yet claiming he is still restrained by French instinct. More recently, art historian Arnauld Pierre reads the paintings as informed by an era of astral photography linked to debates about the origins of life, ideas that preoccupied other artists Léger knew: Paul Klee, Arp, and Duchamp.[101] Fréchuret observes that the comet paintings are exceptional in Léger's oeuvre, which was so focused on geometric order and finished surfaces.[102] The comet paintings were a private commission, and their darkness may be accounted for by the particularly disturbing personal moment in Léger's history. They were also created at a time when the macrocosmic and microcosmic as themes in photography and art called into question the certainties of man.[103] In his 1929 book on art, Ozenfant juxtaposed a microphotograph of a diatom (a water algae) and a telescopic photograph of a star cluster in the midst of a text on the acorn as embracing the universe.[104]

Zervos's interpretation of Léger's non-naturalistic imagery as emotive rather than imitative may mean that "comet" had less of a scientific meaning and more of an affective one aligned with the anxieties of the era and the threats of impending war. The year before Léger completed his comet paintings, the filmmaker Abel Gance released *La Fin du monde* (1930), a futuristic tale about a comet on a collision path with the earth. Léger, who had assisted Gance on *La Roue* (1923), also illustrated Cendrars's apocalyptic tale *La Fin du monde filmée par l'ange de Notre Dame* (1919), in which a spectacular planetary explosion is meant to be a warning about the folly of war. In Gance's version, the director plays the protagonist, a French astronomer named Martial, whose warnings of a comet's impending collision go unheeded. Stock market speculation and decadent partying carry on even as natural disasters and the threat of war mount. Ozenfant, too, demonstrated an interest in cosmic formations, astral and planetary studies, and meteor strikes. In 1928, *Cahiers d'Art* published one of Ozenfant's astral paintings, *Heavens* (1927), a banal artwork diagramming the sun, stars, the moon, Saturn, and other planets.[105] In August 1931, when Léger and Ozenfant were teaching together at their Académie Moderne, they shared an interest in cosmic themes. Ozenfant visited Paris's Musée d'histoire naturelle at the Jardin des Plantes, where he learned about the history of disastrous meteorite strikes on earth, which had produced enormous fires and destroyed miles of forest.[106]

Cosmic themes—constellations, meteors, stars, and other motifs—also became common in Surrealist art as signs of nighttime dream states and the unconscious. By rejecting the legible forms that Ozenfant adopted, Léger's amorphous shapes lend themselves to being read in a nonscientific way as emotional signs engaging with the work of Arp and Miró. In the late 1920s, Arp began producing his constellations series, wooden bas-reliefs of ovoid forms painted in white or black. In 1935, Barr characterized this work as exemplifying "the silhouette of the amoeba" and invented the term "biomorphism" to describe the wider phenomenon.[107] By the time of Zervos's 1932 *Cahiers d'Art* article about Léger's "emotional" new work, including gouaches of biomorphic "cows," Léger's art began to show his debt to Arp's forms. Miró, too, incorporated references to stars, moons, and comets, which appear as signs of the night sky and dreamscapes long before he produced his *Constellations* (1940–41) paintings.

After Miró exhibited *Harlequin's Carnival* (1924) (fig. 46) in the first Surrealist exhibition in 1925 and *La Révolution surréaliste* published the image in the first of

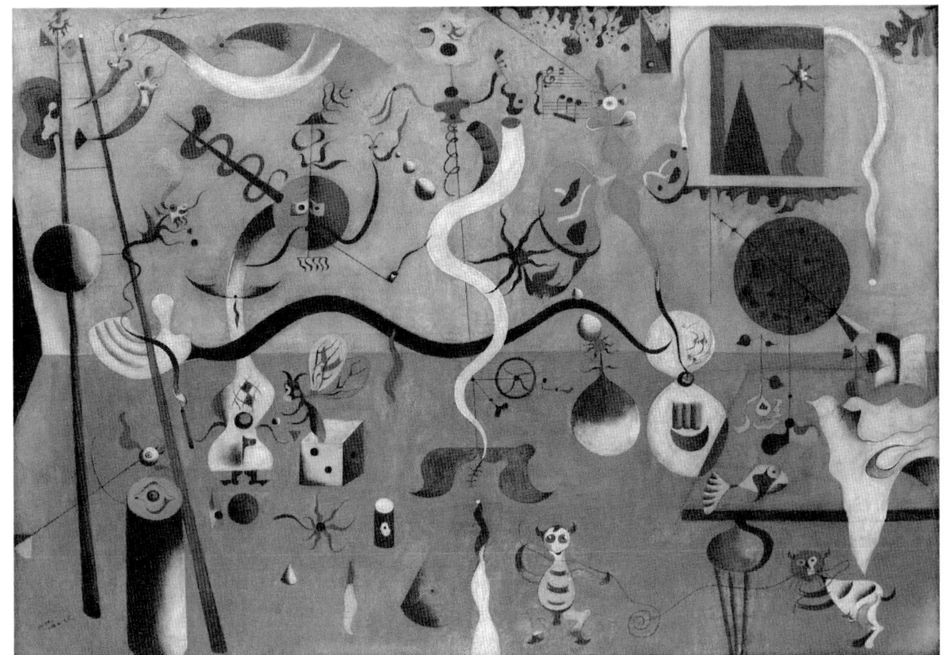

Fig. 46 Joan Miró. *Harlequin's Carnival*, 1924–25. Oil on canvas, 66.04 × 93.027 cm. Room of Contemporary Art Fund, 1940 (RCA1940.8). Buffalo AKG Art Museum / Art Resource, New York. © Successió Miró / Artists Rights Society (ARS), New York / ADAGP, Paris 2024.

December 1926 issue, Léger repeatedly deployed several of Miró's motifs, notably the comet, the ladder, and snaking vertical or horizontal divides.[108] In Miró's *Carnival*, a fork-tailed comet appears at upper left; a ladder missing its lower rungs extends from the painting's lower edge to the comet's terrain; and a vertically positioned, S-shaped wind sock bisects an interior space full of amoebic forms, imaginary animals, musical notes, a guitar, and a window to a night sky. Léger's comet paintings, too, incorporate forked comet tails and snakelike forms. In other work Léger metamorphosed Arp's amoebic forms into clouds and adopted Miró's ladders, both of which become reoccurring motifs in Léger's paintings in the late 1930s and afterward.

While Léger's comets may represent a brief exploration of the cathartic practices of free association, he never acknowledges this kind of investigation. Yet the era's revival of memory may have provoked such associations. Where Léger's comet paintings borrow from Arp's and Miró's forms, it is the limb-like form in the preparatory study that most recalls a celestial sign of nighttime battle imagery. Removed from the final version of the painting, this corporeal fragment suggests a moment of memory retrieval. In September 1931, Léger sketched an almost identical drawing (also with the arm fragment) on the back of a letter to his lover Simone Herman, days before his departure for New York. His letters to her that month convey both a sense that "the machine civilization has perhaps gone too far" and that "catastrophe is in the air."[109] Letters, memoirs, diaries, and novels about World War I often describe the war's battles, typically fought at night, as storms of metallic bits and slaughtered bodies. In one wartime letter, Léger recalled being flung up in the air due to explosions amid the "spectacle" of "slaughter" and a "rain of bullets."[110] In Dorgèles's novel *Wooden Crosses* (1919), one soldier goes out to die in the battlefield "among those broken stones chopped to pieces by the iron storm."[111] And in his diary, Mussolini described battle as a "storm" and "shower" or "rain of shrapnel."[112]

Léger's comets approach the affective release and corporeal disintegration of Masson's imagery, motivated by similar wartime experiences. After exhibiting with Masson in 1925, Léger must have become familiar with Masson's scenes of mythic sacrifice—bodies are torn asunder and limbs flung apart—and perhaps even the massacres series Masson began in 1930 when he shifted alliances from Breton and automatic drawing to Bataille and Dionysic violence. Einstein's article on Masson in *Documents* in 1929 even credits Masson with a painting entitled *Meteors* (1925) in Kahnweiler's Galerie Simon, although no work by that title exists in his catalogue raisonné.[113] But Léger never engages in the kind of automatic drawing or painting that resulted in Masson's oil and sand paintings, such as the *Battle of the Fishes* (1926) or the cathartic violence of the *Massacres* series (1930–34). For Léger, the habits of sublimation and resistance to manifestations of neurasthenia blocked any deeper explorations. While Léger's final comet painting eliminates the recognizable body parts appearing in his preparatory drawing, the theme of amorphous bodies in fragments across the night sky participated in an anxious vision recalling wartime conditions.

Skeletal Flint Rock

Another set of drawings reinforces the evidence that Léger's still life art worked through revived memories of the war. Along with the comet and Arp-like cows, Zervos published two black-ink drawings of flint rock on a yellow ground, another subject of scientific interest whose ambiguous forms fail to resemble the referent, in this case the ocher-colored stone that prehistoric humans first used as tools. In a later version, *Yellow Flint on a Beige Ground* (1932) (fig. 47), two bright yellow flint rocks fill the unmodulated beige ground, sharing the specimen-like display of Léger's holly leaf paintings. But Léger's flint forms are not prehistoric arrowhead tools, which might have suggested interest in the origins and antiquity of art and culture. Although the arc-shaped indentations and irregular surface share some features of the quarried rock, Léger's rocks possess curious digit-like projections and odd circular and oval holes that resemble eye sockets or bullet holes.

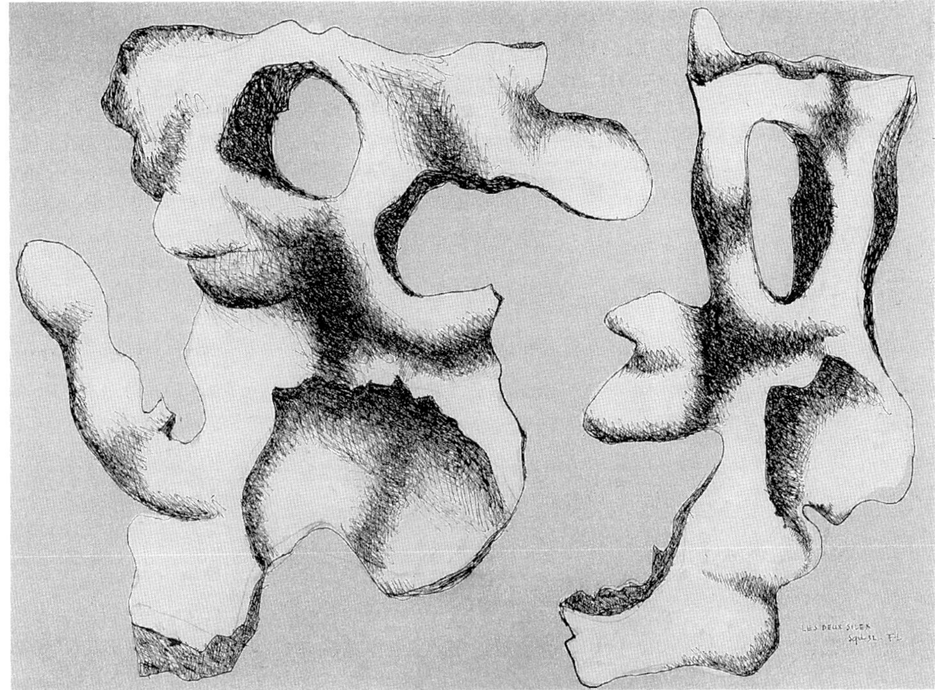

Fig. 47 Fernand Léger, *Yellow Flint on a Beige Ground*, 1932. Ink and gouache, 49 × 67 cm. © Musée(s) de Belfort–Donation Maurice Jardot. © 2024 Artists Rights Society (ARS), New York / ADAGP, Paris.

Léger's flint rock drawings and paintings emerge during a period of archaeological and anthropological discoveries, yet the forms conjure skeletal remains. Léger was familiar with the natural history museums in Paris and New York and their collections of prehistoric rocks and bones. *Cahiers d'Art* and *Documents* published regularly on prehistoric artistic discoveries such as those by archaeologist Leo Frobenius.[114] As art historian Guitemie Maldonado has argued, interwar biomorphism was both a reaction to the past war and a premonition of disaster to come. Many interwar artists collected natural objects (pebbles, stones, bones, shells) to study form and, in doing so, consider questions about the *longue durée* of temporal destructions and transformations.[115] During the period Léger and Ozenfant taught together, Ozenfant went to Paris's Jardin des Plantes and its natural history museum, whose collection he describes in his memoirs: its fossilized skeletons, the prehistoric Menton Man's "ocher" skeleton, Paleolithic objects, fossil imprints, shark bones, meteorites, and geological and mineralogical displays.[116] Several years later, Léger wrote about filling an album with drawings after visiting the Natural History Museum in New York.[117] Léger's "flint rock" titles invite comparison to the geological displays and contemporary inquiry into the origins of human artistic production. But the ambiguous forms and their yellow color may have been modeled on the fossilized skeletons. Such contradictions between the title and the image in *Yellow Flint* blur the distinctions between the rock and the fossilized skeleton, perhaps intentionally aiming to confuse the viewer.

Léger's curious rocks produce disturbing "associations," to use Zervos's term. Of the two "flint rocks," the one at right has a kind of "macchabean grimace" (referencing an Old Testament martyrdom) that Léger had seen among the war's corpses.[118] The holes appearing in the skull-like "rocks" recall alternatively the bullet holes that marked the many soldiers' skeletons littering the contested battle terrains and the trephanned skull, an ancient surgical practice still in use during the war that required a burr hole in the skull. Ozenfant's drawing of a prehistoric trephanned skull, published in his book *Art* (1928), had recently displayed the practice.[119] Two peers in Léger's intellectual milieu, Apollinaire and Braque, had undergone trephination during the war, a memory that could have been revived by the era's imagery and anxieties. Like the comets, Léger's flint rocks are ambiguous forms converging origins and end times and recalling the marks of violence suffered by a once-living body.

That Léger deliberately aimed for ambiguity rather than referentiality is consistent with his thinking about the close-up. Film historian Mary Ann Doane argues that the close-up functions as a kind of "semiotic threat" because it disfigures, makes monstrous, and provides an array of metaphorical possibilities contingent upon the instability and uncertainty of meaning.[120] This characterization of the close-up resonates with the writing of Léger's contemporaries. Eisenstein, who Léger corresponded with and met in 1930 at Congrès du cinéma in Brussels, praised Léger's *Ballet mécanique* for its "psychic side" and "its manipulation of the unconscious."[121] In 1932, curator Sweeney cited Eisenstein's praise of Léger and his understanding of film in terms of contrast and rhythm.[122] Eisenstein had also been the subject of numerous articles in *Variétés*, *Cahiers d'Art*, and other French art journals. He wrote that the close-up of a cockroach was more threatening than a medium-long shot of one hundred elephants.[123] Equally important is Epstein's notion of "magnification" as a way to capture the attention of the distracted viewer. A position somewhere between stasis and "cinematic vivacity," the close-up, Epstein writes, transforms the face into something like the topography of the sky or the sea, a fruit sliced open, or a body slit by a scalpel.[124] Epstein, too, had written about the Impressionist film idea of *photogénie*, an elusive concept developed by Delluc and linked to cinematic poetics, such as magnification and defamiliarizing the familiar.[125] For Eisenstein and Epstein, violence and aggression mark the close-up's magnification and capacity for distortion and defamiliarization.

Léger's interest in the close-up was not simply to valorize the insignificant object but also, like Eisenstein and Epstein, to disturb and confuse the viewer. In his *Ballet mécanique* essay, he cites an example in which the apparent "subject" of a film that the viewer thinks they see—an astronomy image of a planet—is in fact a woman's fingernail magnified "a hundredfold."[126] In 1935, he returns to the same example to explain his idea of a "new reality" through photography's capacity for magnification and abstraction: "I could photograph the fingernail of a modern woman . . . enlarge it a hundredfold, and tell one person, see this is a fragment of a planet in evolution. To another: it is an abstract form."[127] Given his aim of abstraction, Léger's comets, cows, and flint rock may not be what they purport to be but instead distortions that deceive the viewer. In his writing Léger envisions a situation where he retains mastery over the signification process, and the doubled image is a trick he imposes upon the viewer rather than a process like Surrealism's automatic techniques, whose forms are meant to emerge from the unconscious. But it may be that in his pictorial explorations of formal distortions and resignifications, Léger unintentionally disturbed or revived buried memories and emotions in his own unconscious.

Although the comet paintings and flint rock drawings are anomalous in Léger's oeuvre, they inform Léger's development of a new iconography of amoebic clouds, ghostly shadows, and amorphous background shapes that persist late into his career. Signs of corporeal dissolution and indeterminate states, these Surrealist forms operate in Léger's art as psychic threats to be overcome or counterbalanced by competing objects. At first, in *Composition with Two Figures* (1929) and *Dancers with Keys* (1930), Léger's blurred, dissolving forms serve as shadowy backgrounds for floating dancers, architectural plans, and geometric forms that signify the healthy body and the rational mind. In *Mona Lisa with Keys*, the orange ground marked by dark shadows establishes an indeterminate nonspace or background before which elements of Constructivist design compete with displaced signs of war memories. By 1932, the architectural and Constructivist forms have all but disappeared from Léger's oeuvre, replaced by the ladder in Léger's acrobat paintings, including *Composition with Three Figures* (1932), *Marie the Acrobat* (1934), *Sport: Physical Culture Room* (1935), *Adam and Eve* (1935–39), and *Composition with Two Parrots* (1935–39) (fig. 48). In the background, behind the athletes and acrobats and their oddly disjointed, collapsing ladders, their flaccid rope, and deflated drapery, dark organic shapes with bulbous knobby elements appear highlighted in white. These amoebic clouds informed by the photogram's spectral aesthetics suggest an afterlife to Léger's portentous comets.

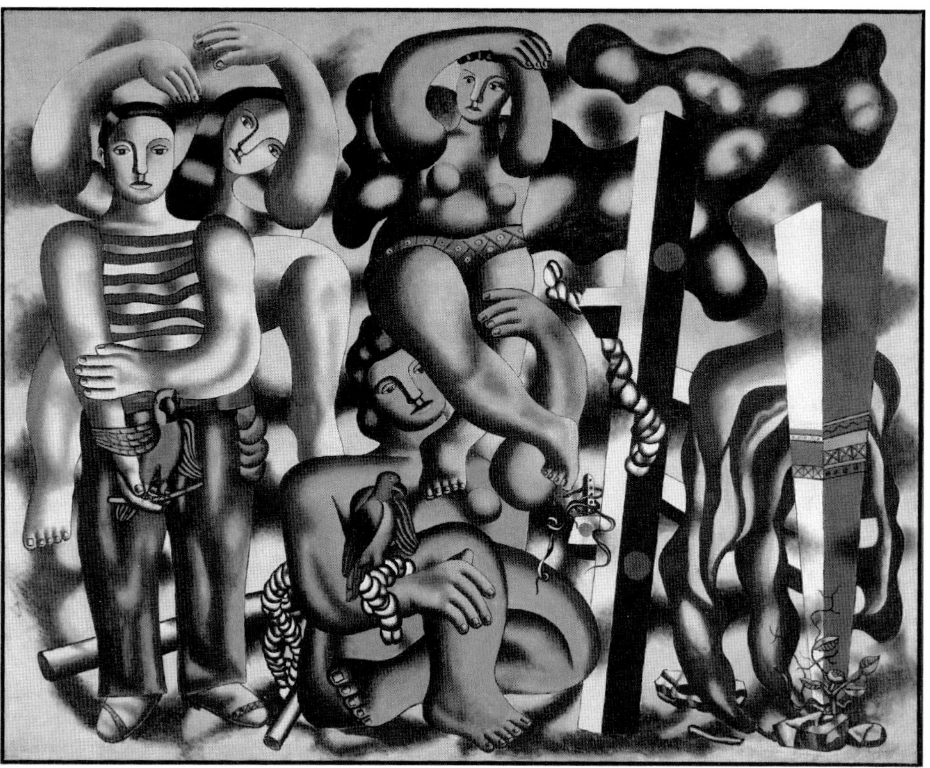

Fig. 48 Fernand Léger, *Composition with Two Parrots*, 1935–39. Oil on canvas, 400 × 480 cm. Photo: Jacques Faujour. Musée National d'Art Moderne / Centre Georges Pompidou, Paris. Digital Image © CNAC/MNAM, Dist. RMN-Grand Palais / Art Resource, New York. © 2024 Artists Rights Society (ARS), New York / ADAGP, Paris.

"We Have Returned to a Wild State"

Where the comets and flint rock enact corporeal dissolutions and betray the traces of violence, slaughter becomes explicit in a set of ink drawings of quarters of beef, also published in *Cahiers d'Art*.[128] In these, Léger brings into view the butchered body, a displaced sign of the soldier's body. The beef drawings return to the theme that preoccupied Léger in his *paysages animés* paintings, particularly *The Cattle Merchant* (fig. 32). In *Ladder, Steps, Roots, and Quarter of Beef* (1932) (fig. 49), for example, Léger no longer anthropomorphizes the living animal whose gaze draws in the viewer. Instead, his ink drawing works to sanitize and cleanse the process of butchery, expressing contradictory desires to remember and transcend death. With the ink drawings of slabs of beef or lamb, Léger sets aside the ambiguous form of the comet to return to the technical precision and clarity that Zervos praised as characteristic of his work.

Léger's drawings of beef betray an ambivalent relationship to slaughter, at once visualizing signs of the slaughtered body while also purifying it of blood and decontextualizing it from the sites of slaughter. Some of the pen-and-ink drawings present geometricized and isolated slabs of meat, while others, such as *Ladder, Steps, Roots, and Quarter of Beef*, create an enigmatic scene bringing together beef with a ladder and a hollowed-out tree stump. The drawing is divided into two parts by a snaking vertical root or limb, returning Léger to his compositional practice of contrasting forms. On the left are two overlapping ladders that bring together two perspectival positions: a rung ladder hanging vertically and parallel to the picture plane and a wide planked ladder whose triangular steps suggest linear recession but that also conjoins with the rung ladder on the bottom step. The ladders lean against a Y-shaped tree trunk that is, however, neither rooted nor grounded. At right is the "quarter of beef," an almost rectangular form divided vertically into three parts and horizontally into wide rows of ribs. Perhaps informed by Miró's "ladder of escape" to a transcendent or dream realm, Léger's ladder can trace its lineage to his prewar *escalier* motif and his wartime incorporation of the stepped shoulders and faces of his *Card Party* soldiers. The compositional elements are corporeal and narrative fragments: a tree trunk severed from its base and roots and cropped of its fruited limbs, ladders that go nowhere, and the ribs of an animal "drawn" and quartered. These motifs—the roots, tree trunks, ladders, and branches of fruit trees—appear repeatedly in other drawings and paintings from the 1930s. While some art historians see the motifs of ladders and tree roots as informed by Léger's rural vacations, the array of objects assembles, I propose, an iconography indexical of war and death: beef recalling the body of the soldier, barren tree fragments reminiscent of the brutalized terrain of no-man's-land, and the ladder leading out of the trench to the site of death.

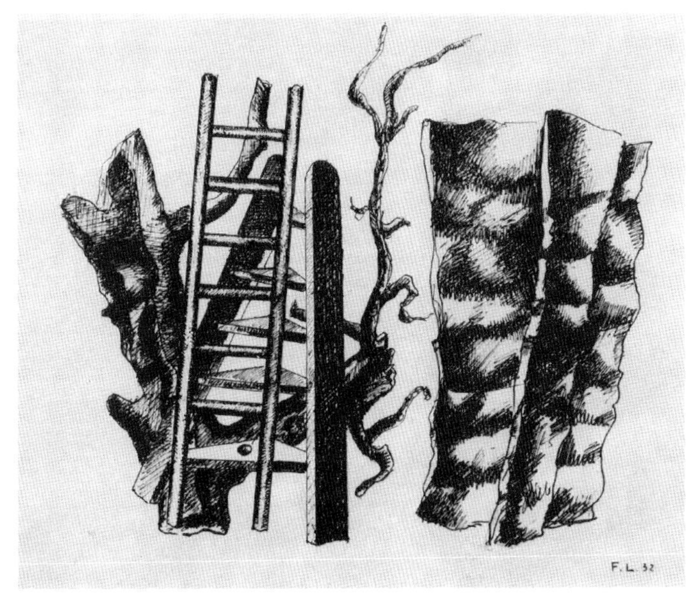

Fig. 49 Fernand Léger, *Ladder, Steps, Roots, and Quarter of Beef*, 1932. Ink drawing, 31.5 × 39 cm. In Jean Leymarie and Jean Cassou, *Fernand Léger, dessins et gouaches* (Paris: Editions du Chêne, 1972), fig. 176. Private collection, Paris. © 2024 Artists Rights Society (ARS), New York / ADAGP, Paris.

Léger's drawings of racks of beef, hung vertically like a butcher shop display, emerged just as the abattoirs of Paris's Les Halles became a reoccurring theme in urban architecture and photography. In 1928, *Variétés* published photographs by Krull and Moholy-Nagy of the butcher shops and sewers of Les Halles.[129] Eli Lotar, the cinematographer for director Jean Painlevé's undersea film *Caprelles et Pantopodes* (1930), which Léger praised, was also a successful photographer whose slaughterhouse images were widely published between 1929 and 1931, first in *Documents*, then in *Variétés* and *VU*.[130] Lotar's series calls attention to the brutal process of butchery in images of a living ox being lowered into the abattoir, the flaying of the animal, a severed ox head, rows of ox shins, and floors covered in looping strokes of blood that trace the dragging of the animal carcass across the floor. Léger's drawings, by contrast, purify form. They function like Purist still lifes, which, as Ozenfant wrote, aimed to cleanse and classicize: "to reject Rembrandt's perishable beef."[131]

In Léger's essay "La Rue, l'objets, spectacles" (1928), the butchery again revives memories of war but blocks explicit expressions of mourning. In *L'Intransigeant* in February 1929, Léger nostalgically and melancholically described a militarized display of legs of lamb as a screen that disrupts access to a lost era: "The beautiful pharmacies on boulevard Sebastopol, the horse butchers on the rue de la Roquette, and, blocked by all that, reduced, absorbed, the good little old 1880 shop, moved one to tears, hidden in the shadow of a hundred legs of lamb aligned militarily by order of size, like a parade."[132] Here, the "hundred legs of lamb aligned militarily by order of size" convey the collectivity, nationalism, mass discipline, and rank of a modern army. These slaughtered masses obscure the prewar Belle Epoque–era "little old 1880 shop." The "parade" of butchered legs recalls and displaces signs of Armistice Day military parades of soldiers and disabled veterans. While it is unclear what the "good old little 1880 shop" was selling, it was a *magasin* (shop) not a *boucherie* (butcher) and was "blocked by all that"—the pharmacies, the horse butchers, and the legs of lamb.

For Léger, born in 1881, the nostalgia for the 1880 shop could signify an association with friends and generational peers who were mobilized in 1914 or who volunteered for the war, as did Apollinaire (born in 1880), the Polish-born poet and art critic who died due to the Spanish flu. When Léger published the essay on February 25, 1929, it was only a few months after the tenth anniversary of the Armistice in November 1928, giving more immediacy to the visual comparisons to military order and parades. The Armistice commemorations did indeed revive war memories for Léger. In the story of the 1880 shop blocked by a militarist parade of butchered lamb legs, Léger reprises the route he could have taken to attend Apollinaire's funeral on November 13, 1918, two days after Armistice. The street of horse butchers that Léger recalls, rue de la Roquette, leads from the Place de la Bastille to the Père Lachaise cemetery, where Apollinaire is buried, a likely route that he and Cendrars would have followed. As Cendrars recalled in his memoirs, he and Léger were cut off from the funeral procession by a group of revelers celebrating the Armistice.[133] The contradictory moods—of mourning and celebration—and the sense of being blocked both reemerge in Léger's story, reviving emotions he must have felt a decade before.

In a striking betrayal of Purist logic, Léger's verbal and textual characterizations of beef and butcheries conjure up the spectacle of a dance of death antithetical to the

Dalcrozian dance of physical culture. When Sweeney first met Léger in the spring of 1930, the encounter turned into a dinner with Einstein, the Russian theater director Vsevolod Meyerhold, and their wives and then ended at Les Halles at 6:00 A.M. Léger, whom Sweeney described as a Norman countryman accustomed to the taste of "rare beef and Calvados," claimed he wanted to create a "Ballet des Boeufs." In a moment of gallows humor, Léger told them: "What a magnificent stage set for a ballet the hanging beef carcasses in the butcher sheds would make."[134] Again, in 1931, after his first trip to New York, Léger conflated slaughter and dance, writing that the sight of "plucked chickens, suspended against the light, presented against a black background . . . a *danse macabre*."[135] The *danse macabre* was an image of skeletal figures dancing with the living that first emerged during the Hundred Years' War in France (1337–1453). Léger's imagined Ballet des Boeufs and *danse macabre* invert the machine aesthetic suppression of the display of death, exemplified by the rhythmic pendular swinging of the rows of mass-produced commodities in the *Ballet mécanique*. Léger's ballet of butchered animals also imagines a motif that would have run counter to the salubrious dancing female nudes of his still life paintings. His proposed Ballet des Boeufs was, however, never staged, undoubtedly because to do so would have returned Léger to the war's horrors. But invoking such a "ballet" swings the pendulum back from the body as machine to the body as "meat," which is how Léger wrote about Verdun. The Verdun battlefield was a "mix of rotten meat and mud"—that is, decaying human flesh mixed with the rain-soaked land where infantry had to dig new trenches and where Léger once had to live for six days.[136]

Paradoxically, the body's bestial display as beef also makes it a sign of abundance and an object of primal desire. Léger's machine aesthetic–era observation that even the shin of an ox became valuable points not only to a commodification of all parts of the animal but also to postwar food scarcity. Again, in 1933, Léger described a period of want and hunger in terms that returned him to the wartime life of the savage and embattled forests. Léger wrote to his lover Herman characterizing his survival as a regression to the wild, the hunt, and the forest, and as a nighttime battle among artists: "[We have] returned to a wild state of hunt—one hunts in the brush of the virgin forest with the unknown blackness around us, little light, finally beginning to see in the night like wolves—the battle between us—looking and listening. Those who fall are buried in the virgin forest . . . all the men I know who have entered into this battle have changed physically—all are thinner—Picabia, Brancusi—I too have lost weight."[137] The dark forest of want signals an economic climate of slow or no sales, one that destroys "those who fall," while those who remain standing (Picabia, Brancusi, Léger) are weakened from hunger. Just as the immediate postwar crisis in artistic value had troubled Léger a decade earlier, the new economic conditions returned him to a primal state of death or survival.

In this era of economic want and hunger, Léger also wrote a letter to Herman enigmatically explaining his drawings as a violent destruction of the metallic and a scene of slaughter: "new and bitter . . . very fine drawings in the genre of Dürer, hard locks, exploding all that because of you—even wicked—they are wicked—I attacked a butchery—I have elements of 'beef' and quarters of meat—all that mixed with ladders, compasses, rope, saw, and all—you are the queen of all these objects my dear the queen who dominates and presides over their birth . . . very sadly, melancholically, tenderly yours."[138] Léger's fantasy envisions an emotional release in which sadism, intimacy, and sublimation are linked. A "wicked" desire motivates metaphors of assault and slaughter ("hard locks, exploding all that"; "I attacked a butchery") followed by an exhausted presentation of gifts (meat, ladder, the drawings), an idealization of the desired ("you are the queen"), and a residue of melancholy. The explosion of "hard locks," like the holly leaf's destruction of the *femme-machine*, violently ends the machine aesthetic era and its regulation of affect. Emotion is released to Herman and through new signs grouped together in ways that no longer serve Purist ideals. The Constructivist signifier (the compass) and building tools (lock, ladder, saw) fail to participate in envisioning utopian futures or, at best, are inadequate for modernist architectural orders.

Yet, despite Léger's discursive release of affect and pictorial trade in the signs of corporeality, its dissolution, and the spectacle of mass slaughter, he is unable to mourn the lost body. Léger's bitter, wicked, and illicit desire hungers for a murdered body that is unavailable to representation. The collection of objects intimates a missing body: a builder, a butcher, a farmer, a lover, or a corpse. Blocked, too, is the process of destruction or slaughter that Lotar depicts. The "ladders, compasses, rope, saw, and all," whose pictorial counterpart could be *Ladder, Steps, Roots, and Quarter of Beef*, enact an incomplete scenario telegraphing what could be a sanitized scene of slaughter. Although blocking from view the horrors of slaughter in Lotar's photography, Léger nevertheless grapples with its visual fragments.

Conclusion

When Léger returns to representing the male body during the Popular Front era, some of his most important works, like *Composition with Two Parrots* (1935–39), bring together the motifs he developed throughout the late 1920s and early 1930s, showing that Léger's thinking about the human body as an object was also bound up with the object as a sign of loss. Protected by the arced arms of a dancing female figure behind him and two darker women at center, the resurrected male is an expressionless acrobat or circus performer whose limbs are as pale, gray, and shadowy as the comets. Like the black-and-white photograph of a dead son whose memory is protected by living women, the monochromatic male body has perhaps only "sentimental value" and serves as a mediating form between the living viewer and lost referent. His world is populated by the new iconography of Léger's still life era: dancing women, a strange ladder whose posts tilt awkwardly and rearrange linear perspective, limp garments, bits of rock that are the only "ground," intestinal rope, an indeterminate background with shadowy forms, and photogram-inspired dark amoebic clouds with bulbous white highlights. The male figure and his three female dancer-acrobat companions are all positioned in the foreground parallel to the picture plane. They are situated in a shallow space that is no longer a shop window to view commodities or the scientific display case for naturalia. In turning to a scene of circus acrobats, work Léger described as life threatening, Léger may have been constituting not a scene of entertainers but an allegory about artistic risk.[139]

Léger's abandonment of the mass-produced commodity and machine aesthetic betrays a lost faith in the postwar economic recovery and the failure of Purism's constant combat with neurasthenia and death in the face of Surrealism's challenge and the visibility of male ruination. Léger's turn to Freudian symbolism, exemplified by his key paintings and drawings for *Variétés*, demonstrates self-conscious efforts at mastering the signs of the unconscious that Bretonian Surrealists turned to for hallucinatory poetics. Yet, because Léger's found-object drawings were published with stories about the desperate and photography of public alcoholics and ragpickers, their compensatory signification was undermined. Revived memories of war and the visibility of "fallen humanity" must have disturbed Léger's psyche or "equilibrium." His attention to the spectral aesthetics of the photogram and the biomorphic forms of Miró and Arp engage with the dissolution of corporeality and are the most potent signs of anxiety and threat. These signs motivated his promoters—Einstein, Ozenfant, Zervos, Tériade, Waldemar George—to reinforce Léger's public persona as a phallic figure for whom the unconscious signified "nothingness." Yet Léger's writing to his lover reveals at least the private release of affect and an expression of melancholy bound up with the destruction of the mechanical and the display of the slaughtered body. While Léger's new monumental paintings of acrobats and circus figures reclaim a compositional and psychic balance between threatening elements and survival, they nevertheless evidence a new consciousness about corporeal risk.

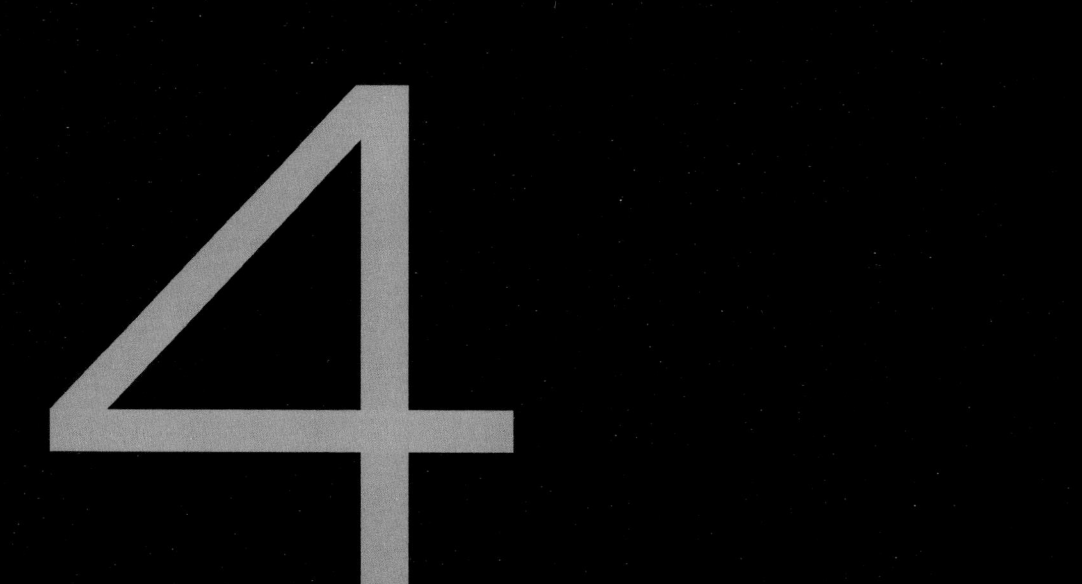

Deterritorialization and Dissociation

Two acrobats in yellow and pink suits take the light. . . . Without a [safety] line, it is a major attraction. . . . Three perilous somersaults in space . . . applause . . . the end of a mass anxiety . . . the acrobat welcomes the applause, waving politely while standing on his fragile trapeze that gently rocks like a ship on water. . . . We live in space more than ever, one pushes all sides in order to evade and leave the constraints of the ground, a competition establishes between flight from the solid and concrete; a nervous mobility takes hold of the world. . . . Our modern space no longer has limits but is a domain of unlimited action. We plunge into it, we live in it, we must survive in it. A dangerous life, the acrobats' protective net has disappeared; it is the life of prey before the rifle.

—LÉGER, "LE CIRQUE" (1949)

Written in 1949 about his long-standing motif of acrobats, Léger's statement adopts a philosophy of artistic risk, instability, and anxiety. In his terms, the acrobatic couple represents a collective state of being, and their perilous movements provoke "mass anxiety" in the spectator. The aerial space of the circus acrobat is also a watery space where the trapeze "rocks like a ship on water," and "we plunge" into "space," which offers flight, freedom, "nervous mobility," and the "life of prey before the rifle," a constant threat of violent death. The pre–World War II acrobats, *Composition with Two Parrots*, with their iconography of losses, prepared the way for a new wartime figure of "mass anxiety": the diver. By the 1940s, the ontological state of Léger's acrobats and divers represents, I propose, a new kind of war trauma, that of national collapse, flight, and exile.

Motivated by the German invasion of France in June 1940 and exile in the United States from 1940 to 1945, Léger transformed his acrobats into a series entitled *Plongeurs* (Divers) (1941–45). Léger announced the new motif in a number of wartime exhibitions, starting with the *Artists in Exile* group show in March 1942 in New York. Two years later, Léger had a solo exhibition at the Jacques Seligmann Gallery accompanied by a brochure explaining the *plongeurs* series' origins "in the fateful summer of 1940" when Léger was in Marseille awaiting "formalities" (probably transit visas) to leave France. There, he observed "the crowds on the beach and in the water" that later inspired the *plongeurs* series.[1] A longer narrative of Léger's Marseille experience does not fully emerge until after the war in a 1953 interview, raising questions not so much about authenticity, truth, or literality but about the function of linking the *plongeurs* images to the traumatic fall of France and Léger's wartime exile in the United States.[2]

Like Léger's 1919 origin story for his machine aesthetic, the Marseille story is a war story produced in multiple iterations and bound up with experiences of fear, the threat of death, and survival. It is an account full of gaps and omissions marking the psychic operations of memory and forgetting, a story often in contradiction with the art it is ostensibly meant to explain. The modernist visual language of the *plongeurs* series—its refusal of a familiar iconography, its geographic and spatial indeterminacy—undermine narration while lending itself to the dissociation of traumatic memory. Like *The Card Party*, the *plongeurs* paintings can be read in terms of multiple overlapping and competing temporalities and spatialities, this time registering the affective dynamics of the exilic status. For Léger during the 1940s, Marseille and New York were liminal spaces of uncertainty and waiting. Marseille was a site of departure from the Nazi invasion and war to safety; New York and the United States became spaces of contingent freedoms, sites where expatriates like Léger anticipated the war's possible outcomes and alternative futures. As I will show, the perspectival multiplicities that occurred in *The Card Party* reoccur in the *plongeurs* series. Even fewer signifiers of place help locate the viewer, rendering temporality even more disoriented.

With the *plongeurs* series, Léger seems to have been "possessed by an image or event," which Caruth characterizes as symptomatic of trauma.[3] In Ricoeur's analysis, the "memory-image" is bound up in the dialectic of remembering, forgetting, and representation, a dialectic that complicates contemporary debates about three types of Freudian "memory-traces": as a documentation or signifier, a psychical impression, or a neuroscientific cerebral trace.[4] As a "memory-image" or signifier of his Marseille experience, Léger's *plongeurs* are a malleable and indeterminate modernist form, contingent upon an event not fully assimilated or narrated—that is, the traumatic separation from the homeland. The images are dissociative at the individual, collective, and national level and suggest a history that is no longer "straightforwardly referential" but, as Caruth has argued, is formed "in the nature of a traumatic departure" and linked to a cyclical process of departure, forgetting, and return.[5]

Léger and his contemporaries understood or interpreted the series as responding to a wide range of sources, often traumatic scenes of social disruption that Léger abstracted. These sources are as diverse as Poussin's *Rape of the Sabine Women* (1637), Michelangelo's Sistine Chapel frescoes, and flood iconography familiar to Léger from the folkloric *images d'Epinal* prints and medieval manuscripts. Yet, despite Léger's repeated turn to traumatic scenes, he uses modernist abstraction to eliminate narrative's referential time and place, a process that can be understood as effecting a dissociation or splitting of the psyche as a defense against shock. Caruth and psychiatrist Bessel van der Kolk have foregrounded the distinction between narrative memory and traumatic memory made by Janet in his work on dissociation, which Janet characterized as an inability more than a refusal to narrate.[6] The traumatic experience destroys mental associations and accounts for amnesia and disconnections in the narration of the event. In Léger's case, that is, and in the context of exile and the traumatic loss of nation, the genres of history painting and portraiture were blocked or inadequate or antithetical to Léger's modernist aesthetics. Instead, his aesthetics serve the dissociated or traumatic memory that the *plongeurs* register.

The *Plongeurs* Images

The *plongeurs* motif is an iconographic innovation that borrows formal elements of Léger's circus imagery only to work through conditions of even greater possibility, danger, and the threat of death. The series includes more than twenty paintings and as many drawings depicting a mass of swimmers in an indeterminate space. The *plongeurs'* often androgynous nudes are a dispersed collective that provides none of the fraternal camaraderie and "resilience" imagined in *The Card Party* (1917) and *The Three Comrades* (1919). Nor are Léger's *plongeurs* engaged in utopic leisure or generative life despite the formal similarities Ozenfant claimed to his painting *The Beautiful Life* (1929).[7] A novel motif displacing more familiar modernist types such as the female nude or the bather, Léger's *plongeurs* are bodies whose scattered movements in an ungrounded space fail to serve the landscape genre. These figures share no common cause, and their competing gazes have no unified vision. I argue that the series suggests a working through of the status of the collective during a period of historical trauma and personal survival. The transformations in the compositions develop ideas about the gendered and racialized body, dynamic movement, and collective relations.

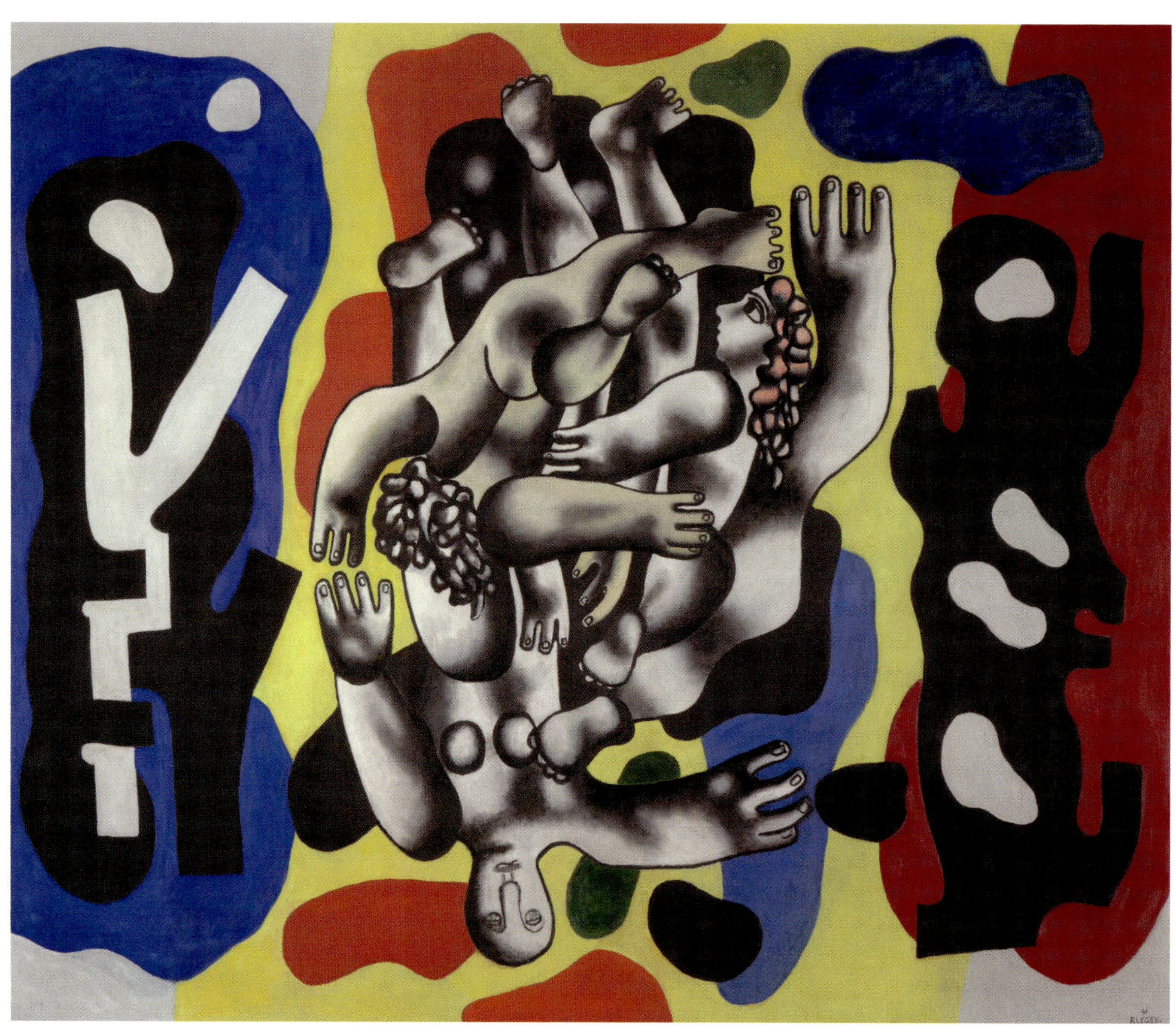

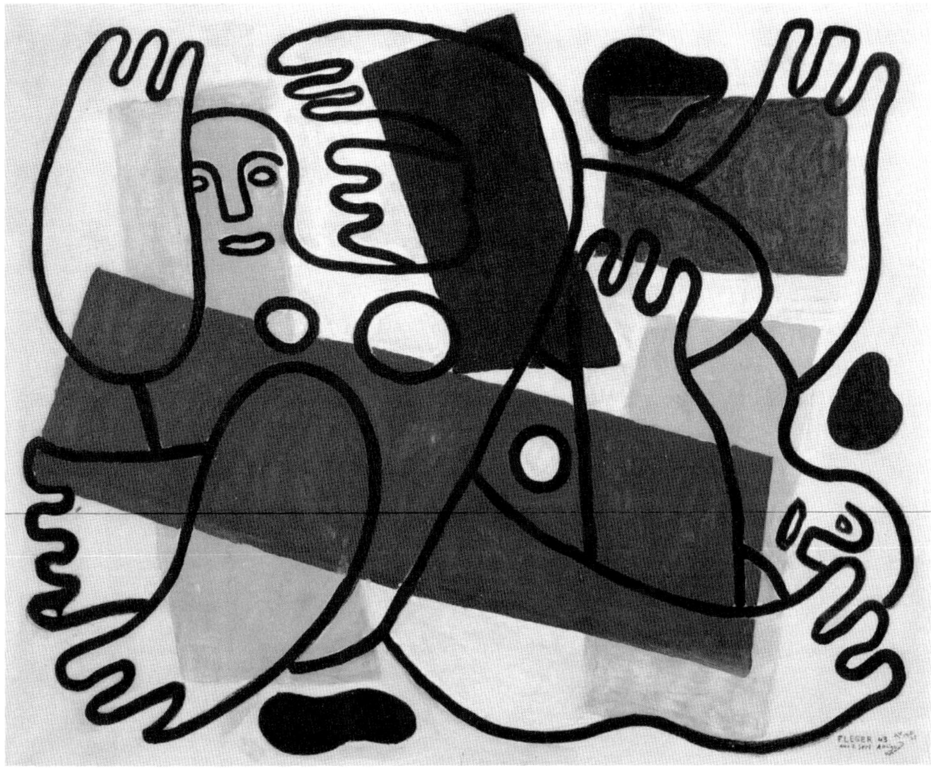

Fig. 50 | opposite Fernand Léger, *Divers on a Yellow Ground*, 1941. Oil on canvas, 186.7 × 217.8 cm. Gift of Mr. and Mrs. Maurice E. Culberg (1953.176). Art Institute of Chicago, Chicago / Art Resource, New York. © 2024 Artists Rights Society (ARS), New York / ADAGP, Paris.

Fig. 51 Fernand Léger, *The Divers*, 1943. Oil on canvas, 88.9 × 106.68 cm. Harvard Art Museums / Fogg Museum, Gift of Mr. and Mrs. Josep Lluís Sert, Inv. no. 1964.60. © Harvard Art Museums / Art Resource, New York. © 2024 Artists Rights Society (ARS), New York / ADAGP, Paris.

Three broad categories of the divers paintings—those with colorless figures, those with outlined bodies, and those Léger called polychrome *plongeurs*—mark Léger's process of working through the fall of the nation and its potential redemption through racialized colors (black, brown, yellow) implicating the colonial subject. The earliest painting, *Divers on a Yellow Ground* (1941) (fig. 50), establishes the figural and spatial paradigms repeated throughout the series—notably, a trio of floating monochromatic nudes, one of which is bald and hangs upside down. In a second stage, exemplified by Harvard University's *The Divers* (1943) (fig. 51), Léger dematerializes the group of *plongeurs* by transforming them into outlined bodies with simplified paper doll–like limbs and shared body parts. Strips of red, yellow, blue, and green seem to pass through the figures, conveying both lightness and a transparent fragility. Finally, in the third stage, *Big Black Divers* (1944) (fig. 52), the bodies are represented as solid planes of unmodulated brown, black, blue, and yellow, suggesting a regenerative primitivism and the racial categories of the French empire. In this stage, a centrally positioned and upright brown body reverses the upside-down figure in *Divers on a Yellow Ground*, offering a sense of gravity that contrasts with the

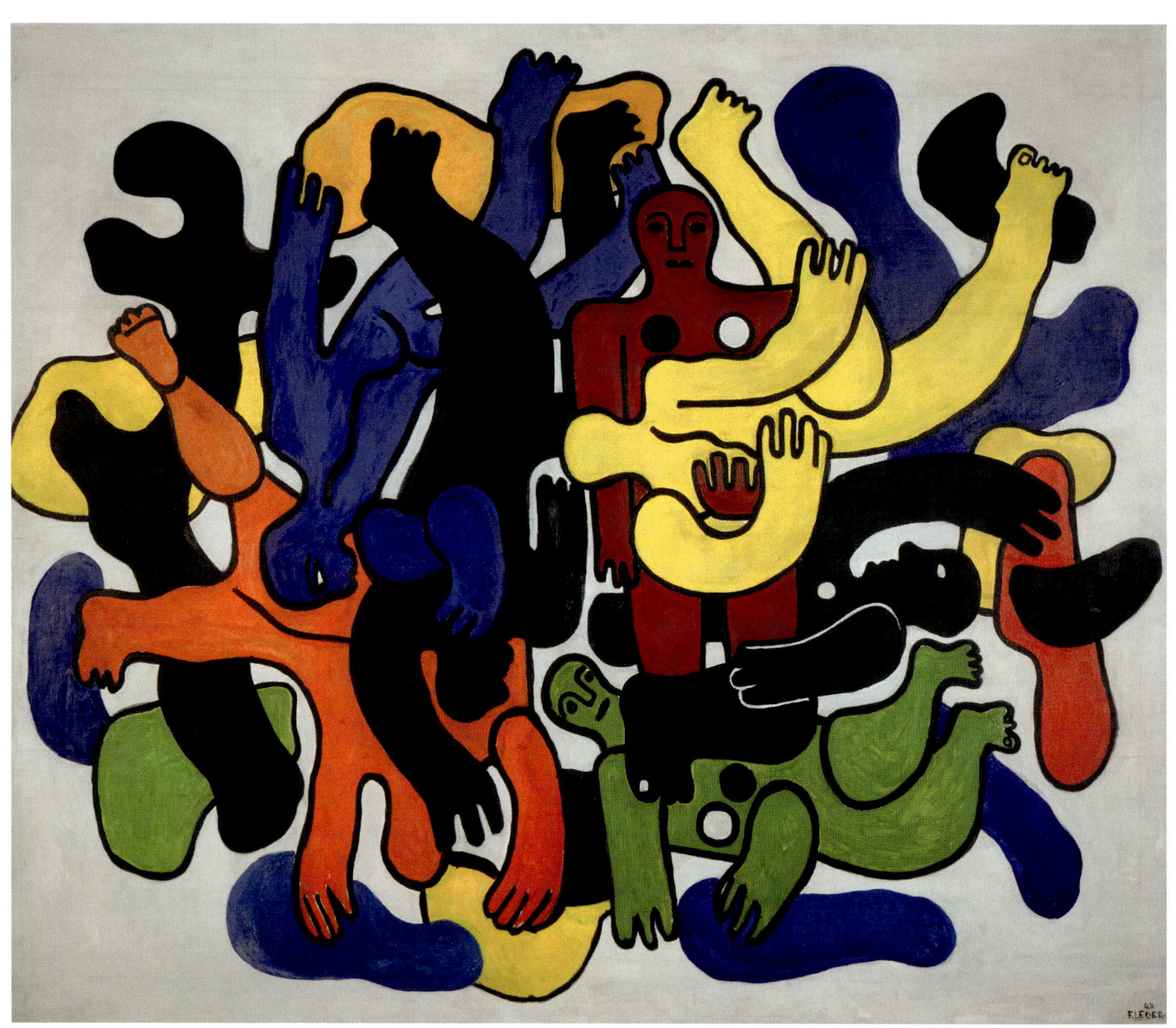

other *plongeurs* paintings. Just as *The Card Party* served as Léger's vehicle for grappling with his experience of the war, so, too, the *plongeurs* pictures work through new historical traumas at the national, collective, and individual levels: France's invasion, a new artistic dispersal, and Léger's exile.

In *Divers on a Yellow Ground*, Léger establishes the corporeal relations of social dispersion and alienation, marking a key theme of the series that resonates with the national collapse in 1940. The figures, indifferent or oblivious to each other, look not to one another but instead gaze upward or outward toward the viewer. A group of female nudes with heavy bodies cluster in the center of the canvas and swim, float, sink, fly, or fall above a scattering of unmodulated amoeba-shaped planes of red, blue, green, and black. Léger's use of monochromatic bodies revives ideas about war as the absence of color as well as the mediating role of black-and-white photography and film. By contrast to his interwar acrobat paintings with their ladders and bits of rock, *Divers on a Yellow Ground* fails to provide any referential earth or sky to establish a gravitational orientation for the viewer or the divers, effecting the kind of *dépaysement* previously identified with Surrealist practice. This *dépaysement*, along with a modernist rejection of long-standing Renaissance pictorial conventions for reading the canvas, has resulted in occasional erroneous reproductions rotating the painting 180 degrees.

Fig. 52 Fernand Léger, *Big Black Divers*, 1944. Oil on canvas, 186 × 221 cm. Photo: Jacques Faujour. Musée National d'Art Moderne / Centre Georges Pompidou, Paris, AM1982–102. Digital Image © CNAC/MNAM, Dist. RMN-Grand Palais / Art Resource, New York. © 2024 Artists Rights Society (ARS), New York / ADAGP, Paris.

The ambiguities in the setting, gravitational orientation, and figural integrity are compounded by the indeterminate yellow "ground," which could be read as a rocky wall, a sandy beach, or yellow sky. An array of feet, arms, and legs intertwine and radiate out from the central mass, making it difficult to tell where one body ends and another begins. Léger makes social disconnection and alienation central to this crowd of divers moving in contradictory directions: two arms form a horizontal bar linking the left and right figures, while the profusion of additional hands and feet render ambiguous which bodies they belong to. The many limbs pull the viewer's gaze upward and downward as well as inward and outward depending upon how one reads the "ground" and where the watery surface might be imagined. Are the figures swimming, sinking, or drowning? The effect of the *plongeurs*' contradictory gazes and movements reinforces gravitational and spatial ambiguities and creates a palimpsest of inconsistent spaces and temporal moments. Only Léger's authorial initials in the lower right anchor the painting and identify its orientation.

In combining spatial ambiguity and spectatorial disorientation, Léger's *plongeurs* paintings convey corporeal states of uncertainty and instability that express the mood of the era. Many contemporaries described the divers as vertiginous, invoking vertigo's symptomology of dizziness, lost balance, and falling. In 1945, Canadian poet and ex-Jesuit François Hertel wrote that the masses have "a vertiginous speed," and in 1960, Aragon observed that Léger's late work was "a world without shadows, a vertiginous world of acrobats, swimmers, and workers."[8] Architectural historian Sigfried Giedion and others compare the painting to the flight of figures in Renaissance and Baroque ceilings, while art historian Meyer Schapiro and Bois emphasize the *plongeurs*' variable orientation and rejection of gravity.[9] For Léger, who suffered periodic bouts of vertigo, the malady may have served as a metaphor for the instability of social-political orders and the disorientating aspects of modernity.

The Fall of France

The year before he completed *Divers on a Yellow Ground*, in the summer of 1940, Léger was part of the mass displacement that became known as *le Traume de 1940* (the Trauma of 1940) or *l'Exode de mai-juin 1940* (the Exodus of May–June 1940). As the German army invaded France from the north, an estimated six million civilians took to the roads, propelling floods of people to head south and resulting in an estimated 100,000 deaths on the road.[10] The German Luftwaffe mounted aerial attacks on fleeing French tanks and civilians in cars, bicycles, and on foot, and civil society collapsed as local and national leaders joined the flight.[11] By the time of the German occupation of Paris on June 14, 1940, Léger had left his farm in Lisores (Normandy), passed through Bordeaux, which was bombed in late June, and was on his way to Vichy and to Marseille, thanks to help from Jean Giraudoux, then minister of information.[12] In mid-September, the Americans Gerald and Sara Murphy wired Léger money for boat passage and visas.[13] Léger was soon on his way out of France and arrived in the United States in mid-November.[14]

Historian Stanley Hoffmann has characterized the Exodus of 1940 as a humiliating national failure and a traumatic "memory that speaks so low and so little," such that for decades it lacked commemoration and became another postwar cultural silence.[15] The invasion provoked national chaos and uncertainty that divided the country and dispersed communities. In 1941, André Labarthe, the journalist and founder of the expatriate paper *La France Libre*, described the invasion of France as the "collapse of a nation" dominated by "haunting images of country roads full of a lost people shot down by birds of death, towns populated by crowds without shelter, [and] temporary governments taking a blind eye to historic decisions."[16] The German *blitzkrieg*, first tested at Guernica during the Spanish Civil War, saw full effect on civilians caught on the road or outside shelters. During the period from mid-June to mid-September, when Léger was on the road heading south with millions of others, the national and municipal boundaries, demarcation lines, and authorities were in flux. Even after General Pétain's concession speech on June 17, until the Armistice was signed on June 22, German bombings still took place. Vichy France, the nominally independent but complicit French government in southern France, was not formed under Pétain's leadership until mid-July. Some French soldiers continued fighting and initiated raids in Rennes, Nantes, Tours, and Bordeaux, creating confusion about France's status and whether those on the road should return home and, if so, which route to take.[17]

The chaotic dynamics of Léger's *plongeurs* series, with its watery metaphor, engages a contemporary discourse describing the German invasion as an apocalyptic inundation that rapidly overtook the nation and subsumed an unprepared populace, drowning many and scattering families. Diluvial imagery dominates the poetry and histories that emerged in 1940 and that continued to be produced about the fall of France. Goll's book-length poem "Jean sans Terre," which Léger illustrated with one drawing, describes the Nazi invasion as a flood. Published in 1940 in the United States in French as part of the collection *Les Chansons de France*, Goll's poem states: "Landless Jean sings an ode to France in May 1940," but there are not enough angels "to fight against the flood and the squads of vultures."[18] Léger's illustration for Goll's poem depicts the prewar outline of France's hexagonal borders overlaid with roses, a romantic memorialization to a beloved lost national body.

Like Goll's use of "flood" to describe the invasion, philosopher Jacques Maritain, in his book on the fall of France, *A Travers le désastre* (1941), casts the collapse and exodus in aquatic language: "When the great flood tide of catastrophe swept everything before it, when the exodus poured upon the highway hordes of men afflicted with acute anguish and misery, each one bore his own affliction with courage and helped his neighbor to bear his."[19] Historians since then have perpetuated similar metaphors. In 1957, historian Jean Vidalenc's book on the Exodus of 1940 repeatedly describes the crowds as "un flot de réfugiés" (a flood of refugees).[20] More recently, historian Emile Temime has written that with the Armistice, signed near Compiègne Forest, and the formation of Vichy France, an "immense wave" of people flooded into Marseille. They were "bottled up in provisional internment sites," cramped hotel rooms, and the streets of Marseille, all anxiously awaiting transit and exit visas.[21] Such textual descriptions of chaos, crowding, people bottled up and moving blindly and often at cross-purposes parallels the spatial and social relations among Léger's *plongeurs*.

Metaphors of drowning and surviving floods reoccur in Léger's writing at times of social crisis, prefacing their reemergence in the *plongeurs* series. In 1933, in a letter to his lover Simone Herman, Léger wrote about drowning and shipwreck to express anxiety about surviving during the shortages and hunger of the Depression: "How many are going to die! Who will float, we are all in the water with our head and our arms appearing and disappearing. What a shipwreck!"[22] In *Divers on a Yellow Ground*, the figures' arms and heads appear and disappear, possibly floating or perhaps drowning. Over a decade later, when Léger described his *plongeurs* series as based upon the sight of divers in Marseille, he replicates his invocation of the avant-garde community as a shipwrecked body with heads and arms appearing and disappearing under water: "Whose head, whose leg, whose arms, you no longer know, you can no longer distinguish them."[23] In the 1933 letter, Léger linked the shipwreck metaphor to conditions of war, economic hardship, and embattlement, writing about his compatriots "engaged in the same battle." They have had to toughen up and "harden" themselves "worse than in the war" for this period that is "unlike any battle I've ever known."

Léger's shipwreck and drowning metaphors reoccur in his writing to characterize modernity's dangers. In 1938, Léger described the state of modern life as threatening rapids: "A crazy speed sweeps the world along and carries it into a whirlpool where thousands of individuals will be hopelessly drowned like butterflies. A dangerous and magnificent life for those who can swim through this beautiful chaos as if it were the sea—'not letting them swallow them up.'"[24] Again, in 1939, in writing about the proliferation of apparently unabated counterfeiting, Léger included himself among those masses losing money and described the financial crisis using metaphors of drowning: "We others 'outside the law' of the larger family—children, artists, irregulars and madmen—have to know how to swim—under the water—steering a course between [Scylla and Charybdis]—to dive but [also] to make it out."[25] Casting himself as an artist *hors la loi* (outside the law or bourgeois norms), Léger envisions himself as swimming in a hostile and threatening sea of financial risk. Léger's *plongeurs* paintings, too, are *hors la loi*, outside any organizing or classificatory schema—neither history nor myth, nor biblical narrative. It is not surprising that Léger would return to the diluvial metaphors he used to characterize times of social chaos and that his contemporaries invoked to describe the fall of France.

Apocalyptic Floods

Interwar publications about medieval manuscripts, which particularly interested modernists, provided an iconography of flooding and deterritorialization that likely motivated some key compositional attributes of Léger's *plongeurs*. Art historian Simon Willmoth has argued that a New York version of the Beatus *Commentary on the Apocalypse* influenced formal elements of Léger's *plongeurs* paintings. Produced in the second half of the eighth century, the Beatus *Commentary on the Apocalypse* is a manuscript about the biblical end of times written by the Spanish monk Beatus de Liébana (Asturias). In succeeding centuries, Spanish and French artists produced illustrated copies of the manuscript that came to modernist attention in the interwar years. In October 1935, on the occasion of his second trip to the United States, when he had an exhibition at MoMA, Léger saw one such Beatus manuscript, *Las Huelgas*

Apocalypse (MS 644) (1220), in the Pierpont Morgan collection. Léger's guide was art historian Meyer Schapiro, who spent an hour discussing it with Léger, an encounter Schapiro later reported to Willmoth.[26] Léger was, according to Schapiro, particularly impressed by the color and spacing. Willmoth draws a connection between the manuscript's bands of color and Léger's conception of "free color," or color operating independently of the figures. In works like Harvard's *The Divers* (1943) (fig. 51), Léger deploys "free color" by using rectangular strips of red, blue, and yellow to cross over transparent figures represented only as black outlines. Finally, Willmoth argues that Léger's interest in such medieval sources was tied to his response to the rise of fascism in 1939, linking apocalyptic floods to social crises.

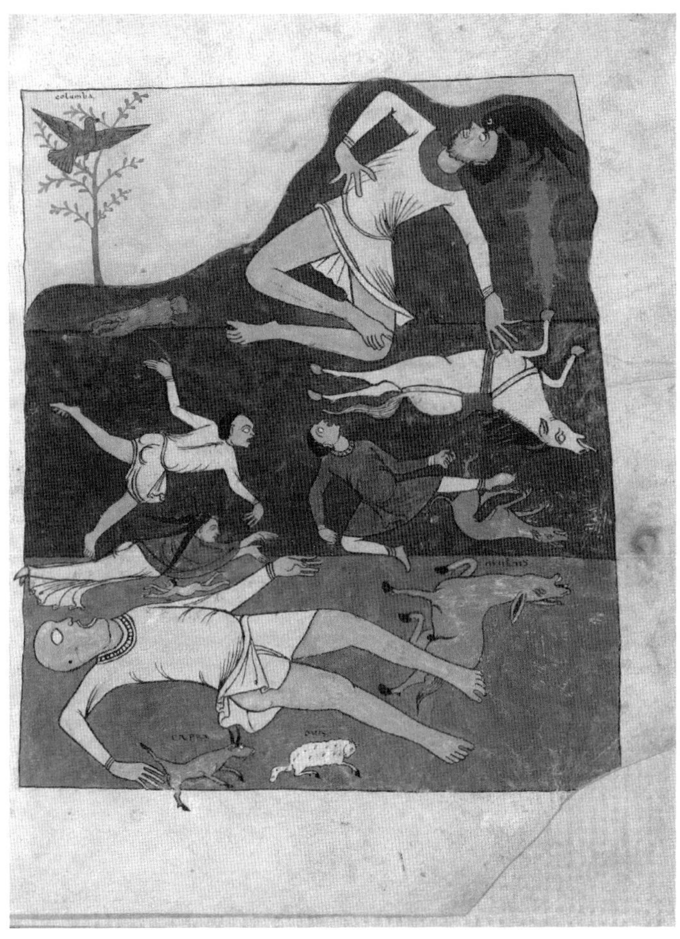

Fig. 53 Stephanius Garsia, *Flood*, in *Commentary on the Apocalypse*, by Beatus of Liebana, MS lat. 8678, fol. 85r, made for the Abbey of Saint-Sever, 1028–72. Ink and tempera on vellum, 36.5 × 28 cm. Courtesy of the Bibliothèque nationale de France.

Léger's turn to medieval representations of the biblical apocalypse brings together his modernist position against mimetic traditions, including the Italian Renaissance, and a visual metaphor for chaotic and life-threatening events. In addition to the Spanish illustrations of the Beatus manuscripts in the Pierpont Morgan collection, Léger likely knew of a French version in the Bibliothèque nationale: the Saint-Sever Beatus Apocalypse manuscript (fig. 53). It was produced in about 1060 in the Benedictine Abbey of Saint-Sever in Landes in southwestern France, and it probably came to Léger's attention thanks to Bataille. In the second issue of *Documents* (April 1929), a periodical coedited by Léger's longtime friend Einstein, Bataille published an article about the Saint-Sever version of the Beatus manuscript and reproduced six images, including the flood scene. Bataille calls attention to the crow in the top register, whose "beak is plunged in the meat of a human head," the "absurdist horror" and "arbitrary deformations" of the large drowned man in the bottom register, and the "unexpected jovial sentiment" in the goat at the bottom of the page.[27]

The Saint-Sever manuscript illustration, with its dead and living humans and animals scattered across three horizontal bands, conveys the chaos and disaster wrought by the apocalyptic flood. Its multiple perspectives and temporal moments seem to enact a traumatic memory. The top register is divided in two parts: at left, a tree with a blue bird perched in its branches arises from a blue mountain set against a yellow ground, perhaps a sign of post-diluvial promise; at right, the blue mountain transforms into a watery burial site for the dead man whose eyes are being plucked out by a crow. The man's crossed legs extend into the middle horizontal band below. This dark red ocher register offers an aerial view of two upturned animals (a horse and a goat) and several figures. One of the figures is a man in yellow who swims toward another in blue whose gaping mouth and sightless gaze signify his apparent drowning. A woman with long black braids and wearing a blue cloak swims along the dividing line between the middle and bottom register, transforming that line into a watery horizon. Below her, in the bottom register, a bald man lies horizontally and faces upward, his mouth agape and his sightless eyes conveying death or lost consciousness. At his side are several animals, one of which is the "jovial" goat who survives him.

Léger borrows from these medieval flood compositions in his *plongeurs* paintings not only in his use of "free color" that Willmoth noted but also in the "arbitrary deformations" that Bataille saw in the Saint-Sever manuscript. Léger's paintings share the shifting and contradictory perspectives and sense of social upheaval in which all are uprooted from the *territoire* that once grounded them. Like the Saint-Sever manuscript, Léger's *plongeurs*, too, are bodies with bald heads, simplified facial features, jutting angled elbows, and fringes of fingers and toes. Léger's *plongeurs* enact similar behaviors to the medieval figures. Like the living depicted in the Saint-Sever flood scene, the figures in Léger's *Divers on a Yellow Ground* seem disinterested in or unaware of each other, preoccupied with their individual pursuits of survival, and unwilling or unable to aid those who have sunk to their death. Like the Saint-Sever figures, who move through floodwaters in contradictory spaces viewed from multiple perspectives, Léger's *plongeurs* enact their drama in an indeterminate spatial context permitting multiple perspectival readings alternatively imagined from above or below or head-on. The effect in each case is to convey vertiginous social and psychic disruption and deterritorialization.

The Hanged Man

During the months from mid-June, when he left his Norman farm in the north of France, traveled to Bordeaux, and finally arrived in Marseille, Léger witnessed desperation and alienation akin to the medieval apocalypse. In the late summer and fall of 1940, Léger wrote several letters to his wife, Lohy, who stayed in France during the war. His letters testify to the death and family separation engendered by chaos on the roads: "I saw the battle of the trains—slept in cattle cars—in train stations, outside . . . women not daring to leave their wagon because of their kids, not eating for two days, pissing on themselves. . . . Children lost, crushed, in train stations where ten thousand people attacked twenty wagons. Bordeaux."[28] Léger's description captures the collective panic caused by inadequate transport, the trials of women who tried to guard their children and keep their families together when men were often still deployed in what became known as the Phoney War, and the brutality of mobs in which the most vulnerable were lost or crushed. Historian Hanna Diamond describes this summer of chaotic flight as a period of "abandonment and disorientation," "panic and fear," when there was an absence of leadership, disruption in communications, and breakdown of families.[29]

By the time Léger arrived in Marseille in the summer of 1940, it had become known as a city of flight, a city of refuge, and a site of internment.[30] Léger's passage through southern France took him to areas that had seen an explosion of refugees and internment camps during the late 1930s in response to the rise of fascism. Camps such as Les Milles (near Aix-en-Provence), where German artists including Ernst, Robert Liebknecht, Leo Marchutz, and Wols were interned in 1940, had previously housed refugees from the Spanish Civil War.[31] Hitler's rise to power had forced masses of Eastern European Jews, communists, and socialists to escape to France. Temime observes that even before the onset of World War II, Marseille became a "major center of the international battle against fascism and Nazism."[32] As the repository for the flood of humanity in flight and the major city near so many internment camps, Marseille became identified with conditions of social disorder, the anxieties that came with homelessness and an undocumented status, and the spaces of confinement and containment: the "hell" of internment and refugee camps, overcrowded housing, and temporary shelters.

Many of Léger's intimates and peers were trapped in France at the time of occupation, and some were unable to escape as he did. Lohy, his first wife, from whom he had long been separated, remained in Bordeaux unable to gain ship's passage. Artists Hans Bellmer and Ernst were initially interned at Camp des Milles, and then Ernst joined Breton and other Surrealists who found refuge at journalist Varian Fry's Air-Bel in Marseille from fall 1940 to early 1941. An American, Fry had formed the International Rescue Committee to assist about two hundred preselected artists and intellectuals believed to be subject to the "surrender-on-demand" clause of the Franco-German Armistice. That clause required a suspected opponent to the Nazi regime to be handed over by Vichy police to German authorities upon demand, leaving many leftists and dissidents vulnerable.[33] Novelist Anna Seghers's *Transit* (1944) and Fry's autobiographical account of his rescue agency in Marseille, *Surrender on Demand* (1945), describe the crowded city full of desperate people navigating the

Kafkaesque labyrinth of interdependent safe conduct passes, transit and exit visas, and ship's passage and other paperwork required for legal departure, a structure that intensified fears and uncertainties.

Fig. 54 Paul Marteau, *The Hanged Man*, card XII, from *Le Tarot de Marseille*, 1930. Courtesy of the Bibliothèque nationale de France.

Other émigrés did not have such good fortune as Fry's select and instead waited unsuccessfully for months or years for transit visas and boat passage. A wave of suicides consumed intellectuals Léger knew, perhaps the best-known case being Walter Benjamin's death on the Spanish border in September 1940. The German Expressionist writer Walter Hasenclever, whose work was reviewed in *L'Esprit Nouveau*, overdosed in Camp des Milles in June 1940.[34] Perhaps most difficult for Léger was the death of Einstein, a publisher, art critic, and longtime friend. Interned in France after fighting in the Spanish Civil War, Einstein killed himself in July 1940 at the Spanish frontier. He had published Léger's work as early as 1925 in *Europa Almanach*, wrote about Léger in *Die Kunst des 20. Jahrhunderts* (Berlin 1926), exhibited Léger's work at the Flechtheim Gallery in 1928, and reviewed Léger's art for *Documents* in 1930. Einstein's German nationality, combined with his Jewish ethnicity, his history of militancy, communist allegiance, service in the Spanish Civil War, and exiled status in France, made him a prime target of Nazi authoritarianism subject to the "surrender-on-demand" clause.

A central figure in many of the *plongeurs* paintings, including *Divers on a Yellow Ground* (1941) and *Polychrome Divers* (1942–46), is a hanging or falling body that signifies, I argue, the conditions of constraint and lost agency suffered by many of those Léger left behind. A central androgynous figure who is bald yet bears breasts hangs upside down and gazes blankly at the viewer. In *Divers on a Yellow Ground*, the figure sinks like a dead person or one who has abandoned hope; their bloated, four-fingered right hand and arm extend parallel to the bottom frame, and their left arm, parallel to the body, almost touches the fingers of another figure. A right foot that could belong to this figure emerges at the top left of the corporeal mass that obscures much of the diver's body. The ambiguously gendered body conveys the dissolution of gendered roles, and its inability to grasp any other hand suggests the rupture of familial structures within the context of the 1940 Exodus.

The *plongeur*'s position resembles the hanged man card of tarot expert Paul Marteau's Le Tarot of Marseille playing cards, published in 1930 (fig. 54). In tarot, the deck of seventy-eight illustrated cards used for reading one's fate, the hanged man typically appears strung up by his left foot, his right leg crossed behind his left and his arms tied behind his back. He signifies constraint, the inability to act, futility, and lost agency, experiences familiar to the desperate crowds trapped in Marseille in 1940. For Léger, whose *The Card Party* painting depicts the popular soldiers' card game *manille* to signify both fate and fraternity, it would not be surprising that he turned to tarot to signify chance and destiny. Tarot occupied many in Marseille in 1940, the best-known example of which may be the Surrealists, who produced their own tarot cards (without the hanged man) while sheltered at Fry's Villa Air-Bel.[35]

Even before 1940, tarot cards entered into vanguard visual vocabulary as a Dadaist and Surrealist sign of chance and the imagination unfettered by the rational mind. Invented in Italy during the Renaissance, tarot cards were produced in Marseille workshops as early as the 1700s. Léger is likely to have known about Marteau's card deck and his illustrated history and guide to the game, *Le Tarot de Marseille* (1919). The book was prefaced by Jean Paulhan, who later became editor from 1925 to 1940 of the leading modernist literary review *La Nouvelle revue française*. Paulhan, who appears in Ernst's painting *Friends' Reunion* (1922), was interested in Dadaist notions of chance and arbitrary destiny. Léger had known Paulhan since 1922, when they had been part of Breton's Congress de Paris planning committee. Marteau's writing on tarot also appeared in *Arts et métiers graphiques*, a monthly illustrated periodical that published Léger's writing the same year.[36] In the context of Marseille 1940 as a state of uncertainty and anxiety, many, perhaps even Léger, must have played the game. Certainly the figure of the hanged man in Léger's *plongeurs* paintings emblematizes the traumatic experience of the millions of refugees in and around Marseille.

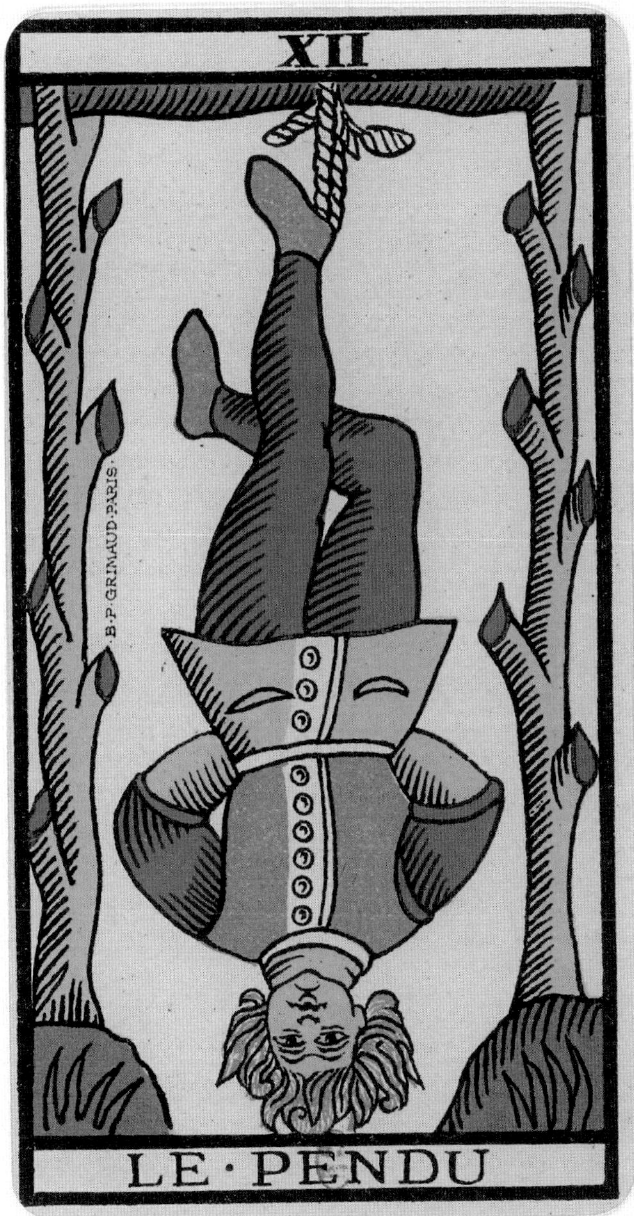

Léger's Marseille Story

By March 1944, when Léger exhibited his new artwork in a solo show at the Jacques Seligmann Gallery in New York, art dealer Germain Seligmann published the first and only wartime version of Léger's traumatic departure through

Marseille. *Plongeurs* images appear on the brochure's cover and dominate the list of sixteen gouaches, drawings, and paintings. In the exhibition brochure, Germain Seligmann writes: "When Fernand Léger was in Marseille in the fateful summer of 1940, awaiting the fulfilling of the formalities necessary to leave France to reach this country, he was strongly attracted by the designs of crowds milling on the beach and in the water. . . . When he found his 'balance' in the new surroundings, he at once went to work carrying out three monumental compositions which he called 'Les Plongeurs' ('The Divers') based on his Marseille inspirations."[37] In Germain Seligmann's terms, Léger lost his "balance" during the invasion of France but found his "ground" in a secure refuge and was then able to produce his "monumental" images of acrobats and divers. The indirectness of the story, recounted by Germain Seligmann rather than Léger, and the sparse details about the German invasion and about Léger's conditions in Marseille, enact a form of self-censorship in the context of the inadequacy of language and narrative. Even while the anecdote offers an individual memory of departure, the figures in the images are so dislocated from any Marseille or wartime referent as to make the relationship almost unrecognizable.

Rather than offering referential signs of Marseille, the *plongeurs* pictures are linked to a personal symbolism that Léger had produced in the 1930s, including acrobat paintings that signify artistic risk and the threat of death. In the early 1940s, Léger made the connection between the *plongeurs* and acrobat series in a letter to Le Corbusier, stating that he was being productive in the United States: "Perhaps the imagination is more creative and rapid here. . . . *The Divers* is freer and more violent than the *Parrots* you saw in Paris. I am in a fight with the human body and pure color."[38] By describing the *plongeurs* as more "free" and more "violent" than the acrobatic paintings, Léger claims that the *plongeurs*' spatial indeterminacy and gravitational loss are simultaneously and contradictorily forms of freedom and violence. Léger's *Composition with Two Parrots* was one of several interwar acrobat-themed paintings, including *Composition with Three Figures* (1932) and *Marie the Acrobat* (1934). *Two Parrots* was first exhibited for one day in March 1940 at the Galerie Mai (sculptor Meric Callery's studio) in Paris before being shipped to New York for a showing in June in Callery's studio there.[39] Its four acrobats stand or dance before a yellow backdrop, while their props (parrots, rope, ladder, and drapery) provide a totemic and personal context that Léger's *plongeurs* lack.

In tracing Léger's wartime exhibition history, it becomes clear that he continued with his prewar *saltimbanques* (or acrobats) as a major theme in his artwork but then shifted to the *plongeurs* in summer 1941. The brochures for Léger's earliest exhibitions in the United States, at the Marie Harriman Gallery in New York (March 1941), the Arts Club of Chicago (May–June 1941), and Mills College in Oakland, California (summer 1941), all list numerous drawings and studies for *saltimbanques*, showing that he was still thinking in terms of the interwar acrobats. The cover of the Mills College brochure even depicts *Composition with Two Parrots*, effectively framing the theme of the exhibited art in terms of those acrobats. But in June 1941 he added some twenty *plongeurs* drawings to the traveling exhibition of his work that started at the Arts Club of Chicago and came to Mills College, where he taught that summer.[40] At that point he wrote to Lohy, then in Vichy France, telling her he was working on a painting—"*Les Plongeurs*, things seen at Marseille last summer"—the first written reference to the series and to its origins in his Marseille passage.[41]

The *Artists in Exile* exhibition, held in March 1942 at the Pierre Matisse Gallery in New York, foregrounded the condition of exile and may have motivated Léger to develop the Marseille story published in the Seligmann brochure. Each artist in the exhibition was represented by only one work. Léger's submission, according to the brochure, was a study for *Study for the Divers* (1942), indicating that he may have thought of the *plongeurs* in terms of the theme of "exile." Many of the fourteen artists who participated came to the United States with the aid of Fry's International Rescue Committee, including Masson, Breton, Chagall, and Ernst, while other artists, like Léger, Ozenfant, and Kurt Seligmann, had been able to leave earlier. The brochure makes clear its aim is to welcome the artists to the United States and to recognize their talent. In his essay "Europe," James Thrall Soby, the collector, critic, and tobacco heir, anticipated that the US public's reaction to the artists could be xenophobia and nationalism. Such attitudes characterize the enemy, he wrote, and instead, the United States should offer "a sympathetic relationship with refugee painters and sculptors." The Greek American Surrealist and art critic Nicolas Calas wrote in his essay "America" that the refugee needs "understanding and encouragement" and that the "immigrant artist must be grafted to American life." The brochure does not provide any accounts from the individual artists about their final days in Marseille, but the exhibition's theme of exile seems likely to have opened the door to exchanges among the artists about their traumatic departures, stimulating Léger's memories about his own passage.

Later that year, in October 1942, Léger exhibited multiple *plongeurs* works in two solo shows: one of paintings at the Paul Rosenberg Gallery and a second of gouaches and drawings in art dealer Curt Valentin's Buchholz Gallery. A *New York Times* review of the two shows briefly references a large canvas entitled *Les Plongeurs* (186.7 × 217.8 cm), which Willmoth identifies as *Divers on a Yellow Ground*.[42] The review emphasizes Léger's refusal of a worldly context for his new figural works. The Buchholz exhibition included two works entitled *Human Bodies in Space* and another identified as *Man in Space, Designs for Murals*, both of which were probably studies for *plongeurs* paintings.[43] The *Man in Space* title, perhaps created by Valentin, may have been informed by cosmic themes and celestial battles in the work of exiled Surrealist artists such as Tanguy, Masson, and Roberto Matta. Masson, for example, had exhibited his painting *The Germ of the Cosmic* (1942) at Valentin's gallery eight months before Léger's show there.

Around the same time as the Rosenberg and Buchholz exhibitions, French filmmaker Thomas Bouchard filmed a documentary of Léger in his New York studio, the only copy of which is in the Harvard Film Archive. Although the film was not screened until after the war, the interviews probably took place in late 1942 or early 1943 based upon Léger's discussion (in French) of the *corps en espace* or "bodies in space" paintings linked to the Buchholz exhibition. Léger states in the film that, in these new works, the human body is now "entirely free," an object "without any feeling other than that of movement or of plastic and dynamic action." He reiterates his modernist position that "the sentimental or literary subject" (narrative form) should be left to the movies.[44] Léger identifies Cézanne as his master and links his recent paintings to the problem of materiality and the modernist body posed by Cézanne. By freeing the body of any worldly context, Léger's "bodies in space" reject even Cézanne's Gulf of Marseille landscape settings, where Léger witnessed his original *plongeurs*. Léger's claim that his bodies are objects "without any feeling" or sentiment revives Purist discourse that served to negate investment in the vulnerabilities of the organic body and the frailties of the postwar man.

Léger's *plongeurs* communicate neither desire nor pain; in that refusal they revive the shocked affectlessness and gender ambiguity of his automatons and robots from the 1920s. The *plongeurs*' bodies, like the *femme-machine* bodies of *Three Women* (fig. 25), are segmented and disconnected, made to be a collective mass rather than individuated as Léger's male workers are. The *plongeurs*' figure of a hanged "man" returns to and reworks the bald androgynous "women" in *Reading* (1924) and *Woman with a Fruit Bowl* (1924) (figs. 27 and 28). Juxtaposed with female figures gendered by their long hair, the bald *plongeurs* recapitulate the instability of gender in times of social change and crisis. While the *plongeurs* have none of the spatial and social specificity of the *Three Women*, their indeterminacy makes them both more "free" and more "violent," less bound by conventional orders but perhaps more vulnerable.

"The Social and Political Order to Come"

Early interpreters of the *plongeurs* saw them as political and social art addressed to a general public akin to the mural-sized paintings and art of the Popular Front era. In 1945, a collection of essays on Léger's wartime artistic production, *Fernand Léger: La Forme humaine dans l'espace* (Human Form in Space), provided the first critical commentary on the *plongeurs* series. Edited by modern art advocate Father Couturier, it included contributions from Giedion, art dealer Samuel M. Kootz, and Hertel. Giedion places the *plongeurs* in the context of the Popular Front mural projects and their public address. He argues for modern art in public life, public buildings, and civic centers, citing the 1937 World's Fair in Paris, and he characterizes the *plongeurs* as the representation of "mass movement."[45] In doing so, he implicates the *plongeurs* in the French national order and a progressive political ideology. Kootz saw dissonance, nervous color, and "a prefiguration of the social and political order to come." Kootz wrote that "the social and political troubles of the moment . . . have a great influence on his [Léger's] unconscious."[46] Such a characterization imagines the paintings as a utopian vision while implicitly acknowledging France's ongoing occupation and its psychic impact on the artist.

Giedion's reading of the *plongeurs* as public art like the Popular Front–era commissions in 1937 is consistent with Léger's ambition of making the *plongeurs* into mural-size canvas paintings. Both the Art Institute of Chicago's *Divers on a Yellow Ground* (1941) (186.7 x 217.8 cm) and the Musée national Fernand Léger's *Polychrome Divers* (1942–46) (250 x 185 cm) are monumental in scale, with figures that are life-size or nearly so, immersing the viewer in the disorientating spatial field. In May 1945, when the Parisian dealer Louis Carré was planning a postwar exhibition of Léger's new work, Léger described the series as a problem of mural painting and movement, writing that there are "forty or so representations of what I call the 'human body in space' solely on the problem of figures in movement. . . . Unfortunately, it's difficult to find walls on which to work all that up."[47] That Léger wanted "walls on which to work all that up" indicates that during the war, he both desired but never received the mural commissions or larger popular audiences he had hoped for.

Léger linked mural art to social revolution, public education, and an engagement with modern art and rationalist architecture, but he rejected the literalness and naturalism of Socialist Realism. From the time of his collaboration with Le Corbusier and in numerous talks and interviews in the 1930s and afterward, Léger argued for mural painting, which for him included wall-sized canvases, as a public art addressed to a popular audience but in a modernist visual language.[48] An extensive scholarly discussion about Léger's mural projects emphasizes the interwar revival of the mural and Léger's position as an avant-garde artist aligned with the left yet critical of Socialist Realism.[49] In the 1930s, Léger invested in the Popular Front's promise of national regeneration and collaborated with the Popular Front on mural commissions. At the time of the 1937 World's Fair in Paris, Léger contributed one of twelve large hanging panels for the Pavillon de la Solidarité, which represented a consolidation of twelve unions into the Confédération Générale du Travail (CGT). Léger also collaborated on several photomontages: with architect and designer

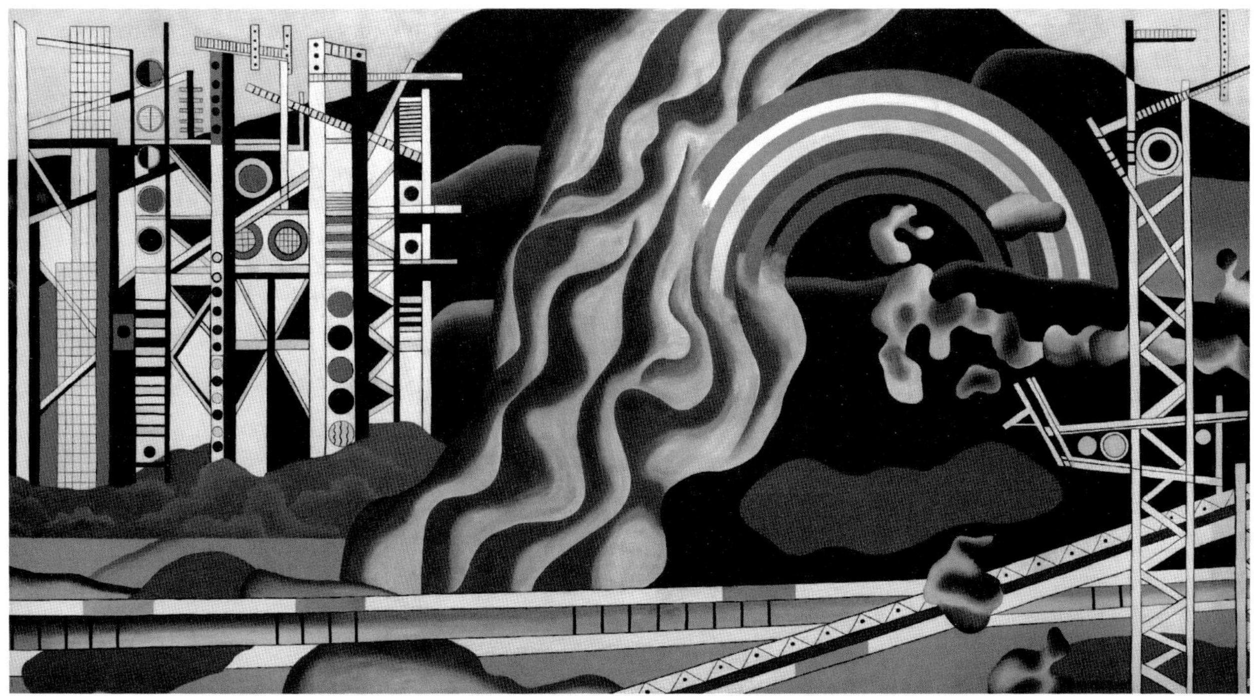

Fig. 55 Fernand Léger, *The Transport of Power*, 1937. Oil on canvas, 491 × 870 cm. Collection du Centre national des arts plastiques, Paris. Photo: Yves Chenot. © 2024 Artists Rights Society (ARS), New York / ADAGP, Paris.

Perriand for the star-shaped, open-air Ministry of Agriculture pavilion and on a now-lost photomontage for Le Corbusier and his cousin the architect Pierre Jeanneret's Pavillon des Temps Nouveaux.[50] The best known of his Popular Front murals is an enormous canvas painting of hydroelectric power, *The Transport of Power* (1937) (fig. 55), created for the Palais de la Découverte, then a new science museum. In contrast to the *plongeurs*' disrupted watery world, *The Transport of Power* channels the flow of water through science in the form of the steel girder power plant with its promising benefits signified by the rainbow at right. Where *The Transport of Power* wants the viewer to be awed by the spectacle of the mechanical sublime, *Divers on a Yellow Ground* immerses the viewer into the *plongeurs*' space and the experience of being uprooted, of being "at sea," and of losing one's balance. And with the fall of France, the social order of the CGT mural dissolved into a disoriented, alienated collective.

Although Léger's Popular Front mural projects had engaged with labor themes and public works projects, he abandoned work themes after the Popular Front's loss of power in 1938 and the fall of France in 1940 and did not return to labor motifs until his late-career constructor series. France's political collapse resulted in the disintegration of the physical and ideological infrastructure that supported leftist public mural projects and their utopian collective iconography. In the United States, the Federal Art Project that had supported so many public murals came to a close in 1943 due in part to the exigencies of war. It is from this uncertain position that Léger complained to Carré in 1945 about failing to find "walls on which to work all that up." With Léger in exile in the United States, despite his recognition and commercial success, his new work received none of the political affiliation, state recognition, or public status of his many interwar projects. The only public projects he created in the United States were his post–World War II ceramic wall hangings for the United Nations building (1952). Other proposed projects never came to fruition.[51] Instead, Léger's only mural versions of the *plongeurs* were produced for a private space, the New York home of the architect Wallace K. Harrison. That enormous mural, an oil and charcoal work on canvas, now hangs in the Museum Ludwig in Cologne.[52] The *plongeurs* were thus doubly unmoored, first by the scenario within the frame and second by the failure to find a permanent public position for their display.

The politics of the *plongeurs* are not literal but participate in an emerging discourse of modernist abstraction that reinforced Léger's thinking about painting as a formal rather than narrative or historical project. Kootz, who exhibited Léger's *plongeurs* in New York in 1945, became a major dealer in Abstract Expressionist art, and his announcement cards for Léger's exhibition also advertise Robert Motherwell, Adolph Gottlieb, and Hans Hoffman. In 1943, Gottlieb and Mark Rothko sent a letter to the *New York Times* refusing to explain their pictures or to provide decorative or academic art to please the public. They also expressed a "spiritual kinship" with "primitive and archaic art" and claimed that the only valid subject matter is "tragic and timeless."[53] Léger's intensifying abstraction in the *plongeurs* series, in which the figures are detached from the specificity of time and space, share the emerging abstractionist position against narrating or explaining art. During the war, abstraction may have been better understood in the existential crisis of Rothko's tragic representations than in the liberatory postwar artistic autonomy of Pollock's drip paintings. Aligned with this thinking, at least one contemporary critic read Léger's *plongeurs* against the prevailing leisure scene interpretation. In response to Léger's 1953 Chicago retrospective curated by Katherine Kuh, which included *Divers on a Yellow Ground*, art critic Kenneth Rexroth claimed that Léger was an "existentialist without a capital E."[54] Whether Léger, who met Jean-Paul Sartre in 1945, read Sartre's *Being and Nothingness* (1943) is unknown, but the *plongeurs*' alienated yet interdependent state lends itself to an interrogation of how to be in relation to the other.[55] If Kootz saw a nervous quality to the *plongeurs* and Rexroth interpreted Léger as an "existentialist," it may be because the forms of history—the nation, the heroic, and the utopian that Socialist Realism relied upon—were for many artists unavailable after the fall of France and were discredited due to the war's atrocities.

Against History

While Léger shared the leftist politics of the Socialist Realists working in France and the United States, his *plongeurs* series reinforces his rejection of their utopian iconography and naturalistic aesthetics. In the United States, he, like the the Mexican muralists, was critical of US capitalism, castigating Wall Street for its speculation, greed, and indifference to suffering.[56] In 1945, he, too, joined the Communist Party and became a target of surveillance by the FBI and attacks by conservative US politicians.[57] During his multiple trips to the United States, Léger encountered mural projects by the Mexican artists that invested in historical narrative, international collaboration, and the heroic worker. In fall 1931, on his first visit to the United States, Léger presented a lecture at the New School for Social Research, which had recently unveiled two major mural productions, according to *New York Times*' reports.[58] These were Mexican muralist José Clemente Orozco's *The Fraternity of All Men at the Table of Brotherhood and Ultimate Universality* (1931–32) (fig. 56), which depicts an imagined gathering of men of all races, including portraits of Vladimir Lenin and Mahatma Gandhi; and American Regionalist artist Thomas Hart Benton's *America Today* (1931), which envisions scenes of city life and leisure, urban industry, and a multiracial group of muscular male dockyard workers loading transoceanic liners. In 1940, the summer before Léger went to teach at Mills College in Oakland, California, Rivera had completed the *Pan American Unity* mural (fig. 57) at San Francisco City College. Léger had known Rivera since the Cubist era, when they participated in the 1910 Société des Indépendants group show. In 1919, after Rosenberg severed his contract with Rivera, Léger expressed frustration at Rivera's anti-Cubist position.[59] Rivera's enormous *Pan American Unity* mural spans the historical past—from the Aztecs to colonial-era liberators (George Washington, Simón Bolívar) and twentieth-century building projects and heroes (Edison). Above and on either side of the massive, centrally positioned, and deified machine are two perspectives of the Olympic diving champion Helen Crlenkovich in midflight. Divers look up from the platforms below; even an Aztec sculptor crosses time and space to join their upward gazes. Léger may have seen the mural during his California summer, possibly on a tour given by his former student Miné Okubo. Okubo studied with him from 1938 until her return to the United States in September 1939, when she then assisted with the Rivera mural project by giving tours; she worked in Oakland until her internment in 1942, an experience she documented in her graphic memoir *Citizen 13660* (1946).[60]

Unlike murals by Orozco, Benton, or Rivera, Léger's *plongeurs* supplant the "great man" and "heroic worker" with anonymity and displace the American regionalist and Socialist Realist iconography with indeterminate space and movement. Rather than presenting a historic moment, an orderly collective, or a vision of a

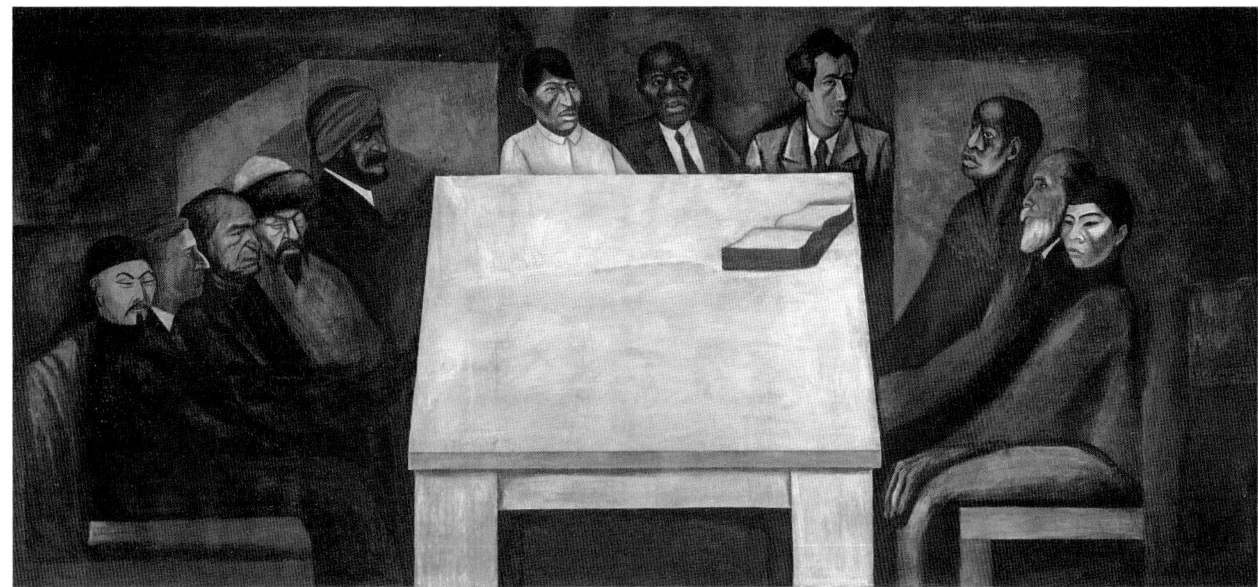

utopian future, Léger's *Divers on a Yellow Ground* imagines mass movements of scattered bodies with an uncertain fate. Léger's figures are neither named heroes like Orozco's and Rivera's nor iconic laborers such as Benton's dockworker. Instead, they are anonymous and androgynous or feminized, undermining the tropes of masculinity invoked by the dockworker or unionized laborers. They fail to enact the gestures and postures of productive or economic motion, transcendent physical feats, or utopian potential. Despite Léger's transit through the docks of Marseille, New York, and Oakland, and his invocation of "Marseille" in his explanation for the origin of the *plongeurs* series, he refuses to depict any referential elements signifying "port" or the port's most iconic figure: the dockworker. A more Socialist Realist artist might have instead transformed their memory of Marseille, a major Mediterranean port, into a paean to labor, as in artist Joseph Inguimberty's *Dockers at the Port of Marseille* (1924) or as Léger's student Georges Bauquier did in *The Dockers* (1951). Instead, the *plongeurs'* nudity and indeterminate space eliminate the signs of class and the tools and spaces of labor. In so doing, they reject a return to Léger's machine aesthetic iconography of mechanics and tugboat captains, factories and capitalist production. In this sense, the *plongeurs* are out of place and outside time, emptying the body of the certainties of the self and signifying the trauma of exile in which the self is divorced from its past.

Léger's *plongeurs* oppose the chronological time, named historical persona, and literal forms of Socialist Realism, a position that was part of his long-standing modernist abstraction and lent to the *plongeurs'* dissociated world. In his earliest

Fig. 56 José Clemente Orozco, *Table of Universal Brotherhood* or *The Fraternity of All Men at the Table of Brotherhood and Ultimate Universality*, 1931–32. Fresco, 198 × 427 cm. New School for Social Research, New York. Courtesy of The New School Art Collection. © 2024 Artists Rights Society (ARS), New York / SOMAAP, Mexico City.

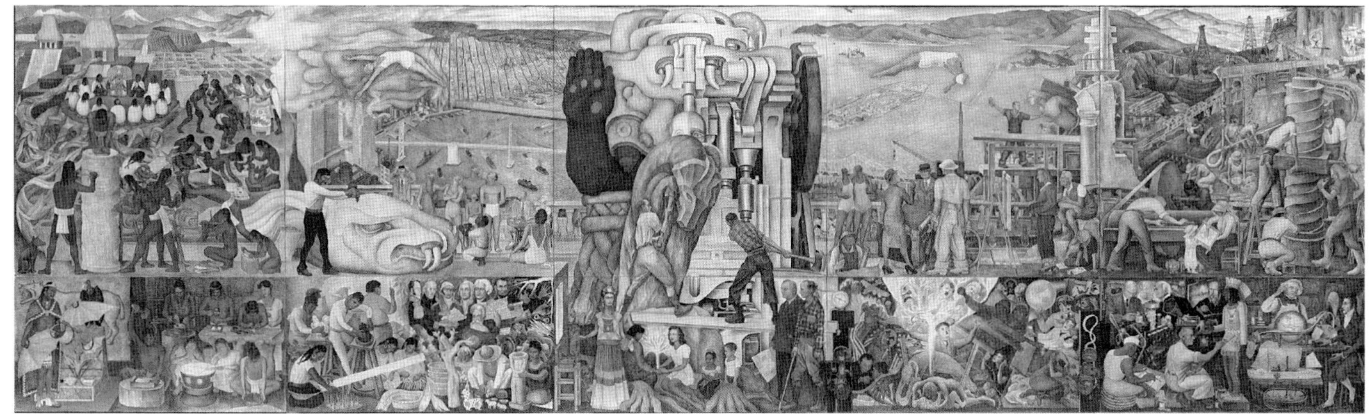

Fig. 57 Diego Rivera, *The Marriage of the Artistic Expression of the North and of the South on this Continent*, also known as *Pan American Unity*, 1940. Fresco, 670.5 × 2255.5 cm. Courtesy City College of San Francisco. © 2024 Banco de México Diego Rivera Frida Kahlo Museums Trust, Mexico City / Artists Rights Society (ARS), New York. Image: Cultural Heritage Imaging.

lectures and writings, Léger had asserted an avant-garde opposition to academic history painting, mimesis, the narrative, and the sentimental.[61] After Socialist Realism became orthodoxy in the Soviet Union in 1934, Aragon organized a debate among vanguard artists, known as the *querelle du realisme* (quarrel over realism), held at the Communist Party's Maison de la Culture and published as a collection of essays.[62] In that debate, Léger argued that "realism" changes from one era and one artist to the next, and he proposed instead a "new realism" founded in modernism and as inventive as the poetics of popular slang. He rejected the claim that modernist art was exclusively for the rich or the bourgeoisie and asserted that the working class only needed leisure time to frequent museums and understand avant-garde art.[63] By the time of Léger's major retrospective at the Chicago Art Institute in 1953, which included *Divers on a Yellow Ground* now in its collection, he emphatically refused to offer any narrative explanation for his paintings. He reiterated to curator Kuh his long-standing position that mural painting should not be about religious, military, or social issues, which could be better handled by books or film. Instead, Léger explained the series of divers, acrobats, and dancers in formal terms as "a new energy—an increased movement in the composition" and an "intensity of contrasts of movement."[64] Not a literal representation of the collective, the *plongeurs* instead represent the dynamics or energy of the group, the "mass movement" that Giedion saw, interpretations that permit Kootz's reading of them in terms of the "social and political troubles of the moment."

One alternative to the literality of Socialist Realist murals that Léger knew well was the most renowned public mural at the 1937 World's Fair in Paris: Picasso's *Guernica* (1937) (fig. 58). When Léger arrived in New York in November 1940, *Guernica* was on display at MoMA. Originally exhibited in the Pavilion of the Spanish Republic, Picasso's interpretation of the German *blitzkrieg* that destroyed the Basque city

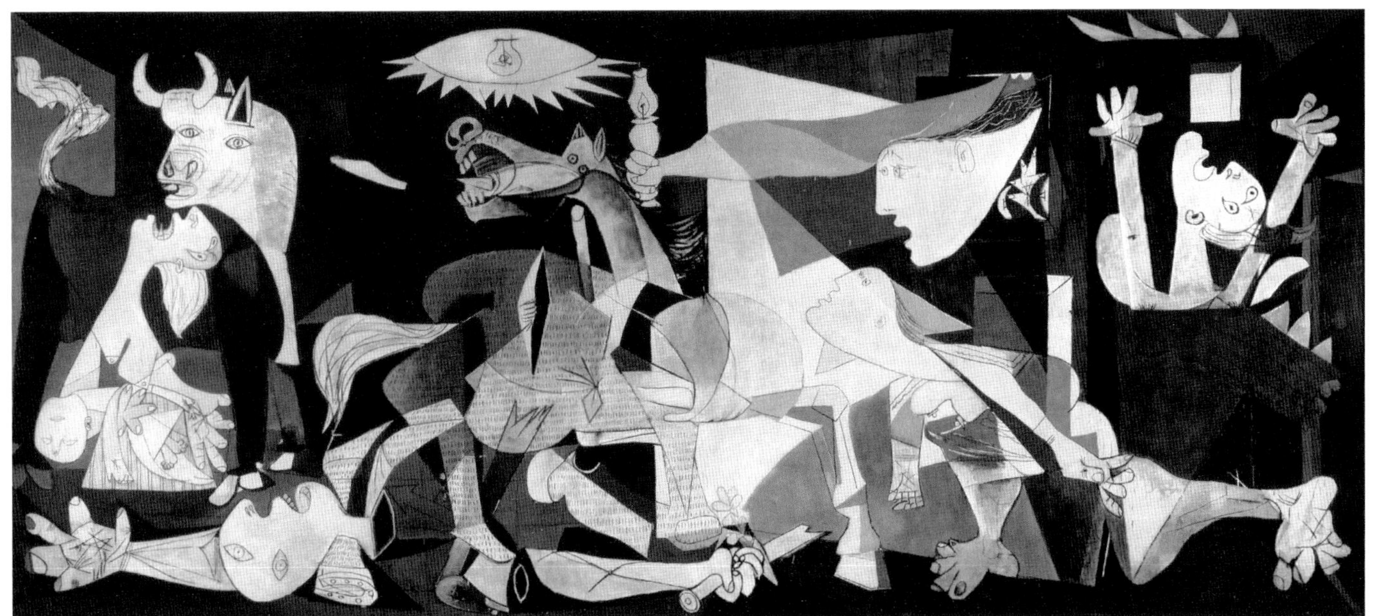

of Guernica surely had new meaning for Léger, who had just survived the summer 1940 blitz aimed at the six million people on the road in France. Historian Annie Cohen-Solal observes that the expatriate artists "all went to MoMA to discover or rediscover Picasso's *Guernica*" and other Surrealist masterworks.[65] *Guernica* quickly achieved an iconic status as a political protest against fascism. After *Guernica* was moved to New York in 1937, Valentin, who later exhibited Léger's *plongeurs* in 1942, published Picasso's drawings and studies as a fundraiser for the Spanish Civil War.[66] In reflecting upon fascism's destruction of republican governments, Léger may well have joined the modernist pilgrimage to see *Guernica*.

Fig. 58 Pablo Picasso, *Guernica*, 1937. Oil on canvas, 350 × 780 cm. Museo Nacional Centro de Arte Reina Sofia, Madrid, Spain / Art Resource, New York. © 2024 Estate of Pablo Picasso / Artists Rights Society (ARS), New York.

That Léger paid attention to Picasso's ideas and methods would not be surprising given their long parallel histories. They both arrived in Paris in 1900 and met that year; they traveled in the same artistic circles, became leading Cubists, regularly exhibited together, and were represented by the same dealers, including Kahnweiler and Rosenberg. By the 1930s, they were cast in opposition or on par with each other; Einstein saw Léger as the "constructor" in opposition to Picasso the Surrealist, while Alfred Neumeyer, director of the Mills Gallery of Art, described Léger as comparable in stature to Picasso.[67] Léger, like Picasso, turned to French masters such as Poussin in responding to traumatic historical moments. During *Guernica's* residency at MoMA, critics compared it to many paintings, including Poussin's *Rape of the Sabine Women* (1637) (fig. 59).[68] In an essay first published in 1945 with his *plongeurs* paintings, Léger, too, identified the Poussin painting as influential for

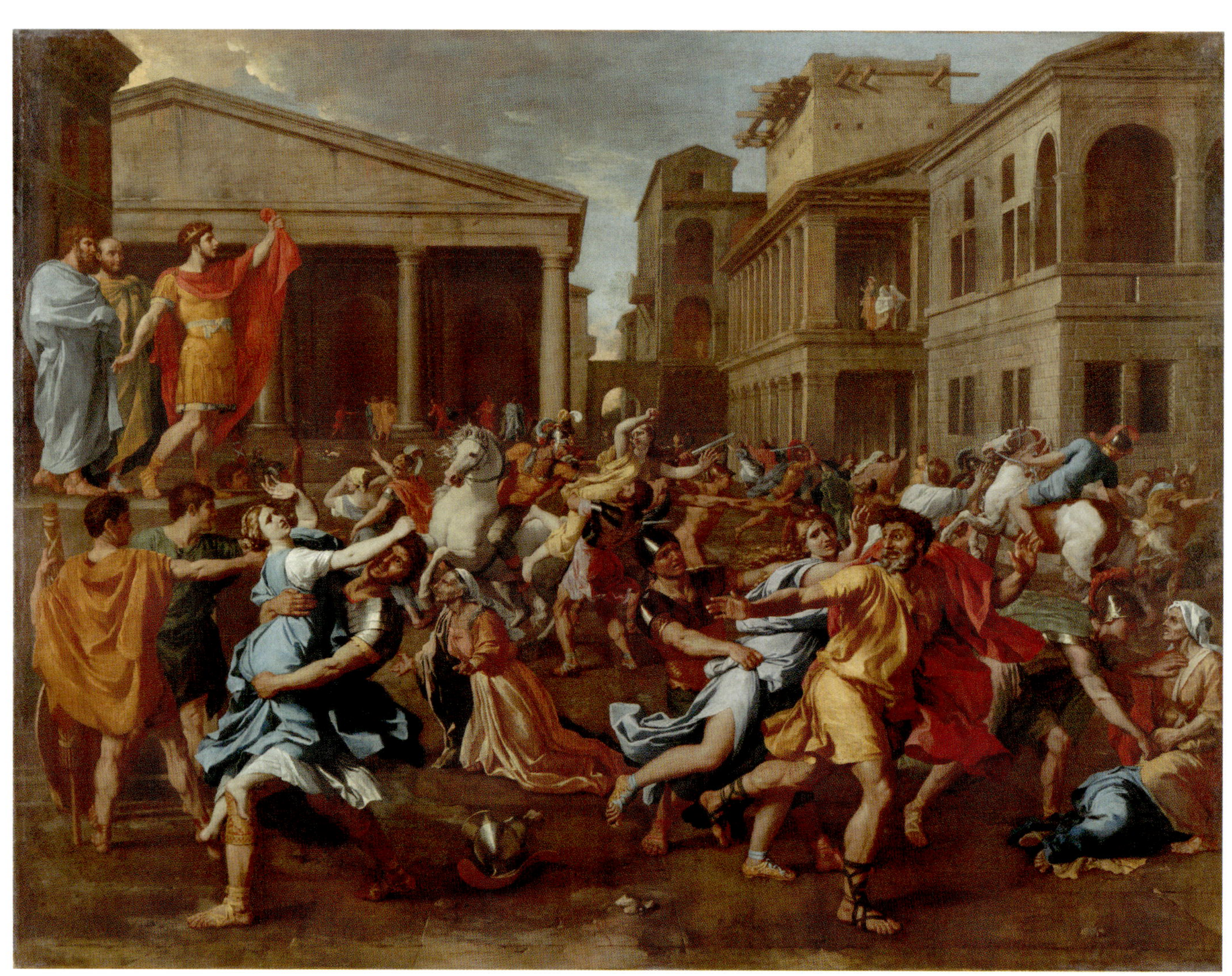

his use of line, color, and compositional structure.[69] But if Léger turned to Poussin in developing his *plongeurs* compositions, he rejected the explicit connection to an iconography of war and assault that Picasso adopted in *Guernica*.

Traumatic Time and Mythic Form

Fig. 59 Nicolas Poussin, *Rape of the Sabine Women*, 1637. Oil on canvas, 159 × 206 cm. Musée du Louvre, Paris, France. © RMN-Grand Palais / Art Resource, New York.

What should we make of the absence of national identity, fraternal solidarity, and utopian visions in the *plongeurs*? How might Léger's rejection of positivist signs or referential form lend itself to traumatic experience? Arising from a specific historic moment, the *plongeurs* series nevertheless dislocates the spectator from historical time and national or geographic spaces and instead immerses the viewer into the timeless but not the utopian, a nonplace that is the antithesis of a *lieux de mémoire*. The series is in this sense haunted by what is missing, what can no longer be materialized, and what has been denied representation: the individual body, the erotic or laboring body, the body invested with a memory of the past and a hope for the future, the spaces of culture and history, the cries of suffering in Picasso's *Guernica*.

Many exiled artists turned to mythic scenes of creation and destruction during the war, but unlike his contemporaries, Léger never adopted titles or an iconography that reference the mythic. Works such as Lipchitz's *Rape of Europa* (1941), Rothko's *Sacrifice of Iphigenia* (1942), and Masson's *Pasiphaë* (1943) turn to antiquity for metaphors of sacrifice and suffering to represent war-torn Europe as a traumatized feminized body. Although Léger returns to the compositional structures of High Renaissance myths of creation and destruction, he does so only to evacuate any legible reference to mythic forms in his *plongeurs* imagery and title, with the result that the *plongeurs* comprise a new typology that obscures—even dissociates—its sources.

In developing his Marseille story, Léger approached the mythic yet never adopted a recognizable iconography. Like his obsessively repeated story of his inspiration from the glint of light on a 75mm cannon, Léger's Marseille story transforms into linguistic control what must have been an overwhelming experience. In an interview in 1954 with the art critic Dora Vallier, Léger reveals that the *plongeurs* that possessed him during the war were produced as part of a process of dissociation from iconic Renaissance imagery, specifically Michelangelo's Sistine Chapel frescoes, with their mythic cataclysms:

> In 1940, I was in Marseille working on my *Plongeurs*, [a composition of] five or six diving figures. Then I left for the United States and [there I] went to the pool one day. There were no longer only five or six divers but a couple hundred [diving] all at once. See if you can distinguish them! Whose head?

> Whose leg? Whose arms? I didn't know any more. So I scattered the limbs in my painting. In doing so, I think I am much closer to the truth than Michelangelo who studied the details of the muscles of each body part. The figures he painted in the Sistine Chapel I saw quite well; they don't fall, they stay fixed in each corner of the building. You can even distinguish the nails of their big toes. As for me, I assure you that when the Marseille boys threw themselves in the water, I didn't have time to notice the details, and my divers, they fell.[70]

Léger's image-memory of *plongeurs* collapses multiple spaces and temporalities and moves between a European past and the moment of dislocation to the site of exile. It transits from Marseille in 1940, the United States during his exile, the Sistine Chapel he surely saw when he went to Italy with Rosenberg in 1924 and certainly knew in reproduction, and a narrative return to Marseille as a scene of chaos. The story suggests an experiential truth cloaked in modernism's anti-Renaissance discourse. It invests contradictory meanings to diving and falling—a watery scene of leisure and a cataclysmic fall—yet evacuated of pleasure or fear. Like Léger's account in 1919 of the glint of light on a 75mm cannon, Léger elides the threat of death that nevertheless appears in the form of fragmented limbs and the fall.

At the onset, he visualizes two opposing social conditions and sites creating the masses: divers in the Marseille harbor and swimmers in an American pool. Where the Marseille harbor had become a site of mass exodus and national, even continental, dismemberment in 1940, US swimming pools were sites of racially segregated leisure metonymic of the scale of the country and its masses. In the summer of 1941, when Léger taught in Oakland, California, he may have learned of Fleishhacker Pool in San Francisco, which was the largest pool in the United States and could accommodate ten thousand swimmers.[71] Léger's statement oscillates between sites of chaos, first located in the masses at an American swimming pool where individual differentiation is impossible. By the end of the passage, he returns to Marseille, and chaos shifts to corporeal experience: he "didn't have time to notice the details" but only the sensation of falling. Léger's Michelangelo is no longer only a referential sign of the Oedipal father to be supplanted by modernism but now a complex sign of losses linked to a European past and a dislocated present. "Michelangelo" is engulfed by "Marseille." Art history, the heroic male body, and the old institutions are swallowed up by exile that renders unrecognizable earlier forms and values.

In the 1920s, the Purists had turned to the athletic and convulsive movements of Michelangelo's Sistine Chapel to explain painting's relationship to architecture and their concept of a *machine à émouvoir*. For Ozenfant and Le Corbusier, the *machine à émouvoir* was a Purist method of analyzing the "plastic elements" of a painting for how the movement of masses and the relationships among volumes, color, and

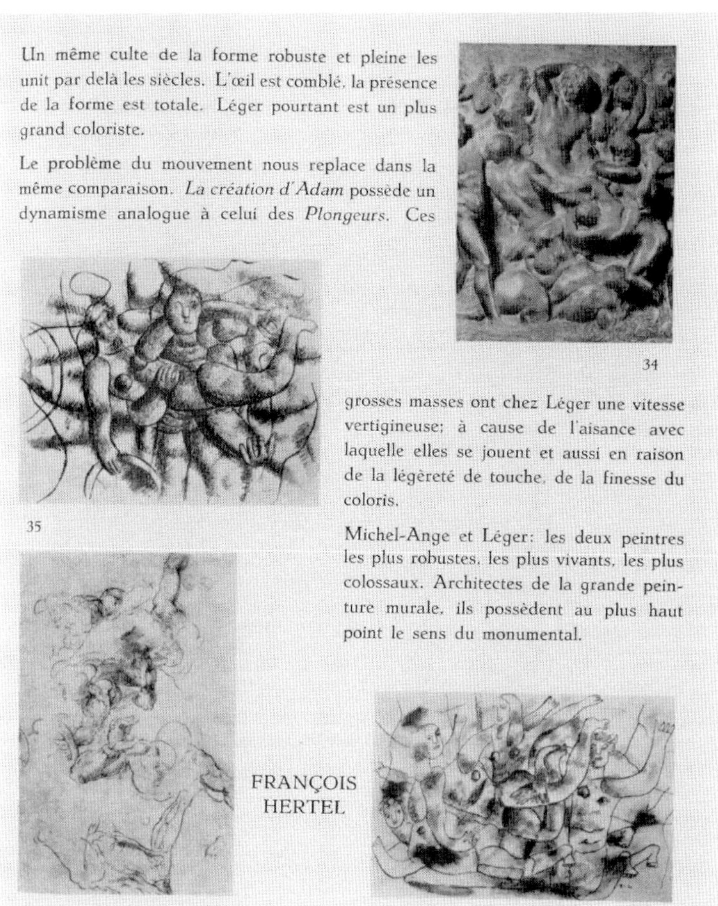

Un même culte de la forme robuste et pleine les unit par delà les siècles. L'œil est comblé, la présence de la forme est totale. Léger pourtant est un plus grand coloriste.

Le problème du mouvement nous replace dans la même comparaison. *La création d'Adam* possède un dynamisme analogue à celui des *Plongeurs*. Ces grosses masses ont chez Léger une vitesse vertigineuse; à cause de l'aisance avec laquelle elles se jouent et aussi en raison de la légèreté de touche, de la finesse du coloris.

Michel-Ange et Léger: les deux peintres les plus robustes, les plus vivants, les plus colossaux. Architectes de la grande peinture murale, ils possèdent au plus haut point le sens du monumental.

34

35

36

FRANÇOIS HERTEL

37

Fig. 60 François Hertel, "Léger, Disciple de Michelange," *La forme humaine dans l'espace* (Montreal: [publisher], 1945): n.p., figs. 34–37. Fig. 34 is Michelangelo's *The Battle of Lapiths and Centaurs* (1492). Fig. 35 is Léger's *Acrobats* (1940), ink drawing, Coll. Louis Carré, Paris. Fig. 36 is a drawing by Michelangelo. Fig. 37 is Léger's *The Divers* (1941), ink drawing, Art Institute of Chicago. © 2024 Artists Rights Society (ARS), New York / ADAGP, Paris. Image courtesy of the Library of Congress, Washington, DC.

composition "give satisfaction to the eye" and "delight the intellect."[72] This conception of painting helps explain early interpretations of the *plongeurs*. In 1945, Hertel wrote that he saw Léger as a "disciple" of Michelangelo and that both artists were "heavy artillery" in the world of painting, both "architects of large mural painting."[73] Hertel juxtaposed Léger's preparatory studies for *plongeurs* with Michelangelo's sketches for the *Last Judgment* as well as the relief sculpture *The Battle of Lapiths and Centaurs* (1492) (figs. 60 and 61). The comparison foregrounds their shared pattern of interlaced limbs, corporeal interdependence, and animated movement leading the eye back and forth between sculptural depth and surface line. While Léger rejects illusionism, the study of anatomy, neo-Platonism, and Christian mythology, his composition nevertheless borrows from the *Last Judgment*'s ideas about movement and space.

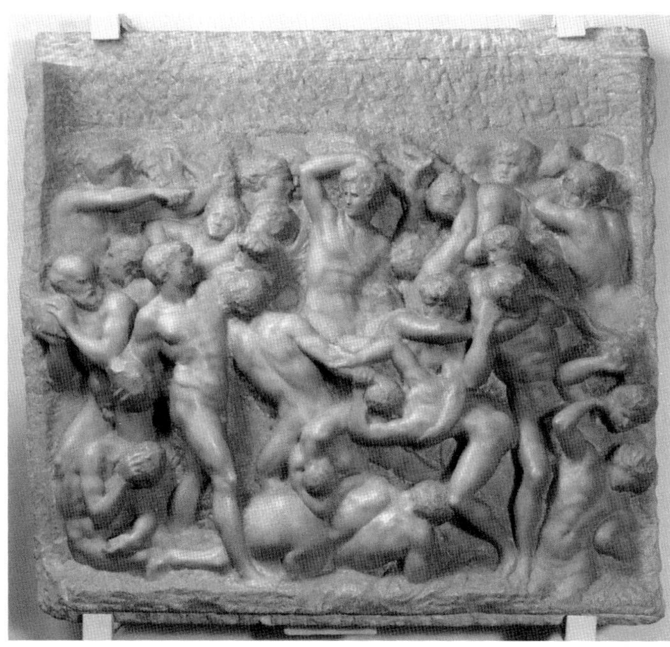

Fig. 61 Michelangelo, *The Battle of Lapiths and Centaurs*, 1492. Marble, 84.5 × 89.2 cm. Casa Buonarroti Florence, Italy. Associazione Metamorfosi, Rome / Photo Scala, Florence / Art Resource, New York.

Léger's *plongeurs* and his Marseille story suggest that, despite his protestations, he sought out Michelangelo, specifically the Sistine Chapel, as a potent cultural symbol. Léger's *plongeurs*, with their contrasting and contradictory movements, borrow from the bodies in Michelangelo's *Last Judgment*, as other scholars have noted. Karin von Maur observes that the dynamism of Léger's *plongeurs* is informed by the representational problem of weightlessness that both Michelangelo and Rubens depict in their hell scenes. She writes that the *plongeurs* are "entirely novel compositions in which the figures are transformed into a rotating, radiating focus of forces in space and time."[74] Two figures in Léger's *Divers on a Yellow Ground*, the bald hanged man and the diagonal swimming woman whose back is to us, quote and mirror two figures in Michelangelo's *Last Judgment*: the falling person at lower left in Michelangelo's earthly realm and the muscular back of a human being flung downward into hell from Charon's boat at lower right. But unlike Michelangelo's earthly figure, who is rescued by a golden-haired angel, Léger's has no savior. In surviving and escaping from the fall of France, Léger produced figures that resonate with the movement in Michelangelo's chaotic scenes invoking the end of times. But Léger's paintings also collapse social hierarchies, theological orders, political movements, and collectives organized in the service of any nation or ideological party.

By suspending moral, spatial, and temporal knowledge, Léger's *Divers on a Yellow Ground* negates the contexts that provide psychic "location" and meaning. Where Michelangelo's altar wall divides the heavens into discrete realms whose porous boundaries are marked by the struggle between angels and demons for the bodies and souls of the saved and damned, in Léger's painting there are no angels or demons interacting with the divers or differentiating land from sky, hellholes from celestial clouds, and salvation from damnation. The divers' ambiguous movements (whether climbing, falling, or diving) suggest that they do not even "know" which direction leads to heaven or hell. In the mobile space of water that defies gravity, other forces push and pull at bodies that have little power over their fate. This dislocation is exacerbated by the sense that some of Léger's figures treat the picture plane as "ground." The diagonal diver in *Divers on a Yellow Ground* has an acutely foreshortened leg, the sole of her foot kicking toward the picture plane. This perspective borrows from the position of a viewer looking up at God's feet and legs in Michelangelo's ceiling fresco *Creation of the Sun, Moon, and Plants*. Léger's painting thus converges multiple viewing positions, as though we simultaneously stand before the *Last Judgment* and look directly up at the *Creation* scene on the ceiling. The movements of the various divers in Léger's painting construct contradictory grounds and sky, making "up" and "down," earth and heaven, contingent upon the particular figure's gaze and position in relation to the "background" forms that can be read alternatively as watery reflections, geological cliff formations, or yellow sky.

Unable to discern the surface of the water, the viewer occupies a state of sensory dislocation outside normal experience, contexts, and spatial rules. The viewer's relationship to the *plongeurs* is disoriented: are we the most lost, having sunk to the depths of a sea, now looking up to figures swimming above us, or are we safe on land observing a chaos beneath us? Or perhaps we swim alongside the *plongeurs* we see before us. While Michelangelo's cosmos offers a hierarchy of good and evil and gods and demons in the highly doctrinal and liturgical context of the Sistine Chapel, "truth" in Léger's painting is displaced from structures of meaning, a dislocation that is artistic, ethical, and physical.

In *Divers on a Yellow Ground*, the multiple perspectives and ungrounded bodies competing and moving through space are counterbalanced with framing panels of fixed bodies that borrow and rework another origin myth: one of Léger's preliminary curtain designs for *The Creation of the World* (1923) (fig. 62) ballet. Léger claimed in his Marseille story that his divers do not remain "fixed in each corner," a claim that is true for most of the series but not for the Chicago painting, which incorporates two abstracted black forms on either side of the *plongeurs*. The compositional similarities between Léger's earlier *Creation* curtain and *Divers on a Yellow Ground* show that Léger returned to and reworked his ideas for the earlier origin myth. Like the two framing elements in the *plongeurs* painting, the *Creation* curtain uses two peripheral figures to draw our attention to the central image. In *Creation*, the female figures imitate wooden Senufo (Côte d'Ivoire) rhythm pounders and stand in symmetrical profile facing the central panel of a *kota* (Gabon) reliquary-type of figure.[75] In *Divers on a Yellow Ground*, however, the framing figures refuse *Creation*'s promise of production, regeneration, or commemoration. By comparison to *Creation*'s anticipation of a new world, the *plongeurs*' abstracted, quasi-figural forms seem to be a regression to an inchoate state of being, neither fully human nor animal, somewhere between vegetative and fetal life. The left might be read as a quasi-figural shape with a rounded "head" aimed toward the bottom frame, its "arm" a small black horizontal bar that holds a large, white, Y-shaped branch. The right form could be read as the silhouette of an erect human-animal whose infantile head we see in profile, its

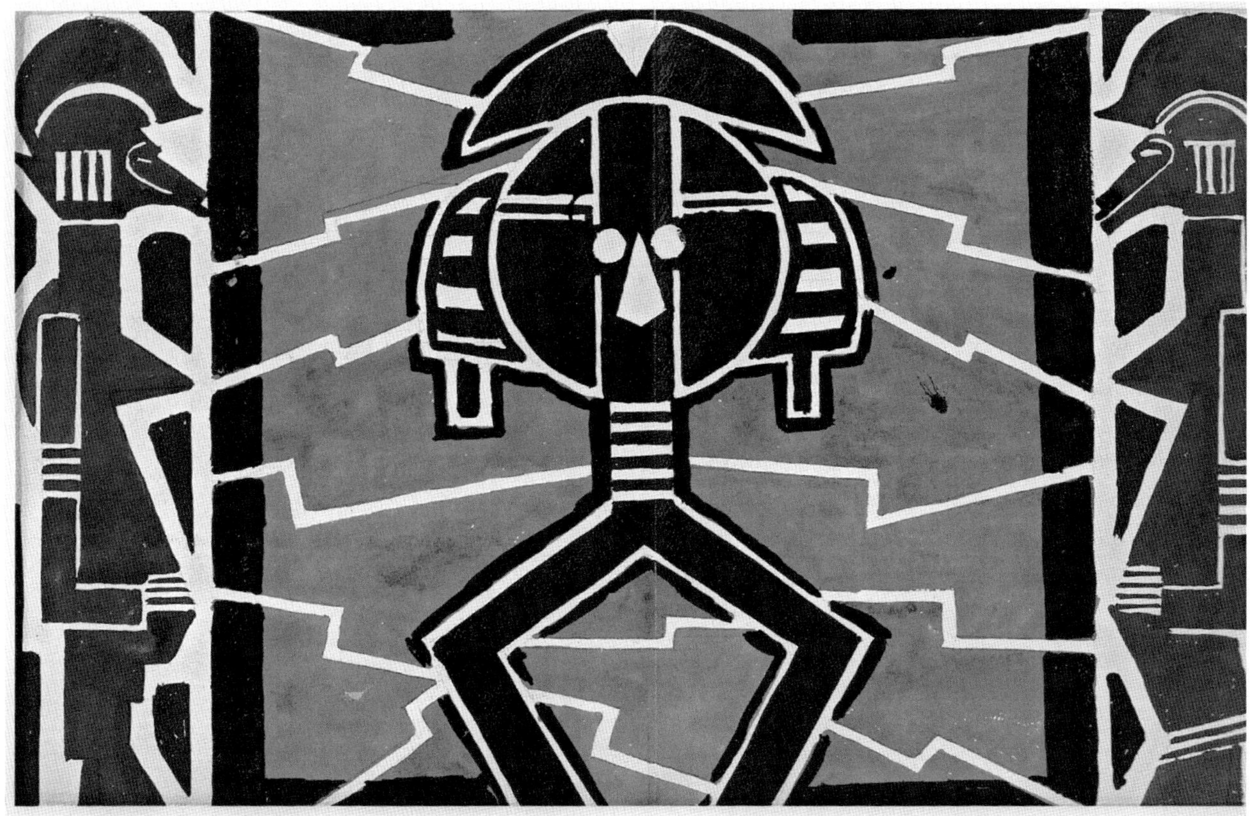

Fig. 62 Fernand Léger, curtain design for *The Creation of the World*, 1923. Gouache and drawing on paper, 31.3 × 49.9 cm. Private collection. In Norman Abramovic and Fabrice Hergott, *La Création du monde: Fernand Léger et l'art africain dans les collections Barbier-Mueller* (Paris: A. Biro, 2000), 102. © 2024 Artists Rights Society (ARS), New York / ADAGP, Paris.

stump arms reaching upward, its feet transformed into a kind of sculptural base, with a tail curling up at lower right. Arrested in the moment of chaotic formation before the intervention of the hand of any god, the *plongeurs* "guardians" signify an undoing of biological and social orders. They posit a dissociated subject position as a counterpart to the swimming figures immersed in a chaotic collapse.

Like Michelangelo's *ignudi* positioned at the corners of the flood scene (fig. 63), Léger's guardians serve as fixed bodies detached physically, spatially, and temporally from the scenes they frame. Léger's framing figures "head" in opposite directions, making the upper and lower frames function as opposing gravitational forces similar to the way that the pedestals of the *ignudi* act as counterweights pulling outward away from the central Genesis scene. Michelangelo's *ignudi* refuse to react to the biblical disasters unfolding before them and instead seem located outside the biblical events they anchor. Léger's abstractions, too, exist outside time and are unable or unwilling to respond; their embryonic silhouettes are without facial features to express affect or eyes to see, perhaps blinded to or castrated by the chaos before them.

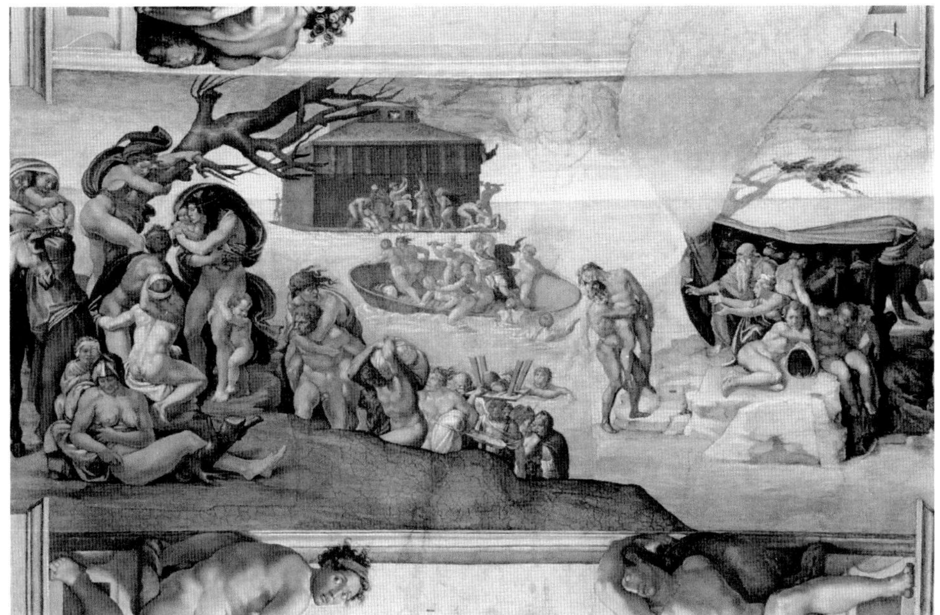

Fig. 63 Michelangelo, flood scene with *ignudi* (male nudes) in corners, 1508–9. Fresco. Sistine Chapel, Vatican Palace, Vatican. Erich Lessing / Art Resource, New York.

Abstraction as Dissociation

Léger's *plongeurs* series exemplifies the ambiguities between narrative and history, art and memory, representation and survival that have motivated trauma studies. Although Léger explained the theme as arising from the sight of divers in the Marseille harbor on the eve of his departure from France, his representational strategies dissociate the viewer from any specific place or time far more even than his long-standing modernist position against history painting. As dislocated figures, the *plongeurs* are far more abstracted from time and place than the acrobats of *Composition with Two Parrots*. Léger's Marseille story may even be apocryphal, but its significance is as a visual scene tied to the moment of flight and exile from the homeland. If it is a testimony or representation of survival, it is oblique and metaphoric, more screen memory than historical fact. In chapter 2, I argued that Léger's gendered figures manifest a complex dynamic of repetition that aims for mastery and drives toward death. Léger's production of the *plongeurs* series, too, suggests that the repetition that aims for mastery is contingent upon and interdependent with the repetition compulsion that immerses the survivor in trauma.

Léger, like many exiled artists, wanted to claim the autonomy of avant-garde art as a Kantian space of freedom above or beyond politics, reinforcing his abstracted forms. In the 1930s, Léger participated in state-sponsored Popular Front projects aligned with its social and political agenda. He supported nonintervention and peace movements in response to the rise of fascism, but his "new realism" rejected doctrinaire Socialist Realism. With the rise of fascism in 1939, *Cahiers d'Art* distributed an inquiry about whether art "can exist outside its historic time," to which Léger replied that "war leaves no place for art."[76] He sought to straddle partisan allegiance and artistic autonomy. While the artist may serve a revolutionary cause by making a photomontage or film or develop a collaboration according to larger shared ideals, Léger claimed that the artist should also have time to conduct studio investigations, "like the scientist in his lab, above the fray." Léger's use of the phrase "above the fray" invokes Rolland's pacifist statement against nationalism and militarism, *Au dessus de la mêlée* (Above the Fray), first published during World War I.[77]

Léger's new series emerges within the context of an expatriate avant-garde that moved away from explicit political context. As curator Sabine Eckmann has shown, many exiled artists—Ernst, Lyonel Feininger, Kurt Schwitters, Beckmann—sought to be "free of politics," yet their insistence upon autonomy often contradicted the social context of their experiences.[78] For example, Beckmann's work reveals the "contradictions between his desire for autonomous, transcendent art and the realities of the day."[79] Similarly, Ozenfant refused to consider himself a refugee, as though he could not fully acknowledge the fall of Europe or a sense of loss, while Masson and Tanguy explained their relocation to Connecticut rather than New York City in terms of individualism and even detachment from the war.[80] New York critics, too, promoted an image of the solitary avant-garde artist rather than a people-in-exile.[81] This distancing from the explicitly political occurred even as mythic themes and cosmic battles served as a form of displaced anxieties, as, for example, in Matta's morphologies of the cosmos or Masson's "telluric landscapes" with their "semi-abstract evocations of fragmentary plant and animal forms."[82] Others produced more enigmatic worlds; Breton saw Tanguy's *The Earth and the Air* (1941) as an "inner world" of "total indeterminacy."[83] The indeterminate worlds of Léger's *plongeurs*, too, might be interpreted as projections of his anxieties about the traumatic fall of France and its uncertain future.

Léger's discourse of being detached or free from politics may have been adopted by his generation in the context of exile, but the language of freedom also cloaked or disavowed the traumatic rupture of exile. Art historians have foregrounded Léger's experience of the United States as offering a sense of autonomy and freedom as well as alienation due to the massive scale of the country's geography and the speed and size of US cities.[84] Léger's exile in the United States permitted him significant professional success thanks to sixteen exhibitions, most of which were in Chicago, San Francisco, and New York.[85] Perhaps because of this success, the discourse of modernist autonomy and art as a space of freedom has long persisted in interpretations of

Léger's *plongeurs*.[86] But this "freedom" within the context of exile does not account for Léger's repeated dissociative processes.

In Léger's conception, "freedom" could also manifest in formal terms as the color that contrasts with the monochromatic or outlined body emptied of identity. In Harvard's *Divers* (1943) (fig. 51), the body is a heavy black outline, a spectral or trace being without mass, counterbalanced with rectangular bands of flat planes of blue, red, and yellow, possibly borrowed from the medieval apocalypse manuscripts. Léger explained these bands of color sweeping over outlined figures as "color in freedom," a motif he credited to publicity projectors that swept bands of colored light over the streets and the people in them.[87] Fréchuret characterizes Léger's bands of color as a "curative element" inspired by the Broadway projectors and in response to New York's severity.[88] Léger seems to have thought of the device as a colorist cure for ordinary people trapped in drab and oppressive worlds. On one occasion during the war when architectural historian Giedion and Moholy-Nagy were visiting Léger's New York studio, Giedion asked about the use of free color. Moholy-Nagy replied, pointing to the skyscrapers: "Don't you see that Léger must get even with those things out there?"[89] Moholy-Nagy thus interpreted the *plongeurs* as a dematerialized release from the oppression of capitalism or urban life, a reading possibly arising from his interest in the X-ray and photogram that dematerialized solid forms as well as from Bauhaus ideas about color's generative and vitalist qualities, ideas that Léger shared. Perhaps, too, Léger sought to release his figures from the weight of the traumatic displacements he witnessed in 1940.

Reconstituting a French Corpus

In grappling with the dissolution of the nation as *territoire* and as social coherence, Léger repeatedly turned to populist and pre-Renaissance French sources sharing common themes while at the same time decontextualizing the iconography. With *Divers on a Yellow Ground*, as I have shown, Léger developed a method of borrowing from the formal and compositional elements of traumatic scenes while emptying the image of narrative, spatial, and social specificity. In the polychrome *plongeurs*, particularly *Big Black Divers* (1944) (fig. 52), Léger borrows from distinctly French sources—the Saint-Sever version of the Beatus Apocalypse, *image d'Epinal* scenes of flooding, and Poussin's *Rape of the Sabine Women* (1637) (fig. 59)—while negating the scene of emotional charge. Affect, if it is felt, is displaced from narrative and facial expression to spatial sensation and social dynamics. Léger's turn to the popular and elite forms of French visual culture operates as both a return to France in the symbolic order as well as a process of dissociation from the traumatic.

Like the Saint-Sever manuscript, an *image d'Epinal* print entitled *Great Floods of 1856* (fig. 64) was a possible compositional model for Léger's *Big Black Divers*. In the 1930s, Léger had belonged to the Association des Écrivains et Artistes Révolutionnaires (Association of Revolutionary Artists and Writers), which promoted medieval manuscript illustration, stained glass, and the *image d'Epinal* as truly French forms.[90] The print, which represents the historic events of a disastrous flooding of the Loire River, brings together a rhythmic effect of primary colors in figure and ground as well as a story of flood and rescue that might also be read in *Big Black Divers*. In the print, buildings collapse in the background while Napoleon III's foot soldiers and equestrian officers rescue boatloads of frightened (and mostly female) survivors. Although the print is gendered in ways that Léger's painting is not, the print's distribution of mostly primary colors across the picture plane is similar to Léger's arrangement of color in his polychrome *plongeurs* in that color repeats, alternates, and organizes a visual path through the image.

Léger had explicitly turned to Poussin's *Sabine Women* as a French model during his Purist period and again in the 1940s. In the 1920s, Poussin was promoted in the pages of *L'Esprit Nouveau*, and Léger cited the French master's juxtaposition of arches and figures as a model for his law of contrasts.[91] In 1945, in his essay on the human body as an object, Léger once again cited the *Sabine Women* as a "concentration of figures radically opposed to the geometric elements of constructions . . . a battle of right angles and curves."[92] Léger's emphasis on geometry, line, and form indicate his debt to art historian Pierre Courthion, whom Léger knew in the 1930s. Courthion had published a biography of Poussin in 1929 and illustrated his book with only two images, one of which was Poussin's *Sabine Women* in the Louvre. In Courthion's interpretation, Poussin's painting has "an almost mathematical solidity, he [Poussin] opposes lines with lines, volumes with volumes, men and women, defense of the Sabine from the attack of the Romans. . . . [it is a] symphony of rhythms that overlap each other: the savage rhythm of the soldiers that brutalize the Sabine they rape; the rhythm accelerated, desperate in the escape at right; the slow and desolate rhythm of the old mother who begs the Romans; the serious rhythm of Romulus who commands."[93]

While Léger does not specify how Poussin informed the *plongeurs* series, his *Big Black Divers* shares Poussin's rhythmic use of color and line to punctuate the composition and convey "dynamic action." Yet where Poussin uses these rhythmic effects to express the drama of historic events, Léger detaches the signifiers of gesture and movement from country, culture, and historical narrative. In Léger's writing, Poussin's "right angles," the rectangular forms of the classical architecture, are juxtaposed against "curves," the raised arms of the abducted women and fighting men. The swimming and kicking limbs of Léger's brown, black, blue, and yellow *plongeurs* structure a rhythmic parallel borrowed from the raised arms that punctuate

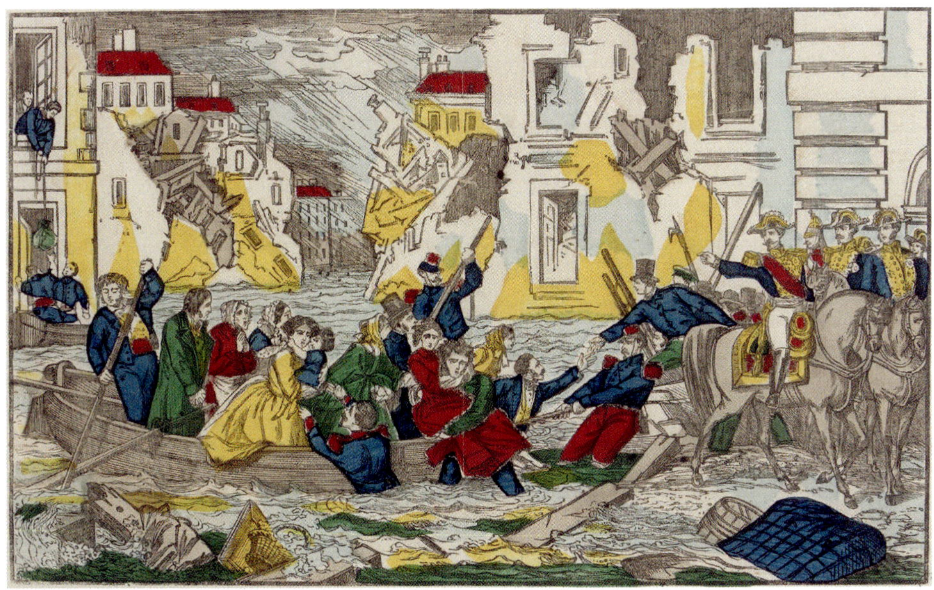

Fig. 64 Jean-Charles Pellerin, *Great Floods of 1856*, n.d. Color lithograph, 32 × 41.7 cm. Musée des Civilisations de l'Europe et de la Méditerranée, Marseille, France, Inv. no. 53.86.4812. Photo: Danièle Adam. © RMN-Grand Palais / Art Resource, New York.

Poussin's composition. Just as the blue and red garments of Poussin's Sabine women and Roman men direct the viewer's gaze across the canvas, so, too, pure color is distributed across Léger's canvas: blue, brown, black, yellow, and green bodies all have their counterparts in watery plaques. But where Poussin's form signifies in terms of pleas for help, resistance, aggression, and defense, such emotion is largely excluded from *Big Black Divers*. So, too, is history: Poussin's painting invokes the brutal myth from ancient Rome while Léger's polychrome *plongeurs* evacuate any temporal, spatial, or historical specificity.

Black and Brown Saviors

Beginning in 1944, as the tides of the war shifted in favor of the Allies with their landing at Normandy in June, the liberation of Paris in August, and the invasion of Germany in September, the constrained figure of the hanged man is counterbalanced or supplanted completely by a standing brown figure. "France" and "Marseille" no longer become equated with social collapse, occupation, and desperate crowds in flight. While early versions of the *plongeurs* paintings, such as *Divers on a Yellow Ground*, worked through the traumatic invasion of France and departure through Marseille, later *plongeurs* paintings offer the possibility of gravity and grounding. In *Big Black Divers*, Léger invests the previously grisaille or outlined figures with flat planes of blue, brown, black, and yellow, colors suggesting a racialized coding. A standing brown figure replaces the hanged man at the center of the canvas in *Divers on a Yellow Ground*, thus providing gravitational orientation and diminishing the vertiginous chaos of earlier versions of the *plongeurs*. Even more, the erect figure no longer aimlessly floats or sinks but, in a gesture of solidarity amid the chaos, catches a falling yellow *plongeur*. This gesture of acrobatic risk and rescue revives one that Léger first introduced in the 1930s and that later reappears in *Acrobat and His Partner* (1948). The erect figure in *Big Black Divers*, too, functions as a point of stasis among the other *plongeurs*. Like Léger's interwar acrobats who stand facing the picture plane, this new diver might be read as confronting or mirroring the viewer.

In gaining gravity and solidarity, the polychrome *plongeurs* suggest a new equilibrium and new affective states that offer a resolution to the anxiety of earlier *plongeurs*. The earliest manifestation of this erect *plongeur* appears in 1942, a year after Léger reunited with composer Darius Milhaud and novelist André Maurois to teach at Mills College. At that time, Léger dedicated a gouache with a standing *plongeur* to Maurois and his wife. It may be that as promising partnerships and exhibition opportunities arose for Léger, he was able to regain his ground and restore his professional persona. Another early painted version of the polychrome *plongeurs*, *Divers with Birds* (1942), depicts a standing brown figure at center. Léger gave it to Maria Martins, a Surrealist sculptor who was a lover of Duchamp and wife of the Brazilian ambassador, when he was soliciting funds from Brazil for a collaboration with Milhaud on a planned opera about "El Libertador" Simón Bolívar.[94] But the emergence of the polychrome *plongeurs* also align with the shifting fortunes of France and its dependence on its colonial terrain and subjects.

The brown, black, and yellow bodies of the polychrome *plongeurs* participate in typologies familiar to the colonial concept of *la plus grande France*, an invocation that came about as France recruited its empire to regain the hexagon. Historian Eric Jennings has argued that the heart of General de Gaulle's Free France was not in London but in sub-Saharan Africa, which provided de Gaulle territory, human resources, and a staging ground from which to reclaim the mainland.[95] By November 1942, Free France regained control of a majority of its colonies. And in June 1943, Algiers became its capital, remaining so until August 1944, when de Gaulle launched his campaign through the port of Marseille. Indexical of the multiethnic ports that Léger passed through from Marseille, France to Oakland, California, *Big Black Divers* engages in a new primitivism in the service of regeneration, opening up other possible meanings for "Marseille."

In the 1930s and 1940s, Marseille had been for Léger a site of libidinal energies and colonized bodies. In the 1930s, he wrote to Herman about a Marseille outside the rules of good taste, a city of prostitution, drugs, and sexual adventure, a multiethnic, messy, vital, and colorful city like New York.[96] In describing the Marseille of

1940 and 1941 at the time of the Nazi invasion and national collapse, Fry wrote that the city was crowded with colonial soldiers in ethnographic dress: soldiers wearing Tunisian red fezzes or *chéchias*, Zouaves in Turkish-style trousers, Moroccan spahis with broad black sashes on their waists, and Senegalese wearing turbans.[97] Léger's polychrome *plongeurs*, like the colorless hanged man and outlined versions, are, however, neither objects of desire nor exotic warriors. Their androgyny, combined with the essentialized ethnic marker of color, simultaneously elides the erotic body while also drawing upon tropes of the primitive. Perhaps the primitive's perceived inability to feel served Léger's aim to evacuate abstraction of feeling.

While Léger may have wanted the polychrome *plongeurs* to signify racial harmony or collaboration, his modernist indeterminacy both opens up meaning to multiple historical and geographic contexts while also eliding their specificity. In 1942, Léger wanted to imagine "America" as a multiethnic society that was the most likely to produce a future racial harmony, yet his public and private writing scarcely comments upon racial or colonial hierarchies in the United States, such as Japanese internment or racial segregation. In an essay on what it meant to "discover America," Léger described the sight of three shopgirls—"a Chinese, a Negress, and a blonde American"—whom he saw chatting with each other just before the store's opening.[98] Léger interpreted them as "three graces" and a "prophetic triptych" of races that "are often fighting and tearing each other apart"; he claimed that if they ever reached an understanding it would be "here under this sun" and "the greatest event in the history of the world." Léger's utopian vision deflects a global, imperial war from view and constructs a feminine version of Orozco's international brotherhood that simultaneously diminishes dispute to feminine bickering. At the same time, it invokes the old trope of empire's global scope configured as female figures representing Africa, Asia, and the Americas. There was another "Marseille" that Léger perhaps could not see, one that existed in the United States as well as in France—that is, the brutality against Africans in Marseille that novelist Claude McKay fictionalized, the French colonialism that poet and politician Aimé Césaire saw as preparation for Nazism, and the oppression that Léger's former student Okubo suffered during internment.[99]

Conclusion

The *plongeurs* series did not continue after the war, which is not surprising given its use as a process of working through the fall of France and the experience of exile, but its afterlife appears in Léger's *France Reborn* (1945) (fig. 65). Created as a commercial poster design for the Art Institute of Chicago's exhibition *Modern Art in Advertising: Designs for the Container Corporation*, held from April 27, 1945, to June 23, 1945,

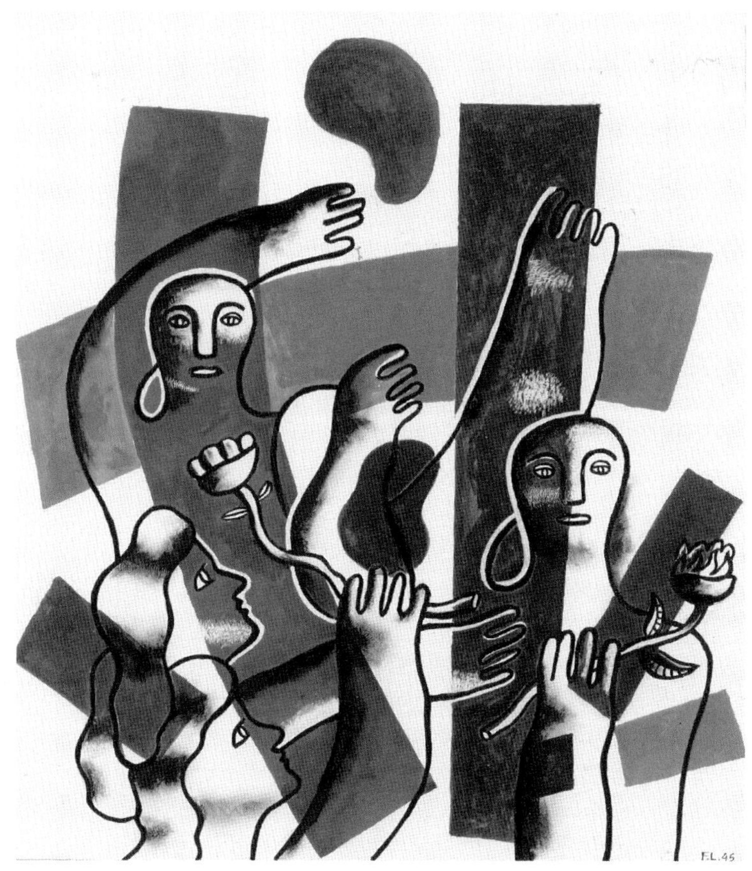

Léger's poster was one of many designs by modern artists recruited to publicize the company's contribution to European relief efforts.[100] Planned after the D-Day invasion on June 6, 1944, the exhibition was still open when victory in Europe was declared on May 8, 1945. Léger's inclusion was in part due to his long-standing friendship with Moholy-Nagy, founder and director of the New Bauhaus in Chicago, who had developed ties with the Art Institute and with industrialists like Walter Paepcke, president of the Container Corporation. Contingent upon US capitalism, the project occurred only months before Léger's inscription into the French Communist Party in October 1945. Léger's image combines the outlined *plongeurs* and "free color" with the gravitational orientation of the erect figure in the polychrome *plongeurs*, but without the colonial referent of colored bodies. At left, two profiled female figures with long hair, one with a flower, gaze upward and gesture toward vertical bands of color in red and blue, colors that stand in for the French *tricoleur*. A vertical band of red arcs through several figures, illustrating the advertising caption: "new lifeblood—supplies in paper packages." The catalog states that Léger wanted the image to express "the French people's feelings of joy and freedom at the end of the war" and that the elevated arms, flowers, and pure color express "the plastic sign of liberation."[101] All erect, the figures find gravity and ground with France's reintegration as free nation. The two figures at left reinscribe gender normativity with their long hair, while the outlined rather than polychrome bodies assert a coded racial hegemony. By the time of the catalog's postwar publication in 1946, the published images became known as the "United Nations series," reinforcing nationalisms contingent upon racial classifications and colonialism.

Fig. 65 Fernand Léger, *France Reborn*, 1945. Watercolor, gouache, and pencil on paper, 66.2 × 55.5 cm. Gift of Container Corporation of America (1984.124.173), Smithsonian American Art Museum, Washington, DC / Art Resource, New York. © 2024 Artists Rights Society (ARS), New York / ADAGP, Paris.

While the *plongeurs*' afterlife in *France Reborn* offers a vision of a collective that has regained its grounding, Léger's *plongeurs* series operates, I argue, as a working through of Léger's traumatic departure from France, exile in the United States, and his search for artistic freedom during the war years. Where *France Reborn* invests in a reconstituted nationalism, the *plongeurs* series used modernist abstraction in a process of dissociation from scenes of violence, itself a form of violent negation. In characterizing the *plongeurs* as "freer" and more "violent" than the interwar acrobats, Léger introduced a new figural type and a vertiginously alienated collective. In doing so, he rejected earlier modernist paradigms and the "literary subject," such as the nude, the landscape, history, and myth. Instead, the paintings immerse the viewer in a collective body enacting social collapse and dissolution or, in the case of the hanged man, entrapment and constraint. In envisioning them as mural paintings for a future canvas or wall format, Léger imagined a collective, even populist, audience and recalled a lost state infrastructure of the Popular Front era. The abstraction of Léger's *plongeurs* series, with its weightlessness and disorientation, offers viewers a contradictory sense of freedom even as it radically undermines the certainties of the self, making "freedom" contingent upon forgetting or erasing trauma from memory or at least from sight.

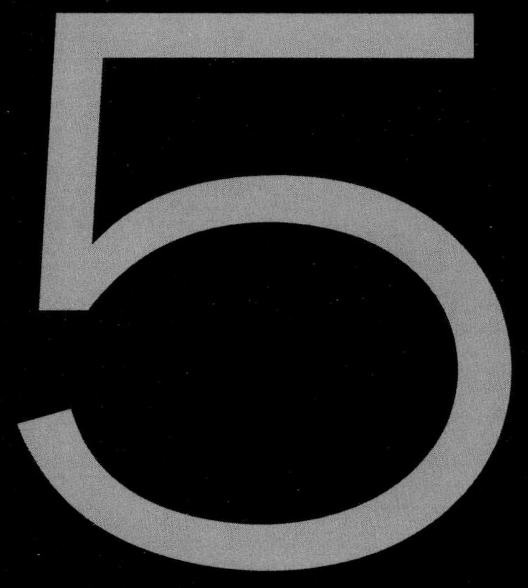

Survival, Nostalgia, and Melancholy

Big Julie (1945) (fig. 66), one of the last major works that Léger produced during his exile, is, like the *plongeurs* series, a manifest scene of leisure—a young woman with her bicycle—that simultaneously encodes the war's losses and a new crisis of masculinity. *Big Julie* is both the culmination of a wartime series of paintings and drawings depicting groups of women bicyclists and a predecessor to postwar scenes of cyclists of various genders. Exemplified by *The Four Cyclists* (fig. 67), the cycling series insists upon leisure in the midst of war, perhaps addressing working-class viewers who Léger hoped would use their leisure time to learn about modern art. Unlike the groups that predominate in the cycling images, however, Julie stands erect and alone with her bicycle, in a dependent yet alienated relationship with the vehicle of her liberation. Her left arm, awkwardly dislocated from her shoulder and twisted backward, means that she leans on rather than holds up her partner. Her columnar body revives the caryatid classicism of the domesticated women in Léger's paintings from the 1920s, while the clay golem-like malleability of her right arm, the acrobatic outfit she wears, and the bicycle wheels' resemblance to juggler's rings invoke the circus scenes of the 1930s. Julie's "other half" seems to be a monument to a failed machine era and an earlier avant-garde: a convoluted and incomplete bicycle that is missing key parts (the seat, the wheel spokes, the pedals) and that hangs like a crucified body upon a Kazimir Malevich–style cross in Pentecostal red. In pairing a muscular female body without a male partner, *Big Julie* seems to mourn the heterosexual dyad while converging masculine and feminine elements in the represented body. The bicycle, claimed as a symbol of leisure, is surprisingly nonfunctioning and useless. The cyclists' terrain, suggested only by a few undulating lines or arcs in the group pictures, disappears completely in *Big Julie*, which seems to position the "objects" in a timeless, even spiritual field.

Fig. 66 Fernand Léger, *Big Julie*, 1945. Oil on canvas, 112 × 127 cm. Acquired through the Lillie P. Bliss Bequest, Museum of Modern Art, New York. Digital Image © The Museum of Modern Art / Licensed by SCALA / Art Resource, New York. © 2024 Artists Rights Society (ARS), New York / ADAGP, Paris.

Commentaries on the cyclist series, by Léger as well as art historians, emphasize the themes of leisure and popular culture and almost never address the paintings' absences. Yet Léger also spoke about *Big Julie* in terms of the "survival" of popular culture and "memory of an old French song," raising questions about what forms of survival and memory are represented. Cycling, a major activity in interwar France and wartime United States, was one of Léger's favorite pastimes but became a complex, emotionally laden signifier in the context of the fall of France and Léger's wartime exile. *Big Julie*'s foregrounding of the female body and its contingent relationship to a missing male partner raise questions about wartime femininity and male absence. In other words, how might the absence of male figures in the cyclist series—and in Léger's wartime work more generally—complicate the possibilities for representation that *Big Julie* engages? What might account for the split field and its dialectics? The painting's binary structure confronts the viewer with a set of competing and contingent relations: the popular and the avant-garde, the organic and the machine, the static and dynamic, the figural and abstract, the autonomous and the sacrificial, the sacred and profane, among others. In this chapter, I argue that the series is bound up with traumas experienced at the national, collective, and individual levels: the exile's alienation from the French homeland, the dispersal of artistic and intellectual circles, and the familial separations and male loss. *Big Julie* is thus a complex field through which the artist works through ideas about the survival of modernism and French culture.

Engaged in a "leisure" activity like Julie's cycling, Léger generated art that blocks themes of war, male workers, and soldiers in order to explore their antithesis. Unlike his situation during World War I, Léger could not claim frontline fraternal camaraderie and did not express a desire to represent the soldier's shocked subjectivity, nor did he attempt to represent the soldier at all. Despite his position far from the warfront and in the land of industry, he could not return to the gendered iconography of the 1920s: columnar or reclining women confined to the domestic space and male laborers—the cattle merchants, tugboat captains, mechanics—moving through the city and factory.

Like Léger's origin stories for his machine aesthetic and *plongeurs*, his anecdotal accounts about the cyclist paintings are fragmentary and elliptical, markers of traumatic ruptures with the nation and with artistic and intellectual communities. In his contradictory accounts of Julie, she is alternatively a sign of liberty in the United States and nostalgia for France, suggesting competing emotions linked to his American opportunities and lost homeland. In 1946, when MoMA purchased *Big Julie*, Léger claimed inspiration from US "bad taste" and cast French "good taste"

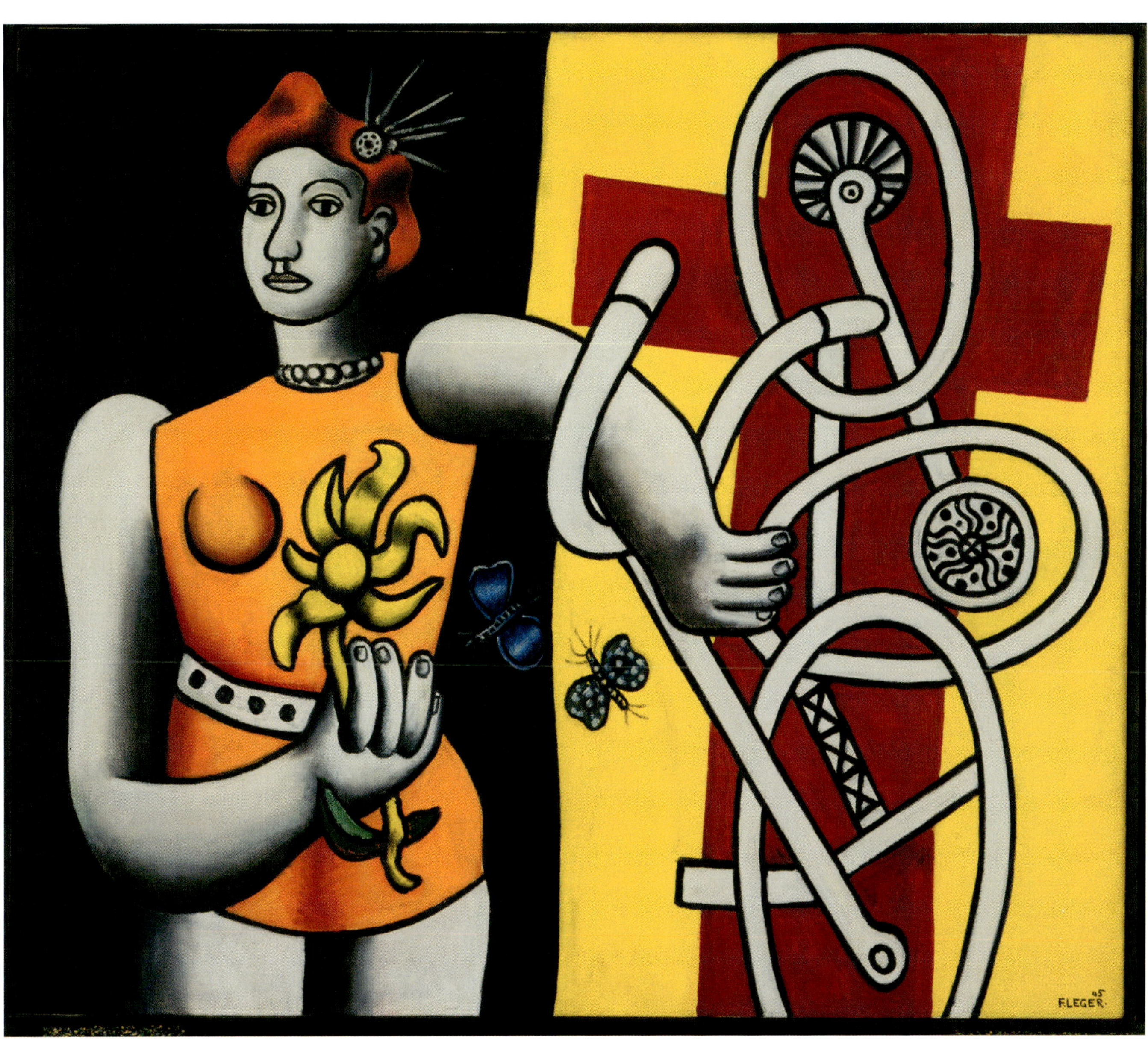
45
F.LEGER.

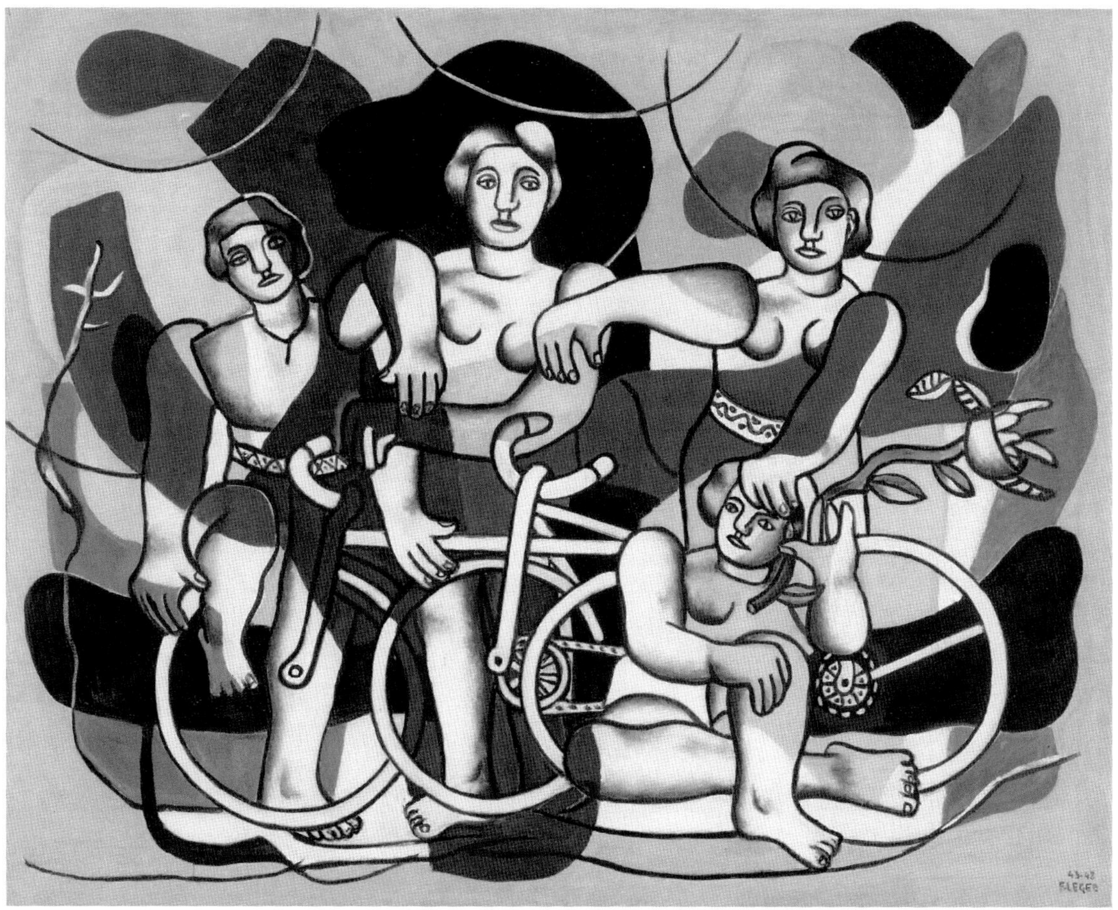

Fig. 67 Fernand Léger, *The Four Cyclists*, 1943–48. Oil on canvas, 130 × 162 cm. Donation of Nadia Léger and Georges Bauquier (Biot), 1969, Inv. no. MNFL98005. Musée National Fernand Leger, Biot, France. © RMN-Grand Palais / Art Resource, New York. © 2024 Artists Rights Society (ARS), New York / ADAGP, Paris.

as a "pitfall" precluding "vigorous survival."[1] But in the documentary on Léger shot during the war by Bouchard, Léger explained the title as "in memory of an old French song."[2] These competing stories might be explained by the different nationalities of the audiences for the MoMA bulletin and the French film. But Léger's responses also suggest that he was keenly aware of iconic cultural forms as repositories of collective memory and social values. France and Frenchness, for example, are alternatively a site of "good taste" to be brought low and the terrain of nostalgia, that archaic malady brought on by being far from the homeland or made modern by the lost attachments of a mobile world. Unlike Léger's story about the 75mm cannon or his Marseille departure, these anecdotes make no claim upon historical events. Yet Léger's comments about "bad taste" as "survival" invite inquiry into the battles fought and the forms that survive.

Bad Taste and US Culture

When MoMA acquired *Big Julie* in 1945, the museum's journal published an interview in which Léger emphasized his appropriation of popular forms. Léger casts Julie as a figure of "bad taste" informed by the sweater girl, burlesque, and Broadway as well as his earlier circus, acrobat, and cyclist paintings:

> For me, the contrast in the United States between the mechanical and the natural is one of great anti-melodic intensity. Bad taste is also one of the valuable raw materials for the country. Bad taste, strong colors—it is all here for the painter to organize and get the full use of its power. Girls in sweaters with brilliant colored skin; girls in shorts dressed more like acrobats in a circus than one would ever come across on a Paris street. If I had only seen girls dressed in "good taste" here I would never have painted my *Cyclist* series, of which *La Grand Julie* in the Museum was the culmination. . . . I always hate to see "good taste" come to the people. For painters like me who are robust it is very dangerous to frequent the beau monde, ballets and the like. French "taste" is a pitfall for the creative artist. . . . Even burlesque shows are infected by "good taste." Still there is no need yet to worry. One only has to study the hand-painted ties on Broadway—a locomotive and four pigeons on a violet and black ground, or a buxom nude on a saffron ground—to realize there is still a vigorous survival.[3]

Léger's statement about *Big Julie* expresses a contradictory identification with the "bad taste" of New York's popular cultural forms, cast as the survival of male desire in the form of the objectified female body, while "good taste" is an infection attributed to a feminized and subjugated France. If there is a contest between the "natural" and "mechanical," Julie is natural or authentic rather than "infected" (or affected), while the mechanical represented by the bicycle is disabled.

Big Julie's libidinal "bad taste" draws from what art critic Clement Greenberg called kitsch: the "inauthentic" commodified mass culture of Hollywood films and popular photography magazines addressed to the "ignorant" to reap "enormous profits" and wipe out folk culture.[4] Léger's bright, unmodulated color engages with the aesthetics of comics in an era when Wonder Woman debuted (in January 1942) swinging through the air like a trapeze artist to rescue a military pilot. With her short shorts and tight sleeveless top, Julie adopts similar attire. Such skimpy garments regularly appeared on the covers of the mass-distribution picture magazines such as *Life* and *Look*, glossy magazines whose broad visual array provided an accessible entrée into US popular culture particularly for the non-English speaker like Léger. Julie's outfit borrows the bust-defining, leg-displaying "sweater girl" aesthetic adopted, for example, by actress Judy Garland on the cover of *Look* in January 2, 1940. Julie's pearl choker and glittering brooch, a round medallion with spiked rays pinned to her brilliant orange-red Communard beret, present an array of contradictory class signals. The faux jewelry are "inauthentic" mass-produced commodities meant to appeal to an "uncultivated" consumer. The brooch imitates the sequined adornments popularized in the genre of the musical, while the tight string of pearls marks the repressed desire of bourgeois self-presentation. Worn together in the context of cycling, they are contradictory and confusing, but they are both signals of a commodified form of class aspiration in the cultural context of a constrained left. As a representative of "the people" rather than the beau monde or elite classes, Julie is more burlesque than ballet, more buxom nudity than sartorial haute couture.

To critics like Greenberg and Harold Rosenberg, Léger's wartime art was symptomatic of the decline and intellectual fall of France. Produced in the wake of Greenberg's landmark essay "Avant-garde and Kitsch" (1939), *Big Julie* grapples with the issues he raises: the relationship between popular and avant-garde forms, the politics of capitalism and art's commodification, audiences and class formation, national identity and survival. Greenberg famously defined kitsch as a dominant but debased culture, precisely the kind that Léger celebrates. By 1954, in response to Léger's retrospective at MoMA, Greenberg complained that the final version of Léger's cyclist series had the feel of an "old popular print." Although Greenberg praised Léger's Cubist work, he saw Léger's post-Cubist work as a "decline" and wrote that the art produced in the United States was "not impressive." Greenberg dismissively asserted: "Nothing in Léger's art has equaled the breadth and finality it had before cubism gave out."[5] Léger, in Greenberg's terms, represented an intellectual fall and failure of avant-gardism.

On the one hand, by 1940, avant-garde art in the European context suffered under totalitarianism's outright attacks, state-sponsored forms of realism in the Soviet Union, and neoclassicisms in Germany and Italy. In 1937, the Nazis organized the Degenerate Art exhibition in order to equate the distorted and fragmented bodies in avant-garde art, including Expressionism, Dadaism, and Surrealism, with mental deficiency, insanity, Judaism, and homosexuality. Even the mechanical-abstracted bodies of Bauhaus artists like Schlemmer and Baumeister came under attack due to the mutability of their forms.[6] On the other hand, there was also a rapprochement between modernism and fascism particularly as the arts lent themselves to ideologies of nationalism, racial authenticity, and the soldierly body.[7] In the 1920s and 1930s, Le Corbusier had become increasingly bound up in complex relationships with French fascist groups—from Ernst Mercier's Redressement Français to

Georges Valois's Action Française. Le Corbusier established the syndicalist journal *Plans* (1931–32), with a Valois follower, and under Vichy, he earned an official role in developing state housing policy.[8]

Léger's investment in US popular culture as a form of survival might be understood as a response to the emasculation of the avant-garde and French art under fascist attack. In the 1930s, Mussolini's favorite artist, Mario Sironi, argued for a revival of figural forms in fresco and mural art. As Golan has shown, Sironi targeted Surrealism by claiming that Italian mural art was a more masculine form than French art and easel painting.[9] The Nazi state valorized the rigid, phallic, neoclassical bodies in the artwork of Arno Breker and Adolf Ziegler. Nazi sculptor Josef Thorak's pair of seventeen-foot hypermuscular male nudes, *Comradeship* (1937), occupied Paris at the World's Fair, and with the Nazi invasion, Breker's colossal bronze *ubermensch* dominated the Tuileries Garden in May 1942. By 1943, "degenerate" art had no market—even in Paris, where the Nazis burned avant-garde work, including art by Léger and Picasso, such that the smoke was visible from the terrace of the Tuileries.[10] As Golan argues, the dichotomy between "an eternally feminine, capricious, and alluring France versus a masculine, super-industrial, pragmatic America and Germany came to the fore."[11] In wartime United States, critics supportive of French art had to "ensure its masculinization." Art was susceptible to being viewed as an "escapist, feminine or all too often homosexual activity" evidenced, for example, by the poet Archibald MacLeish's condemnation in 1942 of French art in the United States as "a rich woman's fashion."

Nevertheless, the exiled in the United States gained a liberty contingent upon access to academia and exhibition opportunities, as curator Stephanie Barron's exhibition *Exiles and Emigrés* (1997) has shown. Major museums such as MoMA arranged for the exhibition and purchase of Surrealist and avant-garde works by established artists, including Léger. The New School for Social Research in New York was the first and most important academic network for many émigré artists, particularly painters and printmakers.[12] Bauhaus architects Van der Rohe, Gropius, and Marcel Breuer perhaps fared best by taking on university leadership positions.[13] Salvador Dalí, who probably achieved the greatest commercial success, adapted to the cultural politics and demands of the wartime era despite criticism of his society portraits, aggressive self-marketing, and regressive Catholicism. Other prominent Surrealists, such as Ernst and Masson, retreated from the public eye.[14] Although favored by New York's three modern art museums, the Surrealists received negative reviews from prominent critics: Greenberg saw Surrealism as an "anti-aesthetic nihilism"; the realist artist George Biddle wrote that Surrealism was an "always decadent and recently dying movement"; and Klauss Mann (son of novelist Thomas Mann) attacked Surrealists as pampered under the protection of millionaire Peggy

Guggenheim while millions died.[15] In this context, Léger fared comparatively well, gaining a temporary teaching post at Mills College in California, speaking engagements throughout the United States, and numerous exhibitions during the war years. Léger's use of popular culture provided an alternative to Surrealism's melancholy and nihilism and surely accounts for his relative success in the United States.

During the interwar years, Léger had seen Parisian popular culture and mass entertainment in contradictory terms—as "raw material" for his pictorial process but also as so "enormous" as to threaten the individual body—conditions only magnified in the US context.[16] In a joint interview in 1954, Léger and Cendrars recalled going to the Casino de Paris, and they remembered Place de Clichy as the site where advertising was born, with its enormous posters and monumental Cadum Baby billboard.[17] Although Léger produced only a couple film posters, for *La Roue* (Abel Gance, 1923) and *L'Inhumaine* (Marcel L'Herbier, 1924), he repeatedly turned to advertising, film, and popular spectacle to garner strategies for attracting viewers. He studied the disruption of the billboard across the landscape, the composition of shop window displays, and the typography of posters.[18] In the 1920s, Léger saw advertising as regenerative: its explosion of color and monumental scale with "enormous letters, its figures four meters tall" was the antithesis of the war, which had been "four years without color" and a "life in silence."[19] In the 1930s, Léger cotaught a course on modern advertising, and by the end of his life, Léger was credited by many—from Kahnweiler to Raynal—with transforming contemporary design.[20] Léger, too, claimed that *The City* (1919) had a major impact on poster design and the decorative arts.[21] Léger's *Big Julie*, however, shifts gears from *The City*'s representation of urban visual culture as a sensory assault understood only in fragments to a diptych of iconic forms. *Big Julie* condenses the kinds of mass visual culture that Greenberg disparaged as kitsch: "rotogravure sections and calendar girls," Hollywood film, magazine covers, and the artist Norman Rockwell.

Potency and Popular Culture

Léger's recriminations against the Casino de Paris, the Alhambra, and other Parisian music halls "infected" with "good taste" may reveal a sense of threat and competition from the blurring of high and low art or culture. Within the textual space of interwar arts and literary presses from *L'Esprit Nouveau* to *Nouvelle revue française*, reviews of Léger's work appeared alongside reviews of performances at the Casino de Paris, putting such music halls in the cultural mix with Léger's art and endowing them with a level of bourgeois respectability that New York burlesque never achieved. The Casino de Paris's pretentions to class finery can be measured, too, by its sets imitating royal palaces and imperial residences, choreography on grand staircases, and the mass spectacle of ballroom dancing. Parisian revues—with their stars in long satin gowns, pearls, feathers, and furs—contrasted with the New York variety or burlesque shows and their shimmying girls in scantier outfits of spangles and shorts. But Léger's recrimination of Casino de Paris for being "infected" with affectations of highbrow culture also registers the threat of libidinal constraint.

Léger's valorization of New York burlesque invests in primitive or libidinal instincts as a sign of "survival" after France, as the signifier of "civilization," had collapsed. Julie's "acrobatic" look draws from the "raw material" or urban culture of burlesque and its properties of seduction while transcending burlesque's low into painting's high status. Made famous by stars such as Gypsy Rose Lee and Mae West, burlesque imagined a sexually knowledgeable, even aggressive, woman whose shows invited male fantasy. By the time of Léger's first visit to New York in 1931, burlesque had risen from its origins in 1912 at the Minsky Brothers' clubs and moved to the Theater Republic on 42nd Street. As historian Robert C. Allen argues, "unruly women" such as Mae West and Gypsy Rose Lee breathed new creative life into burlesque during the interwar period. However, the New York City government became increasingly restrictive and, in 1939, shut down burlesque shows.[22] By the time of Léger's wartime exile, burlesque appeared only in censored film versions, such as Howard Hawks's *Ball of Fire* (1941) and *Lady of Burlesque* (1943), based upon Gypsy Rose Lee's mystery thriller *The G-String Murders* (1941). In Léger's interpretation, a "vigorous survival" of burlesque and bad taste persisted through the "hand-painted ties . . . [of] a locomotive and four pigeons on a violet and black ground, or a buxom nude on a saffron ground." These ties, with their phallic iconography, were known as "swing ties" and had been made famous by African American musicians like Cab Calloway, Count Basie, Duke Ellington, and Fats Waller, making Léger's reference another recruitment of the "primitive" for regeneration.

Léger's invocation of US burlesque and the pinup embraces "bad taste" as a form of "vigorous survival," but both American burlesque and French music hall traditions are linked, more broadly, to the wartime mobilization of female sexuality. In France during World War I and again in the United States during World War II, culturally sanctioned modes of the female display served the needs of heteronormative male sexuality while also raising anxieties about disease and prostitution. During World War I, France had alternatively encouraged women to reward men for bravery, warned soldiers about sexually transmitted disease, and justified an economy of women for the discharge of men's sexual energy.[23] Urban entertainment in Paris became identified with sexual and social transgressions, but cinema, music halls, and theater also served as morale boosters for soldiers on leave and fulfilled a need for "laughter and forgetting."[24] Revues of half-naked women singing patriotic songs in pseudo-military garb functioned to fetishize the female body as both compensation for and displacement of male losses.[25] During World War II, Léger interpreted the US forms of the fetishized female body—the burlesque, pinups "dressed more like acrobats in a circus," and buxom nudes on swing ties—as signs of the survival of masculine libidinal potency. Hollywood stars and pinups Lana Turner and Betty Grable became popular icons for soldiers at the front. In her films, such as *Keep Your Powder Dry* (1945), Turner eroticized the image of the Army woman. Grable advised women to send pinup pictures of themselves to their husbands, a practice promoted in popular women's magazines as a patriotic form of sex appeal. The pinup, "sweater girl," and cheesecake displays were legitimized and even nationalized during the war yet operated within a larger system of contradictory messages about wartime female sexuality.[26]

Léger's Julie encodes an ambivalent combination of sexualized display in the service of the male psyche and a hypertrophic muscularity that challenges it, at once offering visual pleasure and threatening potency. Julie's combination of populist forms and muscularity condenses the collective potency and scale of US popular culture, perhaps best represented by New York City and Times Square. Léger had traveled to the United States twice before (in 1931 and 1935–36) and repeatedly commented on the scale of New York's skyscrapers, Wall Street and capitalism, Times Square, and Radio City Music Hall. For him, New York was "the most colossal spectacle in the world," and Wall Street's corporate architecture was composed of the "biggest banks in the world" that served as "the most arrogant family tombs of the great billionaires . . . like new pharaohs, they have their pyramids."[27] Times Square was the neural network of the commodified and spectacular forms Léger drew upon. It had the largest electric and neon signs (until the lights were dimmed in 1942 in compliance with military orders), a subway stop with the highest number of passengers in the city, theaters seating up to 6,000 people, and a dense offering of news, advertising, restaurants, and hotels.[28]

Missing Men

Léger's economic survival depended upon the wives of those "new pharaohs," who became his patrons during his wartime exile and signified another form of female potency. Julie's columnar pose recapitulates Léger's portrait of one such patron, arts collector Maud Dale (fig. 68), who was the wife of Wall Street banker Chester Dale. Julie reconfigures Mrs. Dale's *Venus pudica* stance into a gesture signaling springtime and sexual blossoming: a yellow flower in full bloom is positioned over Julie's left breast, and two blue butterflies flit between the painting's two halves. Maud Dale had supported Léger's first exhibition (with Picasso and Braque) at MoMA in February 1931, and she wrote the foreword to the catalog. During the

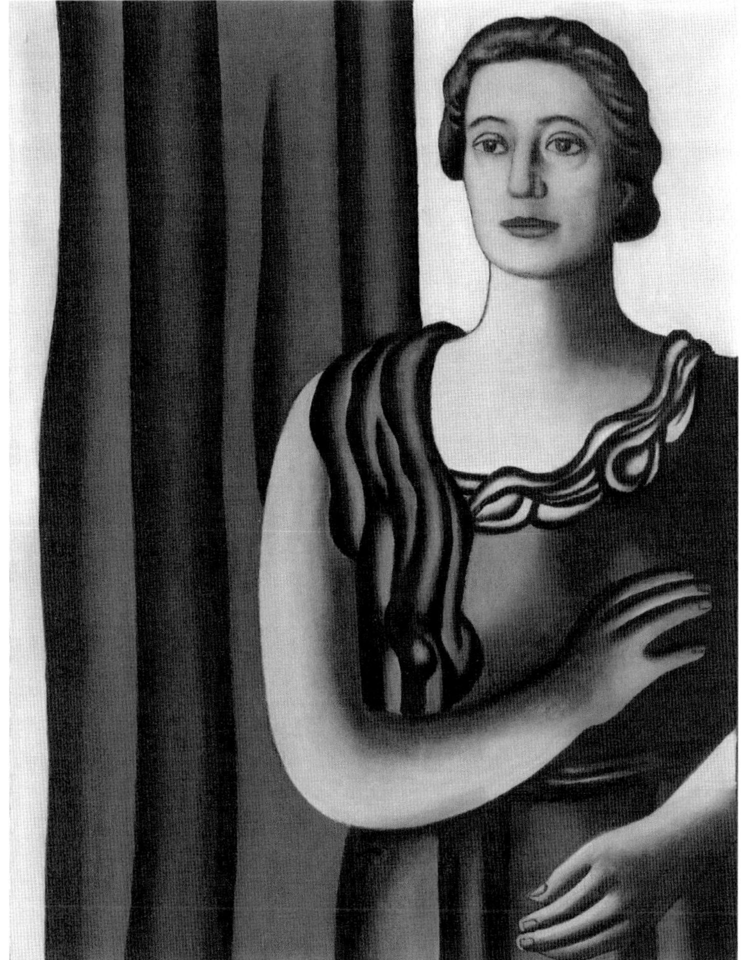

Fig. 68 Fernand Léger, *Maud Dale*, 1935. Oil on canvas, 100.4 × 79.7 cm. National Gallery of Art, Washington, DC. © 2024 Artists Rights Society (ARS), New York / ADAGP, Paris.

war, haute bourgeois women like Mrs. Dale had an increasingly important role in making and shaping the interest in and market for avant-garde art. In 1942, perhaps in response to MacLeish's assertion that French art was too often a rich woman's fashion, Léger complained to MacLeish that leisure in America was the property of the rich rather than the working class. "These LADIES," Léger wrote, ". . . personify 'LEISURE' and MONEY. The art dealers turned these works of art into speculation such as painting = value—gold. . . . Only these Ladies can afford the present huge luxury economy of LEISURE."[29] Ordinary people, Léger protested, "don't have leisure [time] to cultivate themselves . . . [they] work ten hours per day [and] lack hope . . . I would give all the rich ladies in the world for the poor mechanic who came to my studio and told me: that's a pretty painting." In imagining the spectators

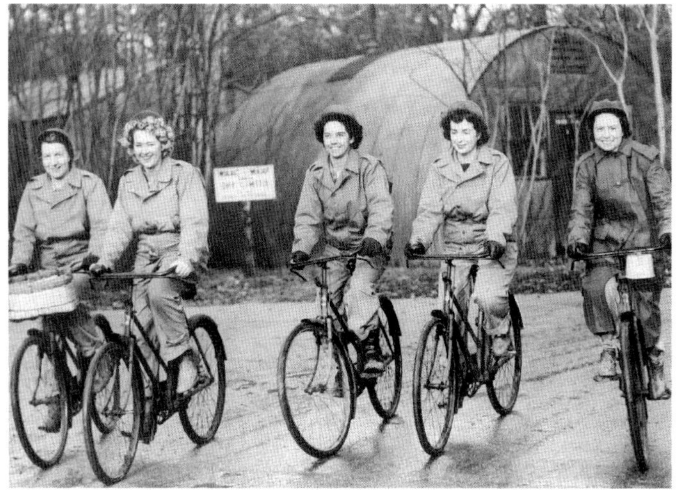

Fig. 69 Women's Army Auxiliary Corps (WAAC) stationed at a US medium bomber station in England ride bicycles on their way to work, December 22, 1943. Photograph. Associated Press File Photo.

Fig. 70 | opposite Adel Precision Products Corp. advertisement, *Saturday Evening Post* 216, no. 45 (May 6, 1944): 99.

of his paintings, Léger wants to supplant the "rich ladies" with the "poor mechanic," but in wartime America, his least likely viewers were young male workers.

Instead, his dependency on the patronage of wealthy women both sustained and undermined artistic autonomy and economic agency. Beholden to potent matrons of the US art scene yet anxious about speculation in the art market, Léger returns to the concerns that troubled him during the Drouot art auctions in the 1920s. Léger's criticism of "rich ladies" targets women like Maud Dale, Sara Murphy, Baroness Hilla Rebay, Dreier, Callery, and Guggenheim, all of whom supported him. Such wealthy philanthropists, art patrons, and art collectors had a major impact on the career and success of exiled artists in the United States and made acquisitions that determined the wartime market value of their work. Maud Dale had first written about Léger for the Société Anonyme exhibition in 1925. Rebay, the Solomon R. Guggenheim Museum's first curator and director when it was known as the Museum of Non-Objective Painting, included fifteen works by Léger in the opening exhibition, *Art of Tomorrow*, in 1939.[30] Dreier, who supported Black Mountain College and established the Société Anonyme exhibitions in 1920, collected and exhibited Léger's work in several of those shows, including his first US solo in 1925.[31] Callery, the inspiration for *Marie the Acrobat*, was an artist and collector who exhibited Léger's *Composition with Two Parrots* twice, first in her Parisian studio in March 1940 and then in New York in June of the same year. Callery also exhibited her collection of art by Léger (six paintings and two drawings) and Picasso (twenty-three oils, twelve drawings, five prints, and one sculpture) for the first time at the Philadelphia Museum of Art in 1945.[32]

But signs of female potency were not limited to Léger's patrons. In 1942, when Léger began the cyclist series, the Woman's Army Auxiliary Corps (WAACs) formed and was publicized with photographs of cycling service women (fig. 69). Léger's *Four Cyclists* share the camaraderie of the collective scene while replacing the military uniforms with acrobatic or leisure wear. Popular culture joined military propaganda in addressing female audiences. Wonder Woman exhorted women to "earn your own living—join the WAACS or WAVES [Women Accepted for Volunteer Emergency Service] and fight for your country!"[33] Women's entry into the military produced debates about gender roles and fears about the threat to family life and marriage. But the potential conflicts between "woman" and "soldier" also permitted a space for the formation of modern lesbian identity.[34] Léger's *Four Cyclists* demonstrate a heightened awareness of female solidarity and autonomy that engages in affectional ties, suggesting such new expressions of female sexuality. The two standing figures at right and left sling their arms over the shoulders of the central cyclist, grazing her breasts, while the right figure tenderly strokes the seated woman's hair.

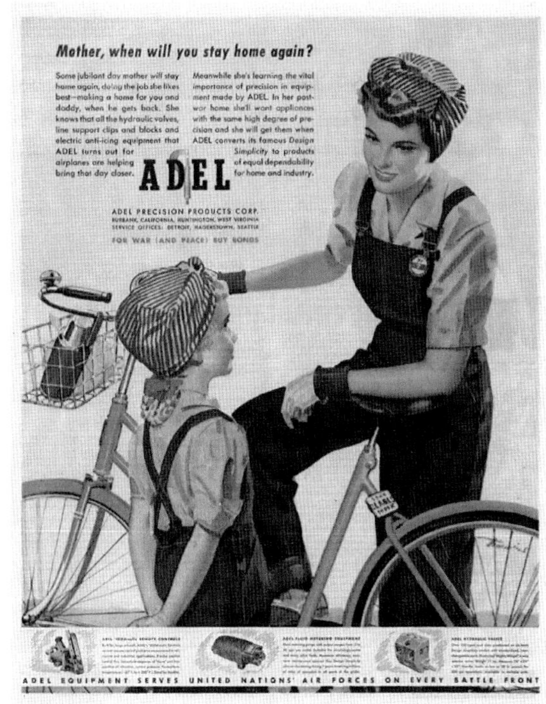

The United States' deployment of women in factory labor surely recalled for Léger similar conditions during World War I in France. From 1914 to 1918, women's apparent displacement of men from the workplace became a subject of anxiety for Apollinaire and many others. Silverman describes the wartime social formation of a workforce without men as a "symbolic impotence" that undermined the dominant fictions of masculinity.[35] A May 6, 1944, *Saturday Evening Post* advertisement by Adel Precision Products (fig. 70) draws upon the visibility of women's wartime factory roles to advertise its products while reassuring readers that the young mother's paid labor is only temporary. Addressed to an imagined daughter of the working woman, the text tells us that she uses "precision equipment" to produce airplanes to help bring closer the day when "mother will stay home again." The image shows the mother in denim overalls pausing before mounting her bicycle as her daughter in matching clothing asks: "Mother, when will you stay home again?"

Perhaps only by occupying the countryside outside the spaces of labor could Léger's muscular cyclists diffuse the anxieties about women's usurpation of men's roles. In imaging a populist female potency outside the world of labor and, in the case of the group images, outside a compulsory heterosexuality, Léger avoided the tensions between maternity and labor that appeared in US popular culture. After the war, in Léger's *Cyclist* (1950) (fig. 71), a female cyclist straddles her bicycle in a pose almost identical to the mother in the Adel products advertisement. But Léger's cyclist has no children and is masculinized by her inflated muscles and a heart-shaped tattoo previously found on the arms of Léger's interwar Adam in *Adam and Eve* (1935–39). Julie's powerful arms in both the 1945 painting and the

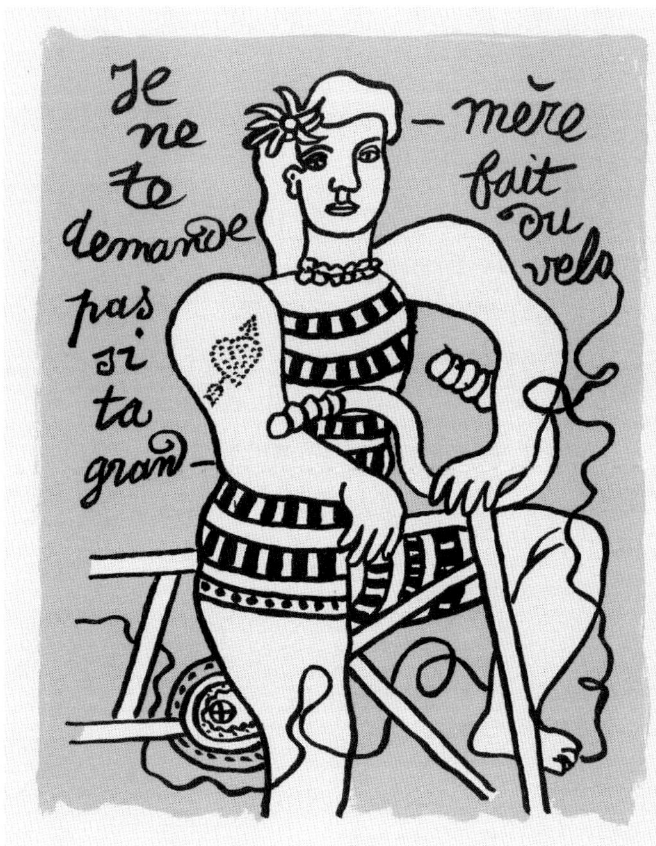

Fig. 71 Fernand Léger, *Cyclist*, 1950. Lithograph, 37.8 × 29.2 cm. Fernand Léger, *Le Cirque*, 111. The Louis E. Stern Collection, Museum of Modern Art, New York. Digital Image © The Museum of Modern Art / Licensed by SCALA / Art Resource, New York. © 2024 Artists Rights Society (ARS), New York / ADAGP, Paris.

1950 lithograph recall the hypertrophic female muscularity on display in Norman Rockwell's *Rosie the Riveter*, published on the cover the *Saturday Evening Post* on May 29, 1943. Julie's diffidence shares Rosie's deliberate detachment from the male viewer, her head and gaze turned away in contrast to the seductive posture and open-mouthed availability of the pinup. Léger's *Circus* Julie, now in possession of the handlebars' phallic form, emphasizes this refusal with the quip: "Je ne te demande pas si ta grand-mère fait du vélo," an idiomatic expression that translates literally to "I won't ask if your grandmother rides a bike" but means approximately "buzz off" or "don't get up in my business."

Embracing an image of feminine power and its disruptions to the heterosexual paradigm, Léger created even more assertive female cyclists after the war. In *Leisure—Tribute to Louis David* (1944–49) (fig. 72), an apparently familial group—two men in suits, two women in cycling outfits, and two children—fail to pair up in conventional ways. The men's hands—one touching the seated woman, the other holding the standing woman's bicycle—suggest proprietary relationships. But the standing cyclist advances her bicycle between the legs of the seated woman in a sexually aggressive move. Léger may have wanted to acknowledge a new postwar culture in which French women had just gained suffrage and philosopher Simone de Beauvoir's *Second Sex* (1949) challenged a naturalized history of gender and male entitlement. French women appeared in visual and literary culture as resistance heroes and veterans of war. In Beauvoir's *Le Sang des autres* (1945), for example, the heroine's independence and sexual maturity depend upon her access to a stolen bicycle.[36] But in 1960, five years after Léger's death, the French state inaugurated the Musée national Fernand Léger with a ceramic facade that quotes *Big Julie*'s compositional structure only to replace Julie with a young man, eliminating the iconography of female potency and so losing Léger's crucial insights about women's transformations during the war.

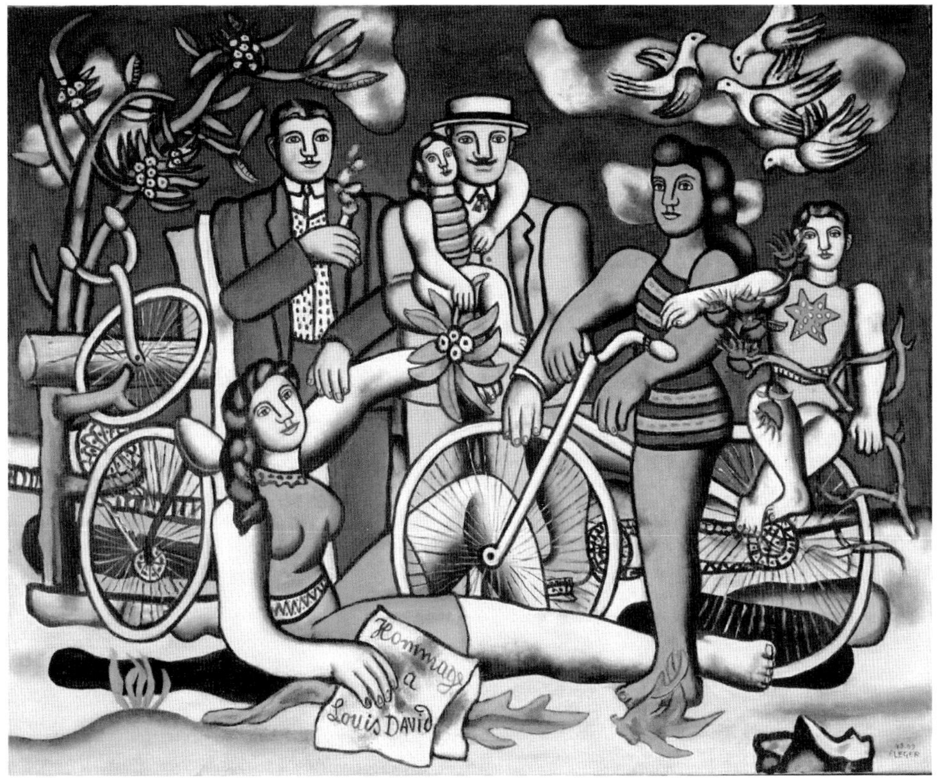

Fig. 72 Fernand Léger, *Leisure—Tribute to Louis David*, 1948–49. Oil on canvas, 154 × 185 cm. Photo: Jean-François Tomasian. Musée national d'art moderne / Centre Georges Pompidou, Paris, Inv. no. AM2992BISP. Digital Image © CNAC/MNAM, Dist. RMN-Grand Palais / Art Resource, New York. © 2024 Artists Rights Society (ARS), New York / ADAGP, Paris.

Nostalgia and Loss

Even as the cyclist paintings express an ambivalent investment in the revivifying and even virile energy of American "bad taste" and its potent women, they simultaneously engage in a nostalgic look back upon an idealized interwar France. In doing so, Léger's comments register both a sense of survival in the context of exile as well as a sense of loss resulting from new historical traumas. In Bouchard's wartime film *Fernand Léger in America: His New Realism* (1942–45), never widely distributed and only recently available to researchers, Léger describes *Big Julie* both in terms of freedom in an expansive US landscape and nostalgia for a lost French world marked by youth and leisure:

> The painting we show you next, called *The Great Julie*, is one of the last completed in America. It is one of a series of bicyclists. This series, also inspired by the American landscape, deals with country girls dressed in bright colors, rolling along the roads in the sunshine on their bikes. Through the composition

> and colors, I believe I have been able to make one feel the joy and liveliness inherent in this everyday sight. Speaking technically, I have achieved a contrast through opposing the static qualities of the girl against the black background, and the dynamic qualities of the wheels on the red background. I have called this canvas *The Great Julie* in memory of an old French song, whose first couplet will end our film: "When I knew you, you were sixteen; you were only a simple working girl, modest as a field flower. Your smile was enough to give pleasure."[37]

Bouchard's film recalls not only the past of the "old French song" about a "modest" (virginal) sixteen-year-old girl but also that of Léger's machine aesthetic era. The film recapitulates the montage structure of the *Ballet mécanique* but replaces the manufactured object with close-ups of market produce and vegetation intercut with details of similar forms in Léger's wartime imagery. Recalling Léger's cattle merchant paintings and perhaps also the slaughter of the war, the camera briefly focuses on the head of a living calf, whose eye gazes at the camera and then cuts to Léger making a pot-au-feu and later coq au vin. But Julie's gravity, detachment, and sexual maturity contradict Léger's statement about "country girls" who recall the feeling of "joy and liveliness." The "landscape" of the cyclist series is less a space of openness and freedom than a stage with a few props in a shallow depth of field, a few referential lines signifying ground, and a single flower.

In the Bouchard film, Léger describes cycling as liberty and leisure, while in other writing, the bicycle is a sign of modernity and mechanization as well as an iconic form of the aestheticized commodity. Léger praised bicycles because, as he told the filmmaker Hans Richter, they are "one of the mechanical things that comes out of our times."[38] He was an avid cyclist who went to the *bals musettes* (popular dance halls) wearing knickerbockers and a cycling cap and once did a 100-kilometer round-trip ride from Arromanches to Deauville.[39] A seductive commodity, the bicycle was both a model for and competitor of fine art. Léger saw the bicycle as a mass-produced object that attracted buyers with its beauty more than its functional uses: "before knowing whether or not they need it, people say 'the beautiful bicycle!'"[40] He recalled once being in a "quartier populaire" in New York City when a crowd of people gathered in front of a vegetable merchant's shop window drawn there by a bicycle in the display.[41]

But the Bouchard film is silent about the wartime conditions for Léger's exile; nor does Léger say anything about the important partnerships and love affairs abruptly and traumatically severed by the war. Two of Léger's most important relationships—with his first wife, Lohy, and with Le Corbusier—were both launched by quasi-mythical cycling encounters. According to a story Cendrars told in the

1950s, Léger met Lohy one day in the spring of 1914 when Léger was with friends (including the poet Paul Fort, Severini's father-in-law). As they were sitting on the terrace of the Closerie des Lilas café, Lohy supposedly arrived as a bride perched on a bicycle in a "vaporous cloud of veils" and collapsed into Léger's arms. Exhausted from having bicycled from her birthplace, the suburb of Vernon some 80 kilometers away, she regained her breath to explain that she had abandoned her groom at the notary just before promising wifely fidelity.[42] Cendrars's nostalgic retrieval of the prewar spring is simultaneously a moment of innocence before the fall of war. In his later years, Léger recalled his first encounter with Le Corbusier in 1920 in a similarly fantastic tale. The future father of the International Style advanced slowly toward Léger on a bicycle, appearing like a "shadow puppet topped with a bowler hat, [and wearing] glasses and a clergyman's raincoat."[43] Both tales, told from the perspective of post–World War II reunions, are comic, nostalgic, and apocryphal, but during the war, the picture was more complex. Le Corbusier gained a position in the Vichy regime while Lohy, having long been separated from Léger and then living with an unreliable partner, was struggling to get by in southern France. Léger's war letters to Lohy show that he was preoccupied with her well-being, sent her money, and told her about his accounts and the locations of his paintings, authorizing her to sell some off as needed.[44] By comparison to World War I, their positions were reversed: she remained in the conflict zone, while he was safe across the seas.

As the activity of women at the homefront and the artist-in-exile, cycling signaled severed relationships and the national trauma of war: the American women whose men were an ocean away, the French artist alienated from his homeland and networks. But should we see Léger's cyclists at leisure as forgetting or even indifferent to their missing men? Or could Léger's foregrounding of leisure in the midst of war have been a kind of claim upon the worker's right to leisure and a symbolic strike against the exigencies of capitalist-militarist economics? Liberty and leisure could have contradictory meanings contingent upon individual and national contexts. In August 1941, after spending three weeks in Los Angeles, Léger complained about an "extreme individual liberty" exemplified by "ultrarapid divorces [and] camouflaged funerals" resulting in "solitude."[45] In March 1942, the Popular Front and its gains for workers, including paid vacation, were on trial when the Vichy government conducted widely reported show trials of several interwar French prime ministers, including Léon Blum. Blum defended the accomplishments of his Popular Front government, including the forty-hour work week and leisure time, and he argued for democracy and a "French faith in our civic liberty."[46] Perhaps Léger's Julie cyclist is a form of solitary and individual liberty or a symbol of hard-won Popular Front freedoms.

Fig. 73 Jean Metzinger, *At the Cycle Racetrack*, 1911–12. Oil and collage on canvas, 130.4 × 97.1 cm. Peggy Guggenheim Collection, Venice (Solomon R. Guggenheim Foundation, New York) 76.2553 PG 18. © 2024 Artists Rights Society (ARS), New York / ADAGP, Paris.

In the early decades of the twentieth century, the bicycle emerged as a sign of liberty and national discovery but also risk. Cycling not only provided leisure and mobility from and through the city but also launched a new speed sport identified with masculinity and danger. In his autobiography, Fauvist artist Vlaminck, who was five years older than Léger and also represented by Kahnweiler in the 1910s, writes about the enormous sense of freedom and discovery he felt bicycling through the French landscape in 1896. Vlaminck describes the challenges of his career as a professional cyclist on a concrete track and the fatalities of speed cycling (then without helmets).[47] As it gained in popularity, cycling influenced fashion, facilitated the birth of tourism in the countryside, and engendered newspaper reports of dangerous exploits and fatal accidents. The Tour de France, established in 1903, was a hallmark event ensuring cycling's cultural importance for France and launching a specialized sports magazine: *Le Vélo*. The leading sporting paper in France, *Le Vélo* was at one point directed by Gaston de Pawlowski, a powerful writer and editor Léger undoubtedly knew about. Pawlowski was also the editor-in-chief of important literary and arts magazines: *Le Rire*, which mockingly reviewed Cubism in the Salon des Indépendants and Salon d'Automne exhibitions early in Léger's career, and *Comoedia*, which reviewed Léger's interwar film, theater, and other work.[48]

Metzinger, another avid cyclist like Vlaminck, produced several prewar Cubist paintings on the theme of cycling, including *At the Cycle Racetrack* (1911–12) (fig. 73). Art historian Fae Brauer interprets the painting as invested in the physical culture movement and the discourse of Bergsonian vitalism (and virility) aimed to subvert the threat of neurasthenia that artists could be susceptible to.[49] Decades later, Léger imagines his female cyclists not on the competition track hunched over their machines nor constituted by the pictorial strategies of a vitalist Cubism but instead paused in their activity to confront the view as though for a snapshot. By the time Léger produced *Big Julie*, war and exile had separated him from many former Cubist compatriots. Gleizes, Metzinger, Vlaminck, and Villon all survived the war years in France; Vlaminck had even shown his willingness to forge alliances with the Nazis.[50]

World War I reinforced the bicycle's signification as a vehicle of liberty and virility, intensifying its associations with mortal risk and then, too, with the war's innovations in corporeal reconstruction. It became both a sign of masculine daring in sport and military service, as recounted by Vlaminck, who did his military service in a bicycle corps that was part of the infantry.[51] Bicycle races, along with boxing matches and theatrical performances, were part of the entertainment at the front as reported in trench journals.[52] But the risks of bicycling became more acute as the war's weaponry became more effective. As Delaporte has written of those who suffered facial injuries—*les gueules cassées*—some 15–20 percent were due to simple accidents such as falls from horses or bicycles.[53] Bicycling also served as a test of the

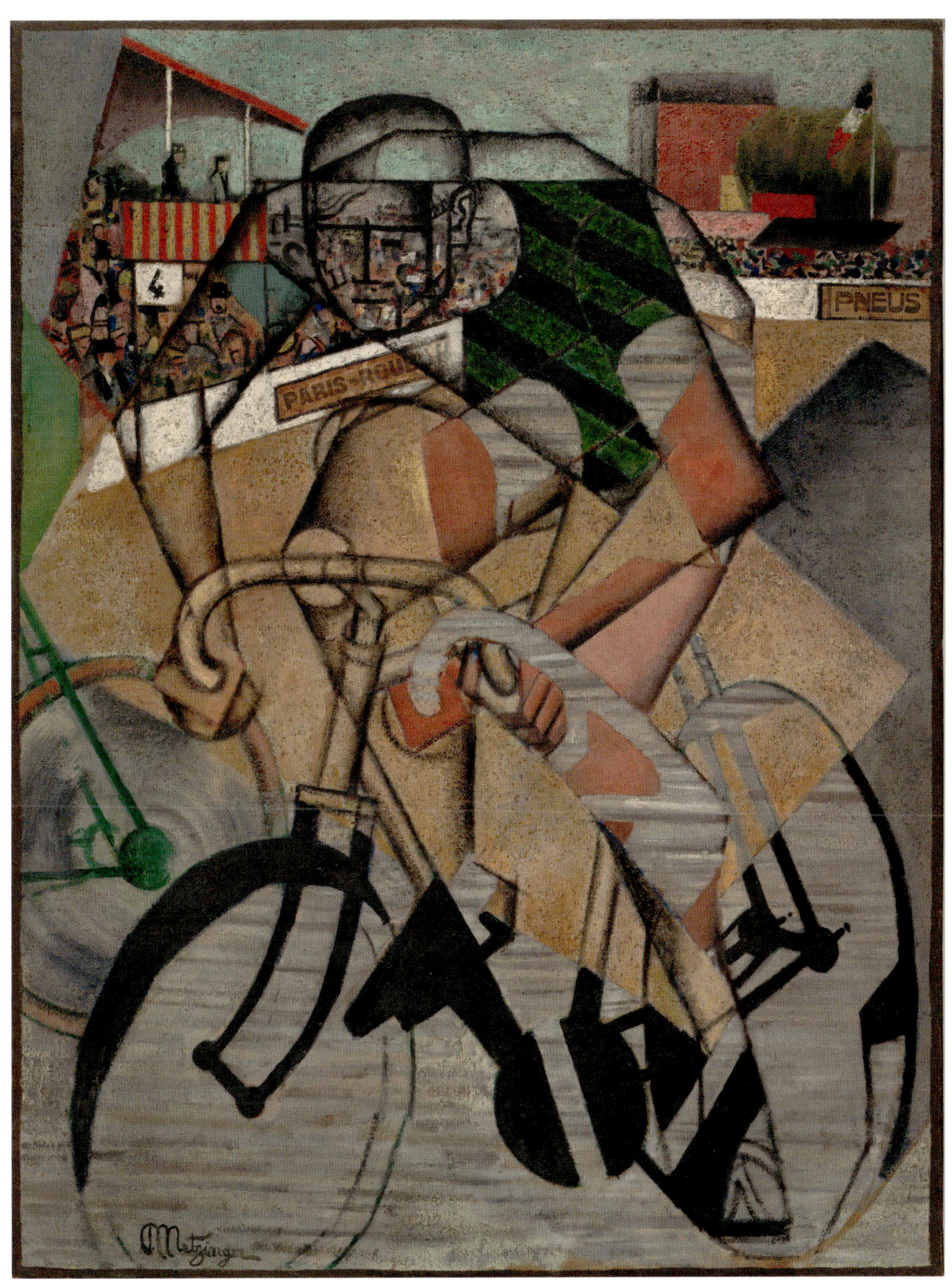
4
PNEUS

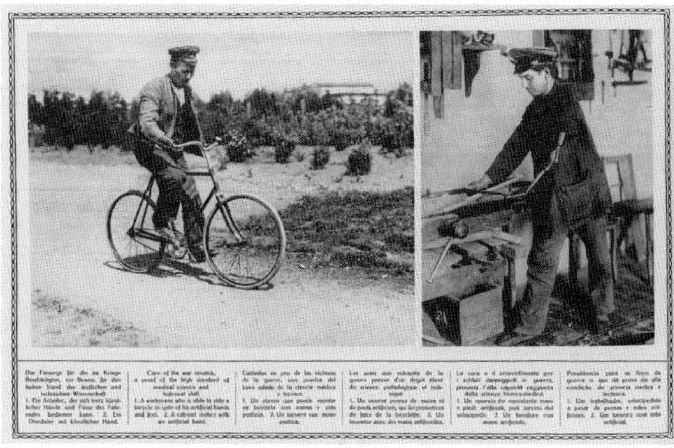

Fig. 74 Uncredited photograph of disabled veterans with prosthetics. *Der Grosse Krieg in Bildern,* no. 7 (1915): 34. The caption, which is in German, English, Spanish, French, Italian, and Portuguese, states: "Care of the war invalids, a proof of the high standard of medical science and technical skill. 1. A workmann [*sic*] who is able to yide [*sic*] a bicycle in spite of his artificial hands and feet. 2. A cabinet makey [*sic*] with an artificial hand." Courtesy of the Library of Congress, Washington, DC.

Fig. 75 | opposite Anonymous photograph of bicycle rack in Rostock, Germany. In *Variétés* 2, no. 8 (December 15, 1929), n.p. Courtesy of the Library of Congress, Washington, DC.

Fig. 76 | opposite French workers on holiday cycling down the Champs-Elysées, Tandem Day, May 14, 1938. Photograph. "La Journée du Tandem." *L'Intransigeant* (May 16, 1938), 10. Courtesy of the Bibliothèque nationale de France.

functionality and aesthetics of prosthetics, as documented in war photography albums, such as one in which an amputee veteran rides a bicycle using an artificial arm (fig. 74).[54] The cyborgian human-bicycle builds upon the bicycle's prewar associations with independence and autonomy and extends these to an image of a reengineered and reconstituted mechanized male body.

By the interwar era, the bicycle as a sign of modernity was identified with masculine autonomy, and athleticism had been compromised by wartime losses. Le Corbusier invested in images of sports and physical culture in the pages of *L'Esprit Nouveau*, including advertising for the Geugeot "cyclo-moto." But bicycling also became a sign of female autonomy from the bloomer era to the interwar New Woman, as in the example of Romains's *La Scintillante* (1924), a play about a female proprietor of a bicycle shop.[55] From theater to photography, bicycles signified within contexts of the lost or alienated social relations of the postwar era. In 1929, at the time of a Brussels performance of Stravinsky's *L'histoire du soldat* (1918), artist Floris Jespers created a backdrop and set using an abstracted bicycle to modernize a narrative based upon a Russian folk tale.[56] In the Faustian story, a soldier gains powers to predict the future but loses his identity and returns to his village unrecognizable to his friends and family. In *Variétés*, photographs by Herbert Beyer, Lux Feininger, and anonymous artists depict the bicycle as urban transportation. One shows a bicycle stand in the center of a largely desolate square in the port city of Rostock, Germany (fig. 75). Racked upright in an assembly-line style, the row of bicycles reminds the viewer of what is absent: the worker at labor. The bicycles are presented in the same position of inactivity that Léger adopts for Julie's bicycle, an inactivity that reinforces absence.

Perhaps the most utopian signification of cycling for Léger's generation was when, during the Popular Front era, the French government promoted bicycling as part of its new vacation law. In 1936, Blum's administration enacted legislation that established paid vacations and inspired a record year of first-time vacationers. As historian Charles Rearick has shown, "the legend of the worker-vacationer" emerged in newspaper and magazine photographs as well as newsreels beginning in the summer of 1936.[57] Rearick writes: "The images of young people taking off on bicycles in 1936 inspired others to do likewise the following year. In August 1937, middle-aged Frenchmen . . . took to the roads as 'cyclotourists' in greater numbers than ever before."[58] In 1938, the newspaper *L'Intransigeant* organized Tandem Day, a cycling event held on May 14 to mark the start of vacation. The newspaper's photographs show couples with matching outfits heading down the Champs-Elysées, linking cycling and leisure to heterosexual romance (fig. 76). "En vélo Simone," or tandem cycling, even became a popular expression for intercourse.[59] Films from the time depict the Popular Front–era vacation as an opportunity for young love and familial leisure. In film director Julien Duvivier's *La Belle Equipe* (1936), vacationers arrive on bicycle at a cooperatively owned café along the Marne River, and in filmmaker Marcel Carné's *Le Jour se lève* (1939), the romantic hero bikes with his lover to the countryside. Both films starred Jean Gabin, who, according to Rearick, developed an image of a "rough-hewn natural working guy, yet a tender-hearted comrade underneath," the ideal type representing the Popular Front constituency.[60] Léger, too, had celebrated athleticism and the Popular Front's vacation legislation in photomontages created with Perriand for the Pavillon de l'Agriculture for the 1937 World's Fair in Paris; these depict a long jumper and a men's athletic team, although not explicitly cycling.[61] The games accompanying the World's Fair included a cycling competition for the male participants.[62]

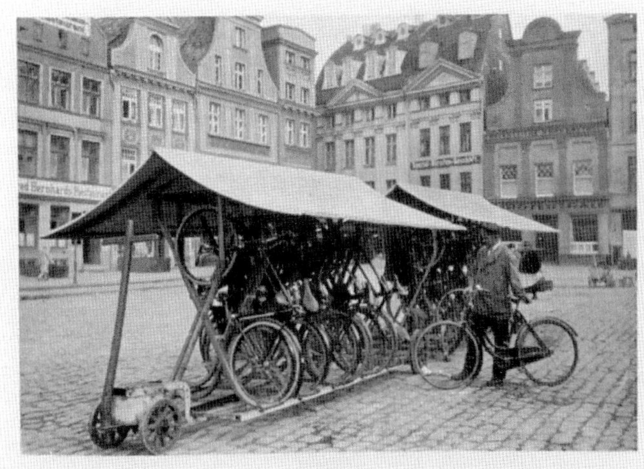

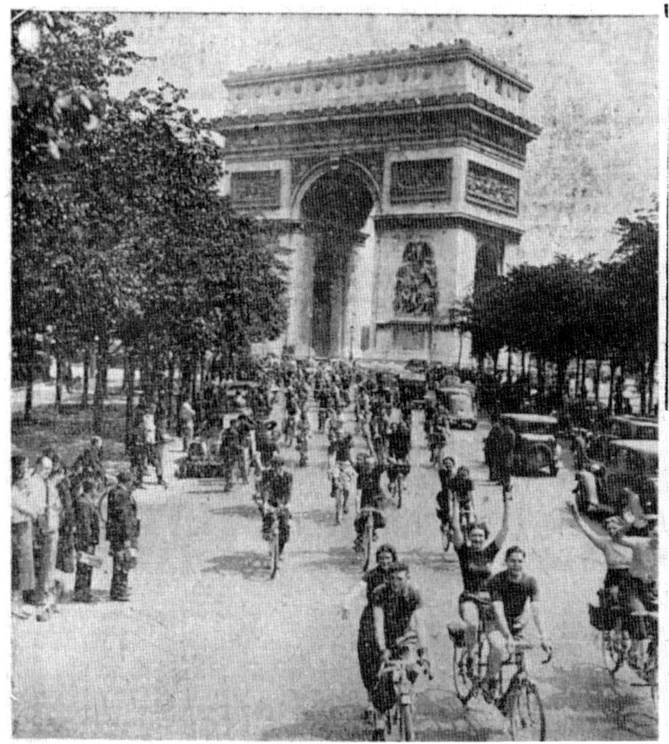

If paintings like *Big Julie* or *The Four Cyclists* are a form of nostalgia or "memory of an old French song," they might be read as a recalling the Popular Front through vacation imagery. In other words, Léger's cyclists convey a kind of *punctum* of Popular Front–era photography recalled through loss. *The Four Cyclists*, for example, borrows from the aesthetics of street photography in that the figures gaze directly at the viewer, and their bodies are frontally positioned in the foreground parallel to the picture plane. The

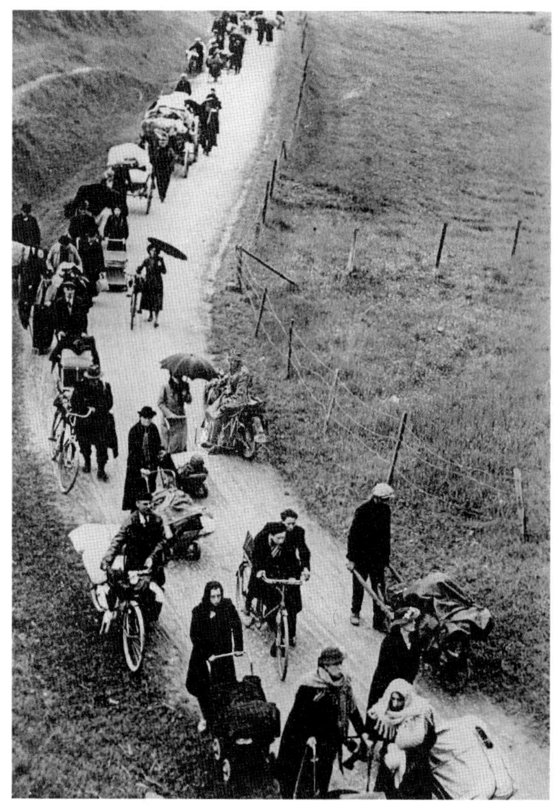

figures' monochromatic bodies recapitulate the flattening impact on mass registered in black-and-white photographs taken under bright sunlight. Their casual postures and momentary pause in their cycling activity capture a sense of normalcy that precludes from sight any reference to the war. In drawing from Popular Front vacation imagery, the cyclist paintings might be understood as a palimpsest or layering of memories that recall the Popular Front vision of the nation through the memory of a traumatic future: the invasion of France and the war to come.

In 1940, cycling again became linked to national trauma as reporters documented the enormous population displacements provoked by the German invasion. The bicycle became an important mode of transportation as many fled their homes with whatever vehicles were available, as documented by photographs of refugees (fig. 77). For Léger, who must have seen such cyclists in his passage through France en route to Marseille, the cyclist series may have been motivated by a conflicted memory of this national humiliation and a simultaneous desire to forget it.

Fig. 77 Unknown photographer, the Exodus of May–June 1940 in France during World War II. RV 533–5. © LAPI / Roger-Viollet.

Léger's memory of the popular song as recounted in the Bouchard film is imbued with a past that he does not explicitly name and memories not made visible in the frame of his cyclist paintings. The idiomatic expression that winds around the postwar Julie of Léger's illustrated book *Circus* (1950) refuses not only male familiarity but also any inquiry into her personal history. From the vantage of that postwar period, the refused conversation blocks not only stories of the Belle Epoque era of the cyclist's grandmother but also any accounting of Julie's wartime survival. Instead, the narrative of Léger's *Circus* (1950) draws from the bicycle's history as a sign of masculine athleticism and risk while transforming Julie into an allegorical symbol of threatened ideals and female resilience. Léger's parable envisions the cyclist in competition with the faster, larger automobile: "Lightly, she brushes past a car on the road. A few centimeters to the right or left and she is destroyed by the four-wheeled beast. A tiny error of judgment on the circus platform where the action takes place five meters above the ground and she is flat on the floor bespattered with blood."[63] This cyclist is a risk-taker, like the acrobat or tightrope-walker, and her bicycle represents a modernity that is outmoded or overwhelmed by more potent mechanical-modern forces. What Léger chose to represent pictorially, however, was not the speed and movement of a Metzinger-like Cubist cyclist, but rather the machine stopped to achieve equilibrium and avoid the spectacle of death.

Diptych for a Divided Nation

In adopting a diptych structure for *Big Julie* and introducing a Latin cross in the right half, Léger arrests time and transforms the cyclist into an icon, an intermediary form between embodiment and spiritual realms. Rather than recalling history in a narrative form, the diptych revives iconic forms removed from chronological time and transcended to a spiritual realm. The temporality of the icon is static and antithetical to the multiple temporalities of traumatic time in operation in *The Card Party*. Rather than *The Card Party*'s phenomenological engagement with a sign of death, *Big Julie* presents the viewer with a memorializing modernist-iconic form. Léger understood that religious iconography was a familiar visual language for popular audiences and sought to deploy its motifs and techniques in his late work. Léger's rapprochement between religion and modernism may have started in 1942, when Father Marie-Alain Couturier saw Léger's exhibition at the Paul Rosenberg Gallery in New York. Couturier was a Dominican priest who had trained as an artist and edited the wartime book on Léger's *plongeurs* series. In the post–World War II era, Couturier became an important connection between the Catholic Church and modern artists, leading to Léger's mosaic facade for Notre Dame de Toute Grace, Assy, Haute Savoie, in 1946. Léger later produced stained-glass and mural designs for other churches: Sacre-Coeur at Audincourt in 1951 and Courfaivre, Switzerland, in 1954.

But even before World War II, Léger was attentive to popular forms of devotional practices. In an essay entitled "Si tu n'aimes pas les vacances" (If You Hate Vacation; 1929), he advocated for cycling through the countryside without a watch and stopping at Lisieux in Normandy to see the diorama dedicated to Saint Thérèse. Newly canonized in 1920 and known as "the *poilu*'s saint" due to some faithful soldiers who advocated for her sainthood, Saint Thérèse has a shrine located in Léger's native region.[64] Visitors could light up the shrine with colorful electric lights, two at a time for every two francs dropped in the box and then, upon leaving the church, cross the street to find a Calvados merchant who had just launched a new drink, the Thérésette.[65] Léger's irreverent description links cycling, popular religious practice, and modern electrification to animate the shrine with colorful lighting, devices aimed to attract believers just as commercial lighting in shop windows drew in consumers.

While *Big Julie*'s bright colors and costuming may draw from US mass culture, her diptych format and the Latin cross backdrop to her bicycle show that Léger also borrowed from Christian iconography to address increasingly religious wartime audiences. Léger's comments about the painting emphasize Julie as a figure of "bad taste" but never directly address the cross as a sign of loss or the painting's dialectic of sacred and profane. Léger's red Latin cross could have reminded viewers of the French Croix de Lorraine adopted by Charles de Gaulle's Free France. A red Latin cross with two crossbars, it became a pervasive icon in French expatriate publications and fundraising posters disseminated in London and New York during the war.[66] Christian iconography, too, became important for American audiences. As historian Michael Snape has shown, religion became a significant factor in American military discipline and public morale during the war. The US Office of War Information produced posters propagandizing Nazism's threats to religion. Church attendance increased among civilians, and surveys document claims to greater Bible reading.[67]

But the cross in Léger's *Big Julie* is not a literal quotation of the Croix de Lorraine. Instead, it borrows strategically from Malevich's *Black Cross* (1915) (fig. 78), recruiting the forms of modernist abstraction that could still be recognizable to a wider audience. Léger's cross adopts the distinctive tilt and unmodulated color of Malevich's cruciform while also similarly extending the horizontal bar almost to the edge of the frame. The uneven vertical division between Julie's black ground at left and the yellow ground at right, a split that breaks at Julie's shoulder level, is roughly parallel to the cross's irregular slight tilt. For Léger, who had many long-standing connections to the Russian vanguard, the Malevich quotation in *Big Julie* was unquestionably intentional.

Léger's citation of Malevich operates as an homage not only to the Russian artist who died in 1935 of cancer but also to the avant-garde communities that the war so traumatically dispersed. Léger's Russian connections date to the Jack of Diamonds exhibition in Moscow in 1912 organized by Mikhail Larionov, Malevich's good friend, and to Vassilieff's academy, where she hosted talks by Léger in 1913 and 1914. In the 1910s and 1920s, Léger met many visiting and expatriate Russians who were in communication with Malevich, including Exter, Larionov, Natalia Goncharova, Mayakovsky, and El Lissitzky.[68] Although Malevich never traveled to France and Léger never made it to Russia, they knew each other's art through exhibitions and publications, including the Salon des Indépendants in 1914, which displayed Malevich's work. In its first issue, *L'Esprit Nouveau* listed Malevich as one of the members of its international network of "collaborators." Regular articles about the Russian vanguard appeared in the Purist press and in other French surveys of contemporary art. During the war, when Léger was working on *Big Julie* in New York City, there

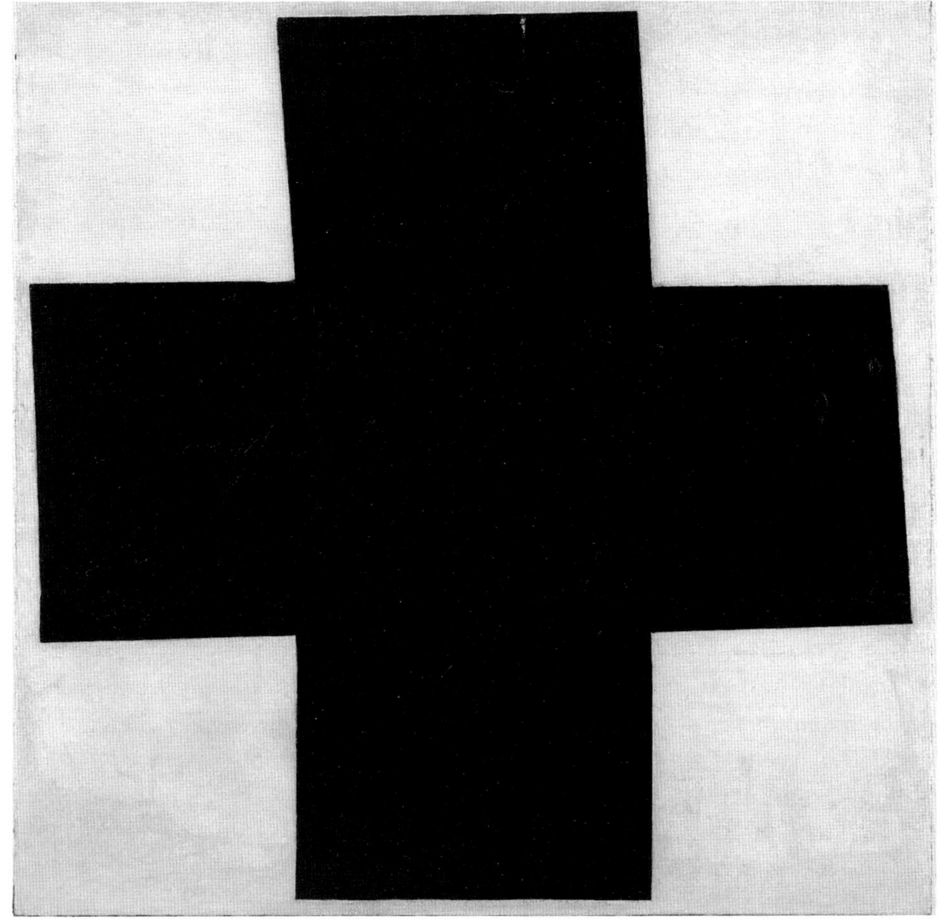

Fig. 78 Kazimir Malevich, *Black Cross*, 1915. Oil on canvas, 80 × 79.5 cm. Photo: Philippe Migeat. Musée National d'Art Moderne / Centre Georges Pompidou, Paris, Inv. no. AM1980-1. Digital Image © CNAC/MNAM, Dist. RMN-Grand Palais / Art Resource, New York.

were several works by Malevich in the MoMA collection. Acquired in 1935 after Malevich's death, these included *Black and Red Cross in Flight* (1920–1921). In 1936, Barr had included both Malevich and Léger as part of MoMA's landmark exhibition *Cubism and Abstract Art* (1936). Léger, who attended the opening in March 1936, may have discussed with Barr the similarities in their painting produced around 1912, a point Barr noted in his catalog.[69]

Although Malevich's writings were not translated into French until decades later, Léger certainly knew of Malevich's ideas through Parisian publications and exhibitions as well as through the Russian expatriate community in Paris. Possibly the most important interpreters of Malevich for Léger were Exter and, to a lesser degree, Nadia Khodassevitch. Exter, who traveled regularly between Russia and France between 1909 and 1914, was part of the Suprematist movement and had a close rapport with Malevich before she turned to Constructivist painting and work in theater and film. After settling permanently in Paris in 1925, Exter taught with Léger at the Académie Moderne for five years.[70] Khodassevitch studied in a branch of Malevich's newly formed UNOVIS (the Union of New Art) while in her teens, but she left Russia in 1921, eventually arriving in Paris in 1925 to study with Léger at his Académie Moderne. From 1932 on, she ran his studio, led communist meetings there, and then in 1952 married him, reinforcing Léger's loyalty to the French Communist Party.[71] From all these networks, Léger must have known that Malevich wrote about him and taught his students about Cubism.[72] Another route of knowledge could have been Léger's friend Einstein, who published a German translation of Malevich's *Suprematist Manifesto* (1915) in 1925.[73] In his manifesto, Malevich identified the cross as one of his "Suprematist elements" along with the square and circle. Like Léger, Malevich advanced a modernist art that was antinaturalistic and against academic forms of representation. Both rejected the hold of the Renaissance and instead engaged with the modern world and its machines. Malevich's Suprematism, too, invoked notions of collectivity and communism that resonated with Léger's ideals.

Paradoxically, while Léger's dyad foregrounds Julie's libidinal body and a sacrificed machine on the cross, Léger remained silent about the war's production of sacrificed youth and missing men. Léger's wartime statement in the Bouchard film nostalgically recalls "an old French song," while his postwar statement in the MoMA bulletin insists upon "bad taste" and "survival." The idealized male body, whether imagined as a Christological body, a competitive cyclist like Metzinger or Vlaminck, or a Popular Front Gabin type, is refused representation and recalled only through his absence. Mounted on a cross, the bicycle can no longer be a mere sign of leisure as it is in Léger's group cyclist paintings. Instead, it gestures toward losses: vanguard communities and networks ruptured by death, distance, and ideological differences, and perhaps even failed investments in a machine aesthetic.

Melancholy and Male Ruination

Even as the crucified bicycle gestures to the lost ideals of the machine aesthetic and Popular Front eras, the absences from Léger's *Big Julie* effect a screening or blocking of masculine ruination and the historical trauma of the fall of France. This ruination, however, comes into view in Léger's dream segment for Richter's six-part, quasi-Surrealist film, *Dreams that Money Can Buy* (1947). Léger first met Richter in 1924 at an international film festival in Vienna, where *Ballet mécanique* was screened. During World War II, Richter took refuge in the United States, where Léger's studio was one of his first stops, and he later became director of the Institute of Film Techniques at the City College of New York. Léger's contribution to *Dreams*, entitled "The Girl with the Prefabricated Heart," was the first one Richter shot. The Léger segment incorporates an earlier version of *Big Julie*, entitled *Julie, the Beautiful Cyclist* (1945), while also displaying the disintegration of the male body in the segment's finale. The narrative of *Dreams* is loosely organized around a disillusioned and unemployed veteran named Joe who has turned his home into a psychiatric office, shifting inquiry from his psychic state to the "clients" that seek his help. The *Julie* painting appears in two contexts in Richter's film. As the film begins, clients arrive in Joe's office, which is decorated with a few artworks, including Léger's *Julie*. They pass before the Léger painting, making it serve as an enigmatic symbol susceptible to Joe's dream analysis (fig. 79).

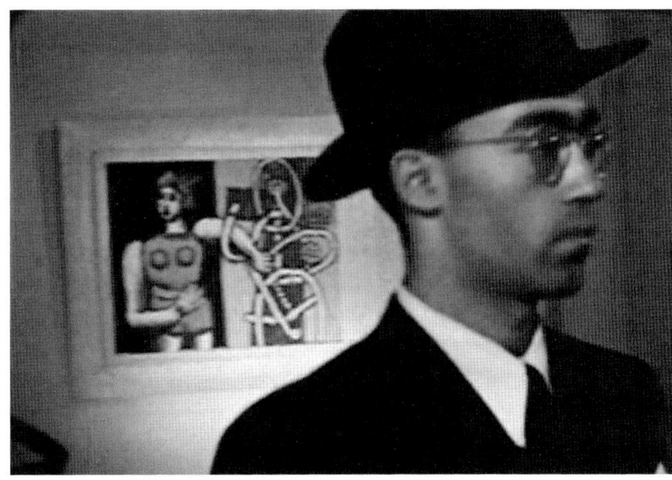

Fig. 79 Fernand Léger, film still from "The Girl with a Prefabricated Heart" segment in *Dreams that Money Can Buy* (Hans Richter, 1947), minute 06:52. Léger's *Julie, the Beautiful Cyclist* (1945), now in the Menil Collection in Houston, Texas, is on the wall behind the first client, Mr. A. © 2024 Artists Rights Society (ARS), New York / VG Bild-Kunst, Bonn / ADAGP, Paris.

In the second context, Léger's painting appears in his seven-minute dream segment. One of six dream sequences, Léger's segment parodies the Hollywood musical through a song that tells the story of the courtship and marriage of two mannequins who are the alter egos of Joe and a young female client. Léger's painting is one of the many gifts the male suitor gives to the female mannequin, also named Julie. Made on a limited budget, the film suffers from flawed sound, color, and lighting, and it instead relies on voice-over to suggest the thoughts, desires, and fears of the characters as well the societal demands they want to resist.[74] In Léger's segment, an extradiegetic "love" song, "The Girl with the Prefabricated Heart," replaces the voice-over of the other sequences to tell the story of Julie the mannequin. Mannequin Julie begins as a disassembled body, foregrounding her artificiality and reconstruction, recalling and displacing the reconstructed male bodies and prosthetic limbs Léger saw during World War I and its aftermath. An uncanny hand severed from the mannequin's body rises up to begin her assembly. According to the song, she is a "goddess" who "grew untouched by human hand"; she is "grade A" and made of "chromium nerves," "a platinum brain," "nylon hair," and a "prefabricated heart." Idealized beauty made mechanical is now seen as false rather than futuristic and utopian as it had been in the 1920s. Feminine heartlessness replaces the Purist-era suppression of sentiment and presages Julie's indifference and betrayal of her suitor.

Mannequin Julie's initial baldness recalls the female figures that appeared in Léger's paintings *Reading* (1924) and *Woman with a Fruit Bowl* (1924) (figs. 27 and

28). In the 1920s and again with the *plongeurs*, Léger's bald women signified in terms of gender instabilities and anxieties. Julie's momentary baldness in the *Dreams* segment reveals her modernity. As an exemplar of the assembly-line process, the mannequin Julie circles around and admires her reflection, a dance reprising the circular and elliptical choreography of the rows of kitchen pots in Léger's *Ballet mécanique* (1924). Fully formed, she is an impenetrable idealization viewed from a heroicizing low-angle close-up. Her mannequin mate is a nameless but bourgeois dandy in a tuxedo only known as "a mail-order male . . . from Yale." He is handsome and rich with "biceps of stainless steel." Their courtship and her bridal gown are marked by artificiality and death. Modern life in the United States is exemplified by "sterilized flowers" and "air-conditioned air." A spectral veil drifts downward, and the song explains that her gown is an "atomic weave" made "in a four-billion-dollar machine." The song narrates a dystopic view of contemporary life contingent upon the death of nature and art in the atomic era initiated by the bombings of Hiroshima and Nagasaki on August 6 and 9, 1945.

The segment's apparent critique of American alienation from nature is only obliquely a critique of militarism and mass production. Joe, the film's veteran turned dream analyst, never looks inward or references the war neurosis that plagued his generation. Imagined as a master rather than a subject of dream analysis, Joe is symptomatic of a new cultural silence about psychic shock and breakdowns, the most emblematic example of which may be the fate of filmmaker John Huston's documentary on shell-shocked veterans, *Let There Be Light* (1945); shot in Long Island, New York, it was censored until 1981. Instead, the war's production of male loss is supplanted by anxieties about modern women, heterosexuality, and the future of gender relations. The client who provokes the Julie dream is a young woman who resists Joe's advances. Just as Joe provides dream interpretation or psychiatric readings to his clients, the mail-order male mannequin offers to interpret Julie's dreams. As narrated in the song, the Yale male wants to compel Julie's thoughts to "move in harmony with mine," lyrics timed for his presentation of the *Julie* painting. The song tells us that "nature" (a live bird) and "art" (the Léger painting) will not woo her. Even the faux diamonds and pearls fail. Her last-minute refusal to marry quickly becomes a sign of frigidity, even lesbianism, since she relies on her "sisters" who are "Amazons" that rush "to her aid and [save] the day." Her thoughts, which the male suitor can read, are depicted as animated "wheels" emerging from *Julie*'s bicycle, transforming the gift into a sign of her desired autonomy. Female thought and rationality become equated with indifference to emotion and to her suitor's suffering and death. As the song explains: "Girls of wax cannot use devotion; they might melt if they felt an emotion." In the final minutes, the mannequin Julie in her bridal gown rides on her bicycle alone; "her loneliness she must insist on," the song tell us.

Intercut with her cycling, the male mannequin in groom's clothing falls to the ground and loses his head, "lifeless . . . and . . . wifeless" (fig. 80). As the female mannequin "rides on through the evening . . . Isolde without Tristan," she ironically moves nowhere on a stationary bicycle. Artificial flowers rain down on her but celebrate neither a wedding nor a victory parade. Julie's autonomy, made contingent upon male ruination, serves nothing.

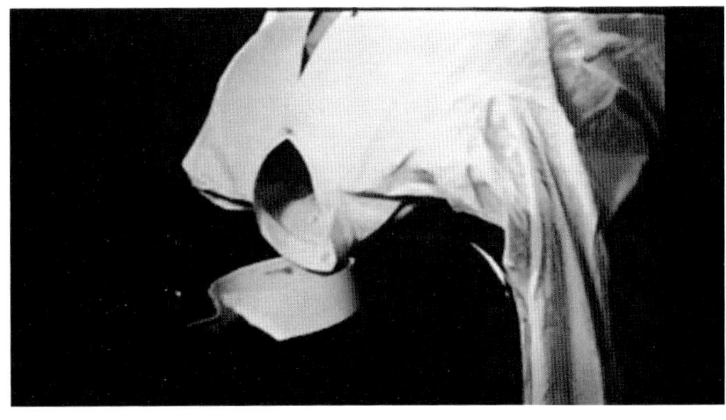

Fig. 80 Fernand Léger, film still from "The Girl with a Prefabricated Heart" segment in *Dreams that Money Can Buy* (Hans Richter, 1947), minute 28:08. © 2024 Artists Rights Society (ARS), New York / ADAGP, Paris / VG Bild-Kunst, Bonn.

Richter stated that Léger wanted to make a film about "American folklore" by animating the mannequins they saw together on their visit to New York's Grand Street where rows of shop windows displayed the mass production of bridal gowns.[75] Bouchard, too, included a scene of these bridal shops in his film on Léger, presumably based upon his conversations with Léger about the film. According to Richter, Léger insisted that the female mannequin bicycle away at the end of the story because he saw the bicycle as an invention of his era. But the scene also recalls Cendrars's apocryphal tale of Lohy, who had abandoned her groom on their wedding day to remain independent. As an expression of cynicism about societal investment in bourgeois sexuality and marriage, Léger's mannequin Julie is the successor to the mechanical bride of Duchamp's *The Bride Stripped Bare by Her Bachelors, Even* (1915–23) and a precursor to media theorist Marshall McLuhan's *The Mechanical Bride: Folklore of Industrial Man* (1951).[76] In McLuhan's analysis of the postwar culture of consumption, girdle advertisements and bridal imagery marked the era's mass-produced romance, assembly-line weddings, and mechanized life, or what he described as "collective dreams" and "synthetic gods and goddesses."

What may be most surprising for those accustomed to thinking of Léger in terms of his good humor and utopian machine aesthetic is the film segment's melancholia and male ruination. Twenty years after his machine aesthetic era and the *Ballet mécanique*, Léger has lost his Purist-era investment in counterbalancing the signs of neurasthenia and death (the Chaplin marionette's frenetic movement and collapse) with the industrial era's mass production of beauty (the manufactured object). In the Richter film, manufactured beauty is false and betrays man, leaving him lifeless and wifeless. Reviews of the film, which won a prize at the Venice Film Festival in 1947 and premiered in New York in 1948, cast it as a Surrealist film but often negatively so.[77] However, a couple reviews identify Léger's segment as the most accessible.[78] The New York brochure for the film premiere includes brief comments on the film's psychology by Dada poet and historian Richard Huelsenbeck, then a practicing psychiatrist in New York, and by Frankfurt School cultural critic Siegfried Kracauer, also a refugee in New York. Huelsenbeck saw the film as depicting the "inner movement" and "tensions" of mental life.[79] Kracauer interpreted the film as a critique of mechanized modern society: "Both the Léger and Richter episodes are very explicitly in defiance of our mechanical civilization. They mock at it or present the seeming normality as a distortion of the really normal . . . Melancholia, our lot as creatures, alternatives [*sic*] with the gaiety which is inseparable from artistic fulfillment."[80] In Richter's dream sequence, the sixth and final segment of the film, Joe enacts the symptomology of the shell-shocked veteran. He is impotent with women and alienated from his former life and friends, who turn out to be card-playing dummies. God and philosophy fail him, and the voice-over tells us that, like his clients, he feels empty and numb: "my senses were numb. I sense nothing, I felt nothing." Kracauer's reading of Léger's and Richter's episodes as a mix of gaiety and melancholia accords with Léger's interpretation of modern life as comic and tragic.

In foregrounding failed dreams and ruined masculinity, Richter's film and Léger's segment adopt the forms of film noir and almost acknowledge a profound sense of nothingness at the core of masculine subjectivity. They incorporate key features of the film noir genre developed in the postwar period: voice-over narration, an imposition of bourgeois rules and norms, jumbled flashbacks, dream sequences, menacing shadows, popular psychology, close-ups and other acute or dramatic camera angles, and a mannequin-like quality to a deadpan couple. Not surprisingly, film noir found its predecessors in interwar French film as war loomed. Historian David Slavin argues that films produced in France after the fall of the Popular Front, such as Carné's *Le Quai des brumes* (1938), convey a disillusion that reversed the classic Hollywood paradigm and placed a failed masculinity on display.[81]

The *Julie* painting's appearance in Richter's film reorients its meaning from the summer joy Léger claimed to the context of melancholy that Kracauer observed in that segment. In Freud's analysis, melancholia and mourning are linked. The work of mourning is a reaction to loss and a process in which the mourner recognizes that the loved object no longer exists and withdraws its attachment. In melancholia, the process of mourning is blocked due to an ambivalence about the lost object, now withdrawn from consciousness, resulting in a symptomology of dejection, lost interest in the outside world, lost capacity to love, and lowered self-regard.[82] Sometimes, according to Freud, the process ends with an abandonment of the object as valueless. Such a position appears in Léger's repeated disinvestment from the body: in his 1915 letter in which the economically ruined male body has mere "sentimental value" that is "not worth anything," and in his *Dreams* sequence, with its disintegrating "mail order male . . . from Yale." Art historian Lisa Saltzman has asked whether painting can "perform the work of mourning, or is it melancholic, a petrified object, an allegorical fragment, a ruin, whose meaning, whose resolution, is necessarily deferred in an endless chain of signification?"[83] Applying this question to Léger's *Big Julie*, we might interpret its iconicity as a vehicle for memorialization—that is, an investment in the image's mediating role, one that can never fully access the lost object nor disinvest from it. Instead, the painting's objects reify struggles Léger returned to throughout his career: the dilemma of the human body as an object and the problem of formal and psychic equilibrium.

Conclusion

As a profoundly ambivalent painting, *Big Julie*, although manifestly about cycling and leisure, does more to mourn lost ideals and failed investments in the male body, the machine aesthetic, and the redemptive possibilities for art in the modern world. It occupies a complex position between narratives of summer vacation as a sign of populist power and allegories of male sacrifice, between inviting the viewer to desire *Big Julie*'s corporeality and apparent autonomy and invoking anxiety about the sources of her power, between seeing her body as the signifier of a nation populated by women and reading her as the reassembled body of a fractured people. Like other wartime pictures, the cyclist series, with *Big Julie* as its culmination and Richter's film as its animation, works through a series of problems about the artist's role in the social order. The painting also points to Léger's anxieties about his gendered subjectivity, offering a shifting identification—either with the cyclist as a sign of liberty, just as Léger sought freedom in the United States through the transcendent realm of art, or with the sacralized and fetishized bicycle, as a sign of memorialized losses. Structured as a diptych, Julie nevertheless collapses multiple binaries: fine art borrows from mass culture for its icons, the "living" and organic become automatons while the mechanical is anthropomorphized, religious iconography is secularized, and a phallic femininity cohabits with a castrated masculinity, both foregrounding and destabilizing the heterosexual paradigm. Like *The Card Party*, *Big Julie* is a composition engaged with concepts of survival and memorialization, but instead of imaging a hypertrophic new man emerging from the war, it envisions a phallic new woman. In its dialectic, the painting looks both to a past of modernism, masculinity, and the machine aesthetic and to a future of popular culture and new forms of femininity, one ruined and abstract, the other potent but figural.

Conclusion

How did machine modernisms register the trauma of World War I and grapple with its aftermath? What are the possibilities and contingencies of trauma's representation or its unavailability to cognition? What are the conditions for survival or resilience, and how are these bound up with subject formation? What does Fernand Léger's example teach us about trauma, resilience, and gender? This book has presented a series of case studies from Léger's oeuvre as a lens into the conditions and contradictions of trauma and offers a new interpretation of Léger and the traumatized masculine subjectivity of his era. Prior scholarship has often seen Léger as someone who survived the war unscathed rather than being profoundly disturbed by the wars and social upheavals of his era. This book proposes new readings of some of Léger's most iconic works: *The Card Party* (1917) as a confrontation with death and *Big Julie* (1945) as a memorializing icon. It calls attention to less studied examples of his work, such as his still life pictures from the 1930s and his contribution to the film *Dreams that Money Can Buy* (Richter, 1945). It also draws upon little-known sources, such as Bouchard's 1945 film on Léger in exile in the United States. Through a discourse analysis of Léger's writing, published talks, and private letters, I draw out Léger's ambivalent feelings about the war, reoccurring anxieties about the economy and the value of art and man, and blockages at the level of representation. While widely known as a leading machine modernist, Léger was also a survivor of multiple historical traumas, including World War I's trench warfare and France's social collapse and mass exodus in June 1940. These experiences were felt on the individual, collective, and national level and left their mark on his art and writing. But Léger's art is rarely explicitly "about" trauma. Instead, trauma's traces emerge through contradictions, absences, and ambivalences in his work.

In foregrounding the impact and legacy of the war, I show how Léger both participated in national discourses and went against the grain. During World War I, the French state suppressed the image of its war dead and disfigured and permitted the representation of the amputee only with prosthetics. Yet Léger's *Card Party* deploys a prewar Cubist visual language to show disfigured and amputee soldiers confronting a figure of death or loss. At the same time, Cubism, unlike more naturalistic aesthetics, refuses knowledge of the internal psyche and its wounds. Interpretations of the painting as fascist, hardened soldiers miss the dialectic between the fractured interior and breached corporeal shell, and no prior reading has accounted for the way it stages a confrontation with death. These, I have argued, are crucial aspects of the monumental painting. Nor have prior interpretations examined the context of the painting's production during Léger's hospitalization for nerves and at a moment when he assumed he would be returned to the front, a context that helps explain its temporal and spatial simultaneity. The painting is exceptional in its attention to the soldier's body and in its uses of Cubism to subvert censorship while also acknowledging the limits of sight. By contrast, in 1916, Picasso and Severini had turned away from Cubism and Futurism's fractured forms to advance new classicisms.

Despite wartime letters describing his symptoms, Léger remained silent about the conditions of his hospitalization for the rest of his life and instead, in his late career, claimed to be a loyal comrade who had no fear and refused to leave his troupe even after opportunities to transfer into the camouflage unit. Much of the scholarly literature has taken Léger at his word rather than interpreting his statements and silences as a process of fashioning his public persona. That persona conformed to notions of a virile fraternal masculinity while suppressing stigmatized nervous conditions and failures of masculinity. Similarly, Léger's bellicose claim in 1919 that the glint of light upon a 75mm cannon was the model for his new machine aesthetic has not been previously examined for its contradictions with his pictorial production and the historic need to camouflage such guns. My study has analyzed Léger's public and private writings within the discourse of his era, reading them for how the trauma and memory of the war are configured through omissions, fragments, or, in the case of 75mm cannon discourse, through an identification with the aggressor weapon.

In the interwar era, France engaged in a cultural silence about psychic wounds, but French scholarship on the history of early twentieth-century psychiatry has only recently begun its analysis of the period. During the interwar years, monuments proliferated, but official commemorations constrained outpourings of grief. National attention shifted to reconstructing buildings, bodies, and the economy. Histories of the postwar return-to-order and interwar classicism include Purist aesthetics and

Léger's art, yet such histories have not accounted for their contradictory desires to forget the war while still combating its legacy. While Purism encouraged an amnesia about or blindness toward the war's damage, its periodical *L'Esprit Nouveau* repeatedly sought to use machine modernisms like Léger's in a battle against melancholy, neurasthenia, and death, represented by artists like Grosz and Dix. Léger's machine aesthetic writings, too, seek to overcome death in that the paradigm and predecessor for the mass-produced commodity is scavenged war debris, revealing a self-conscious process of purification, fetishization, and commodification. But a sense of embattlement pervades Léger's work.

The ways Léger departs from interwar classicisms and Purist dictates have not been closely considered but, I have argued, help complicate our understanding of aftermath cultures. Léger engaged with a national iconography of male workers as mechanics, tugboat captains, and typographers, but his "classical," columnar female figures are often confined within claustrophobic interiors. Léger's puppetlike male figures gain value from their proximity to the economic engine rather than power over it, while his female figures encode what Butler calls the "regulation of affect" or what Bennett terms the "mechanisms of constraint." Unlike Severini's or Picasso's return-to-order women, Léger's women never suckle infants and are rarely maternal contrary to the biopolitics of the period. On the rare occasions that Léger provides a close study of the male body, such as with his Chaplin puppet or *The Mechanic* (1920), the body is alternatively falling apart or sutured at the seams. Here, the postwar man is what Léger described as a "hypertrophic" man who could be "stretched to breaking."[1] Léger's landscapes, too, have none of the nostalgia of his contemporaries and instead depict crypt-like houses and cattle on their way to slaughter, recalling the soldier's passage to war. Léger's writing, too, betrays anxieties about new economic battles, the arbitrary monetary value of his work in a volatile economy, and the destroyed male body as having mere "sentimental value."

From the 1930s to 1945, the male body is made largely absent through long periods of Léger's artistic production, perhaps because of its mere "sentimental value." The suppression of masculinity is, however, a rarely discussed aspect of his oeuvre. The limits and failure of Purist rationalism and Léger's machine aesthetic became increasingly evident in the late 1920s and early 1930s in the context of Surrealism's iconography of corporeal dissolution, revived memories of war in 1928, and documentary film and photography showing the human toll exacted by the global economic crisis. That Léger was aware of the limits of rationality emerges in his Berlin talk in 1928 and in his abandonment of his machine aesthetic. Trauma to the male body becomes "visible" in Léger's art primarily through signs of absence and displacement: in the 1930s, when Léger's still life objects (holly leaves, comets, slabs of beef) exhibit the traces of violence that had been visited upon the male body, and in *Big Julie* with its castrated bicycle on a Malevich cross. The shocking scene of the male mannequin's dismemberment in Léger's segment for *Dreams that Money Can Buy*, like the Chaplin puppet's disintegration at the end of the *Ballet mécanique*, are rare representations of male ruination in Léger's oeuvre. Perhaps because of Léger's persona as a virile man of the people, a public image launched in the 1930s and entrenched in the 1950s by the French Communist Party, his doubts, ambivalences, and blockages have rarely been explored.

Rather than necessarily explicitly representing any traumatic scene, Léger's art periodically revives the sensory conditions of his traumatic experiences. *The Card Party* enacts both a form of repetition compulsion, returning the artist to the scene of disaster—that is, the war as a site of death and lost agency, as well as a pictorial process aimed to achieve mastery over those conditions. In *The City*, the fragmentation of forms signifying the sights and sounds of the city revive the sensory experience of the battlefield and the simultaneous loss of agency or ability to see, know, and master the scene. On the other hand, Léger's *Three Women* might be understood not only as the desired and feared potency of the *femme-machine* but also as the disciplining of powerful emotions. By 1930, when memories of the war appeared in novels and memoirs and a "fallen humanity" became increasingly visible, Léger produced his extraordinary and anomalous comet triptych, which revives a sense of immersion in a nighttime battle. So, too, Léger's *plongeurs* series recapitulates the feelings of vertigo, falling, and drowning that emerged in the discourse about the traumatic fall of France in 1940. With the end of the war and Léger's return to France, the *plongeurs* evaporate, and equilibrium, a Purist concept, returns.

Léger's highly ambivalent attitude toward feeling and sentiment are, I have proposed, the result of an incomplete process of mourning marked by blockages and discontinuities between writing and image. The sentiment largely precluded from pictorial visualization, however, sometimes finds its melancholy expression in his intimate letters to his lover Simone Herman, as in his letter to her about breaking into a butchery for her, his queen. If Léger ever achieves mourning, it may be in the acrobatic paintings from the 1930s and 1940s, such as *Composition with Two Parrots*, where the male acrobat gains a kind of "sentimental value," or in *Big Julie*, when read as a memorializing icon for the absent male body, replaced by the crucified bicycle.

Léger repeatedly wrote that he wanted color to be therapeutic in response to war as a time and space without color or vitality. In his writing, the absence of color could signify the numbing and deadening effects of mechanized labor for the soldier or the factory laborer. Color frequently offers vitalism and regeneration: in the reconstruction bond posters he saw during his wartime hospitalization, the Bergsonian *élan vital* of the soldier, the animation of urban dynamism, farm machinery transformed into primordial birds, the bright and colorful factory, primitive and primitivist bodies, and the polychrome hospital. But the location of color more often lies outside the human body, which is rarely a source of vitalism. In reanimating the pictorial space with color, what comes to life is not so much the organic but the overwhelming machinery of capitalism particularly in the 1920s. In a rare exception, in *Big Black Divers* (1945), color deeply infuses the body, converging the tropes of racial typologies with a regeneration that is ahistorical and dissociated.

Masculinity may have been enacted through Léger's artistic process and staged in scenes of "dynamism," "classicism," or "equilibrium," but he was also repeatedly threatened by what could not be mastered. His rejection of naturalistic and academic forms of portraiture and history painting paradoxically meant that he engaged in a modernist aesthetics profoundly implicated in the limits of sight, consciousness, knowledge, and narrative. Léger's art alternates between a desire to forget trauma and its willful repression, its abstraction and dissociation, its resurfacing and displacements. Rather than producing a narrative that externalizes trauma, Léger's antimimetic practices refuse what can never be fully known and what the artist may never really have been able to retrieve. Vulnerable to destructive militarisms and capitalisms, the human body, especially the male body, comes in and out of visibility in Léger's oeuvre. His *mécaniciens* and tugboat captains from the 1920s move through spaces that are only apprehended in fragmentary and montage form. His acrobats and constructors from the late 1930s through the post-1945 era engage in life-threatening work on incomplete architectural structures, suggesting that by the end of his career, Léger thought of reconstructions and utopias as fragile, transitory, and even illusory. In his scenes of cycling and picnics, Léger invites the viewer to see themselves at rest away from the shock of modern life, yet he may have simultaneously created the conditions for remembering losses mediated by the image or outside the frame. Perhaps in his late work, Léger was less positivist and more postmodern than his manifest scenes of leisure might suggest.

Notes

Unless otherwise indicated, all translations are my own.

Introduction

1. LaCapra, *Writing History*, 23.
2. Fernand Léger, "L'Art et le peuple" (1946), in *Fonctions*, 247.
3. Cooper, *Fernand Léger.* The story has been repeated in many contexts, for example: Bauquier, *Vivre dans le vrai*, 64; Le Noci, *Fernand Léger*; Cork, *Bitter Truth*, 86.
4. Barbusse, *Lettres à sa femme*, 361–66; Mussolini, *My Diary*, 24.
5. Apollinaire, "Une Conférence de Fernand Léger."
6. Romoff, "Fernand Léger"; Hoppe, untitled essay on Léger; Guy Dornand, "Léger raconté par lui-même," *Plume*, no. 6 (1954): 57, quoted in Derouet, "Léger et le cinéma," 121; Bauquier, *Vivre dans le vrai*, 54; Kahnweiler, "Fernand Léger," 48.
7. Léger, "Correspondence (March 1922)," 11.
8. Léger, *Correspondance de guerre*, Letter No. 12 (April 12, 1915), 32, 35 (emphasis in the original).
9. Léger was hospitalized among the gassed, meaning among those with respiratory injuries. Derouet, foreword to Léger, *Correspondance de guerre*, 5. Prior to the publication of the war letters, most biographers only mention the gassing and none of the other reasons for his hospitalization. See, for example, Bauquier, *Vivre dans le vrai*, 76; De Francia, *Fernand Léger*, 38. On his diagnosis, see Léger, *Correspondance de guerre*, Letter No. 40 (September 9, 1917), 82, and No. 41 (October 4, 1917), 82–84.
10. See, for example, Léger, *Correspondance de guerre*, Letter No. 18 (September 14, 1915), 46–47.
11. For a summary of this literature, see Silverman, *Male Subjectivity*, 62–63.
12. As historian Ruth Leys has shown, the history of psychic trauma is one of shifting debates over etiology, diagnosis, and remedies. Only recently have histories of psychiatry begun to assess the French context during World War I, the range of diagnoses and psychiatric practices, and the implications for soldiers and veterans. See especially the work of Louis Crocq, Hervé Guillemain and Stéphane Tison, Laurent Tatu and Julien Bogousslavsky, Gregory M. Thomas, Marc Roudebush, and Jay Winter.
13. Babinski, *Hysteria or Pithiatism.*
14. Sigmund Freud, introduction to *Psychoanalysis and the War Neurosis* (1919), in *Standard Edition*, 207–10.
15. Gregory Thomas claims that most soldiers suffering from war trauma were deemed shirkers under Babinski's diagnosis. Thomas, *Treating the Trauma*, 71–92. Yet Crocq identifies "at least" twelve primary diagnostic categories and outlines four periods during the war, each with their own vocabulary for psychic ills. Crocq, *Les Blessés psychiques*, 43–44, 52. See also Guillemain and Tison, *Du Front à l'asile.*
16. Touret, "Cendrars (1887–1961)," 106.
17. Cendrars, "Construction," 273.
18. Audoin-Rouzeau, "L'Extraordinaire de la grande guerre," 27–28.
19. Cyrulnik, *Whispering of Ghosts*, 123, 170.
20. Leys, *Trauma*, 124.
21. Ricoeur, *Memory, History, Forgetting*, 4.
22. LaCapra, *Writing History*, 31–37, 89; Caruth, *Trauma*, 9; Felman and Laub, *Testimony*, 6.
23. An outline of the Leys-Caruth debate follows. Ruth Leys devotes the last chapter of her book to Caruth's writing, arguing in part that it is caught up in the double bind of what Leys calls a mimetic/antimimetic paradigm in the genealogy of trauma. It is this paradigm, its formation and transformation in the history of psychiatry, that is the subject of her book. Leys

posits that in the mimetic position, the patient becomes reimmersed in the traumatic event under hypnosis when self-other differentiation between the patient and therapist dissolves; any description of the event produced through hypnosis is susceptible to the suggestion of the therapist. In the antimimetic position, an imagined specular distance assumes a separation between self and other, differentiating the patient from the traumatic event and so permitting narration and mastery over the experience. In Leys's analysis, the history of trauma is a "history of forgetting," and today's psychotherapeutic commonplaces (hypnosis therapy and dissociation diagnosis) mean that we have "not grasped the scandalous nature of the traumatic cure." Leys, *Trauma*, 119, 220–65. In defending Caruth's work, Felman credits Caruth with important insights into aftermath culture, the enigma of survival, as well as with modeling new modes of reading and listening. In an extraordinary eight-page note, Felman also discredits Leys's work on trauma, arguing that Leys misinterprets Freud and Caruth and that Leys's theorization produces an impasse rather than insights for clinical practice. Felman, *Juridical Unconscious*, 173–81n1. LaCapra assesses Caruth and Felman as producing some of the "most powerful and thought-provoking recent criticism." Caruth's analysis, he writes, opens itself up to "reinscription or emulation" of traumatic literary texts and, at times, enacts a "feel" for the traumatic experience that simultaneously results in imprecise critical analysis. He questions Caruth's dependence upon psychiatrist Bessel van der Kolk's argument of trauma's literal neurological imprint on the right side of the brain, which is not accessible to symbolization or verbalization and can only become represented in language when translated to the left or linguistic side of the brain. This use of Van der Kolk is, in LaCapra's terms, "an intricate displacement and disguise of the de Manian variant of deconstruction." LaCapra, *Writing History*, 106–9.

24. Cyrulnik, preface to *Résilience et relations humaines*.
25. Pollock, *Visual Politics*, 18–20.
26. See, for example, Winter's *Remembering War*.
27. Butler, *Frames of War*, 41, 78.
28. Silver, *Chaos and Classicism*, 19–20.
29. Léger, "L'Esthétique de la machine, l'ordre géométrique et le vrai" (1924), in *Fonctions*, 103–9, at 107–8 (hereafter "L'Esthétique de la machine" II).
30. See, for example, Foster, *Prosthetic Gods*, 120.
31. Léger, *Correspondance de guerre*, Letter No. 13 (May 30, 1915), 35–39.
32. See, for example, Felman and Laub, *Testimony*, 2–6; Felman, *Juridical Unconscious*, 2, 171.
33. Saltzman and Rosenberg, eds., *Trauma and Visuality*, x.
34. Pollock, introduction to *Visual Politics*, 12; Bennett, *Empathic Vision*, 1, 9–11.
35. Audoin-Rouzeau and Becker, *14–18: Understanding the Great War*, 175–86.
36. Benjamin, "Storyteller."
37. Masson, *Entretiens*, 33.
38. Danchev, *Georges Braque*, 138–39. Only a few months before his death, Braque told André Verdet that "art is a wound that becomes light," a comment on the therapeutic value of art and perhaps also his war experience. Verdet, *Entretiens*, 49–50.
39. Kimyongür, *Memory and Politics*, 15–16.
40. Silverman, *Male Subjectivity*, 59.
41. Caruth, *Unclaimed Experience*, 58; see also Caruth, *Trauma*, 6–8.

Chapter 1

1. For Léger's descriptions of his maladies, see Léger, *Correspondance de guerre*, Letter No. 39 (n.d.), 82; No. 40 (n.d.), 82–83; No. 41 (October 4, 1917), 83–84; No. 42 (December 7, 1917), 84–85; No. 45 (n.d.), 87; and No. 47 (n.d.), 88, 90.
2. Léger, *Correspondance de guerre*, Letter No. 42 (December 7, 1917), 84–85.
3. Here, I use Bennett's term "sense-memory," to designate the realm of "affective memory" and "lived bodily response[s] to trauma." Bennett, *Empathic Vision*, 25, 40.
4. On the uniforms and war medals, see Meyer, *La Vie quotidienne des soldats*, 44, 79, 179.
5. Bogousslavsky and Tatu, *Blaise Cendrars*, 86.
6. Wittman, *Tomb of the Unknown Soldier*, 3–16, 35, 45.
7. Léger, "Les Realisations picturales actuelles" (1914), in *Fonctions*, 49.
8. Kosinski, "Essentially Modern, Quintessentially French"; Sund, "Fernand Léger and Unanimism."
9. See Léger's praise of Romains's play, *Amedée ou les six messieurs en rang* (1924) in "Le Spectacle" (1924), in *Fonctions*, 116.
10. Goldberg, *En l'honneur.*

11. Goldberg, *En l'honneur*, 28; Léger, "Un Nouvel espace en architecture" (1949), in *Fonctions*, 257–61.
12. Verdet, *Entretiens*, 75.
13. On the forms of wartime *manille*, see Du Bled, *Histoire anecdotique*, 266–72. I am grateful to David Parlett for identifying the card game as *manille*.
14. Originally published in *Valori plastici*, no. 2/3 (February/March 1919): 3, this statement was republished in Léger, "Correspondence (March 1922)."
15. Horne, *Verdun 1916*, 13.
16. Meyer, *La Vie quotidienne*, 301, 311–12.
17. Letter from Braque to Kahnweiler dated October 8, 1919, quoted in Léger and Rosenberg, *Correspondance d'affaires*, Letter No. 13 (January 9, 1918), 24n1.
18. Léger, *Correspondance de guerre*, Letter No. 3 (October 5, 1914), 10–14, and No. 27 (October 25, 1916), 62–64.
19. Alexandre, *Art et Camouflage*, 23–26.
20. Bogousslavsky and Tatu, *Cendrars*, 188.
21. Touret, "Cendrars (1887–1961)," 106.
22. Bogousslavsky and Tatu, *Cendrars*, 187–88.
23. Ibid., 75.
24. Léger, *Correspondance de guerre*, Letter No. 12 (April 12, 1915), 32–35, and No. 37 (n.d.), 79–80. In response to Cendrars's expressions of fear, see Tatu and Bogousslavsky, "Writers as Shell Shock Witnesses," 47, 56; Bogousslavsky and Tatu, *Cendrars*, 188.
25. Cooper, *Fernand Léger*.
26. Léger, *Correspondance de guerre*, Letter No. 12 (April 12, 1915), 32–35, and No. 28 (October 30, 1916), 64–67.
27. Cendrars, "Construction," 273.
28. Cendrars, "Fernand Léger," *La Rose rouge*, no. 13 (July 3, 1919): 145–47, in *Oeuvres Complètes*, 4:190–91.
29. Coulondre, "La Partie de cartes."
30. Cork, *Bitter Truth*, 164–65.
31. Green, *Léger and the Avant-Garde*, 133–34.
32. Green, "La Peinture de Léger," 54.
33. Green, "Different Cubist Trajectories," 59.
34. Dagen, *Silence des peintres*, 201, 326.
35. Rochlitz, "La 'matière première,'" 15.
36. Michaud, *Fabriques de l'homme nouveau*, 18, 21.
37. Garnier and Le Bon, *1917*, 184; Dagen, *Silence des peintres*, 182–83; Michaud, *Fabriques de l'homme nouveau*, 18; Green, "La Peinture de Léger."
38. De Francia, *Fernand Léger*, 39.
39. Marcus, "Fernand Léger," 57–58.
40. Kosinski, *Fernand Léger*, 89.
41. Audoin-Rouzeau, "Correspondance de guerre," 55; Maingon and Tatu, "Creative Minds."
42. See Léger, *Correspondance de guerre*, Letter No. 17 (September 14, 1915), 47; No. 20 (October 15, 1915), 48–50; No. 21 (January 6, 1916), 50–53; No. 44 (December 1917), 86.
43. Nicot, *Les Poilus ont la parole*, 33–60.
44. Sigmund Freud, *War Neurosis* (1919), in *Standard Edition*, 207–10.
45. Silverman, *Male Subjectivity*, 55–65.
46. Ibid., 55.
47. Ibid., 58–59.
48. Ibid., 59.
49. Ibid., 61.
50. Audoin-Rouzeau, preface to *Les Gueules cassées*, 16; Becker and Audoin-Rouzeau, *La France, la nation, la guerre*, 303–4.
51. Delaporte, *Les Gueules cassées*, 30.
52. Mosse, "Shell-Shock as a Social Disease," 101.
53. Gilbert and Gubar, *No Man's Land*, 2:258–323.
54. Goldberg, *"Woman, Your Hour Is Sounding,"* 141–80.
55. Apollinaire, "Les Femmes et la Guerre," *Mercure de France* (October 1, 1917), in *Oeuvres en prose complètes*, 500–501.
56. Demm, *Censorship and Propaganda*, 77–79.
57. Silverman, *Male Subjectivity*, 63–64.
58. Amar, *Physiology of Industrial Organisation*. See also Panchasi, *Future Tense*, 15–42.
59. Bogousslavsky, *Cendrars*, 88. By contrast, the sculptor Maurice Prost, who lost his left arm in the war, commissioned a specialized prosthetic for purposes of sculpting in hard stone. Maingon and Tatu, "Creative Minds," 41.
60. Biernoff, *Portraits of Violence*, 99–106; Powell, "About-Face."
61. Powell, "About-Face," 604, 614. See also Powell, *Bodies of Work*.
62. Leys, *Trauma*, 84.
63. Micale, "Jean-Martin Charcot"; Thomas, *Treating the Trauma*, 22–27, 34–38.
64. Babinski, *Hysteria or Pithiatism*, 223. On the prohibition of women, see Leys, *Trauma*, 91; Roudebush, "Battle of Nerves."
65. Thomas, *Treating the Trauma*, 43–60.
66. Ibid., 22–24.
67. Léger, *Correspondance de guerre*, Letter No. 9 (December 17, 1914), 26–28; No. 11 (February 23, 1915), 30–32; and No. 15 (August 12, 1915), 40–42.
68. See, for example, Léger, *Correspondance de guerre*, Letter No. 2 (August 17, 1914), 9–10; No. 5 (October 30, 1914), 16–18; No. 7 (November 8, 1914), 20–23; and No. 9 (December 17, 1914), 26–28.

69. Nicot, *Les Poilus ont la parole*, 56, 117–21; Turbergue, *1914–1918*, 11, 72.
70. Panchasi, "Reconstructions," 119; see also Turbergue, *1914–1918*, 72.
71. See Guillemain and Tison's extensive study of *cafard* in the trenches as well as their discussion of Voivenel's books. Guillemain and Tison, *Du Front à l'asile*, 78–80.
72. Lagrange, "La Grande Guerre."
73. Maingon, "La Grande Guerre."
74. Léger, *Correspondance de guerre*, Letter No. 44 [November 1917], 86.
75. Léger, "Les Origins de la peinture contemporaine et sa valeur representative" (1913), in *Fonctions*, 37.
76. Barbusse, *Lettres à sa femme*, letter dated February 16, 1916, 239–40.
77. Léger, *Correspondance de guerre*, Letter No. 31 (December 14, 1916), 74–75.
78. Bonnat, *Album National de la Guerre*.
79. Ozenfant, *L'Elan* (December 15, 1915), quoted in Dagen, *Silence des peintres*, 52.
80. Silver, *Esprit de corps*, 53–57; Léger, *Correspondance de guerre*, Letter No. 22 (January 22, 1915), 53–54.
81. "L'Exposition du *Crapouillot*."
82. Silver, *Esprit de corps*, 54.
83. Véray, "Photographie et cinéma."
84. Guillot, "Sur le front photographique," 67; Dagen, *Silence des peintres*, 52–55.
85. Beurier, "Death and Material Culture," 113; Beurier, *Photographer La Grande Guerre*, 71–107.
86. Guillot, "Sur le front photographique."
87. Véray, "1914–1918."
88. For the film showing reeducated farmers engaged in farm labor, see the French Army Archives, Etablissement de Communication et de Production Audiovisuelle de Défense, Film 14.18 B 730 (1917). For the January 1919 photographs of an amputee farmworker at the Maison Blanche reeducation camp, see Lyford, *Surrealist Masculinities*, 55–56.
89. Garnier and Le Bon, *1917*, 334.
90. Lyford, *Surrealist Masculinities*, 59–62.
91. Ibid., 47–54.
92. See, for example, "Carte panoramique"; "Un Bombardement."
93. Amad, "From God's-Eye to Camera-Eye."
94. Green, *Léger and the Avant-Garde*, 101–2.
95. "Les Hommes Restent Calmes"; "La Fin tragique."
96. Antliff and Leighten, *Cubism and Culture*, 71–95. See also Antliff and Leighten's commentaries on Bergson throughout *Cubism Reader*.
97. See Folgarait, *Painting 1909*, 23–42.
98. Cottington, *Cubism and Its Histories*, 91–92.
99. Léger, "Les Réalisations picturales actuelles" (1914), in *Fonctions*, 39–54, at 46.
100. For a fuller discussion of Bergson's impact on the French avant-garde artists, see especially Brauer, *Vitalist Modernism*; Folgarait, *Painting 1909*; and Antliff, *Inventing Bergson*.
101. Léger, *Correspondance de guerre*, Letter No. 23 (January 29, 1916), 54–58.
102. Antliff, *Inventing Bergson*.
103. Audoin-Rouzeau, *Men at War*, 54; Meyer, *La Vie quotidienne*, 44.
104. Winter and Baggett, *Great War*, 59.
105. Antliff and Leighten, *Cubism and Culture*, 146.
106. Léger, "L'Art et le peuple" (1946), in *Fonctions*, 247–55, at 247.
107. Dagen, *Silence des peintres*, 43–44.
108. Jones, *Irrational Modernism*, 58–60, 100.
109. Léger, *Correspondance de guerre*, Letter No. 3 (October 5, 1914), 10–14.
110. Ibid., Letter No. 7 (November 8, 1914), 20–23.
111. Ibid., Letter No. 4 (October 27, 1914), 14–16.
112. Ibid., Letter No. 6 (November 3, 1914), 18–20.
113. Ibid., Letter No. 23 (January 19, 1916), 54–58.
114. Ibid., Letter No. 27 (October 25, 1916), 62–64; No. 28 (October 30, 1916), 64, 66–67; and No. 29 (November 7, 1916), 67–68, 70, 72.
115. Ibid., Letter No. 39 [August 1917], 82.
116. Ibid., Letter No. 41 (October 4, 1917), 83–84.
117. Ibid. On Parmentier, see Walusinski, "Jean-Martin Charcot's House Officers," 29–30.
118. Léger, *Correspondance de guerre*, Letter No. 42 (December 7, 1917), 84–85.
119. Chatelin and Martel, *Blessures du crâne*, 162–67.
120. Thomas, *Treating the Trauma of War*, 56–58. See also Crocq, *Les Blessés psychiques*, 33–39.
121. Crocq, *Les Blessés psychiques*, 72–76, 168.
122. Léger, *Correspondance de guerre*, Letter No. 41 (October 4, 1917), 83–84.
123. Léger, *Léger och Norden*, 25.
124. Sanouillet, *Dada in Paris*, 11; Jones, *Irrational Modernism*, 29, 66.
125. Sanouillet, *Dada in Paris*, 52–53.
126. Léger, *Correspondance de guerre*, Letter No. 23 (May 29, 1916), 54–58.
127. Ibid., Letter No. 48 (n.d.), 90–91. The 1917 still life is signed and dedicated on the back to Dr. Bigard and remains in a private collection. Bauquier, *Catalogue raisonné*, 1:190.
128. Léger, *Correspondance de guerre*, Letter No. 30 (November 23, 1916), 72–74.
129. Verdet, *Entretiens*, 76.

130. Kern, *Culture of Time and Space*, 288–308.
131. Derouet, introduction and chronology to Léger, *Correspondance de guerre*, 6.
132. Léger, *Correspondance de guerre*, Letter No. 26 (August 1, 1916), 61–62. In an editorial note, Christian Derouet identifies the site as Madame Bongard's gallery adjoining her brother Paul Poiret's fashion studio. However, as engineer and art critic Billy Klüver has shown, there were several galleries operating in and adjoining Poiret's studio, including the Galerie Barbazanges and Salon d'Antin. Klüver, *Picasso*, 61–65.
133. Klüver, *Picasso*, 65–67.
134. Ibid., 167–85.
135. Ozenfant, "Notes on Cubism," *L'Elan* (December 1, 1916), quoted and translated in Eliel, "Purism in Paris," 12.
136. Quoted in Silver, *Esprit de corps*, 56.
137. Ibid., 80–84.
138. Léger, *Correspondance de guerre*, Letter No. 20 (October 15, 1915), 48–50.
139. Delaporte, *Les Gueules cassées*, 52–53.
140. Scarry, *Body in Pain*, 4.
141. Demm, *Censorship*, 17.
142. Kosinski, "Des 'contrastes de formes'"; Handler, "1914–20"; Cork, *Bitter Truth*, 163.
143. Léger, *Correspondance de guerre*, Letter No. 27 (October 25, 1916), 62–64.
144. Léger, "Les Réalisations picturales actuelles" (1914), in *Fonctions*, 39–54, at 47.
145. Léger, *Correspondance de guerre*, Letter No. 40 [September 1917], 82–83.
146. Pointon, "Kahnweiler's Picasso."
147. Brooke, *Albert Gleizes*, 46–49.
148. Léger, *Correspondance de guerre*, Letter No. 33 (February 13, 1917), 75–77.
149. Ibid., Letter No. 20 (October 15, 1915), 48–50.
150. Ibid., Letter No. 22 (January 22, 1915), 53–54.
151. Ibid., Letter No. 7 (November 8, 1914), 20–23.
152. Ibid., Letter No. 8 (November 25, 1914), 24.
153. Ibid., Letter No. 23 (January 29, 1916), 54–58.
154. Ibid., Letter No. 33 (February 13, 1917), 75–77.
155. Ibid., Letter No. 3 (October 5, 1914), 10–14; No. 27 (October 25, 1916), 62–64; and No. 30 (November 23, 1916), 72–74.
156. Rondeau, *Fernand Léger*, 134.
157. Duhamel, *New Book of Martyrs*, 2.
158. Léger, *Correspondance de guerre*, Letter No. 33 (February 13, 1917), 75–77.
159. Léger, "Couleur dans le monde" (1937), in *Fonctions*, 206.
160. Schulz-Hoffman, "Beckmann, Matisse and Léger."
161. Salmon, "La Semaine artistique."
162. Léger, "Les Réalisations picturales actuelles" (1914), in *Fonctions*, 39–54, at 50–51; Fréchuret, "Fernand Léger," 107.
163. Sanouillet, *Dada in Paris*, 510.
164. Léger, "Le Spectacle, lumière, couleur, image mobile, objet-spectacle" (1924), in *Fonctions*, 130–31.
165. Flouquet, "Fernand Léger nous parle de l'importance de la couleur," *Le Monde*, no. 53 (July 13, 1929): 7, quoted in Fréchuret, "Fernand Léger," 109.
166. Léger, "Couleur dans le monde" (1937), in *Fonctions*, 205–25, at 205.
167. Léger, "L'Architecture moderne et la couleur, ou la création d'un nouvel espace vital" (1946), in *Fonctions*, 239–45, at 243.
168. Léger, "Un Nouvel espace en architecture" (1949), in *Fonctions*, 259. On the friendship between Marie Vassilieff and Léger, see Bernès and Noël, *Marie Vassilieff*, 21–24; Noël, *Fernand Léger*, 63.
169. Fréchuret, "Fernand Léger."
170. Gage, *Color and Meaning*, 250–52.
171. Ibid., 265, 314, and colorplate 103.
172. See ibid., 304n23.
173. Becker and Audoin-Rouzeau, *La France*, 285–313.
174. Léger, *Correspondance de guerre*, Letter No. 2 (August 17, 1914), 9–10.
175. Ibid., Letter No. 3 (October 5, 1914), 10–14.
176. Ibid.
177. Ibid., Letter No. 9 (December 17, 1914), 26–28.
178. Ibid., Letter No. 4 (October 27, 1914), 14–16.
179. Ibid., Letter No. 11 (February 23, 1915), 30–32, and No. 23 (January 19, 1916), 75.
180. Ibid., Letter No. 12 (April 12, 1915) (emphasis in the original), 32–35.
181. LaCapra, *Writing History*, 23, 81.
182. Léger, "L'Art et le peuple" (1946), in *Fonctions*, 247–55, at 247.
183. Cooper, *Fernand Léger*.
184. See Léger, *Correspondance de guerre*, Letter No. 17 (September 14, 1915), 46; No. 20 (October 15, 1915), 48, 50; No. 21 (January 6, 1916), 50, 53; and No. 44 [December 1917], 86–87.
185. Caruth, *Unclaimed Experience*, 58. For example, Michael Rothberg writes that trauma "draws our attention to the survival of subjects in and beyond sites of violence and in *proximity* to death." Rothberg, "Preface," xiv.
186. Silverman, *Male Subjectivity*, 63.
187. Léger, "Les Origines de la peinture contemporaine" (1913), in *Fonctions*, 26–39; Léger, "Avenement de l'objet."

188. Severini, *Life of a Painter*, 94, 159.
189. *Archivi del Futurismo* (Rome, 1958), 1:106, quoted in Green, *Léger and the Avant-Garde*, 43.
190. Léger, "Les Origines de la peinture contemporaine et sa valeur representative" (1913), in *Fonctions*, 25–38, at 33.
191. See, for example, Léger, *Correspondance de guerre*, Letter No. 5 (October 30, 1914), 16–18; No. 27 (October 25, 1916), 62–64; and No. 29 (November 7, 1916), 67–72.
192. Léger, *Correspondance de guerre*, Letter No. 33 (February 13, 1917), 75–77.

Chapter 2

1. On his stay in Vernon, see Léger, *Correspondance de guerre*, Letter No. 49 (June 18, 1918), 92, and No. 50 (June 1918), 93–95.
2. On the Paris bombings, see Léger and Rosenberg, *Correspondance d'affaires*, Letter No. 22 (March 26, 1918), 28.
3. Léger, *Correspondance de guerre*, Letter No. 41 (October 4, 1917), 83–84.
4. Ibid., Letter No. 48 (n.d.), 99n1. On Léger's prewar lung congestion in 1906, see Bauquier, *Vivre dans le vrai*, 21.
5. Léger, *Correspondance de guerre*, Letter No. 47 (n.d.), 88–90.
6. Ibid., Letter No. 44 [December 1917], 86–87.
7. Léger and Rosenberg, *Correspondance d'affaires*, Letter No. 36 (July 8, 1918), 39.
8. Green, *Léger and the Avant-Garde*, 153–57; Green, "Fernand Léger's Multiplicative Vision."
9. Léger, *Correspondance de guerre*, Letter No. 7 (November 8, 1914), 20–23.
10. Foster, *Prosthetic Gods*, 120, 124.
11. Léger, "Le Spectacle" (1924), in *Fonctions*, 115–16.
12. Cyrulnik, *Whispering of Ghosts*, 97.
13. Audoin-Rouzeau, preface to *Les Gueules cassées*, 16; Becker and Audoin-Rouzeau, *La France*, 303–4.
14. Frader, *Breadwinners and Citizens*, 8.
15. Childers, *Fathers, Families and the State*, 42–81.
16. Higonnet, *Behind the Lines*.
17. Roberts, *Civilization Without Sexes*; Reynolds, *France Between the Wars*.
18. Ricoeur, *Memory, History, Forgetting*, 454.
19. Winter, "Thinking About Silence."
20. Theodosiou, *Le Deuil inachevé*, 146–54.
21. Sherman, *Construction of Memory*; Wittman, *Tomb of the Unknown Soldier*, 35.
22. Audoin-Rouzeau and Becker, *Understanding the Great War*, 177.
23. Leys, *Trauma*, 7.
24. Thomas, *Treating the Trauma*, 88–89, 167–69.
25. Crocq, *Les Blessés psychiques*, 167–70; Guillemain and Tison, *Du Front à l'asile*, 12–15.
26. Thomas, *Treating the Trauma*, 124–45.
27. Silver, *Chaos and Classicism*, 19.
28. Cendrars, "Pourquoi le 'cube' s'effrite?," *La Rose rouge*, no. 3 (May 15, 1919), 33–34, in *Oeuvres Complètes*, 6:39–42; Cendrars, "Fernand Léger," *La Rose rouge*, no. 13 (July 3, 1919), 145–47, in *Oeuvres Complètes*, 6:45–47.
29. Green, *Cubism and Its Enemies*, 58; see Green's description of this wartime shift in Green, "Different Cubist Trajectories."
30. Danièle Pauly locates the meeting between Léger and Le Corbusier around early 1921 at La Coupole. Pauly, *Le Corbusier*, 131. However, art appraiser Pierre Guénégan believes it was in 1920. Guénégan, "Le Purisme," 268.
31. Ozenfant and Jeanneret, *After Cubism*, 132.
32. Ozenfant and Jeanneret, "Le Purisme."
33. Gronberg, "Making up the Modern City."
34. Guénégan, *Le Purisme*; Guénégan, "Le Purisme."
35. Raynal, "Fernand Léger."
36. Léger and Rosenberg, *Correspondance d'affaires*, Letter No. 56 (September 6, [1919]), 56–61.
37. See, for example, Silver, *Chaos and Classicism*.
38. Green, "Fernand Léger."
39. Gordon, "Girls, Girls, Girls."
40. Jones, *Irrational Modernism*, 148.
41. Richards, *Le Corbusier*, 87.
42. Rosenblatt, "Empathy and Anaesthesia."
43. Coulondre, "'It's Geometry in Spasm!'"
44. Pinturrichio, "Le Carnet des ateliers," *Le Carnet de la semaine*, no. 156 (June 2, 1918) and no. 157 (June 9, 1918), cited in Léger and Rosenberg, *Correspondance d'affaires*, Letter No. 39 (August 23, 1918), 42–43n1.
45. Léger and Rosenberg, *Correspondance d'affaires*, Letter No. 39 (August 23, 1918), 42.
46. Ibid.; Rosenberg to Léger, Letter No. 55 (August 24, 1919), 53–56; and Léger to Rosenberg, Letter No. 56 (September 6, [1919]), 56, 58–61.
47. Léger, "L'Esthétique de la machine" II, 107.
48. Léger, "Le Spectacle" (1924), in *Fonctions*, 115–16.
49. Léger, "Couleur dans le monde" (1937), in *Fonctions*, 205–25, at 207.

50. Derouet, introduction to Léger, *Correspondance de guerre*.
51. See also Green, *Cubism and Its Enemies*, 45–46.
52. *L'Esprit Nouveau* published reports on the Kahnweiler and Uhde sales under the title "Echos de l'Hôtel Drouot" in at least seven issues from November 1920 to early 1921. Ozenfant and Jeanneret published the sale prices of the works in issues 13 and 15 of *L'Esprit Nouveau*.
53. Léger and Rosenberg, *Correspondance d'affaires*, Letter No. 95 (May 15, 1921), 84.
54. Rosenberg, "Sequestres 'Uhde et Kahnweiler.'"
55. Derouet, introduction to Léger and Rosenberg, *Correspondance d'affaires*, 5–17, 13; Léger to Rosenberg, *Correspondance d'affaires*, Letter No. 118 (n.d.), 96n4.
56. "Pour M. Vauxcelles." In a series of articles published in *Le Carnet de la semaine* in February and March 2022, Pinturrichio (Vauxcelles's pseudonym) charged that he was the victim of anti-Semitic attacks leveled against him by Ozenfant and Jeanneret and continued to insist on the devaluation of Cubist painting. For the private letters exchanged between Vauxcelles and *L'Esprit Nouveau* and the summons (later retracted) filed on February 21, 1922, against *Le Carnet de la semaine* for defamation, see the *L'Esprit Nouveau* Files, Vauxcelles Affair Folder A.1 (8). IV, items 370–76, Archives of the Le Corbusier Foundation, Paris.
57. Quoted in Pinturrichio, "Carnet des ateliers" (February 26, 1922).
58. Schuker, *End of French Predominance*, 4–26.
59. Léger, *Correspondance de guerre*, Letter No. 13 (May 30, 1915), 35–39.
60. Léger, "Les Origines de la peinture contemporaine" (1913), in *Fonctions*, 35.
61. Léger, "L'Esthétique de la machine, l'objet fabriqué, l'artisan et l'artiste" (1923–24), in *Fonctions*, 87–109, at 87 (hereafter "L'Esthétique de la machine" I).
62. "Domaine de l'esprit nouveau."
63. La Direction, "Ce que nous avons fait."
64. Le Corbusier, *Toward an Architecture*, 94.
65. Antliff and Leighten, "La Cité française," 139.
66. Antliff and Leighten, "Fascism, Modernism, and Modernity."
67. Boyer, *Le Corbusier*, 280.
68. Le Corbusier, *Toward an Architecture*, 294–307.
69. Léger, "L'Esthétique de la machine" I, 97–98.
70. Léger, "L'Esthétique de la machine" II, 103, 106.
71. On the several contributors to the *Ballet mécanique* and its multiple versions, see especially Piccinini, "Aux origines du *Ballet mécanique*"; Posner, "Les Différentes versions"; and Posner, "Chronologie." On debates about the various roles of each contributor, see also Delson, *Dudley Murphy*, 41–68.
72. Léger, *Correspondance de guerre*, Letter No. 29 (November 7, 1916), 67–30.
73. Picinnini, "1924."
74. Affron, "Léger's Modernism," 140.
75. Silverman, *Male Subjectivity*, 63.
76. Raynal, "Fernand Léger."
77. "La Leçon de la machine"; Léger, "L'Esthétique de la machine" I, 99.
78. Chenevier, "La Vie française"; Chenevier, "Economique"; Laffitte, "A propos de la Grande Crise."
79. "Note de l'Administration"; Cohen, introduction to *Toward an Architecture*, 26.
80. Ozenfant, "Note de la Direction."
81. La Direction, "Ce que nous avons fait."
82. Izdebska, "La Poésie russe"; Ehrenbourg, "Le Théâtre Russe."
83. Photograph of model for Tatlin's Monument to the Third International, *L'Esprit Nouveau*, no. 14 (January 1921): 1683; Pugni, "Russie."
84. "[Red Cross Appeal for Russia]," *L'Esprit Nouveau*, no. 15; "[Red Cross Appeal for Russia]," *L'Esprit Nouveau*, no. 16.
85. Eliel, "Purism in Paris," 13.
86. Westheim, "Allemagne."
87. George, "Willy Baumeister."
88. Boehm, "Corps-tableau," 77.
89. Ibid., 66–82.
90. Paret, "Oskar Schlemmer's *Triadic Ballet*," 177.
91. Boulard, "Allemagne."
92. Doherty, "'See, We Are All Neurasthenics!,'" 93.
93. Liliane Meffre explains Einstein's connections to Grosz, Dix, Goll, and Flechtheim. Meffre, *Carl Einstein*, 82–87.
94. Mijolla, "Psychoanalysis and Psychoanalysts."
95. Allendy and Laforgue, "Le Conscient et l'inconscient"; see also Allendy, "Hormones et Sexualité."
96. Allendy, "Le Complexe d'Oedipe."
97. Allendy, "Névroses."
98. Allendy and Laforgue, *La Psychanalyse et les névroses*.
99. Laforgue, *Le Rêve et la psychanalyse*, xviii, xxiii, 98.
100. Léger, "L'Esthétique de la machine" II, 108.
101. Léger and Rosenberg, *Correspondance d'affaires*, Letter No. 56 (September 6, 1919), 56–61.
102. Léger, "L'Esthétique de la machine" I, 99.

103. Léger, "Notes sur la vie plastique actuelle" (1923), in *Fonctions*, 61–67, at 67.
104. Engel, "Mechanical Empire," 40.
105. Green, *Léger and the Avant-Garde*, 233.
106. See Green, "There Is No Antiquity," 3.
107. Hemingway, *Moveable Feast*, 84.
108. Carden-Coyne, *Reconstructing the Body*, 1–21.
109. Foster, *Compulsive Beauty*, 62–74.
110. Sargeant, "Dancing on Fire and Water."
111. Gauthier, "Léger cinéphile."
112. Cendrars, "Charlot" (1952), in *Oeuvres Complètes*, 15:149–56. As early as 1924, Cendrars praised Chaplin's impact on soldiers' morale. See Gauthier, "Léger cinéphile," 113.
113. Guttierez, "Charlot-Léger, 'l'homme-image.'"
114. Léger, "Le Ballet-spectacle, l'objet-spectacle" (1923), in *Fonctions*, 69–73, at 70.
115. Léger, "Autour du 'Ballet mécanique'" (1924–25), in *Fonctions*, 133–39, at 137.
116. Bellow, "Fernand Léger's Mechanical Ballets," 399, 425.
117. Goll, "La Chaplinade"; Tokine, "Yvan Goll."
118. Bergson, "Laughter"; Freud, *Jokes*, 284–85.
119. Tokine, "L'Esthétique du Cinéma."
120. Faure, "Charlot."
121. "Les Livres reçus"; Raynal, "Les Livres."
122. Epstein, "Magnification," 238.
123. Sargeant, "Dancing on Fire and Water," 198.
124. McCabe, *Cinematic Modernism*, 14, 71.
125. Winter, *Remembering War*, 55.
126. Jones, *Irrational Modernism*, 152–54.
127. Foster, *Prosthetic Gods*, 165–66.
128. Delevoy, *Fernand Léger*, 59.
129. Faniest, *Léger*, 29.
130. Epstein, "Fernand Léger."
131. Léger, "Le Spectacle" (1924), in *Fonctions*, 111–31.
132. Léger, "Les Réalisations picturales actuelles" (1914), in *Fonctions*, 40.
133. Léger, "L'Esthétique de la machine" II, 107.
134. Léger, "Le Spectacle" (1924), in *Fonctions*, 130.
135. Léger, *Correspondance de guerre*, Letter No. 11 (February 23, 1915), 30–32.
136. Green, "La Peinture de Léger," 46, 53.
137. Léger, *Correspondance de guerre*, Letter No. 27 (October 25, 1916), 62–64.
138. Kahnweiler, *Rise of Cubism*, 18; Epstein, "Fernand Léger."
139. Léger, *Correspondance de guerre*, Letter No. 10 (January 1, 1915), 28–30.
140. Vallye, "Painter on the Boulevard," 1, 4.
141. Simmel, *Simmel on Culture*, 174–85.
142. Léger, *La Correspondance de guerre*, Letter No. 3 (October 5, 1914), 10–14.
143. Edited letter from Fernand Léger to Alfred H. Barr Jr., November 20, 1943, in Herbert, *From Millet to Léger*, appendix A, 174–77.
144. Léger, "Un Nouveau réalisme, la couleur pure et l'objet" (1935), in *Fonctions*, 187–93.
145. Butler, *Frames of War*, 39.
146. Bennett, *Empathic Vision*, 1.
147. Green, *Léger and the Avant-Garde*, 231.
148. Léger, *Correspondance de guerre*, Letter No. 48 (n.d. [after December 1917]), 90–91.
149. Westheim, "Kunst in Frankreich," 13.
150. Barr, *Modern Painting*, 29. See also Barr, *Masters of Modern Art*, 85.
151. Review of Le Salon d'automne, 14–23.
152. Léger, "Correspondence (March 1922)."
153. Green, *Léger and the Avant-Garde*, 223–50; Foster, *Prosthetic Gods*, 120.
154. Léger quoted in Bauquier, *Vivre dans le vrai*, 111.
155. Rexroth, "Heroic Object and Fernand Léger."
156. Roberts, *Civilization Without Sexes*, 63–87.
157. Léger, *Correspondance de guerre*, Letter No. 49 (June 18, 1918), 92–93.
158. Silver, *Chaos and Classicism*, 29.
159. Bissière, "Ingres," 397; Allendy, "Névroses."
160. Léger and Rosenberg, *Correspondance d'affaires*, Rosenberg to Léger, Letter No. 55 (August 24, 1919), 53–56, and Léger to Rosenberg, Letter No. 56 (September 6, [1919]), 56, 58–61.
161. Hiver, "Le Salon d'Automne," *Montparnasse* (October 1, 1922): 1, translated in Green, *Fernand Léger and the Avant-Garde*, 240.
162. Léger, "Le Spectacle" (1924), in *Fonctions*, 119, 121.
163. Léger, "L'Esthétique de la machine" II, 108.
164. Winter, *Remembering War*, 50, 214.
165. Loverdo and Mallet, *Les Abattoirs Publics*.
166. Vlaminck, *Dangerous Corner*, 89.
167. Stiles, *Concerning Consequences*, 6–7.
168. Audoin-Rouzeau and Becker, *Understanding the Great War*, 182–202.
169. LaCapra, *Writing History*, 23–24, 49–52.

Chapter 3

1. Silver, *Esprit de corps*, 374; Eliel, "Purism in Paris," 64–65.
2. Derouet, "Fernand Léger et les *Cahiers d'Art*."
3. Rochlitz, "La 'matière première,'" 18.
4. Zervos, "Fernand Léger et le Dévelopement," 152.
5. Zervos, "Une Nouvelle étape."
6. Zervos, "Fernand Léger et la Poésie," 99.

7. See, for example, Bouhours, "La Question de l'objet"; Chavanne, "Il faut toujours laisser une route libre"; Fréchuret, "Le Réel transposé"; Gay, "Biomorphisme"; Gay, "Objets décontexualisés"; Maillard, "Abecédaire"; Pierre, "Semence d'étoile"; Freeman, "L'Evénement d'objectivité plastique."
8. Jardot, introduction to *Fernand Léger: La Poésie de l'objet*, 8.
9. Taylor, *Life of Forms in Art*, 57–90; Maldonado, *Biomorphisme*, 19–32.
10. Golan, *Modernity and Nostalgia*, 68–69; Gay, "Biomorphisme"; Maillard, "Abecédaire."
11. Golan, *Modernity and Nostalgia*, x, 61.
12. Monod-Fontaine, "Silex et draperies."
13. Caruth, *Trauma*, 3–9.
14. Leys, *Trauma*, 101–3.
15. Ibid., 229–97.
16. See, for example, Caruth's analysis of the film *Hiroshima mon Amour* (Renais, 1959) in Caruth, *Unclaimed Experience*, 25–56; Leys, *Trauma*, 9, 104–16.
17. Leys, *Trauma*, 105–19.
18. Léger, "Autour du 'Ballet mécanique'" (1924–25), in *Fonctions*, 133–39.
19. Léger, "Avenement de l'objet."
20. Zervos, "Fernand Léger et la Poésie," 99.
21. Taylor, *Life of Forms in Art*, 4–5, 65; Maldonado, *Biomorphism*, 36.
22. Ozenfant and Jeanneret, "Formation de l'optique moderne."
23. See Léger's introduction to the photography book by Moholy-Nagy's student Moi Ver, *Paris*.
24. Moholy-Nagy, *Painting, Photography, Film*, 77.
25. Desnos, "Surrealisme."
26. Fotiade, *Pictures of the Mind*, 7.
27. Otto, *Haunted Bauhaus*, 7, 45–50.
28. Léger, "Actualités." James Johnson Sweeney translated and published the talk in English: Sweeney, "Léger and the Cult of the Close-up."
29. F. L., "L'Exposition de la photographie.'"
30. Philippon and Poirier, *Joseph Babinski*, 43–46; Béhar, *André Breton*, 130.
31. Aragon and Breton, "Le Trésor des Jésuites."
32. Aragon, "Calligrames"; "Collaborators"; Epstein, "Le Phénomène littéraire"; Raynal, "Revue de l'année 1920–1921."
33. Sanouillet, *Dada in Paris*, 104.
34. Béhar, *André Breton*, 138.
35. These include Léger's contribution of a painting to the first Dada event in January 1920; his attendance at multiple Dada festivals in February, March, and May 1920; and his role as one of the organizers for the 1921 Congress of Paris. Sanouillet, *Dada in Paris*, 104, 125–27, 238, 556n15.
36. Hunkeler, *Paris et le nationalisme*, 205–46.
37. "Exhibition reviews."
38. See Fauchereau, *La Querelle du realisme*.
39. Lomas, *Haunted Self*, 72.
40. Caws, *Surrealism*, 29.
41. Ibid., 27, 113.
42. Foster, *Compulsive Beauty*, 136–37.
43. Bois and Krauss, *Formless*, 13–40.
44. Stich, *Anxious Visions*, 27.
45. Lyford, *Surrealist Masculinity*, 85, 141–67.
46. Ades, *Masson*, 200.
47. Baron, "Décadence de la vie."
48. Einstein, "André Masson."
49. See, for example, Arnoux, "Notes du Front."
50. Léger, "New York" (1931), in *Fonctions*, 158.
51. Guy Dornand, "Léger raconte par lui-même," *Plume*, no. 6 (1954): 57, quoted in Derouet, "Léger et le cinéma," 121.
52. Halbwachs, *Les Cadres Sociaux de la mémoire*.
53. See, for example, Winter, *Remembering War*; Becker, *Maurice Halbwachs*, 193–230; Audoin-Rouzeau and Becker, *14–18: Understanding the Great War*, 182–202.
54. Fussell, *Great War*, 336–62.
55. Palmer, *Memories from the Frontline*, 12–13, 191–202.
56. Scott, "Evidence of Experience."
57. Flückiger and Leroy, *Blaise Cendrars*, 189–90. Cendrars literary specialists Jean-Carlo Flückiger and Claude Leroy compare Cendrars's *Moravagine* to Céline's later novel *Voyage au bout de la nuit* (1932) in terms of the types of madness represented in both novels. They note that Cendrars felt Céline plagiarized him and never acknowledged his influence.
58. Bogousslavsky and Tatu, *Blaise Cendrars*, 186–88.
59. Léger, "Couleur dans le monde" (1937), in *Fonctions*, 205–25, at 222.
60. Millington, *Fascism in France*, 31.
61. Bergen, "Practice of Giant Photomontage," 215–17.
62. Epstein, "Freud."
63. For a full discussion of Dr. René Allendy, see Frémont, *Dr. René Allendy*. Regarding Allendy's networks, see Birksted, *Le Corbusier*, 279; Palermo, *Fixed Ecstasy*, 190, 213; Meffre, "Carl Einstein et le Dr René Allendy."
64. Allendy and Laforgue, "La Pensée primitive"; Allendy and Laforgue, "Le Conscient and l'inconscient."
65. Allendy, "Le Rêve."
66. Laforgue, *Le Rêve et la psychanalyse*, 131.

67. Allendy, "La Valeur psychologique."
68. Léger's new still life drawings first appear in the December 15, 1928 (vol. 1, no. 8) and January 15, 1930 (vol. 2, no. 9) issues of *Variétés*.
69. Léger, "Couleur dans le monde" (1937), in *Fonctions*, 205–25.
70. MacOrlan, "Tragédies et divertissements populaires."
71. Fierens, "Des rues et des carrefours"; Vitrac, "L'Ephémère/Fantasmagorie"; Audard, "La Maison du sommeil"; and Bost, "Littérature Allemande."
72. MacOrlan, "George Grosz"; MacOrlan, "Le Fantastique." For MacOrlan's writing on Atget and Krull, see MacOrlan and Abbott, *Atget*, and MacOrlan, *Germaine Krull*.
73. See, for example, Jeanneret, "La Rhythmique," and Jeanneret, "La Rhythmique (fin)."
74. See, for example, Léger, "Ecole de publicité." See also Derouet, "Léger et la publicité."
75. Zervos, "Fernand Léger et le Dévelopement," 152.
76. Einstein, "Léger."
77. Regarding his nervous breakdown, see Ehrenburg, *Memoirs 1921–1941*, 10. Regarding Einstein's war service, see Kiefer, "Carl Einstein," 103.
78. George, "Fernand Léger," 310.
79. George, "Grandeur et misères d'une Victoire," 4–5.
80. "Fernand Léger," special issue, *Cahiers d'Art* 29 (1954), n.p.
81. Ibid.
82. Lista, "La Poétique du cubo-futurisme," 43.
83. See, for example, Léger, "Notes sur la vie plastique actuelle" (1923), in *Fonctions*, 61–67, at 65; "L'Esthétique de la machine" I, 95–96.
84. Léger, "L'Esthétique de la machine" II, 108.
85. Léger, *Correspondance de guerre*, Letter No. 3 (October 5, 1914), 10–14.
86. Ibid., Letter No. 8 (November 25, 1914), 24.
87. Demm, *Censorship and Propaganda*, 91.
88. Allendy, "La Valeur psychologique," 98–101.
89. Browne, "Scavengers of Paradise," 262.
90. Foster, *Compulsive Beauty*, 144–48.
91. For the archival information on the Ypres photograph, see In Flanders Fields Museum, Ieper (Ypres), Belgium, Research Centre, Robert Antony photography, inventory number IFFFC042 001088. I am indebted to Ruth Hommelen for identifying the origins of the two photographs and for her insights into the Belgian photographers, Georges Champroux and Robert Antony (also known as Antony d'Ypres).
92. Léger, "Le Beau et le vrai."
93. Fotiade, *Pictures of the Mind*, 77–154.
94. Foster, *Compulsive Beauty*, 33, 159–60.
95. Léger, *Correspondance de guerre*, Letter No. 6 (November 3, 1914), 18–20.
96. Monod-Fontaine, "Silex et draperies," 183.
97. Zervos, "Fernand Léger et la Poésie."
98. Rothschild, *Making It New*, 57, 67–74.
99. Rondeau, *Fernand Léger*, 8–9.
100. Zervos, "Une Nouvelle étape."
101. Pierre, "Semence d'étoile"; Gay, "Objets décontextualisés."
102. Fréchuret, "Le Réel transposé," 17.
103. Maldonado, *Biomorphisme*, 36–37.
104. Ozenfant, *Foundations of Modern Art*, 256–58.
105. Cassou, "Ozenfant."
106. Ozenfant, *Journey Through Life*, 143.
107. Mundy, "Naming of Biomorphism," 66–68.
108. In 1934, shortly after moving to Paris, Kandinsky went through a similar borrowing process from Miró's *Carnival*. Barnett, "Kandinsky and Science," 213–14.
109. Léger, *Correspondance poste restante*, Letter No. 15 (September 26, 1931), 27–28, and No. 16 (September 27, 1931), 28–29.
110. Léger, *Correspondance de guerre*, Letter No. 10 (January 1, 1915), 28–30.
111. Dorgelès, *Wooden Crosses*, 282.
112. Mussolini, *My Diary*, 22, 45.
113. Einstein, "Quelques Peintures importantes," 104.
114. Derouet, "Léger 1934," 12.
115. Maldonado, *Biomorphisme*, 30, 124–26.
116. Ozenfant, *Journey Through Life*, 137–43.
117. Léger, *Correspondance poste restante*, Letter No. 156 (February 14, 1936), 125.
118. Léger, *Correspondance de guerre*, Letter No. 3 (October 5, 1914), 10–14.
119. Ozenfant, *Foundations of Modern Art*, 212.
120. Doane, "Close-Up."
121. Albera, "Léger et le cinéma," 71. Léger's correspondence with Eisenstein is published in Le Noci, *Fernand Léger*.
122. Sweeney, "Léger and the Cinesthetic."
123. Eisenstein, "En gros plan," 112.
124. Epstein, "Magnification."
125. Epstein, "L'Element photogénique."
126. Léger, "Autour du 'Ballet mécanique'" (1924–25), in *Fonctions*, 133–39, at 134. This story of the magnified fingernail became part of his conception of the "new realism" reiterated in later writing. See, for example, Léger, "Le Beau et le vrai."
127. Léger, "Un Nouveau réalisme, la couleur pure et l'objet" (1935), in *Fonctions*, 187–93, at 190–91.

128. Zervos, "Fernand Léger et la Poésie," 103.
129. Krull, "Aux Halles de Paris"; Moholy-Nagy, "Un Égout des halles de Paris."
130. Lotar, "Aux abbatoirs de la Villette" (1929), 328, 330; Lotar, "La Viande"; Lotar, "Aux abbatoirs de la Villette" (1930), 698–99. Léger is credited by a reviewer of *Pantopodes* with saying it was "the most beautiful ballet he had seen." Les deux Aveugles, "Miracle."
131. Ozenfant, *Foundations of Modern Art*, 284–86.
132. Léger, "La Rue, l'objets, spectacles" (1928), in *Fonctions*, 141–44.
133. Cendrars and Leroy, *Blaise Cendrars*, 175–78.
134. Sweeney, "Léger's Art Is the Man," 28, 42, 44.
135. Léger, "New York" (1931), in *Fonctions*, 151–62, at 159.
136. Léger, *Correspondance de guerre*, Letter No. 28 (October 30, 1916), 64–67.
137. Léger, *Correspondance poste restante*, Letter No. 94 (November 25, 1933), 76–77.
138. Ibid., Letter No. 83 (September 5, 1933), 69–70.
139. Léger, "Le Cirque" (1949), in *Fonctions*, 263–76.

Chapter 4

1. Germain Seligmann, untitled essay in brochure for the exhibition *Fernand Léger: "Les Plongeurs"* (New York: Jacques Seligmann, 1944), n.p., in Artist Files, Library of The Museum of Modern Art, New York.
2. Verdet, *Entretiens*, 99, 103–4.
3. Caruth, introduction to *Trauma*, 4.
4. Ricoeur, *Memory, History, Forgetting*, 415–19.
5. Caruth, *Unclaimed Experience*, 11, 15.
6. Van der Kolk and Van der Hart, "Intrusive Past," 167.
7. Ozenfant, *Foundations of Modern Art*, 334–37.
8. Hertel, "Léger, Disciple de Michel-Ange"; Aragon, "Fernand Léger."
9. Giedion, "L'Art se prépare," 51; Schapiro, "Semiotics of Visual Art"; Bois, "Winks of Recognition," 141.
10. Diamond, *Fleeing Hitler*, 143.
11. Azéma, "Le Choc armé et les débandandes."
12. Bauquier, *Vivre dans le vrai*, 202.
13. Lanchner, "Fernand Léger: American Connections," 69n200.
14. Erickson, chronology to Lanchner, *Fernand Léger*, 277.
15. Hoffmann, "Le Trauma de 1940," 137.
16. Labarthe, "La Bataille de France."
17. Diamond, *Fleeing Hitler*, 114–17.
18. Carmody, *Yvan Goll*, 78–79.
19. Maritain, *France My Country*, 72.
20. Vidalenc, *L'Exode de mai-juin 1940*, 61, 300–326.
21. Temime, *Histoire de Marseille*, 272.
22. Léger, *Correspondance poste restante*, Letter No. 94 (November 25, 1933), 76–77.
23. Léger quoted in Mathey, *Fernand Léger*, 296.
24. Léger, "Couleur dans le monde" (1937), in *Fonctions*, 205–25, at 222.
25. Léger, *Correspondance poste restante*, Letter No. 250 (May 19, 1939), 188.
26. Willmoth, "Léger in America."
27. Bataille, "L'Apocalypse de Saint-Sever."
28. Letter from Léger to Lohy dated August 23, 1940, published in Bauquier, *Vivre dans le vrai*, 195.
29. Diamond, *Fleeing Hitler*, 77, 97.
30. See, for example, Guiraud, *Marseille à l'époque de Vichy*, 89–91.
31. On the artists at des Milles, see Bouches-du-Rhône, *Des peintres au camp des Milles*.
32. Temime, *Histoire de Marseille*, 277, 279, 284.
33. Berman, "Moral Triage or Cultural Salvage?"
34. Fry, *Surrender on Demand*, 30–32.
35. Durozoi, *History of the Surrealist Movement*, 386.
36. Marteau, "Sur quatres lames du Tarot."
37. Germain Seligmann, untitled essay in brochure for the exhibition *Fernand Léger: "Les Plongeurs"* (New York: Jacques Seligmann, 1944), n.p., in Artist Files, Library of the Museum of Modern Art, New York.
38. Le Corbusier quoted in Lanchner, "Fernand Léger: American Connections," 53.
39. Maillard, "Des projets muraux," 94; Affron, "Fernand Léger in New York," 184.
40. Erickson, chronology to Lanchner, *Fernand Léger*, 278.
41. Letter from Léger to Lohy dated July 6, 1941, in Bauquier, *Vivre dans le vrai*, 209.
42. Edward Alden Jewell, "Art Shows Given by Fernand Léger," *New York Times* (October 13, 1942): 20, cited in Willmoth, "Léger in America," 49.
43. Announcement card for Buchholz Gallery's exhibition of Fernand Léger's gouaches and drawings, October 12–31, 1942. Museum of Modern Art, New York, Artist Scrapbooks, Chadwyck-Healey (Arlington, VA, 1988).
44. Transcript and English translation of Thomas Bouchard's film *Fernand Léger in America: His New Realism* (1945), in Katharine Kuh Papers, 1943–59, Box 10, Folder 5 and Box 11, Folder 2,

Art Institute of Chicago Archives. The half-hour film and the Thomas Bouchard Archives are now available at the Harvard Film Archives, Harvard University.
45. Giedion, "L'Art se prépare," 50–52.
46. Kootz, "Peinture Moderne et Expression Sociale," 59–60.
47. Fernand Léger, letter to Louis Carré, in Derouet, chronology and bibliography to *Fernand Léger*, 337.
48. See, for example, Léger, "Le Mur, l'architecte, le peintre" (August 1933), in *Fonctions*, 171–86.
49. See, for example, Baudin-Renneau, *Fernand Léger*; Brunhammer, *Fernand Léger*; Affron, "Couleur dans le monde"; and Willmoth, "Le Mur, l'architecture, le peintre."
50. Bergen, "Practice of Giant Photomontage," 221–32; Affron, "Couleur dans le monde," 77–78.
51. Maillard, "Des projets muraux."
52. See Baudin, "Fernand Léger and Wallace K. Harrison"; Kramer, "Emancipated Drawing."
53. Adolph Gottlieb and Mark Rothko, letter to the *New York Times* (1943), in Landau, *Reading Abstract Expressionism*, 149.
54. Rexroth, "Heroic Object and Fernand Léger."
55. See Léger's letters to Nadia Bauquier dated August and September 1945, published in Bauquier, *Vivre dans la vrai*, 247, 249.
56. For Léger's paraphrasing of Marx on price, value, and profits, see his reference to the cotton market in Léger, "Le Mur, l'architecte, le peintre" (1933), in *Fonctions*, 171–84, at 177.
57. Erickson, chronology to Lanchner, *Fernand Léger*, 282.
58. Willmoth, "Léger in America," 45.
59. Léger and Rosenberg, *Correspondance d'affaires*, Letter No. 40 (September 6, 1918), 43–44.
60. Robinson and Creef, *Miné Okubo*, 46–49. Regarding Okubo's tours, see "Rikka–to a total new generation" [unidentified periodical] (Toronto, Ontario, Canada) 5 (Winter 1984): 4, in Archives of American Art, Roy Leeper and Gaylord Hall Collection of Miné Okubo papers. Léger never took a public position on Japanese internment, perhaps because his status in the United States was subject to regular review.
61. Léger, "Les Origines de la peinture contemporaine et sa valeur representative" (1913), in *Fonctions*, 25–38.
62. Fauchereau, *La Querelle du realisme*.
63. Léger, "Le Nouveau réalisme continue" (1936), in *Fonctions*, 195–203.
64. Kuh, *Fernand Léger*, 51–55.
65. Cohen-Solal, "Ultimate Challenge," 212.
66. Valentine Gallery, *American Artists Congress*.
67. Einstein, "Léger."
68. Golan, *Muralnomad*, 174.
69. Léger, "A propos du corps humain," 66–67.
70. The most complete statement, including the last two sentences about the Sistine Chapel, appears in the 1956 retrospective on Léger. Mathey, *Fernand Léger*, 296.
71. Wiltse, *Contested Waters*, 98.
72. De Fayet, "La Sixtine." See also Ozenfant and Jeanneret, "Les Idées de l'Esprit Nouveau." De Fayet is sometimes claimed as a pseudonym for Le Corbusier. See, for example, Boyer, *Le Corbusier*, 21.
73. Hertel, "Léger, Disciple de Michel-Ange," figs. 30–37.
74. Maur, "Rhythm and the Cult of the Body," 39. See also Martin and Ramond, "Les 'armes offensives,'" 18.
75. Abramovic and Hergott, *La Création du monde*, 102–3.
76. Duthuit, "Enquête," including Léger's response on pp. 70 and 72.
77. Rolland, *Au-dessus de la mêlée*, 21–38.
78. Eckmann, "Considering (and Reconsidering) Art and Exile," 31.
79. Buenger and Holz, "Antifascism or Autonomous Art?," 59.
80. Golan, "On the Passage," 129–30.
81. Ibid., 134.
82. Eckmann, "Art and Exile," 167.
83. Ibid., 172, 178.
84. Nanney, "Léger et les Etats-Unis."
85. Maillard, "Des projets muraux," 94.
86. See, for example, Nettelbeck, *Forever French*, 68; De Francia, *Fernand Léger*, 136.
87. Léger, "On Monumentality and Color"; Vallier, "La Vie fait l'oeuvre de Léger," 154.
88. Fréchuret, "Fernand Léger," 106.
89. Giedion, "Some Words on Fernand Léger," 54.
90. Ory, *La Belle Illusion*, 95–96.
91. De Fayet, "Nicholas Poussin"; De Fayet, "Peinture ancienne et peinture moderne"; Léger, "Notes sur la vie plastique actuelle" (1923), in *Fonctions*, 63.
92. Léger, "A propos du corps humain." See also Léger's comments about the Poussin painting in Verdet, *Entretiens*, 104–5.
93. Courthion, *Poussin*, 46–47.
94. Hedel and Teixeira de Barros, *Fernand Léger*, 17–18.
95. Jennings, *Free French Africa*.
96. See especially Léger, *Correspondance poste restante*, Letter No. 22 (October 31, 1931),

34–36; No. 78 (August 28, 1933), 67–68; No. 112 (July 20, 1934), 90–91; No. 135 (July 18, 1935), 109–10; and No. 170 (July 18, 1936), 136–37.

97. Fry, *Surrender on Demand*, 21.
98. Léger, "Découvrir l'Amérique."
99. Césaire, *Discourse on Colonialism*, 36.
100. Erickson, chronology to Lanchner, *Fernand Léger*, 281, Affron, "Fernand Léger in New York," 187–88.
101. Jacobson, *Modern Art in Advertising*, figs. 50 and 51.

Chapter 5

1. Sweeney, "Eleven Europeans in America," 13–15.
2. English transcript of Thomas Bouchard's film in which Léger demonstrates his artistic process, *Fernand Léger in America*, in Katharine Kuh Papers, Art Institute of Chicago Archives.
3. Sweeney, "Eleven Europeans in America," 15.
4. Greenberg, "Avant-Garde and Kitsch."
5. Greenberg, "Master Léger."
6. Chametzky, "From *Werkbund* to *Entartung*."
7. See, for example, Hahn, "Bauhaus and Exile."
8. Antliff, "La Cité française," 134–37; Richards, *Le Corbusier*, 37–47, 59–65.
9. Golan, "From Monument to Muralnomad," 188; Golan, *Muralnomad*, 37.
10. Bertrand Dorléac, *Art of the Defeat*, 17, 89.
11. Golan, "On the Passage," 133–34.
12. Barron, "European Artists in Exile"; Golan, "On the Passage," 142–43.
13. See Hahn, "Bauhaus and Exile"; Schulze, "Bauhaus Architects."
14. Eckmann, "Surrealism in Exile," 149, 162, 166–67.
15. Golan, "On the Passage," 132–33.
16. Léger, "L'Esthétique de la machine" I (1923–24), in *Fonctions*, 100. See also Léger's description of urban visual culture as "an inexhaustible mine of raw material" in "Le Ballet-spectacle, l'object-spectacle" (1923), in *Fonctions*, 69–73.
17. Galerie Louis Carré, *Entretien*, 26–27.
18. Léger, "La Rue, objets, spectacles" (1928), in *Fonctions*, 142–44.
19. Léger, "Couleur dans le monde" (1937), in *Fonctions*, 206–7.
20. Derouet, "Léger et la publicité"; Chavanne, "Il faut toujours laisser une route libre."
21. Verdet, *Entretiens*, 77.
22. Allen, *Horrible Prettiness*, 31, 250–51, 277–81.
23. Grayzel, *Women's Identities at War*, 121–56.
24. Rüger, "Entertainments."
25. Ibid., 119.
26. Hegarty, *Victory Girls*, 1–6, 110–27.
27. See, for example, Léger, "New York" (1931), in *Fonctions*, 151–62. See also Léger, "Un Nouveau réalisme, la couleur pure et l'objet" (1935), in *Fonctions*, 187–93.
28. Lankevich, *Postcards from Times Square*, 70, 97.
29. Letter from Fernand Léger to Archibald MacLeish, October 29, 1942. File on Léger's *Three Women*, Department of Painting and Sculpture Study Center, the Museum of Modern Art, New York.
30. Rebay, *Art of Tomorrow*, 4.
31. On Katherine Dreier's support for Black Mountain College, see Barron, "European Artists in Exile," 24. On the history of the Société Anonyme, see Gross, *Société Anonyme*, and Herbert, Apter, and Kenney, *Société Anonyme*.
32. Philadelphia Museum of Art, "Callery Collection."
33. See Emad, "Reading Wonder Woman's Body," 962.
34. Hampf, "Dykes or Whores."
35. Silverman, *Male Subjectivity*, 63–64.
36. Vassallo, "Simone de Beauvoir's *Le Sang des autres*."
37. English transcript of Bouchard's film *Fernand Léger in America*, in Katharine Kuh Papers, Art Institute of Chicago Archives.
38. Mekas, Bachmann, and Danisk Filmmuseum, "Interviews with Hans Richter," 31.
39. Lunel, "D'un lointain souvenir . . ."; Richter, "In Memory of Two Friends."
40. Léger, "Couleur dans le monde" (1937), in *Fonctions*, 214.
41. Dora Vallier, "La Vie fait l'oeuvre de Léger," 166.
42. Bauquier, *Vivre dans le vrai*, 47, 63; Cendrars, "La Grande copine" (1955), in *Oeuvres Complètes*, 15:3–8.
43. The story appears in an early version of Léger's "Color in Architecture," in Papadaki, *Le Corbusier*, 78–80.
44. See letters from Léger to Lohy dated from October 7, 1940 to February 18, 1942 in Bauquier, *Vivre dans le vrai*, 195–222.
45. Léger, "Los Angeles . . ."
46. Birnbaum, *Blum*, 118–42. See, for example, the *New York Times* coverage: Warren, "Averted Civil War," 8, and Warren, "Leon Blum."
47. Vlaminck, *Dangerous Corner*, 45–57.
48. *Comoedia* published reviews of the ballet *Skating Rink*, for which Léger did set and

costume designs, and the film *La Roue*, for which Léger designed a poster. See, for example, Rieu, "Skating Rink."

49. Brauer, "Vitalist Cubisms," 31.
50. Bertrand Dorléac, *Art of the Defeat*, xiv, 86.
51. Vlaminck, *Dangerous Corner*, 49–50.
52. Turbergue, *1914–1918*, 67.
53. Delaporte, *Les Gueules cassées*, 58.
54. See Perry, "Re-Arming the Disabled Veteran," 93.
55. A photograph of the set, which includes at least five bicycles, appears in *Bulletin de l'effort moderne*, no. 9 (November 1924): n.p.
56. See the photography spread in *Variétés* 1, no. 11 (March 15, 1929): n.p.
57. Rearick, *French in Love and in War*, 207.
58. Ibid., 211.
59. Bouhours, "La Question de l'objet," 33.
60. The "Gabin myth," developed in his films from the 1930s, is a jaunty hero, a good comrade to his male buddies, and an outsider who gains love—only to lose it all through betrayal or revenge, resulting in murder or suicide. Rearick, *French in Love and War*, 152, 222–27.
61. Bergen, "Practice of Giant Photomontage."
62. Rocca Serra, "Les Jeux internationaux universitaires."
63. Léger, *Le Cirque* (1950), translated in *Léger's Circus*, 5.
64. Regarding the "poilu's saint," see Audoin-Rouzeau and Becker, *14–18: Understanding the Great War*, 131.
65. Léger, "Si tu n'aimes pas les vacances."
66. Le Tacon, *La Croix de Lorraine*, 129–45.
67. Snape, *God and Uncle Sam*, 256–78.
68. Regarding Jeanne Lohy's friendship with Larionov and Gontcharova, see Léger, *Correspondance de guerre*, Letter No. 23 (January 29, 1916), 54–58. On Léger's many Russian connections, see Marcadé, "Léger et la Russie."
69. Barr, *Cubism and Abstract Art*, 122.
70. Marcadé, "Léger et la Russie," 61.
71. Wilson, "Artiste, Muse et égérie Russe?"; Du Chatenet, *Nadia Léger*, 606–9.
72. For Malevich's writing on Léger, see especially Malevich, "Léger, Gris, Herbin, Metzinger."
73. Malewitsch, "Suprematismus."
74. See, for example, the Catalog of the Film and reviews collected in Hans Richter Archive, A.III.1, *Dreams that Money Can Buy*, Press Clipping File, Archives of the Museum of Modern Art, New York.
75. Mekas, Bachmann, and Danisk Filmmuseum, "Interviews with Hans Richter," 30.
76. McLuhan, *Mechanical Bride*, 93–97.
77. Seymour Peck, "*Dreams* is Surrealist, Freudian and Disturbing," *PM Reviews* (April 25, 1948): n.p., Richter, A.III.1, Museum of Modern Art Archives, New York. In France, Henri Langlois panned the film as too influenced by rich donors and Hollywood. Bargues, "*Dreams*."
78. Pelswick, "How Abstract Can You Get?"; Crowther, "Screen."
79. Richard Huelsenbeck, "Psychology and Film," in Catalog of the Film, Richter, A.III.1, Museum of Modern Art Archives, New York.
80. Siegfried Kracauer, "Art and the Movies," in Catalog of the Film, Richter, A.III.1, Museum of Modern Art Archives, New York.
81. Slavin, *Colonial Cinema*, 173.
82. Sigmund Freud, "Mourning and Melancholy" (1917), in *Standard Edition*, 14:243–58.
83. Saltzman, *Anselm Kiefer*, 75.

Conclusion

1. Léger, "L'Esthétique de la machine" II, 103–9.

Bibliography

Abramovic, Norman, and Fabrice Hergott. *La Création du monde: Fernand Léger et l'art africain dans les collections Barbier-Mueller*. Paris: A. Biro, 2000.

Ades, Dawn. *André Masson: Catalogue Raisonné de l'oeuvre peint, 1919–1941*. 3 vols. Vaumarcus: ArtAcatos, 2010.

——. *The Colour of My Dreams: The Surrealist Revolution in Art*. Vancouver: Vancouver Art Gallery, 2011. Exhibition catalog.

Affron, Matthew. "Couleur dans le monde: Léger et le Photomontage." In Lecoq-Ramond and Widerkehr, *Fernand Léger*, 65–78.

——. "Fernand Léger in New York, 1940–45." In Barron, *Exiles and Emigrés*, 184–89.

——. "Léger's Modernism: Subjects and Objects." In Lanchner, *Fernand Léger*, 121–48.

Albera, François. "Léger et le cinéma." In *Fernand Léger: Od malarstwa do architektury / De la couleur au mur*, edited by Sylvie Forestier, 65–73. Warsaw: Zacheta Narodowa Galeria Sztuki, 2006. Exhibition catalog.

Alexandre, Patrice, ed. *Art et Camouflage*. Paris: Beaux-Arts de Paris, 2019.

Allen, Robert C. *Horrible Prettiness: Burlesque and American Culture*. Chapel Hill: University of North Carolina Press, 1991.

Allendy, René, and René Laforgue. "Le Conscient et l'inconscient." *L'Esprit Nouveau*, no. 21 (March 1924): n.p.

——. "La Pensée primitive." *L'Esprit Nouveau*, no. 20 (January–February 1924): n.p.

——. *La Psychanalyse et les névroses*. Paris: Payot, 1924.

Allendy, René. "Le Complexe d'Oedipe." *L'Esprit Nouveau*, no. 28 (1925): n.p.

——. "Hormones et Sexualité." *L'Esprit Nouveau*, no. 23 (1924): n.p.

——. "Névroses." *L'Esprit Nouveau*, no. 24 (1924): n.p.

——. "Le Rêve." *L'Esprit Nouveau*, no. 25 (1924): n.p.

——. "La Valeur psychologique de l'image." *L'Art cinématographique* 1 (1926): 75–104.

Amad, Paula. "From God's-Eye to Camera-Eye: Aerial Photography's Post-humanist and Neo-humanist Visions of the World." *History of Photography* 36, no. 1 (February 15, 2012): 66–86.

Amar, Jules. *The Physiology of Industrial Organisation and the Re-employment of the Disabled*. Translated by Bernard Miall. London: The Library Press Limited, 1918.

Antliff, Mark. "La Cité française: Georges Valois, Le Corbusier, and Fascist Theories of Urbanism." In *Fascist Visions: Art and Ideology in France and Italy*, edited by Matthew Affron and Mark Antliff, 134–70. Princeton, NJ: Princeton University Press, 1997.

——. "Fascism, Modernism, and Modernity." *Art Bulletin* 84, no. 1 (March 2002): 148–70.

——. *Inventing Bergson: Cultural Politics and the Parisian Avant-Garde*. Princeton, NJ: Princeton University Press, 1993.

Antliff, Mark, and Patricia Dee Leighten. *Cubism and Culture*. New York: Thames & Hudson, 2001.

——. *A Cubism Reader: Documents and Criticism, 1906–1914*. Chicago: University of Chicago Press, 2008.

Apollinaire, Guillaume. "Une Conférence de Fernand Léger." *Les Soirées de Paris* (June 15, 1914): n.p. Reprinted in *Apollinaire on Art: Essays and Reviews 1902–1918*, edited by LeRoy C. Breunig, translated by Susan Suleiman, 382–83. Boston: ArtWorks, 2021.

——. "Les Femmes et la Guerre." *Mercure de France* (October 1, 1917). In *Oeuvres en prose complètes*, edited by Michel Caizergues and Michel Décaudin, 3:500–501. Paris: Gallimard, 1993.

Aragon, Louis. "Calligrames." *L'Esprit Nouveau*, no. 1 (October 1920): 103.

——. "Fernand Léger" (1960). In *Ecrits sur l'art moderne*, 193–202. Paris: Flammarion, 1981.

Aragon, Louis, and André Breton. "Le Trésor des Jésuites." *Variétés* 2 (June 1929): 47–61.

Archives of American Art. Roy Leeper and Gaylord Hall Collection of Miné Okubo papers.

Archives of the Le Corbusier Foundation, Paris. *L'Esprit Nouveau* Files, Vauxcelles Affair Folder A.1 (8). IV, items 370–76.

Archives of the Museum of Modern Art, New York. Hans Richter Archive. A.III.1. *Dreams that Money Can Buy* Press Clipping File.

Archives of the Museum of Modern Art, New York. Artist Files. Fernand Léger.

Arnoux, Alexandre. "Notes du Front: Armistice." *L'Intransigeant* (November 12, 1928): 1.

Audard, Pierre. "La Maison du sommeil." *Variétés* 2, no. 9 (January 15, 1930): 624–26.

Audoin-Rouzeau, Stéphane. "Correspondence de guerre." In "Fernand Léger." Special issue, *Europe* 75, nos. 818–19 (June–July 1997): 51–57.

——. "L'Extraordinaire de la grande guerre." In *La Grande Guerre dans tous les sens*, edited by Stéphane Audoin-Rouzeau and Nicolas Beaupré, 18–45. Paris: Odile Jacob, 2021.

——. *Men at War 1914–18 National Sentiment and Trench Journalism in France During the First World War.* Translated by Helen McPhail. Providence, RI: Berg, 1992.

——. Preface to *Les Gueules cassées: Les Blessés de la face de la Grande guerre*, by Sophie Delaporte, 13–28. Paris: Edition Noêsis, 1996.

Audoin-Rouzeau, Stéphane, and Annette Becker. *14–18: Understanding the Great War.* Translated by Catherine Temerson. New York: Hill and Wang, 2002.

Audoin-Rouzeau, Stéphane, and Nicolas Beaupré, eds. *La Grande Guerre dans tous les sens.* Paris: Odile Jacob, 2021.

Audoin-Rouzeau, Stéphane, and Jean-Jacques Becker, eds. *Encyclopédie de la Grande Guerre, 1914–1918: Histoire et Culture.* Paris: Bayard, 2004.

Azéma, Jean-Pierre. "Le Choc armé et les débandandes." In *La France des années noires, De la défaite à Vichy*, edited by Jean-Pierre Azéma and François Bédarida, 1:97–129. Paris: Seuil, 1993.

Babinski, Joseph. *Hysteria or Pithiatism, and Reflex Nervous Disorders in the Neurology of War.* London: University of London Press, 1918.

Barbusse, Henri. *Lettres à sa femme, 1914–1917.* Paris: Buchet/Chastel, 2006.

Bargues, Cécile. "*Dreams*: Le Rêve américain de Hans Richter." In Dopffer and Guttierez, *Fernand Léger et le cinéma*, 174–77.

Barnett, Vivian Endicott. "Kandinsky and Science: The Introduction of Biological Images in the Paris Period." In *Biocentrism and Modernism*, edited by Oliver A. I. Botar and Isabel Wünsche, 207–26. Burlington, VT: Ashgate, 2011.

Baron, Jacques. "Décadence de la vie." *La Révolution surréaliste*, no. 3 (April 15, 1925): 14–15.

Barr, Alfred H., Jr. *Cubism and Abstract Art.* New York: Museum of Modern Art, 1936.

——. *Masters of Modern Art.* New York: Simon and Schuster, 1954.

——. *What Is Modern Painting?* New York: Museum of Modern Art, 1943.

Barron, Stephanie. "European Artists in Exile." In Barron, *Exiles and Emigrés*, 11–29.

——, ed. *Exiles and Emigrés: The Flight of European Artists from Hitler.* Los Angeles: Los Angeles County Museum of Art, 1997. Exhibition catalog.

Bataille, Georges. "L'Apocalypse de Saint-Sever." *Documents*, no. 2 (May 1929): 74–84.

——. *Documents.* Reprint. Paris: Mercure de France, 1968.

Baudin, Katia. "Fernand Léger and Wallace K. Harrison: An American Dream Come True." In *Fernand Leger: Painting in Space*, edited by Katia Baudin-Renneau, 186–93. Cologne: Museum Ludwig, 2016.

Baudin-Renneau, Katia, ed. *Fernand Léger: Painting in Space.* Cologne: Museum Ludwig, 2016.

Bauquier, Georges, ed. *Fernand Léger: Catalogue raisonné de l'oeuvre peint.* 8 vols. Paris: A. Maeght, 1990–2003.

——. *Fernand Léger: Vivre dans le vrai.* Paris: A. Maeght, 1987.

Becker, Annette. *Maurice Halbwachs: Un Intellectuel en guerres mondiales, 1914–1945.* Paris: A Viénot, 2003.

Becker, Jean-Jacques. *The Great War and the French People.* New York: St. Martin's Press, 1986.

Becker, Jean-Jacques, and Stéphane Audoin-Rouzeau. *La France, la nation, la guerre: 1850–1920.* Paris: Sedes, 1995.

Béhar, Henri. *André Breton: Le Grand indésirable.* Nouvelle ed. Paris: Fayard, 2005.

Bellow, Juliet. "Fernand Léger's Mechanical Ballets: On Dance and the Machine Aesthetic." *Modernism/Modernity* 29, no. 2 (April 2022): 399–430.

Benjamin, Walter. "The Storyteller" (1936). In *Illuminations*, edited by Hannah Arendt, 83–109. Translated by Harry Zohn. New York: Schocken Books, 1986.

Bennett, Jill. *Empathic Vision: Affect, Trauma, and Contemporary Art.* Stanford, CA: Stanford University Press, 2005.

Bergen, Véronique. "The Practice of Giant Photomontage." In *Charlotte Perriand:*

Inventing a New World, edited by Sébastien Cherruet and Jacques Barsac, 213–44. Paris: Fondation Louis Vuitton, 2019. Exhibition catalog.

Bergson, Henri. "Laughter" (1900). In *Comedy*, edited by Wylie Sypher, 79–83. 1956. Repr., Baltimore: Johns Hopkins University Press, 1980.

Berman, Elizabeth Kessin. "Moral Triage or Cultural Salvage? The Agendas of Varian Fry and the Emergency Rescue Committee." In Barron, *Exiles and Emigrés*, 99–112.

Bernès, Claude, and Benoît Noël. *Marie Vassilieff (1884–1957): L'oeuvre artistique, l'académie de peinture, la cantine de Montparnasse*. Sainte-Marguerite-des-Loges: Editions BVR, 2017.

Bertrand Dorléac, Laurence. *Art of the Defeat, France 1940–1944*. Translated by Jane Marie Todd. Los Angeles: Getty Research Institute, 2008.

Bertrand Dorléac, Laurence, and Maurice Fréchuret. *Exils: Réminiscences et nouveaux mondes*. Paris: Réunion des musées nationaux-Grand Palais, 2012.

Beurier, Joëlle. "Death and Material Culture: The Case of Pictures During the First World War." In *Matters of Conflict: Material Culture, Memory and the First World War*, edited by Nicholas J. Saunders, 109–22. London: Routledge, 2004.

——. *Photographer La Grande Guerre: France-Allemagne; L'héroïsme et la violence dans les magazines*. Rennes: Presses Universitaires de Rennes, 2016.

Biernoff, Suzannah. *Portraits of Violence*. Ann Arbor: University of Michigan Press, 2017.

Birksted, J. K. *Le Corbusier and the Occult*. Cambridge, MA: MIT Press, 2009.

Birnbaum, Pierre. *Léon Blum: Prime Minister, Socialist, Zionist*. New Haven, CT: Yale University Press, 2015.

Bissière. "Ingres." *L'Esprit Nouveau*, no. 4 (January 1921): 388–400.

Blossfeldt, Karl. *Karl Blossfeldt: Art Forms in Nature; the Complete Edition*. Edited by Gert Mattenklott. Munich: Schirmer Art Books, 1999.

Boehm, Gottfried. "Corps-tableau et machine-tableau: Les Travaux de Baumeister dans les années 20 et son amitié avec Léger." In *Willi Baumeister et la France: Arp, Cahn, Cézanne, Delaunay, Gleizes, Helion, Le Corbusier, Léger, Miro, Ozenfant, Picasso, Mondrian/Seuphor*, 66–82. Paris: Réunion des Musées nationaux, 1999.

Bogousslavsky, Julien, and Laurent Tatu. *Blaise Cendrars ou la légende du légionnaire*. Paris: Auzas éditeurs-Imago, 2015.

Bois, Yve-Alain. "Winks of Recognition." In Ciuha, *Fernand Léger*, 139–46.

Bois, Yve-Alain, and Rosalind Krauss. *Formless: A User's Guide*. New York: Zone Books, 1997.

"Un Bombardement des positions Allemands devant Fleury." *Le Miroir* (November 5, 1916): 11.

Bonnat, Léon Joseph Florentin. *Album National de la Guerre, publié par le comité de la 'Fraternité des artistes' sous le haut patronage de monsieur Raymond Poincaré*. Paris: Bernheim-Jeune, 1915.

Bost, Nico. "Littérature Allemande: Jeunes Générations." *Variétés* 2, no. 9 (January 15, 1930): 656–60.

Bouches-du-Rhône, Conseil général, Espace 13. *Des peintres au camp des Milles: Septembre 1939–Été 1941: Hans Bellmer, Max Ernst, Robert Liebknecht, Leo Marshutz, Ferdinand Springer, Wols*. Arles: Actes sud, 1997.

Bouhours, Jean-Michel. "La Question de l'objet vu du cinéma." In Chavanne, *Fernand Léger*, 26–34.

Boulard, Paul. "Allemagne." *L'Esprit Nouveau*, no. 27 (November 1924): n.p.

Boyer, Christine M. *Le Corbusier: The Writings of an Architect*. New York: Princeton Architectural Press, 2010.

Brauer, Fae. "Vitalist Cubisms: The Biocultures of Virility, Militarism and La Vie Sportive." In *Sport and the European Avant-Garde (1900–1945)*, edited by Andreas Kramer and Przemysław Strożek, 19–56. Leiden: Brill, 2022.

——, ed. *Vitalist Modernism: Art, Science, Energy and Creativity*. New York: Routledge, 2023.

Braun, Emily, and Rebecca Rabinow, eds. *Cubism: The Leonard A. Lauder Collection*. New Haven, CT: Yale University Press, 2014.

Brooke, Peter. *Albert Gleizes: For and Against the Twentieth Century*. New Haven, CT: Yale University Press, 2001.

Browne, Colin. "Scavengers of Paradise." In *The Colour of My Dreams: The Surrealist Revolution in Art*, edited by Dawn Ades, 245–62. Vancouver: Vancouver Art Gallery, 2011. Exhibition catalog.

Brueggemann, Aminia M., and Peter Schulman, eds. *Rhine Crossings: France and Germany in Love and War*. Albany: State University of New York Press, 2005.

Brunhammer, Yvonne. *Fernand Léger: L'oeuvre monumental*. Milan: 5 continents, 2005.

Buelens, Gert, Sam Durrant, and Robert Eaglestone, eds. *The Future of Trauma Theory: Contemporary Literary and Cultural Criticism.* London: Routledge, 2014.

Buenger, Barbara Copeland, and Keith Holz. "Antifascism or Autonomous Art? Max Beckmann, Wassily Kandinsky, John Heartfield, Kurt Schwitters, Oskar Kokoschka." In Barron, *Exiles and Emigrés*, 57–98.

Buszek, Maria Elena. *Pin-up Grrrls: Feminism, Sexuality, Popular Culture.* Durham, NC: Duke University Press, 2006.

Butler, Judith. *Frames of War: When Is Life Grievable?* London: Verso, 2009.

C., S. de. "Le Miracle de Kerensky." *L'Illustration*, no. 3887 (September 1, 1917): 239–42.

Carden-Coyne, Ana. *Reconstructing the Body: Classicism, Modernism, and the First World War.* Oxford: Oxford University Press, 2009.

Carmody, Francis J., ed. *Yvan Goll, Jean sans terre: A Critical Edition with Analytical Notes.* Berkeley: University of California Press, 1962.

"Carte panoramique de la Citadel de Verdun avec ses forts et les points de combat." *Le Miroir* (March 12, 1916): 8–9.

Caruth, Cathy, ed. Introduction to *Trauma: Explorations in Memory*, edited by Cathy Caruth, 3–12. Baltimore: Johns Hopkins University Press, 1995.

——. *Trauma: Explorations in Memory.* Baltimore: Johns Hopkins University Press, 1995.

——. *Unclaimed Experience: Trauma, Narrative, and History.* Baltimore: Johns Hopkins University Press, 1996.

Cassou, Jean. "Ozenfant." *Cahiers d'Art* 3, no. 10 (1928): 437.

Caws, Mary Ann, ed. *Surrealism.* London: Phaidon, 2004.

Cendrars, Blaise. "Construction" (1919). In *Complete Poems*, edited by Blaise Cendrars and Ron Padgett, 80. Berkeley: University of California Press, 1992.

——. *J'ai tué.* Paris: Crès, 1918.

——. *J'ai tué.* Paris: A la belle édition, 1919.

——. *Oeuvres Complètes.* Paris: Club français du livre, 1968–71.

Centre Georges Pompidou. *Fernand Léger.* Paris: Centre Georges Pompidou, 1997. Exhibition catalog.

——. *Fernand Léger: La Poésie de l'objet, 1928–1934.* Paris: Centre Georges Pompidou, 1981. Exhibition catalog.

Césaire, Aimé. *Discourse on Colonialism.* Translated by Joan Pinkham. New York: Monthly Review Press, 2000.

Chametzky, Peter. "From *Werkbund* to *Entartung*: Willi Baumeister's 'Wall Pictures.'" In *The Built Surface*, vol. 2, *Architecture and the Pictorial Arts from Romanticism to the Twenty-First Century*, edited by Karen Koehler, 160–85. Aldershot: Ashgate, 2002.

Chatelin, Charles, and Thierry de Martel. *Blessures du crâne et du cerveau formes cliniques, traitement médico-chirurgical.* Paris: Masson, 1917.

Chavanne, Blandine, ed. *Fernand Léger: Reconstruire le réel.* Paris: Réunion des Musées nationaux, 2014. Exhibition catalog.

——. "Il faut toujours laisser une route libre pour les artistes." In Chavanne, *Fernand Léger*, 21–23.

Chenevier, R. "Economique: Où mène la politique anti-Sovietique." *L'Esprit Nouveau*, no. 9 (June 1921): 1045–51.

——. "La Vie française." *L'Esprit Nouveau*, no. 6 (March 1921): 705–14.

Childers, Kristen Stromberg. *Fathers, Families and the State in France, 1914–1945.* Ithaca, NY: Cornell University Press, 2003.

Ciuha, Delia, ed. *Fernand Léger.* Ostfildern: Hatje Cantz, 2008. Exhibition catalog.

Cohen, J. L. Introduction to *Toward an Architecture*, by Le Corbusier, translated by John Goodman, 1–78. Los Angeles: Getty Research Institute, 2007.

Cohen-Solal, Annie. "The Ultimate Challenge for Alfred H. Barr, Jr.: Transforming the Ecology of American Culture, 1924–1943." In *Abstract Expressionism: The International Context*, edited by Joan Marter, 196–214. New Brunswick, NJ: Rutgers University Press, 2004.

"Collaborators." *L'Esprit Nouveau*, no. 1 (October 1920): 117.

Cooper, Douglas. *Fernand Léger, Dessins de guerre, 1915–1916.* Paris: Berggruen, 1956.

Cork, Richard. *A Bitter Truth: Avant-Garde Art and the Great War.* New Haven, CT: Yale University Press in association with Barbican Art Gallery, 1994.

Cottington, David. *Cubism and Its Histories.* Manchester: Manchester University Press, 2004.

Coulondre, Ariane. "La Partie de cartes, 1917." In *Fernand Léger: Le Beau est Partout*, edited by Ariane Coulondre, 62. Metz: Centre Pompidou-Metz, 2017.

——. "'It's Geometry in Spasm!' Cubism and the Press (1908–1919)." In *The Cubist Cosmos: From Picasso to Léger*, edited by Brigitte Léal, Christian Briend, and Ariane Coulondre,

244–50. Kunstmuseum Basel. Munich: Hirmer, 2019. Exhibition catalog.
Courthion, Pierre. *Poussin*. Paris: Plon, 1929.
Couturier, Marie-Alain, ed. *Fernand Léger: La Forme humaine dans l'espace*. Montreal: Les Editions de l'arbre, 1945.
Crocq, Louis. *Les Blessés psychiques de la Grande Guerre*. Paris: Odile Jacob, 2014.
Crowther, Bosley. "The Screen." *New York Times* (April 24, 1948): 11.
Cyrulnik, Boris. Preface to *Résilience et relations humaines: Couple, famille, institution, entreprise, cultures*, edited by Roland Coutanceau and Rachid Bennegadi, xiii–xxiv. Paris: Dunod, 2014.
——. *Whispering of Ghosts: Trauma and Resilience*. New York: Other Press, 2003.
Dagen, Philippe. *Le Silence des peintres: Les Artistes face à la Grande Guerre*. Paris: Fayard, 1996.
Danchev, Alex. *Georges Braque*. New York: Arcade Publishing, 2005.
De Fayet. "Nicholas Poussin." *L'Esprit Nouveau*, no. 7 (April 1921): 751–70.
——. "Peinture ancienne et peinture moderne." *L'Esprit Nouveau*, nos. 11–12 (1921): 1316–19.
——. "La Sixtine." *L'Esprit Nouveau*, no. 14 (January 1922): 1610–22.
De Francia, Peter. *Fernand Léger*. New Haven, CT: Yale University Press, 1993.
Delaporte, Sophie. *Les Gueules cassées: Les Blessés de la face de la Grande guerre*. Paris: Edition Noêsis, 1996.
"Délégation des mutilés aux Champs-Elysées." *Le Miroir* (July 20, 1919): 6.
Delevoy, Robert L. *Fernand Léger: Etude biographique et critique*. Geneva: Skira, 1962.
Delson, Susan B. *Dudley Murphy, Hollywood Wild Card*. Minneapolis: University of Minnesota, 2006.
Demm, Eberhard. *Censorship and Propaganda in World War I: A Comprehensive History*. London: Bloomsbury Academic, 2019.
Derouet, Christian. Foreword to *Fernand Léger: Une Correspondance de guerre à Louis Poughon, 1914–1918*, edited by Christian Derouet, 3–5. *Les Cahiers du Musée national d'art moderne*, hors-série / archives. Paris: Centre Georges Pompidou, 1997.
——. Chronology and bibliography to *Fernand Léger*, by Centre Georges Pompidou, 293–358. Paris: Centre Georges Pompidou, 1997. Exhibition catalog.
——. "Fernand Léger et les *Cahiers d'Art*." In Lecoq-Ramond and Widerkehr, *Fernand Léger*, 37–64.
——. "Fernand Léger's Americas." In Ciuha, *Fernand Léger*, 85–97.
——. Introduction and chronology to *Fernand Léger: Une Correspondance de guerre à Louis Poughon, 1914–1918*, edited by Christian Derouet, 5–7. *Les Cahiers du Musée national d'art moderne*, hors-série / archives. Paris: Centre Georges Pompidou, 1997.
——. "Léger et la publicité." In Centre Georges Pompidou, *Art and Pub: Art and Publicité 1890–1900*, 358–67. Paris: Editions du Centre Pompidou, 1990. Exhibition catalog.
——. "Léger et le cinéma." In *Peinture-Cinéma-Peinture*, edited by Germain Viatte, 121–43. Paris: Hazan, 1990. Exhibition catalog.
——. "Léger 1934: La Tentation du réalisme." In Centre Georges Pompidou, *Fernand Léger: La Poésie de l'objet*, 12–16.
Desnos, Robert. "Surréalisme." *Cahiers d'Art*, no. 8 (October 1926): 210–13.
Les deux Aveugles. "Miracle." *L'Intransigeant* (December 23, 1930): 6.
Diamond, Hanna. *Fleeing Hitler: France 1940*. New York: Oxford University Press, 2007.
Dickerman, Leah, ed. *Dada: Zurich, Berlin, Hannover, Cologne, New York, Paris*. New York: National Gallery of Art, 2005.
Doane, Mary Ann. "The Close-Up: Scale and Detail in the Cinema." *Differences: Journal of Feminist Cultural Studies* 14, no. 3 (Fall 2003): 89–111.
Doherty, Brigid. "'See, We Are All Neurasthenics!' or, the Trauma of Dada Montage." *Critical Inquiry* 24 (Autumn 1997): 82–132.
"Domaine de l'esprit nouveau." *L'Esprit Nouveau*, no. 1 (October 1920): n.p.
Dopffer, Anne, and Julie Guttierez, eds. *Fernand Léger et le cinéma*. Paris: Réunion des musées nationaux, 2021. Exhibition catalog.
Dorgelès, Roland. *Wooden Crosses* (1919). New York: G. P. Putnam's Sons, 1921.
Du Bled, Victor. *Histoire anecdotique et psychologie des jeux de cartes, dés, échecs*. Paris: Librairie Delagrave, 1919.
Du Chatenet, Aymar. *Nadia Léger: L'histoire extraordinaire d'une femme de l'ombre*. Paris: IMAV Editions, 2019.
Duffy, Jean H. "In the Wake of Trauma: Visualising the Unspeakable/Unthinkable in Marie Darrieussecq and Hélène Lenoir." *Word and Image* 27, no. 4 (October–December 2011): 416–28.
Duhamel, Georges. *The New Book of Martyrs* (1917). Translated by Florence Simmonds. London: Wm. Heinemann, 1918.

Durozoi, Gérard. *History of the Surrealist Movement.* Chicago: University of Chicago Press, 2002.
Duthuit, Georges. "Enquête." *Cahiers d'Art* 14, nos. 1–4 (1939): 65–73.
"Echos de l'Hôtel Drouot." *L'Esprit Nouveau*, no. 2 (November 1920): n.p.
"Echos de l'Hôtel Drouot." *L'Esprit Nouveau*, no. 3 (December 1920): n.p.
"Echos de l'Hôtel Drouot." *L'Esprit Nouveau*, no. 4 (January 1921): 48.
"Echos de l'Hôtel Drouot." *L'Esprit Nouveau*, no. 5 (February 1921): 607.
"Echos de l'Hôtel Drouot." *L'Esprit Nouveau*, no. 13 (December 1921): 1563.
"Echos de l'Hôtel Drouot." *L'Esprit Nouveau*, no. 15 (February 1921): 1825.
"Echos de l'Hôtel Drouot." *L'Esprit Nouveau*, no. 16 (1921): 1964.
Eckmann, Sabine. "Considering (and Reconsidering) Art and Exile." In Barron, *Exiles and Emigrés*, 30–42.
———. "Surrealism in Exile." In Barron, *Exiles and Emigrés*, 147–82.
Ehrenbourg, Elie. "Le Théâtre Russe pendant la Révolution." *L'Esprit Nouveau*, no. 13 (December 1921): 1515–19.
Ehrenburg, Ilya. *Memoirs: 1921–1941.* Translated by Tatania Shebunina. Cleveland: World Publishing, 1965.
Einstein, Carl. "André Masson, étude ethnologique." *Documents* 1, no. 2 (May 1929): 93–102.
———. "Léger: Œuvres récentes." *Documents* 2, no. 4 (1930): 190–97.
———. "Quelques Peintures importantes d'André Masson." *Documents* 1, no. 2 (May 1929): 103–5.
Eisenstein, Sergei. "En gros plan" (1940). In *Au-delà des étoiles,* translated by Jacques Aumont, 111–13. Paris: Union Général d'Editions, 1974.
Eliel, Carol, ed. *L'Esprit Nouveau: Purism in Paris, 1918–1925.* New York: Abrams, 2001. Exhibition catalog.
———. "Purism in Paris, 1918–1925." In Eliel, *L'Esprit Nouveau*, 10–69.
Emad, Mitra C. "Reading Wonder Woman's Body: Mythologies of Gender and Nation." *Journal of Popular Culture* 39, no. 6 (December 2006): 954–84.
Engel, Nadine. "A Mechanical Empire: Man Machines from Futurism to Constructivism." In *The Assembled Human: Der Montierte Mensch*, edited by Nadine Engel and Anna Fricke, 32–50. Museum Folkwang. Bielefeld: Kerber, 2019. Exhibition catalog.
Epstein, Jean. *Écrits sur le cinéma, 1921–1953.* Vol. 1, *1921–47.* Edited by Marie Epstein. Paris: Seghers, 1974.
———. "L'Element photogénique" (1924). In *Jean Epstein: Les Ecrits sur le cinéma* (1921–1953), edited by Marie Epstein, 145–47. Paris: Seghers, 1974.
———. "Fernand Léger." *Les Feuilles libres* (March–April 1923): 26–31. In *Jean Epstein: Les Ecrits sur le cinéma* (1921–1953), edited by Marie Epstein, 115–18. Paris: Seghers, 1974.
———. "Freud ou le Nic-Carterianisme en Psychologie." *L'Esprit Nouveau*, no. 16 (1922): 1857–64.
———. "Magnification" (1921). In *French Film Theory and Criticism, A History/Anthology, 1907–1939*, vol. 1, part 3, *1920–1924*, edited by Richard Abel, 235–41. Princeton, NJ: Princeton University Press, 1988.
———. "Le Phénomène littéraire." *L'Esprit Nouveau*, nos. 11–12 (1921): 1215–22.
Erickson, Kristen. Chronology. In Lanchner, *Fernand Léger*, 262–88.
Ernst, Max. *Natural History.* Paris: Galerie Jeanne Bucher, 1925–26.
"Exhibition reviews." *L'Esprit Nouveau*, nos. 11–12 (1921): 1303.
"L'Exposition du *Crapouillot*, Galerie Druet." *Le Crapouillot* (November 1918): 4–5.
F. L. [Fernand Léger]. "L'Exposition de la photographie à la Galerie 'l'Epoque.'" *Variétés* 1, no. 7 (November 15, 1928): n.p.
Faniest, Pierre. *Léger, Nadia . . . et moi.* Châteauneuf-de-Grasse (Alpes-Maritimes): Editions de Bergier, 2002.
Fauchereau, Serge, ed. *La Querelle du réalisme.* Paris: Éditions Cercle d'Art, 1987.
Faure, Elie. "Charlot." *L'Esprit Nouveau*, no. 6 (March 1921): 657–66.
Felman, Shoshana. *The Juridical Unconscious: Trials and Traumas in the Twentieth Century.* Cambridge, MA: Harvard University Press, 2002.
Felman, Shoshana, and Dori Laub. *Testimony: Crises of Witnessing in Literature, Psychoanalysis, and History.* New York: Routledge, 1992.
"Fernand Léger." Special issue, *Europe* 49, nos. 508–9 (August–September 1971).
"Fernand Léger." Special issue, *Europe* 75, nos. 818–19 (June–July 1997).
"Fernand Léger." Special issue, *Cahiers d'Art* 29 (1954).
Fierens, Paul. "Des rues et des carrefours: Venus et les Mannequins ou de l'Automne au Printemps." *Variétés* 1, no. 8 (December 15, 1928): 433–35.

——. "Fernand Léger." *La Renaissance* (August 1929): 380–87.

"La Fin tragique d'une Partie de Cartes." *Le Miroir* (June 6, 1915): 14.

Flückiger, Jean-Carlo, and Claude Leroy. *Blaise Cendrars sous le signe de Moravagine*. Caen: Lettres modernes minard, 2006.

Folgarait, Leonard. *Painting 1909: Pablo Picasso, Gertrude Stein, Henri Bergson, Comics, Albert Einstein, and Anarchy*. New Haven, CT: Yale University Press, 2017.

Fontaine, André. *Le Camp d'étrangers des Milles, 1939–43 (Aix-en-Provence)*. Aix-en-Provence: Edisud, 1999.

Foster, Hal. *Compulsive Beauty*. Cambridge, MA: MIT Press, 1993.

——. *Prosthetic Gods*. Cambridge, MA: MIT Press, 2006.

Fotiade, Ramona. *Pictures of the Mind*. Bern: Peter Lang, 2018.

Frader, Laura Levine. *Breadwinners and Citizens: Gender in the Making of the French Social Model*. Durham, NC: Duke University Press, 2008.

Fréchuret, Maurice. "Fernand Léger, le médecin coloriste." In *L'Art médicine*, edited by Maurice Fréchuret and Thierry Davila, 103–14. Paris: Réunion des musées nationaux, 1999.

——. "Le Réel transposé." In Chavanne, *Fernand Léger*, 12–19.

Freeman, Judi. "L'Evénement d'objectivité plastique–Léger's Shift from the Mechanical to the Figurative, 1926–1933." In Serota, *Fernand Léger*, 19–32.

Frémont, Marguerite. *La Vie du Dr. René Allendy, 1889–1942*. Chastelnau-le-Lez: Climats, 1994.

French Army Archives. Etablissement de Communication et de Production Audiovisuelle de Défense. Film 14.18 B 730 (1917).

Freud, Sigmund. *Jokes and Their Relation to the Unconscious*. Translated and edited by James Strachey. New York: W. W. Norton, 1960.

——. *The Standard Edition of the Complete Psychological Works of Sigmund Freud*. Translated and edited by James Strachey. London: Hogarth Press, 1953–74.

Fromaigeat, E. L. "La Musique en Russie soviétique." *L'Esprit Nouveau*, no. 3 (December 1920): 297–302.

Fry, Varian. *Surrender on Demand*. New York: Random House, 1945.

Fussell, Paul. *The Great War and Modern Memory* (1975). London: Oxford University Press, 2013.

Gage, John. *Color and Meaning: Art, Science and Symbolism*. Berkeley: University of California Press, 1999.

Galerie Louis Carré. *Entretien de Fernand Léger avec Blaise Cendrars et Louis Carré sur Le Paysage dans l'oeuvre de Léger*. Paris: Galerie Louis Carré, 1956.

Garnier, Claire, and Laurent Le Bon, eds. *1917*. Metz: Centre Pompidou-Metz, 2012. Exhibition catalog.

Gauthier, Christophe. "Léger cinéphile." In Dopffer and Guttierez, *Fernand Léger et le cinéma*, 112–17.

Gay, Diana. "Biomorphisme." In Chavanne, *Fernand Léger*, 80–82.

——. "Objets décontextualisés." In Chavanne, *Fernand Léger*, 104–6.

George, Waldemar. "Fernand Léger." *Arts* 15 (May 1929): 303–13.

——. "Grandeur et misères d'une Victoire. Fernand Léger." *Formes: Revue international des arts plastiques* (July 1930): 4–5.

——. "Willy Baumeister." *L'Esprit Nouveau*, no. 15 (December 1921): 1790–94.

Giedion, Sigfried. "L'Art se prépare à la vie publique." In Couturier, *Fernand Léger*, 37–52.

——. "Some Words on Fernand Léger" (1955). In *Architecture, You and Me: The Diary of a Development*, 52–55. Cambridge, MA: Harvard University Press, 1958.

Gilbert, Sandra M., and Susan Gubar. *No Man's Land: The Place of the Woman Writer in the Twentieth Century*. 2 vols. New Haven, CT: Yale University Press, 1989.

Guiraud, Jean-Michel. *La Vie intellectuelle et artistique à Marseille à l'époque de Vichy et sous l'occupation, 1940–1944*. Marseille: Éditions Jeanne Lafitte, 1998.

Golan, Romy. "From Monument to Muralnomad." In *The Built Surface*, vol. 2, *Architecture and the Pictorial Arts from Romanticism to the Twenty-First Century*, edited by Karen Koehler, 186–208. Aldershot: Ashgate, 2002.

——. *Modernity and Nostalgia: Art and Politics in France Between the War*. New Haven, CT: Yale University Press, 1995.

——. *Muralnomad: The Paradox of Wall painting 1927–37*. New Haven, CT: Yale University Press, 2009.

——. "On the Passage of a Few Persons Through a Rather Brief Period of Time." In Barron, *Exiles and Emigrés*, 128–46.

Goldberg, Nancy Sloan. *En l'honneur de la juste parole: La Poésie française contre la Grande Guerre*. New York: Peter Lang, 1993.

——. *"Woman, Your Hour Is Sounding": Continuity and Change in French Women's Great War Fiction, 1914–1919*. New York: St. Martin's Press, 1999.

Goll, Yvan. "La Chaplinade ou Charlot poète." *La Vie des lettres* [1921–1922]: 534–51.

Gordon, Terri J. "Girls, Girls, Girls: Re-membering the Body." In *Rhine Crossings: France and Germany in Love and War*, edited by Aminia M. Brueggemann and Peter Schulman, 87–118. Albany: State University of New York Press, 2005.

Grayzel, Susan R. *Women's Identities at War: Gender, Motherhood, and Politics in Britain and France During the First World War*. Chapel Hill: University of North Carolina Press, 1999.

Green, Christopher. *Cubism and Its Enemies: Modern Movements and Reaction in French Art, 1916–1928*. New Haven, CT: Yale University Press, 1987.

——. "Different Cubist Trajectories: The Work of the Paris-Based Cubists, 1914–18." In *Cubism and War: The Crystal in the Flame*, edited by Christopher Green, 44–63. Barcelona: Ediciones Polígrafa, 2017. Exhibition catalog.

——. "Fernand Léger: 'Mass-Produced' Classics, 1920–35." In *Modern Antiquity: Picasso, de Chirico, Léger, Picabia*, edited by Christopher Green and Jens M. Daehner, 93–97. Los Angeles: J. Paul Getty Museum, 2011.

——. "Fernand Léger's Multiplicative Vision for a Postwar Generation." In *Cubism: The Leonard A. Lauder Collection*, edited by Emily Braun and Rebecca Rabinow, 202–13. New Haven, CT: Yale University Press, 2014.

——. *Léger and the Avant-Garde*. New Haven, CT: Yale University Press, 1976.

——. "La Peinture de Léger pendant et après la guerre." In *Fernand Léger: Le Rythme de la vie moderne, 1911–1924*, edited by Dorothy Kosinski, 45–55. Paris: Flammarion, 1994. Exhibition catalog.

——. "There Is No Antiquity." In *Modern Antiquity: Picasso, de Chirico, Léger, Picabia*, edited by Christopher Green, Jens M. Daehner, Silvia Loreti, and Sarah Cochran, 1–15. Los Angeles: J. Paul Getty Museum, 2011.

Greenberg, Clement. "Avant-Garde and Kitsch" (1939). In *Art and Culture: Critical Essays*, 3–21. Boston: Beacon Press, 1961.

——. "Master Léger" (1954). In *Art and Culture: Critical Essays*, 96–104. Boston: Beacon Press, 1961.

Gronberg, Tag. "Making up the Modern City: Modernity on Display at the 1925 International Exhibition." In Eliel, *L'Esprit Nouveau*, 101–28.

Gross, Jennifer R., ed. *The Société Anonyme: Modernism for America*. New Haven, CT: Yale University Press, 2006.

Der Grosse Krieg in Bildern. Berlin: Georg Stilke, 1915–18.

Guénégan, Pierre. "Le Purisme–Amédée Ozenfant un Esprit nouveau." In *Le Corbusier and the Age of Purism*, edited by Hiroya Murakami, 261–70. Tokyo: Shimbun, 2019. Exhibition catalog.

——. *Le Purisme et son influence internationale: 50 artistes emblématiques*. Paris: Lanwell & Leeds, 2020.

Guillemain, Hervé, and Stéphane Tison. *Du Front à l'asile, 1914–1918*. Paris: Alma, 2013.

Guillot, Hélène. "Sur le front photographique, la propagande officielle par l'image." In Musée de l'Armée, *Vu du Front: Représenter la Grande Guerre*, 64–72. Paris: Musée de l'Armée, 2014. Exhibition catalog.

Guttierez, Julie. "Charlot-Léger, 'l'homme-image.'" In Dopffer and Guttierez, *Fernand Léger et le cinéma*, 118–23.

Hahn, Peter. "Bauhaus and Exile: Bauhaus Architects and Designers Between the Old World and the New." In Barron, *Exiles and Emigrés*, 211–24.

Halbwachs, Maurice. *Les Cadres Sociaux de la mémoire*. Paris, 1925.

Hampf, Michaela. "Dykes or Whores: Sexuality and the Women's Army Corps in the U.S. During World War II." *Women's Studies International Forum* 24, no. 1 (January 2004): 13–30.

Handler, Beth. "1914–20, World War I and the Mechanical Period." In Lanchner, *Fernand Léger*, 174–77.

Hanson, Anne Coffin. *Severini futurista, 1912–1917*. New Haven, CT: Yale University Art Gallery, 1995. Exhibition catalog.

Bouchard, Thomas. *Fernand Léger in America: His New Realism*. 1945. Harvard Film Archives, Harvard University.

Hedel, Brigitte, and Regina Teixeira de Barros. *Fernand Léger: Rélations et amitiés brésiliennes*. Version française. São Paulo: Pinacoteca do Estado de São Paulo, 2009. Exhibition catalog.

Hegarty, Marilyn E. *Victory Girls, Khaki-Wackies, and Patrioutes: The Regulation of Female Sexuality During World War II*. New York: New York University Press, 2008.

Hemingway, Ernest. *A Moveable Feast* (1964). New York: Charles Scribner's Sons, 1992.

Herbert, Robert. *From Millet to Léger: Essays in Social Art History.* New Haven, CT: Yale University Press, 2002.

——. "Léger, Renaissance and Primitivism." In *Hommage à Michel Laclotte: Etudes sur la peinture du Moyen-Age et de la Renaissance*, edited by Pierre Rosenberg, 642–47. Paris: Electa, 1994.

Herbert, Robert L., Eleanor S. Apter, and Elise K. Kenney, eds. *The Société Anonyme and the Dreier Bequest at Yale University: A Catalogue Raisonné.* New Haven, CT: Yale University Press, 1984.

Hertel, François. "Léger, Disciple de Michel-Ange." In Couturier, *Fernand Léger*, n.p.

Higonnet, Margaret R., ed. *Behind the Lines: Gender and the Two World Wars.* New Haven, CT: Yale University Press, 1987.

Hoffmann, Stanley. "Le Trauma de 1940." In *La France des années noires*, vol. 1, *De la défaite à Vichy*, edited by Jean-Pierre Azéma and François Bédarida, 131–50. Paris: Seuil, 1993.

"Les Hommes Restent Calmes sous la Mitraille." *Le Miroir* (December 27, 1914): 5.

Hoppe, Ragnar. Untitled essay on Léger. In "Fernand Léger," edited by Christian Zervos. Special issue, *Cahiers d'Art* 8, nos. 3–4 (1933), n.p.

Horne, Alistair. *The Price of Glory; Verdun 1916.* New York: St. Martin's Press, 1963.

Hunkeler, Thomas. *Paris et le nationalisme des avant-gardes: 1909–1924.* Paris: Editions Hermann, 2018.

Izdebska, H. "La Poésie russe des journées bolsheviques." *L'Esprit Nouveau*, nos. 11–12 (1921): 1231–37.

Jacobson, Egbert. *Modern Art in Advertising: Designs for Container Corporation of America.* Chicago: P. Theobald, 1946.

James, Martin S. "Léger at Rousses Point, 1944: A Memoir." *Burlington Magazine.* 130, no. 1021 (April 1988): 277–82.

Jardot, Maurice. Introduction to *Fernand Léger: La Poésie de l'objet*, by Centre Georges Pompidou, 8–11.

Jeanneret, Albert. "La Rhythmique." *L'Esprit Nouveau*, no. 2 (November 1920): 183–89.

——. "La Rhythmique (fin)." *L'Esprit Nouveau*, no. 3 (December 1920): 331–38.

Jennings, Eric. *Free French Africa in World War II: The African Resistance.* New York: Cambridge University Press, 2015.

Jones, Amelia. *Irrational Modernism: A Neurasthenic History of New York Dada.* Cambridge, MA: MIT Press, 2004.

Kahnweiler, Daniel-Henry. "Fernand Léger." In "Fernand Léger." Special issue, *Europe* 49, nos. 508–9 (August–September 1971): 46–48.

——. *The Rise of Cubism.* 1920. Translated by Henry Aronson. New York: Wittenborn, Schultz, 1949.

Katharine Kuh Papers, 1943–1959, Box 10, Folder 5 and Box 11, Folder 2, Art Institute of Chicago Archives.

Kern, Stephen. *The Culture of Time and Space 1880–1918.* Cambridge, MA: Harvard University Press, 1983.

Kiefer, Klaus H. "Carl Einstein and the Revolutionary Soldiers' Councils in Brussels." In *The Ideological Crisis of Expressionism: The Literary and Artistic German War Colony in Belgium, 1914–1918*, edited by Rainer Rumold and O. K. Werckmeister, 97–114. Columbia, SC: Camden House, 1990.

Kimyongür, Angela. *Memory and Politics: Representations of War in the Work of Louis Aragon.* Cardiff: University of Wales Press, 2007.

Klüver, Billy. *A Day with Picasso.* Cambridge, MA: MIT Press, 1997.

Koehler, Karen, ed. *The Built Surface.* Vol. 2, *Architecture and the Pictorial Arts from Romanticism to the Twenty-First Century.* Aldershot: Ashgate, 2002.

Kootz, S. M. "Peinture Moderne et Expression Sociale." In Couturier, *Fernand Léger*, 53–62.

Kosinski, Dorothy. "Des 'contrastes de formes' jusqu'à la fin de la Première Guerre Mondiale." In *Fernand Léger: Le Rythme de la vie moderne, 1911–1924*, edited by Dorothy Kosinski, 89. Paris: Flammarion, 1994. Exhibition catalog.

——. "Essentially Modern, Quintessentially French: Léger's Prewar Landscapes." In *Cubism: The Leonard A. Lauder Collection*, edited by Emily Braun and Rebecca Rabinow, 164–69. New Haven, CT: Yale University Press, 2014.

——, ed. *Fernand Léger: Le Rythme de la vie moderne, 1911–1924.* Paris: Flammarion, 1994. Exhibition catalog.

Kramer, Andreas, and Przemysław Strożek, eds. *Sport and the European Avant-Garde (1900–1945).* Leiden: Brill, 2022.

Kramer, Daniel. "Emancipated Drawing as Modernist Figure Painting: Fernand Léger's Mural *Les Plongeurs*." In Ciuha, *Fernand Léger*, 98–101.

Krull, Germaine. "Aux Halles de Paris" *Variétés* 1, no. 8 (December 15, 1928): n.p.

——. Untitled photographic essay, *Variétés* 2, no. 11 (March 15, 1930): n.p.

Kuh, Katherine. *Fernand Léger*. Chicago: Chicago Art Institute, 1953.

Labarthe, André. Annual Review, "La Bataille de France." *La France Libre* 1, no. 3 (January 1941): 218–19.

LaCapra, Dominick. *Writing History, Writing Trauma*. Baltimore: Johns Hopkins University Press, 2001.

La Direction. "Ce que nous avons fait, ce que nous ferons." *L'Esprit Nouveau*, nos. 11–12 (1921): 1211–14.

Laffitte, Paul. "A propos de la Grande Crise." *L'Esprit Nouveau*, no. 16 (1922): 1888–1902.

Laforgue, René, ed. *Le Rêve et la psychanalyse*. Paris: Grande Librairie Médicale A Maloine, 1926.

Lagrange, François. "La Grande Guerre au musée de l'Armée." In Musée de l'Armée, *Vu du Front: Représenter la Grande Guerre*, 136–40. Paris: Musée de l'Armée, 2014. Exhibition catalog.

Lanchner, Carolyn, ed. *Fernand Léger*. New York: Museum of Modern Art, 1998. Exhibition catalog.

——. "Fernand Léger: American Connections." In Lanchner, *Fernand Léger*, 15–70.

Landau, Ellen G. *Reading Abstract Expressionism: Context and Critique*. New Haven, CT: Yale University Press, 2005.

Lankevich, George. *Postcards from Times Square*. Garden City, NY: Square One Publishers, 2001.

Léal, Brigitte, Christian Briend, and Ariane Coulondre, eds. *The Cubist Cosmos: From Picasso to Léger*. Kunstmuseum Basel. Munich: Hirmer, 2019. Exhibition catalog.

"La Leçon de la machine." *L'Esprit Nouveau*, no. 25 (1924): n.p.

Lecoq-Ramond, Sylvie, and Léna Widerkehr, eds. *Fernand Léger*. Lyon: Musée des Beaux-Arts de Lyon, 2004. Exhibition catalog.

Le Corbusier. *Toward an Architecture* (1923). Translated by John Goodman. Los Angeles: Getty Research Institute, 2007.

Léger, Fernand. "Actualités." *Variétés* 1, no. 10 (February 15, 1929): 522–25.

——. "Avenement de l'objet." *Le Mois*, no. 41 (June 1934). Reprinted in Centre Georges Pompidou, *Fernand Léger: La Poésie de l'objet*, 25–27.

——. "Le Beau et le vrai." *Beaux arts* (February 9, 1934): 2. Reprinted in Centre Georges Pompidou, *Fernand Léger: La Poésie de l'objet*, 24.

——. *Cirque*. Paris: Tériade, 1950.

——. "Correspondence (March 1922)." *Bulletin de l'effort moderne*, no. 4 (April 1924): 10–12.

——. "Découvrir l'Amérique" (1942). In *Mes voyages*, 61–62. Paris: Ecoles des loisirs, 1997.

——. "Ecole de publicité de la Grande Chaumière." *Arts et Métiers Graphiques*, no. 42 (August 15, 1934): 73.

——. *Fernand Léger: Une Correspondance de guerre à Louis Poughon, 1914–1918*. Edited by Christian Derouet. *Les Cahiers du Musée national d'art moderne*, hors-série / archives. Paris: Centre Georges Pompidou, 1997.

——. *Fernand Léger: Une Correspondance poste restante*. Edited by Christian Derouet. *Les Cahiers du Musée national d'art moderne*, hors-série / archives. Paris: Centre Georges Pompidou, 1997.

——. *Fonctions de la peinture*. Paris: Gallimard, 1997.

——. *Léger och Norden*. Edited by Christian Derouet, Margareta Helleberg, and Nina Öhman. Stockholm: Moderna Museet, 1992.

——. "Los Angeles . . ." (n.d.). In *Mes voyages*, 48–49. Paris: Ecoles des loisirs, 1997.

——. "On Monumentality and Color" (1943). In *Architecture, You and Me: The Diary of a Development*, by Sigfried Giedion, 40–47. Cambridge, MA: Harvard University Press, 1958.

——. "A propos du corps humain considéré comme un objet." In Couturier, *Fernand Léger*, 63–75.

——. "Si tu n'aimes pas les vacances." *L'Intransigeant* (October 21, 1929): 5.

Léger's Circus. London: South Bank Centre, 1988. Exhibition catalog.

Léger, Fernand, and Léonce Rosenberg. *Correspondance d'affaires, Fernand Léger, Léonce Rosenberg, 1917–1937*. Edited by Christian Derouet. *Les Cahiers du Musée national d'art moderne*, hors-série / archives. Paris: Centre Georges Pompidou, 1996.

Le Noci, Guido. *Fernand Léger: Sa vie, son oeuvre, son rêve*. Milan: Apollinaire, 1971.

Le Tacon, François. *La Croix de Lorraine: Du Golgotha à la France libre*. Metz: Serpenoise, 2012.

Leymarie, Jean, and Jean Cassou. *Fernand Léger, dessins et gouaches*. Paris: Editions du Chêne, 1972.

Leys, Ruth. *Trauma: A Genealogy*. Chicago: University of Chicago Press, 2000.

Lista, Giovanni. "La Poétique du cubo-futurisme chez Fernand Léger." In *Fernand Léger*, edited by Hélène Lassalle, 29–44. Milan: Mazzotta, 1990. Exhibition catalog.

"Les Livres reçus." *L'Esprit Nouveau*, nos. 11–12 (1921): 1367.

Lomas, David. *The Haunted Self: Surrealism, Psychoanalysis, Subjectivity.* New Haven, CT: Yale University Press, 1999.

Lotar, Eli. "Aux abbatoirs de la Villette." *Documents*, no. 6 (November 1929): 328, 330.

——. "Aux abbatoirs de la Villette." *VU* (May 20, 1931): 698–99.

——. "La Viande." *Variétés* 2, no. 10 (March 15, 1930): n.p.

Loverdo, Jean de, and Leon Mallet. *Les Abattoirs Publics.* Paris: H. Dunod & E. Pinat, 1906.

Lunel, Armand. "D'un lointain souvenir . . ." In "Fernand Léger." Special issue, *Europe* 49, nos. 508–9 (August–September 1971): 42–45.

Lyford, Amy. *Surrealist Masculinities: Gender Anxiety and the Aesthetics of Post–World War I Reconstruction in France.* San Francisco: University of California Press, 2007.

MacOrlan, Pierre. "Le Fantastique." *L'Art cinématographique* 1 (1926): 1–19.

——. "George Grosz." Preface to exhibition catalog, *Exposition George Grosz* (Paris: Joseph Billiet, 1924). In *Paris-Berlin 1900–1933*, edited by Pontus Hulten, 47. Paris: Centre Georges Pompidou, 1992.

——. *Germaine Krull.* Paris: Gallimard, 1931.

——. "Tragédies et divertissements populaires: L'Aube." *Variétés* 1, no. 8 (December 15, 1928): 430–32.

MacOrlan, Pierre, and Berenice Abbott. *Atget: Photographe de Paris.* Paris: Jonquières, 1930.

Maingon, Claire. "La Grande Guerre exposée à Paris: 1914–1918." In Musée de l'Armée, *Vu du Front: Représenter la Grande Guerre*, 113–21. Paris: Musée de l'Armée, 2014. Exhibition catalog.

Maingon, Claire, and Laurent Tatu. "Creative Minds in the Aftermath of the Great War: Four Neurologically Wounded Artists." In *Neurological Disorders in Famous Artists*, part 4, edited by Julien Bogousslavsky and Laurent Tatu, 37–46. Frontiers of Neurology and Neuroscience 43. Basel: Karger, 2018.

Maillard, Nelly. "Abecédaire." In Chavanne, *Fernand Léger*, 126–30.

——. "Des projets muraux pour les E.U." In *Fernand Léger: Od malarstwa do architektury / De la couleur au mur*, edited by Sylvie Forestier, 89–97. Warsaw: Zacheta Narodowa Galeria Sztuki, 2006. Exhibition catalog.

Maldonado, Guitemie. *Biomorphisme 1920–1950.* Paris: Galerie Le Minotaure, 2019. Exhibition catalog.

Malevich, Kazimir. "Léger, Gris, Herbin, Metzinger" (1929). In *K. S. Malevich, Essays on Art 1915–1933*, 1:62–73. 2 vols. 2nd ed. New York: George Wittenborn, 1971.

Malewitsch, K. "Suprematismus." *Europa Almanach* (Potsdam) 1 (1925): 142–44.

Marcadé, Jean-Claude. "Léger et la Russie." In "Fernand Léger." Special issue, *Europe* 75, nos. 818–19 (June–July 1997): 58–72.

Marcus, Daniel. "Fernand Léger: Objects, Abstraction, and the Aesthetics of Mud." In *Nothing but the Clouds Unchanged*, edited by Gordon Hughes and Philipp Blom, 54–61. Los Angeles: Getty Research Institute, 2014.

Maritain, Jacques. *France My Country: Through the Disaster.* New York: Longmans, Green, 1941.

Marteau, Paul. "Sur quatres lames du Tarot." *Arts et métiers Graphiques*, no. 41 (May 15, 1934): 16–17.

Marter, Joan, ed. *Abstract Expressionism: The International Context.* New Brunswick, NJ: Rutgers University Press, 2004.

Martin, François-René, and Sylvie Ramond. "Les 'armes offensives' du peintre: L'histoire de l'art selon Fernand Léger." In Lecoq-Ramond and Widerkehr, *Fernand Léger*, 9–20.

Masson, André. *Entretiens avec Georges Charbonnier.* Paris: René Julliard, 1958.

Mathey, François. *Fernand Léger, 1881–1955.* Musée des arts décoratifs. Paris: F. Hazan, 1956. Exhibition catalog.

Maur, Karin von. "Rhythm and the Cult of the Body: Leger and the Ideal of the New Man." In Serota, *Fernand Léger*, 33–42.

McCabe, Susan. *Cinematic Modernism: Modernist Poetry and Film.* Cambridge: Cambridge University Press, 2005.

McKay, Claude. *Banjo: A Story Without a Plot.* New York: Harper & Bros., 1929.

McLuhan, Marshall. *The Mechanical Bride: Folklore of Industrial Man* (1951). Madeira, CA: Gingko Press, 2002.

Meffre, Liliane. *Carl Einstein et la problématique des avant-gardes dans les arts plastiques.* Bern: Peter Lang, 1989.

——. "Carl Einstein et le Dr René Allendy: Un Nouveau regard sur l'art?" In *Carl Einstein et Benjamin Fondane: Avant-gardes et emigration dans le Paris des années 1920–1930*, edited by Liliane Meffre and Olivier Salazar-Ferrer, 51–60. Collection "Comparatisme et Société" no. 6. Brussels: Peter Lang, 2008.

Mekas, Gideon Jonas, Gideon Bachmann, and Danisk Filmmuseum. "From Interviews with Hans Richter During the Last Ten Years." *Film Culture* 31 (1963): 26–35.

Meyer, Jacques. *La Vie quotidienne des soldats pendant la Grande Guerre*. Paris: Hachette, 1991.

Micale, Mark S. "Jean-Martin Charcot and *les névroses traumatiques*: From Medicine to Culture in French Trauma Theory of the Late Nineteenth Century." In *Traumatic Pasts: History, Psychiatry, and Trauma in the Modern Age, 1870–1930*, edited by Mark Micale and Paul Lerner, 115–39. Cambridge: Cambridge University Press, 2001.

Michaud, Eric. *Fabriques de l'homme nouveau: De Léger à Mondrian*. Paris: Editions Carré, 1996.

Mijolla, Alain de. "Psychoanalysis and Psychoanalysts in France Between 1939 and 1945." *International Forum of Psychoanalysis* 12, nos. 2–3 (2003): 136–56.

Millington, Chris. *A History of Fascism in France: From the First World War to the National Front*. London: Bloomsbury Academic, 2020.

Moholy-Nagy, László. "Un Égout des halles de Paris." *Variétés* 1, no. 8 (December 15, 1928): n.p.

——. *Painting, Photography, Film* (1927). Cambridge, MA: MIT Press, 1967.

Moi Ver. *Paris: 80 Photographs*. Paris: J. Walter, 1931.

Monod-Fontaine, Isabelle. "Silex et draperies, les années trente de Fernand Léger." In "Fernand Léger." Special issue, *Europe* 75, nos. 818–19 (June–July 1997): 182–84.

Mosse, George L. "Shell-Shock as a Social Disease." In "Shell Shock," edited by Jay Winter. Special issue, *Journal of Contemporary History* 35, no. 1 (January 2000): 101–8.

Mundy, Jennifer. "The Naming of Biomorphism." In *Biocentrism and Modernism*, edited by Oliver A. I. Botar and Isabel Wünsche, 61–76. Burlington, VT: Ashgate, 2011.

Murakami, Hiroya, ed. *Le Corbusier and the Age of Purism*. Tokyo: Shimbun, 2019. Exhibition catalog.

Musée de l'Armée. *Vu du Front: Représenter la Grande Guerre*. Paris: Musée de l'Armée, 2014. Exhibition catalog.

Mussolini, Benito. *My Diary, 1915–17*. Translated by Rita Wellman. Boston: Small, Maynard, 1925.

Nanney, Lisa. "Léger et les Etats-Unis." In "Fernand Léger." Special issue, *Europe* 75, nos. 818–19 (June–July 1997): 73–82.

Nettelbeck, Colin W. *Forever French: Exile in the United States, 1939–1945*. New York: Berg, 1991.

New Burlington Galleries. *Picasso's Guernica with 67 Preparatory Paintings, Sketches and Studies*. London: New Burlington Galleries, 1938.

Nicot, Jean. *Les Poilus ont la parole: Lettres du front, 1917–1918*. 2nd ed. Paris: Editions Complexe, 2003.

Noël, Benoît. *Fernand Léger: Un Normand planétaire*. Sainte-Marguerite-des-Loges: Editions BVR, 2020.

"Note de l'Administration." *L'Esprit Nouveau*, no. 17 (June 1922): n.p.

Ory, Pascal. *La Belle Illusion: Culture et Politique sous le signe du Front populaire, 1935–1938*. Paris: Plon, 1994.

Otto, Elizabeth. *Haunted Bauhaus: Occult Spirituality, Gender Fluidity, Queer Identities, Radical Politics*. Cambridge, MA: MIT Press, 2019.

Ozenfant, Amedée. *Foundations of Modern Art* (1928). New American edition. Translated by John Rodker. New York: Dover Publications, 1952.

——. *Journey Through Life: Experiences, Doubts, Certainties, Conclusions*. Translated by Helen De Vere Beauclerk and Violet M. Macdonald. New York: Macmillan, 1939.

——. "Note de la Direction." *L'Esprit Nouveau*, no. 27 (November 1924): n.p.

——. "Notes on Cubism." *L'Elan*, no. 10 (December 1916). In Eliel, *L'Esprit Nouveau*, 12.

Ozenfant, Amedée, and Charles-Edouard Jeanneret. *After Cubism* (1918), translated by John Goodman. In Eliel, *L'Esprit Nouveau*, 129–67.

——. "Formation de l'optique moderne." *L'Esprit Nouveau*, no. 21 (March 1924): n.p.

——. "Les Idées de l'Esprit Nouveau." *L'Esprit Nouveau*, no. 15 (February 1922): 1703–8.

——. "Le Purisme." *L'Esprit nouveau* no. 4 (January 1921): 369–86.

"La Paix et la guerre." *Variétés* 2, no. 8 (December 15, 1929): n.p.

Palermo, Charles. *Fixed Ecstasy: Joan Miró in the 1920s*. University Park: Penn State University Press, 2008.

Palmer, Jerry. *Memories from the Frontline: Memoirs and Meanings of the Great War from Britain, France and Germany*. London: Palgrave Macmillan, 2018.

Panchasi, Roxanne. *Future Tense: The Culture of Anticipation in France Between the Wars*. Ithaca, NY: Cornell University Press, 2009.

——. "Reconstructions: Prosthetics and the Rehabilitation of the Male Body in World War I France." *Differences: Journal of Feminist Criticisms* 7, no. 5 (Fall 1995): 109–40.

Papadaki, Stamos. *Le Corbusier.* New York: Macmillan, 1948.
Paret, Paul Monty. "Oskar Schlemmer's *Triadic Ballet* and the Trauma of War." In *Nothing but the Clouds Unchanged*, edited by Gordon Hughes and Philipp Blom, 172–79. Los Angeles: Getty Research Institute, 2014.
Pauly, Danièle. *Le Corbusier: Drawing as Process.* Translated by Genevieve Hendricks. New Haven, CT: Yale University Press, 2018.
Pelswick, Rose. "How Abstract Can You Get?" *New York Journal American* (April 24, 1948): 2.
Perry, Heather R. "Re-Arming the Disabled Veteran: Artificially Rebuilding State and Society in World War One Germany." In *Artificial Parts, Practical Lives: Modern Histories of Prosthetics*, edited by Katherine Ott, David Serlin, and Stephen Mihm, 75–101. New York: New York University Press, 2002.
Philadelphia Museum of Art. "The Callery Collection: Picasso-Léger." *Philadelphia Museum Bulletin* 40, no. 204 (January 1945): 35–48.
Philippon, Jacques, and Jacques Poirier. *Joseph Babinski.* Oxford: Oxford University Press, 2009.
"[Photography spread.]" *Variétés* 1, no. 11 (March 15, 1929): n.p.
Piccinini, Mauro. "Aux origines du *Ballet mécanique* 1923: La Création du cinéma vorticiste." In Dopffer and Guttierez, *Fernand Léger et le cinéma*, 148–51.
——. "1924: De la (peu) commune collaboration." In Dopffer and Guttierez, *Fernand Léger et le cinéma*, 152–55.
Pierre, Arnauld. "Semence d'étoile: Le Cosmos biomorphique de Fernand Léger." In Chavanne, *Fernand Léger*, 89–103.
Pinturrichio. "Carnet des ateliers." *Le Carnet de la semaine* (February 26, 1922): 8.
Pointon, Marcia. "Kahnweiler's Picasso; Picasso's Kahnweiler." In *Portraiture: Facing the Subject*, edited by Joanna Woodall, 189–202. Manchester: Manchester University Press, 1997.
Pollock, Griselda. *Visual Politics and Psycho-analyses: Art and the Image in Post-Traumatic Cultures.* London: I. B. Tauris, 2013.
Posner, Bruce. "Chronologie des différentes versions de *Ballet mécanique*." In Dopffer and Guttierez, *Fernand Léger et le cinéma*, 206–7.
——. "Les Différentes versions de *Ballet mécanique*." In Dopffer and Guttierez, *Fernand Léger et le cinéma*, 162–67.
"Pour M. Vauxcelles." *L'Esprit Nouveau*, no. 14 (1921), 1671, republished in *L'Esprit Nouveau*, no. 15 (December 1921), 1815.
Powell, Julie M. "About-Face: Gender, Disfigurement and the Politics of French Reconstruction, 1918–24." *Gender and History* 28, no. 3 (November 2016): 604–22.
——. *Bodies of Work: The First World War and the Transnational Making of Rehabilitation.* Cambridge: Cambridge University Press, 2023.
Pugni, Ivan. "Russie." *L'Esprit Nouveau*, no. 22 (1924): n.p.
Raynal, Maurice. "Fernand Léger." *L'Esprit Nouveau*, no. 4 (January 1921): 427–34.
——. "Les Livres." *L'Esprit Nouveau*, no. 14 (1922): 1655–57.
——. "Revue de l'année 1920–1921. Lettres." *L'Esprit Nouveau*, nos. 11–12 (1921): 1282–89.
Rearick, Charles. *The French in Love and War: Popular Front Culture in the Era of the World Wars.* New Haven, CT: Yale University Press, 1997.
Rebay, Hilla. *Art of Tomorrow.* New York: Solomon R. Guggenheim Museum, 1939.
"[Red Cross Appeal for Russia]." *L'Esprit Nouveau*, no. 15 (February 1922): 1814.
"[Red Cross Appeal for Russia]." *L'Esprit Nouveau*, no. 16 (1922): 1969.
Red Cross Work on Mutilés: At Paris (1918). U.S. Army / Allied Expeditionary Force. 4mm film; black and white, silent. OHA 252. Otis Historical Archives, National Museum of Health and Medicine. http://scalar.usc.edu/works/red-cross-work-1918/red-cross-work-on-mutils-at-paris-1918 (accessed June 29, 2019).
Review of Le Salon d'automne. *Le Crapouillot* (November 1, 1921): 14–23.
Rexroth, Kenneth. "Heroic Object and Fernand Léger." *The Nation* (1953). Republished in *Bird in the Bush: Obvious Essays*, 224–34. New York: New Directions, 1959.
Reynolds, Siân. *France Between the Wars: Gender and Politics.* London: Routledge, 1996.
Richards, Simon. *Le Corbusier and the Concept of the Self.* New Haven, CT: Yale University Press, 2003.
Richter, Hans. "In Memory of Two Friends, Fernand Léger, 1881–1955." *College Art Journal* 15, no. 4 (Summer 1956): 340–43.
Ricoeur, Paul. *Memory, History, Forgetting.* Translated by Kathleen Blamey and David Pellauer. Chicago: University of Chicago Press, 2004.

Rieu, Marcel. "Skating Rink." *Comoedia* (January 20, 1922): n.p.
Roberts, Mary Louise. *Civilization Without Sexes: Reconstructing Gender in Postwar France, 1917–1927.* Chicago: University of Chicago Press, 1994.
Robinson, Greg, and Elena Tajima Creef, eds. *Miné Okubo: Following Her Own Road.* Seattle: University of Washington Press, 2008.
Rocca Serra, Paul de. "Les Jeux internationaux universitaires." *Exposition 1937*, no. 5 (September 1936): 6–7. In *Exposition 1937, Pavillons Françaises.* Paris: Editions Art et Architecture, 1937.
Rochlitz, Rainer. "La 'matière première' de Fernand Léger." In Centre Georges Pompidou, *Fernand Léger*, 13–20.
Rolland, Romain. *Au dessus de la mêlée.* Paris: Libraire Paul Ollendorf, 1915.
Romoff, Serge. "Fernand Léger." *L'Humanité* (July 23, 1928): 4.
Rondeau, Tristan, ed. *Fernand Léger: Lettres à Charlotte et André Mare (1906–1932).* Livarot Pays d'Auge: Editions BVR, 2019.
Rosenberg, Léonce. "Sequestres 'Uhde et Kahnweiler.'" *Bulletin de l'Effort moderne* (January 1924): 13–16.
Rosenblatt, Nina. "Empathy and Anaesthesia: On the Origins of a French Machine Aesthetic." *Grey Room*, no. 2 (Winter 2001): 79–97.
Rothberg, Michael. "Preface: Beyond Tancred and Chlorinda." In Buelens, Durrant, and Eaglestone, *Future of Trauma Theory*, xi–xviii.
Rothschild, Deborah Menaker. *Making It New: The Art and Style of Sara and Gerald Murphy.* Berkeley: University of California Press, 2007.
Roudebush, Marc. "A Battle of Nerves: Hysteria and Its Treatments in France During World War I." In *Traumatic Pasts: History, Psychiatry, and Trauma in the Modern Age, 1870–1930*, edited by Mark Micale and Paul Lerner, 253–79. Cambridge: Cambridge University Press, 2001.
Rüger, Jan. "Entertainments." In *Capital Cities at War: Paris, London, Berlin, 1914–1919*, edited by J. M. Winter and Jean-Louis Robert, 2:105–40. Cambridge: Cambridge University Press, 1997.
Salmon, André. "La Semaine artistique." *L'Europe Nouvelle* (February 22, 1919): 387–88.
Saltzman, Lisa. *Anselm Kiefer and Art After Auschwitz.* Cambridge: Cambridge University Press, 1999.
Saltzman, Lisa, and Eric M. Rosenberg. *Trauma and Visuality in Modernity.* Hanover: Dartmouth College Press and University Press of New England, 2006.
Sanouillet, Michel. *Dada in Paris.* (1965) Translated by Sharmila Ganguly, revised and expanded by Anne Sanouillet. Cambridge, MA: MIT Press, 2012.
Sargeant, Amy. "Dancing on Fire and Water: Charlot and *L'Esprit nouveau.*" In *Slapstick Comedy: AFI Film Reader Series*, edited by Tom Paulus and Rob King, 193–206. New York: Routledge, 2010.
Saunders, Nicholas J., ed. *Matters of Conflict: Material Culture, Memory and the First World War.* London: Routledge, 2004.
Scarry, Elaine. *The Body in Pain: The Making and Unmaking of the World.* Oxford: Oxford University Press, 1985.
Schapiro, Meyer. "On Some Problems in the Semiotics of Visual Art." *Semiotica* 1 (1969): 223–42.
Schuker, Stephen. *The End of French Predominance in Europe: The Financial Crisis of 1924 and the Adoption of the Dawes Plan.* Chapel Hill: University of North Carolina Press, 1976.
Schulze, Franz. "The Bauhaus Architects and the Rise of Modernism in the United States." In Barron, *Exiles and Emigrés*, 225–34.
Schulz-Hoffman, Carla. "Beckmann, Matisse and Léger." In *Max Beckmann and Paris: Matisse, Picasso, Braque, Léger, Rouault*, edited by Tobia Bezzola and Cornelia Homburg, 79–91. St. Louis: St. Louis Museum of Art and Zurich: Taschen, 1999. Exhibition catalog.
Scott, Joan. "The Evidence of Experience." *Critical Inquiry* 17 (Summer 1991): 773–97.
Serota, Nicholas, ed. *Fernand Léger: The Later Years.* Munich: Prestel, 1987.
Severini, Gino. *The Life of a Painter: The Autobiography of Gino Severini.* Translated by Jennifer Franchina. Princeton, NJ: Princeton University Press, 1995.
Sherman, Daniel. *The Construction of Memory in Interwar France.* Chicago: University of Chicago Press, 2000.
Silver, Kenneth E., ed. *Chaos and Classicism.* New York: Guggenheim Museum of Art, 2010. Exhibition catalog.
———. *Esprit de corps: The Art of the Parisian Avant-Garde and the First World War, 1914–1925.* Princeton, NJ: Princeton University Press, 1989.
Silverman, Kaja. *Male Subjectivity at the Margins.* New York: Routledge, 1992.
Simmel, Georg. *Simmel on Culture: Selected Writings.* London: Sage, 1997.

Slavin, David Henry. *Colonial Cinema and Imperial France, 1919–1939: White Blind Spots, Male Fantasies, Settler Myths.* Baltimore: Johns Hopkins University Press, 2001.

Snape, Michael. *God and Uncle Sam: Religion and America's Armed Forces in World War II.* Woodbridge: Boydell & Brewer, 2015.

Soussloff, Catherine M. *The Subject in Art: Portraiture and the Birth of the Modern.* Durham, NC: Duke University Press, 2006.

Stich, Sidra. *Anxious Visions: Surrealist Art.* Berkeley, CA: Abbeville Press and University Art Museum, 1990. Exhibition catalog.

Stiles, Kristine. *Concerning Consequences: Studies in Art, Destruction, and Trauma.* Chicago: University of Chicago Press, 2016.

Sund, Judy. "Fernand Léger and Unanimism: Where There's Smoke . . ." *Oxford Art Journal* 7, no. 1 (1984): 49–56.

Sweeney, James Johnson. "Eleven Europeans in America." *Bulletin of the Museum of Modern Art* 13, nos. 4–5 (1946): 2–39.

——. "Léger and the Cinesthetic." *Creative Art: Magazine of Fine and Applied Art* 10, no. 1 (1932): 440–45.

——. "Léger and the Cult of the Close-Up." *Arts* 17 (May 1931): 561–68.

——. "Léger's Art Is the Man." *New York Times Magazine* (October 18, 1953): 28, 42, 44.

Tatu, Laurent, and Julien Bogousslavsky. "Writers as Shell Shock Witnesses During World War I." In *Neurological Disorders in Famous Artists*, part 4, edited by Julien Bogousslavsky and Laurent Tatu, 47-48. Frontiers of Neurology and Neuroscience 43. Basel: Karger, 2018.

Taylor, Brandon. *Life of Forms in Art: Modernism, Organism, Vitality.* London: Bloomsbury Visual Arts, 2020.

Temime, Emile. *Histoire de Marseille de la révolution à nos jours.* Marseille: Perrin, 1999.

Theodosiou, Christina. *Le Deuil inachevé: La Commemoration de l'Armistice du 11 novembre 1918 en France dans l'entre-deux-geurres.* Paris: Editions de la Sorbonne, 2018.

Thomas, Gregory M. *Treating the Trauma of the Great War: Soldiers, Civilians, and Psychiatry in France, 1914–1940.* Baton Rouge: Louisiana State University Press, 2009.

Tokine, R. "L'Esthétique du Cinéma." *L'Esprit Nouveau*, no. 1 (October 1920): 84–89.

——. "Yvan Goll." *L'Esprit Nouveau*, no. 14 (1922): 1586–90.

Touret, Michèle. "Cendrars (1887–1961)." In *1917*, edited by Claire Garnier and Laurent Le Bon, 106. Metz: Centre Pompidou-Metz, 2012. Exhibition catalog.

Turbergue, Jean-Pierre. *1914–1918: Les Journaux de Tranchées.* Paris: Éditions Italiques, 1999.

Valentine Gallery. *The American Artists Congress Presents the Masterpiece* Guernica *by Pablo Picasso Together with Drawings and Studies for the Benefit of the Spanish Refugee Relief Campaign.* New York: Valentine Gallery, 1937.

Vallier, Dora. "La Vie fait l'oeuvre de Léger: Propos de l'artiste recueillis." In "Fernand Léger." Special issue, *Cahiers d'Art* 29 (1954): 133–77.

Vallye, Anna. "The Painter on the Boulevard." In *Léger: Modern Art and the Metropolis*, edited by Anna Vallye, 1–72. Philadelphia: Philadelphia Museum of Art, 2013. Exhibition catalog.

Van der Kolk, Bessel A., and Onno van der Hart. "The Intrusive Past: The Flexibility of Memory and the Engraving of Trauma." In *Trauma: Explorations in Memory*, edited by Cathy Caruth, 158–82. Baltimore: Johns Hopkins University Press, 1995.

Vassallo, Helen. "'Cette nuit, aura-t-elle une aube?' The Fate of the (Anti)-Heroine in Simone de Beauvoir's *Le Sang des autres* and Régine Deforges' *La Bicyclette bleue*." In *French and Francophone Women Facing War / Les Femmes face à la guerre*, edited by Alison S. Fell, 171–91. Oxford: Peter Lang, 2009.

Véray, Laurent. "1914–1918, the First Media War of the Twentieth Century." *Film History* 22, no. 4 (2010): 408–24.

——. "Photographie et cinéma." In *Encyclopédie de la Grande Guerre, 1914–1918: Histoire et Culture*, edited by Stéphane Audoin-Rouzeau and Jean-Jacques Becker, 701–16. Paris: Bayard, 2004.

Verdet, André. *Entretiens, notes et écrits sur la peinture.* Paris: Editions Galilée, 1978.

Vidalenc, Jean. *L'Exode de mai-juin 1940.* Paris: Presses Universitaires de France, 1957.

Vitrac, Roger. "L'Ephémère/Fantasmagorie." *Variétés* 2, no. 9 (January 15, 1930): 617–22.

Vlaminck, Maurice de. *Dangerous Corner* (1929). New York: Abelard-Schuman, 1961.

Walusinski, Olivier. "Jean-Martin Charcot's House Officers at La Salpêtrière Hospital." In *Following Charcot: A Forgotten History of Neurology and Psychiatry*, edited by Julien Bogousslavsky, 9–35. Frontiers of Neurology and Neuroscience 29. Basel: S Karger AG, 2011.

Warren, Lansing. "Averted Civil War, Blum Says at Trial. The Former French Premier Defends

40-Hour-Week of His Regime as Aid to All." *New York Times* (March 11, 1942): 8.

——. "Leon Blum Warns Court Liberty Will Live. Predicts His Conviction, but Declares It Will Contribute to Revival of Freedom." *New York Times* (March 12, 1942): 13.

Westheim, Paul. "Allemagne: La Situation des arts plastiques." *L'Esprit Nouveau*, no. 20 (January–February 1924): n.p.

——. "Kunst in Frankreich." *Das Kunstblatt* 6 (1922): 8–25.

Willmoth, Simon. "Léger in America." In Serota, *Fernand Léger*, 49–54.

——. "Le Mur, l'architecture, le peintre, Fernand Léger et ses collaborations artistiques 1925–1955." In *Fernand Léger*, edited by Hélène Lassalle, 45–58. Milan: Mazzotta, 1990. Exhibition catalog.

Wilson, Sarah. "Artiste, Muse et égérie Russe? L'histoire extraordinaire de Nadia Khodassievitch-Léger." In Lecoq-Ramond and Widerkehr, *Fernand Léger*, 89–98.

Wiltse, Jeff. *Contested Waters: A Social History of Swimming Pools in America*. Chapel Hill: University of North Carolina Press, 2007.

Winter, Jay M. *Remembering War: The Great War Between Memory and History in the Twentieth Century*. New Haven, CT: Yale University Press, 2006.

——, ed. "Shell Shock." Special issue, *Journal of Contemporary History* 35, no. 1 (January 2000).

——. "Thinking About Silence." In *Shadows of War: A Social History of Silence in the Twentieth Century*, edited by Efrat Ben-Ze'ev, Ruth Ginio, and J. M. Winter, 3–31. Cambridge: Cambridge University Press, 2010.

Winter, J. M., and Blaine Baggett. *The Great War and the Shaping of the 20th Century*. New York: Penguin Studio, 1996.

Wittman, Laura. *The Tomb of the Unknown Soldier, Modern Mourning, and the Reinvention of the Mystical Body*. Toronto: University of Toronto Press, 2011.

Zervos, Christian, ed. "Fernand Léger." Special issue, *Cahiers d'Art* 8, nos. 3–4 (1933).

——. "Fernand Léger et la Poésie de l'objet." *Cahiers d'Art* 9, nos. 1–4 (1934): 99–108.

——. "Fernand Léger et le Dévelopement de sa conception des objets dans l'espace." *Cahiers d'Art* 4, no. 4 (1929): 149–56.

——. "Une Nouvelle étape dans l'oeuvre de Fernand Léger." *Cahiers d'Art* 7, nos. 6–7 (1932): 264–66.

Index

Note: All artworks are by Fernand Léger unless otherwise noted. Page numbers in italics indicate illustrations.

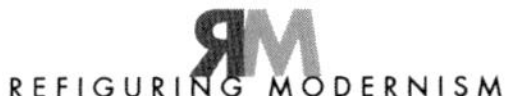
REFIGURING MODERNISM

ARTS

LITERATURES

SCIENCES

(A Series Edited By)

Jonathan Eburne

Refiguring Modernism features cutting-edge interdisciplinary approaches to the study of art, literature, science, and cultural history. With an eye to the different modernisms emerging throughout the world during the twentieth century and beyond, we seek to publish scholarship that engages creatively with canonical and eccentric works alike, bringing fresh concepts and original research to bear on modernist cultural production, whether aesthetic, social, or epistemological. What does it mean to study modernism in a global context characterized at once by decolonization and nation-building; international cooperation and conflict; changing ideas about subjectivity and identity; new understandings of language, religion, poetics, and myth; and new paradigms for science, politics, and religion? What did modernism offer artists, writers, and intellectuals? How do we theorize and historicize modernism? How do we rethink its forms, its past, and its futures?

(Other Books in the Series)

David Peters Corbett, *The World in Paint: Modern Art and Visuality in England, 1848–1914*

Jordana Mendelson, *Documenting Spain: Artists, Exhibition Culture, and the Modern Nation, 1929–1939*

Barbara Larson, *The Dark Side of Nature: Science, Society, and the Fantastic in the Work of Odilon Redon*

Alejandro Anreus, Diana L. Linden, and Jonathan Weinberg, eds., *The Social and the Real: Political Art of the 1930s in the Western Hemisphere*

Margaret Iversen, *Beyond Pleasure: Freud, Lacan, Barthes*

Stephen Bann, ed., *The Coral Mind: Adrian Stokes's Engagement with Architecture, Art History, Criticism, and Psychoanalysis*

Charles Palermo, *Fixed Ecstasy: Joan Miró in the 1920s*

Marius Roux, *The Substance and the Shadow*

Aruna D'Souza, *Cézanne's Bathers: Biography and the Erotics of Paint*

Abigail Gillman, *Viennese Jewish Modernism: Freud, Hofmannsthal, Beer-Hofmann, and Schnitzler*

Stephen Petersen, *Space-Age Aesthetics: Lucio Fontana, Yves Klein, and the Postwar European Avant-Garde*

Stefanie Harris, *Mediating Modernity: Literature and the "New" Media, 1895–1930*

Michele Greet, *Beyond National Identity: Pictorial Indigenism as a Modernist Strategy for Andean Art, 1920–1960*

Paul Smith, ed., *Seurat Re-viewed*

David Prochaska and Jordana Mendelson, eds., *Postcards: Ephemeral Histories of Modernity*

David Getsy, *From Diversion to Subversion: Games, Play, and Twentieth-Century Art*

Jessica Burstein, *Cold Modernism: Literature, Fashion, Art*

Adam Jolles, *The Curatorial Avant-Garde: Surrealism and Exhibition Practice in France, 1925–1941*

Juli Highfill, *Modernism and Its Merchandise: The Spanish Avant-Garde and Material Culture, 1920–1930*

Damien Keane, *Ireland and the Problem of Information: Irish Writing, Radio, Late Modernist Communication*

Allison Morehead, *Nature's Experiments and the Search for Symbolist Form*

Laura Kalba, *Color in the Age of Impressionism: Commerce, Technology, and Art*

Catherine Walworth, *Soviet Salvage: Imperial Debris, Revolutionary Reuse, and Russian Constructivism*

Jo Applin, Catherine Spencer, and Amy Tobin, eds., *London Art Worlds: Mobile, Contingent, and Ephemeral Networks, 1960–1980*

Erik M. Bachman, *Literary Obscenities: U. S. Case Law and Naturalism after Modernism*

Lori Cole, *Surveying the Avant-Garde: Questions on Modernism, Art, and the Americas in Transatlantic Magazines*

Elizabeth Pender and Cathryn Setz, eds., *Shattered Objects: Djuna Barnes's Modernism*

Sam Rose, *Art and Form: From Roger Fry to Global Modernism*

Diederik Oostdijk, *Bells for America: The Cold War, Modernism, and the Netherlands Carillon in Arlington.*

Jessica Gerschultz, *Decorative Arts of the Tunisian École: Fabrications of Modernism, Gender, and Power*

Anna Lovatt, *Drawing Degree Zero: The Line from Minimal to Conceptual Art*

Molly Warnock, *Simon Hantaï and the Reserves of Painting*

Octavio González, *Misfit Modernism: Queer Forms of Double Exile in the Twentieth-Century Novel*

Mark Antliff, *Sculptors Against the State: Anarchism and the Anglo-European Avant-Garde*

Elliott H. King and Abigail Susik, eds., *Radical Dreams: Surrealism, Counterculture, Resistance*

Katie L. Price and Michael R. Taylor, eds., *'Pataphysics Unrolled*

Giovanni Casini, *Léonce Rosenberg's Cubism: The Galerie L'Effort Moderne in Interwar Paris*

William Gallois, *Qayrawān: The Amuletic City*